Political Violence in Kenya

Land, Elections, and Claim-Making

KATHLEEN KLAUS
University of San Francisco

CAMBRIDGE
UNIVERSITY PRESS

University Printing House, Cambridge CB2 8BS, United Kingdom

One Liberty Plaza, 20th Floor, New York, NY 10006, USA

477 Williamstown Road, Port Melbourne, VIC 3207, Australia

314–321, 3rd Floor, Plot 3, Splendor Forum, Jasola District Centre, New Delhi – 110025, India

79 Anson Road, #06–04/06, Singapore 079906

Cambridge University Press is part of the University of Cambridge.

It furthers the University's mission by disseminating knowledge in the pursuit of education, learning, and research at the highest international levels of excellence.

www.cambridge.org
Information on this title: www.cambridge.org/9781108488501
DOI: 10.1017/9781108764063

First published 2020

Printed in the United Kingdom by TJ International Ltd, Padstow Cornwall

A catalogue record for this publication is available from the British Library.

Library of Congress Cataloging-in-Publication Datas
Names: Klaus, Kathleen F., 1985– author.
Title: Political violence in Kenya : land, elections, and claim-making / Kathleen F. Klaus.
Description: Cambridge, United Kingdom ; New York, NY : Cambridge University Press, 2020. | Includes bibliographical references and index.
Identifiers: LCCN 2019052354 (print) | LCCN 2019052355 (ebook) | ISBN 9781108488501 (hardback) | ISBN 9781108764063 (ebook)
Subjects: LCSH: Political violence – Kenya. | Land tenure – Political aspects – Kenya. | Elections – Corrupt practices – Kenya. | Ethnic conflict – Kenya.
Classification: LCC HN793.Z9 V5575 2020 (print) | LCC HN793.Z9 (ebook) | DDC 303.6096762–dc23
LC record available at https://lccn.loc.gov/2019052354
LC ebook record available at https://lccn.loc.gov/2019052355

ISBN 978-1-108-48850-1 Hardback

For Jeffrey

Contents

Figures

Maps

Tables

Acknowledgments

In December of 2007, I was living in southern Malawi on a Fulbright fellowship. I was conducting interviews with land poor Malawians, trying to understand why – years after the end of authoritarian rule – people were not demanding land reform. One evening, while listening to the BBC crackle through my radio, a headline caught my attention. Election violence had broken out in Kenya. The expatriate community in Malawi complained of having to cancel their holiday safaris. Meanwhile, journalists spoke of "tribal clashes," shuttered businesses, and chaos in the streets. Despite the stream of crisis reporting that regularly emanated from the BBC, this particular story stuck out. Election violence was not supposed to happen in Kenya, not in 2007 anyhow. But something else caught my attention as well: the media's emphasis on the tribal and atavistic roots of the crisis. I reflected on my research in Malawi: the centrality of land in people's everyday lives and local politics. I knew little about Kenya at the time. But I did know that like Malawi, tea and coffee estates covered some of the most productive land. And like Malawi, I knew that land mattered to most Kenyans. And later, I'd learn just how much it mattered. At the time however, I knew only that the stories I heard about Kenya's election violence were far too simple. Land, I guessed, had something to do with it too.

This was the question I would ask, in different ways and over the next many years, while a graduate student at the University of Wisconsin-Madison. My undergraduate mentors from Smith College – Cathy and David Newbury, and Greg White – helped me think through difficult questions about politics and history in Africa, navigate the challenges of fieldwork, and land at the University of Wisconsin. I am grateful for their time and their unyielding encouragement.

At Wisconsin, my dissertation advisor, Scott Straus, pushed me to think about land – and to keep thinking about land – from my earliest days of graduate school. Scott, along with Michael Schatzberg and Aili Tripp, created a vibrant intellectual environment to learn and converse about the study of African politics. I also owe thanks to my other committee members: David Weimer, who worked patiently with me to analyze my survey results, and Erica Simmons, who pushed me on my concept of land narratives.

Other faculty at UW-Madison provided feedback at various stages of the book project, including Nadav Shelef, Noam Lupu, Jonathan Renshon, Aseema Sinha, and Jim Delehanty. And while Howard Schweber never commented directly on my work, he officiated my marriage on an island in Vermont, so that has to count for something. Thanks also to my many graduate school companions: Brandon Kendhammer, Alice Kang, Jen Petersen, Jeremy Menchik, Charlie Taylor, Taylor Price, Barry Driscoll, Mehreen Zahra-Malik, Galina Belokurova, Kyle Marquardt, Emily Sellars, Inken von Borzyskowski, Nick Barnes, and Marie-Ange Bunga. The experience was richer with all of you.

My deepest gratitude goes to my research assistants, respondents, and colleagues in Kenya, all of whom made this book possible. The Institute for Development Studies at the University of Nairobi served as my official host. At the University of Nairobi, I benefited from the time and insights of Winnie Mitullah and Karuti Kanyinga. My survey would not have been possible without the expertise and generosity of Abel Oyuke and Sam Balongo. Thanks also to Ambreena Manji, David Anderson, and Fibian Lukalo for their insights and expertise on land issues in Kenya. I benefited from a fabulous team of enumerators, including May Koko, Caroline Magani, Peter Kimani, Kevin Rotich, Nelson Ngige, Benjamin Ayega Anyona, Alice Mbuvi, and Kriss Cheupe. When conducting qualitative interviews across Nakuru County, I was lucky to have Jeff Osemo, Martin Munene, James Cherono, and Dominic Gicheru by my side. Research in Mauche would not have been possible without the kindness of Philip Rotich. Eunice Adhiambo Odhiambo made research in Kwale both possible and enjoyable. My greatest thanks go to my research assistants from Kilifi County: Rebecca Munga and Goodluck Mbaga. I thank them for sharing their time, stories, friendship, and a bit of their life with me. I've learned so much from both of them and I look forward to our next adventure. I also thank Njeri Kangethe for being my "Kenyan mom." She made sure I was safe and sound and, of course, well fed. It was also during my fieldwork that I met Mai Hassan. Since our first chance encounter in Nakuru, I've enjoyed and benefited from our many conversations about land and politics in Kenya. Thanks for being a sounding board, Nairobi roommate, running partner, friend, and collaborator.

The Social Science Research Council and the National Science Foundation provided generous funding for my fieldwork in Kenya, while the United States Institute of Peace, the Harry Frank Guggenheim Foundation, and the Strauss Center for International Law and Security at UT-Austin supported the completion of the dissertation.

I've benefited from the support of many scholarly communities. While finishing my dissertation at the Strauss Center for International Law and Security at UT-Austin, Steven Brooke and Andrew Boutton were great writing partners, while Jason Brownlee offered valuable mentorship. Bruce Carruthers and the Buffett Institute for Global Studies at Northwestern University provided me with the time and space to revise my book, start new projects, meet new people, and learn from a fantastic group of scholars. Rachel Riedl was a wonderful mentor, always willing to meet for coffee, go for a run, or advise on a job talk. Rachel, along with Michael Albertus, Leo Arriola, Ana Arjona, and Robert Braun, participated in my book workshop, hosted by the Buffett Institute and the Program for African Studies, at Northwestern University. Their thoughtful and incisive feedback improved this book greatly. I am very grateful for their time. My fellow postdocs at Northwestern – Maria Akchurin, Nermeen Mouftah, Martha Wilfahrt, Basak Taraktas, Erin Moore, and Sinan Erensu – provided friendship and community. I owe Martha Wilfahrt special thanks for the many drafts she's edited.

Many others have provided feedback and support during the writing of the book, including Cathy Boone, Nic Cheeseman, Sebastian Elischer, Susanne Mueller, Shelby Grossman, Anne Meng, and Alex Dyzenhaus. During the American Political Science Association Africa Workshop in Nairobi, I had great conversations with Beth Whitaker and Aditi Malik, along with the other participants. Thanks also to Yoni Morse, for his hospitality during the Connecticut winter. Brian Ekdale and Melissa Tully have been great hosts in Nairobi and Iowa City. Kim Yi Dionne invited me to writing retreats in the Northampton woods and helped me share my work with a larger public. It's been a pleasure working with both Matthew Mitchell and Jeremy Horowitz on articles related to this book.

Since moving to San Francisco, I've enjoyed participating in the Africa Research Workshop at University of California, Berkeley. I thank Leo Arriola for organizing these gatherings and including me. Workshop participants, including Fiona Shen Bayh, Danny Choi, Justine Davis, and Paul Thissen, provided excellent feedback and engagement. At the University of San Francisco, Jessica Blum and Omar Miranda have been great friends and writing partners. Annick Wibben, Dana Zartner, Kathy Coll, and Sadia Saeed have also provided support. In addition to helping design the figures in this book, Noopur Agarwal is a great friend, providing constant encouragement during the final months of revisions.

My parents, Ellen, Marshall, and my aunt, Moira, have cheered me on at every step of writing this book. My mom showed me the world from an early age and what it takes to survive and thrive as a woman in academia. My dad helped me keep perspective. And my grandmother, who earned her PhD in the 1960s with three kids in tow, reminded me that the dissertation was the easy part. Maureen provided my home away from home while in graduate school.

Finally, thanks to Jeffrey for being my partner through it all – late nights at the library in Madison, *matatu* rides in Kakamega, evictions in Accra, helping me field a survey in Kenya, and moving me to Austin, Evanston, Middletown, and finally, out to San Francisco. Thanks for your patience, editorial eye, and most of all, ensuring that we live well and do good work.

Abbreviations

ADC	Agricultural Development Corporation
CIPEV	Commission of Inquiry into Post-Election Violence
DRC	Democratic Republic of the Congo
ECK	Electoral Commission of Kenya
GEMA	Gikuyu, Embu, and Meru Association
ICC	International Criminal Court
IDP	Internally displaced persons
KADU	Kenya African Democratic Union
KANU	Kenya Africa National Union
KDF	Kenya Defense Forces
KICC	Kenyatta International Conference Centre
LBC	Land-buying company
LDSB	Land Development and Settlement Board
MAS	Million-Acre Settlement Scheme
NARC	National Rainbow Coalition
ODM	Orange Democratic Movement
PEV	Post-Election Violence
PNU	Party of National Unity
SS	Settlement scheme
TNA	The National Alliance Party
URP	United Republican Party

1 | *Introduction*

Mauche Settlement Scheme, Rift Valley Kenya, December 2007

On the evening of December 30, 2007, Kenya's Electoral Commission (ECK) announced the winners of the general election. Residents in the farming community of Mauche had gathered around radios and televisions in local bars and cafés to listen to the electoral results. Community members, most of whom identified as Kalenjin, were confident that their candidate, Raila Odinga, from the opposition Orange Democratic Movement (ODM) party, would win. The mood shifted quickly, however, as the incoming electoral returns pointed to a victory for the incumbent candidate from the Party of National Unity (PNU). ODM supporters in Mauche and elsewhere viewed the PNU win as a sign that the incumbent party had rigged the election. Anxiety and tension grew as residents watched TV images of a prominent ODM candidate, William Ruto, dragged offstage by Kenya's military police.[1] A young resident recounts, "When we saw this we knew the whole of the Kalenjin community had no one to champion for their rights, so the youths from the Kalenjin community proceeded to attack the Kikuyu."[2] Another resident explains how some community members "resorted to fighting" when their candidate didn't win because "they knew the next thing was their eviction."[3] That evening, Mauche

---

[1] William Ruto was an important leader in the Kalenjin community and ODM party. He was pulled offstage during the ECK announcement of Molo constituency. In 2010 the International Criminal Court accused him of involvement in the 2007–2008 postelectoral violence. In 2013, he became Deputy President of Kenya.

[2] Interview-Mauche SS-Nakuru, October 8, 2012 (1). The Kikuyu are the largest ethnic community in Kenya (20 percent of national population) and provided the largest political support base for the incumbent government in 2007.

[3] Interview-Mauche SS-Nakuru County, October 4, 2012 (3).

residents crossed into the neighboring village of Likia and began torching the homes and properties of their Kikuyu neighbors.[4]

Ogilgei Settlement Scheme, Rift Valley, Kenya, December 2007

Less than twenty miles down the road, Kalenjin and Kikuyu farming communities also border one another. Yet Kalenjin residents in Ogilgei provide very different accounts of the 2007 election. Rather than recounting episodes of violence or eviction, residents emphasize that here, "it was peaceful." It was stable enough in fact, that the government designated the ethnically mixed area as a temporary camp for the internally displaced. Most residents of Ogilgei did not believe that electoral results signaled imminent eviction from their land. Violence never escalated during the 2007–2008 postelectoral period, nor had it in previous elections.

The contrasting accounts of Mauche and Ogilgei motivate the book's main puzzle: Why does election violence escalate in one local context, but not another seemingly similar context? Why, for example, might violence escalate between two farming communities, while a short distance away similar farming communities remain peaceful? Why do certain regions, constituencies, neighborhoods, or villages experience significant levels of violence while seemingly similar areas do not?

The book explains this puzzle of local variation by suggesting that the occurrence of violence is a joint production between political elites and ordinary citizens.[5] Indeed, elites must have an incentive to use violence. Yet we know far less about why and when ordinary citizens participate. Explaining spatial variation thus raises a second and closely related research question: why and when do ordinary citizens participate in election violence?

I argue that in contexts where land shapes livelihood and identification, and where property rights institutions are weak, land, and

---

[4] Most Kikuyu, who comprise the country's largest ethnic group, voted for the incumbent candidate, Mwai Kibaki, leader of the PNU.
[5] This concept of the "joint production" of violence builds on Stathis Kalyvas's argument that violence in civil war is jointly produced between national-level actors and allies at the local level (see Kalyvas 2006, 2003).

specifically, collective narratives around land, can provide a key device around which elites and citizens coordinate the production of electoral violence. Drawing primarily on evidence from Kenya's 2007-2008 postelection violence, the book finds that electoral violence escalated between neighboring and ethnically distinct farming communities only when a subset of residents in each community linked the outcome of elections with their ability to access, reclaim, or secure their land. In these cases, violence became a means of ensuring their preferred candidate at all costs, or a mechanism to preempt or defend against their own eviction.

The opening vignette illustrates the centrality of land: many of the Kalenjin residents of Mauche who attacked their Kikuyu neighbors linked the incumbent victory of Mwai Kibaki with their imminent eviction. Lacking title deeds and tenure security, violence acquired a defensive logic: "evict them before they can evict us." Yet in the nearby farming community of Ogilgei, Kalenjin farmers had few reasons to attack their Kikuyu neighbors despite the divisive appeals of politicians. Notably, because Kalenjin residents and their Kikuyus neighbors were both land secure, neither side linked the election outcome with their tenure security.

The Puzzle

In the postelectoral period of Kenya's 2007 general election, the country experienced its most devastating episode of electoral violence in its history. According to official reports, at least 1,300 people were killed and nearly 700,000 people were displaced from their homes (Government of Kenya 2008). Importantly, however, there were significant differences in the sites and scale of violence across the country. The map below illustrates the spatial variation in the level of violence across Kenya's forty-seven counties, which I measure by the number of reported deaths.[6] Map 1.1 shows that the majority of election-related

---

[6] These measures are based on the Uppsala Conflict Data Program at the Peace Research Institute Oslo (UCDP/PRIO Armed Conflict Dataset), the Armed Conflict Location and Event Data Project (ACLED), and the Commission of Inquiry into Post Election Violence (CIPEV) report (Government of Kenya 2008). See appendix for coding details.

County-Level Electoral Violence: 2007–08

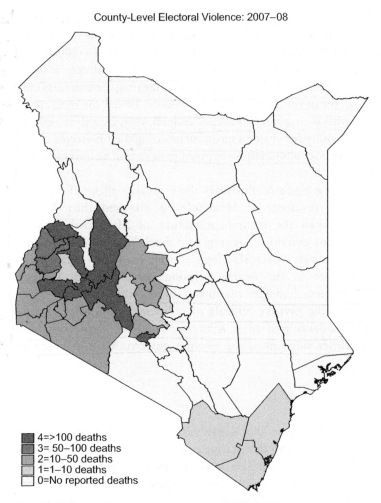

4=>100 deaths
3= 50–100 deaths
2=10–50 deaths
1=1–10 deaths
0=No reported deaths

Map 1.1 County-level election violence: 2007–2008.

deaths occurred in seven out of Kenya's forty-seven counties, most of which were clustered together (darkest shading).

Some of the highest death tolls were in Nairobi, the country's capital city, as well as in the more rural counties of Nakuru and Uasin Gishu, where between 200 and 400 people died and thousands of people were displaced. Yet even within counties with such high death tolls, many residents did not experience physical violence directly. Instead, residents watched or listened as violence escalated elsewhere: in a nearby village, trading center, or distant city.

What accounts for this significant variation in electoral violence across and within counties? Many existing studies analyze the broad institutional and political factors that help explain cross-national or temporal patterns of electoral violence (e.g. Fjelde & Höglund 2016a; Arriola & Johnson 2012; Straus & Taylor 2012). Theories emphasize the strategic calculations of national elites, the type of constitutional design and electoral rules, state capacity, ethnic polarization, and the role of election observers (e.g. Asunka et al. 2019; Daxecker 2014).

Yet most instances of electoral violence are highly localized. As the opening vignette of Mauche and Ogilgei illustrates, electoral violence does not occur uniformly, even in areas with similar political or demographic profiles. While this may seem like an obvious point to some readers, the implication is that while macro-level variables can explain broad cross-national or temporal patterns in electoral violence, the occurrence of electoral violence is often a function of much more local or regional dynamics. However, because most studies focus on macro-level explanations of violence, few can specify how local-level factors and mechanisms interact with macro-level forces to enable and restrain the organization of electoral violence (Balcells & Justino 2014; Kalyvas 2006). Importantly, there are a growing number of studies that focus on the subnational dynamics of election violence (e.g. Gutiérrez-Romero 2014; Dercon & Guiterrez-Romero 2012; Boone 2011; Wilkinson 2004) or on the interaction between micro- and macro-level factors (Söderberg Kovacs & Bjarnesen 2018). Yet we still know very little about why electoral violence varies so significantly within subnational spaces.[7]

Summary of Argument

This book aims to provide a theory of electoral violence that can help explain the significant local variation in violence that so often characterizes episodes of electoral violence in Kenya and elsewhere. Broadly,

---

[7] This research agenda draws inspiration from civil war scholars who focus on the interaction between micro- and macro-level factors (e.g. Balcells 2017; Balcells & Justino 2014; Kalyvas 2006; Weinstein 2006; Wood 2003).

I argue that the occurrence of electoral violence emerges as a joint production between elites and ordinary citizens. This concept borrows from civil war scholars, notably Kalyvas (2003), who argues that civil war is a "joint process" that relies on national elites seeking power at the center who must ally with local actors seeking to gain advantage locally (2003: 486). Drawing on this theory, I analyze electoral violence as a process of social and political mobilization that requires coordination between elites and ordinary actors rather than an event based solely on elite calculations.

I argue that in certain contexts, land narratives can serve as a key device around which elites and citizens coordinate the use of violence. The material and symbolic power of these land narratives varies locally and is often historically rooted. Narratives are the stories people tell "to makes sense of their world and environments" (Autesserre 2014: 6).[8] Land narratives are the ways people talk about and make sense of their claims and rights relative to others. They are the stories that group members tell to express beliefs about the legitimacy or injustice of the land distribution process, fears of losing land, and strategies of asserting claims to land and territory.

To understand how these land narratives can serve as a mechanism through which elites and ordinary citizens organize and restrain violence, the book analyzes the escalation of electoral violence as a process that includes two main causal paths or stages. In the first stage, I theorize the formation of contentious land narratives, analyzing how and why the salience and content of these narratives varies spatially and temporally. I argue that a key source of variation is the parity in land rights between two distinct but proximate groups. The book identifies three scenarios. The first is a scenario of *land equality*: two nearby but ethnically distinct groups both benefit from similar land rights (e.g. all households have a title deed). The second is a scenario of *moderate land inequality*, where members of one ethnic community hold slightly stronger land rights relative to a neighboring group. In a third scenario, there is *significant land inequality* between a landholding and landless class (e.g. landlords and tenants). Importantly, it is in the second scenario – moderate land inequality between ethnic groups – where salient and contentious land narratives are most likely to form.

---

[8] See also Patterson and Monroe 1998; Goffman 1974; Berger & Luckmann 1967.

The second stage of the book analyzes the organization of electoral violence: how and when elites compel ordinary citizens to participate in violence. I argue that under certain conditions, contentious land narratives provide elites with an effective tool to mobilize election-related violence. Specifically, I demonstrate how land narratives shape the mechanisms of political mobilization, the material and symbolic motives for citizen participation, and the logics of targeting.

A key premise is that the occurrence of electoral violence is far less common than the spaces where I observe or predict contentious land narratives. Therefore, I do not claim that contentious land narratives cause or predict violence. Rather, I treat land narratives as a mechanism linking inequality in tenure rights with the escalation of violence. My main interest is in explaining why land narratives enable elites to organize violence in some cases but not others.

In order for electoral violence to escalate, several factors must come into play. First, leaders are only able to invoke a logic for violence where they can also tap into salient and contentious local land narratives – narratives that emphasize anxieties of losing land and anger over previous acts of land grabbing or unjust allocation. Second, these narratives rarely emerge randomly or from elite manipulation alone. Instead, these narratives provide the strongest collection action frame where they are based on very local-level experiences of perceived inequality, injustice, or exclusion.[9] Specifically, I find that land narratives are much more salient where there is land inequality between neighboring ethnic communities who are also political rivals. Contentious land narratives emerge most often when one community holds title deeds to their land and the other community does not. Third, even where there is land inequality and contentious land narratives, elites are only able to use land narratives as tools to organize violence where there is a tradition of political elites acting as strong and credible "land patrons" – a political leader who provides or protects land rights in exchange for loyalty or political support. In these scenarios, followers are more likely to believe that their candidate has the capacity and political will to protect or alter the distribution of land rights in their favor. In these spaces – as in parts of Nakuru County – elections can signal a rare window of opportunity to gain and secure land, and equally, a moment to lose.

---

[9] I borrow the term "collective action frame" from Bedford & Snow (2000).

In examining electoral violence as a coproduction between political elites and ordinary citizens, the book explains why elites succeed in organizing violence in some localities, yet across most others, they face significant constraints.

Summary of Methodology

The theory that I've outlined here draws on fifteen months of multi-method fieldwork that I conducted in Kenya between 2010 and 2013. The fieldwork consisted of two main data collection strategies. The first stage was qualitative in nature and involved what I call a "two-stage comparative case study" – a series of case comparisons across Nakuru County, located in the Rift Valley, and Kwale and Kilifi counties, located in Coast region. In selecting cases, I used a "most-similar" research design. Doing so enabled me to evaluate a series of hypotheses linking land rights with the occurrence of electoral violence, while considering alternative explanations. Specifically, I used this strategy to examine the determinants of contentious land narratives between groups (stage 1) and the determinants of electoral violence (stage 2).

I limited my universe of cases to settlement schemes and land-buying companies (LBCs): agricultural communities where the state or an elected official leverages significant control over the distribution of land and tenure rights. The research design thus enables me to control for a number of factors across cases. Yet it also creates an important scope condition, limiting the generalizability of my theory to spaces where the state controls rights to land. In total, I conducted 230 in-depth interviews with residents of these settlement schemes and LBCs, in addition to focus groups with elders and youths in each case study area. This qualitative stage of the research was crucial for a few reasons. First, interview questions touched on a number of sensitive issues, including land documentation, perceptions of security, views of ethnic others, and one's experience with election violence. I prioritized creating an interview dynamic that encouraged respondents to feel comfortable speaking openly and honestly. To do so, I conducted one-on-one interviews in the privacy of a respondent's home and in the language that the respondent preferred.[10] Further, in nearly every

---

[10]   In most cases, respondents chose to speak in Swahili, though some preferred their mother tongue (e.g. Kalenjin or Kikuyu). A few opted for English.

case-study community, I made repeated visits. This iterative engage-ment also helped me gain the trust of community members. The format of the qualitative interview, which relied on a structured ques-tionnaire, was also important in that it enabled respondents to take the time they needed: to ask for clarification or to expand on certain questions or issues. In this regard, the interview format enabled respondents to answer questions on their own terms; to tell their own stories. While this helped to elicit trust, this last point also allowed me to understand how individuals use particular frames or narratives. It was only by conducting in-depth, qualitative interviews that I could identify the salient narratives that community members used, and further, how such narratives varied, in subtle and explicit ways, across.

The second main data collection strategy was a household-level survey with 750 respondents, which I conducted in two counties in the Rift Valley region (Nakuru and Uasin Gishu) and two in the Coast region (Kwale and Kilifi). The survey is novel and important in part because there is no reliable, individual-level data on election violence. Instead, and with a few notable exceptions, most studies on cross-national and Kenya-specific studies of election violence rely on event-count datasets. While these sources are invaluable, they tend to conceal the more micro-level variation in violence. In addition, these datasets typically rely on media or government reports of violence, which introduces political and reporting bias. While the survey data I present is limited in geographic scope, it enables me to extend my inferential scope by testing the hypotheses I examined in the first stage of data collection (qualitative inter-views) across a larger number of observations. Further, it is one of the few datasets on election violence in Kenya that relies on the responses of "ordinary citizens" rather than bureaucrats, political elites, or media outlets. I expand on the book's methodology and research design in the next chapter.

Defining Electoral Violence

Electoral violence is not unique to Kenya, nor is it isolated to countries in Africa. As the violence and hate speech following the 2016 presiden-tial election in the US demonstrates, electoral violence can occur in a range of country settings with different colonial and conflict histories, and levels of economic development and democratic consolidation.[11] By one estimate, 19 percent of all elections held between 1945 and 2010 experienced significant violence while protests accompanied another 14 percent.[12] Since 1981, 37 percent of elections have been violent (NELDA).[13] Across Africa, highly repressive or large-scale violence has affected 20 percent of all elections held between 1990 and 2008 (Straus & Taylor 2012).[14] By 2013, 48 percent of voters surveyed across thirty-three African countries reported that they feared election violence (Mares & Young 2016),[15] and while recent attention has focused on electoral violence across Africa, most incidents of election violence have occurred in South Asia (e.g. India and Pakistan) and Latin America (e.g. Colombia and Guatemala).[16]

Importantly, the way that scholars choose to conceptualize and measure election-related violence, including decisions about how to establish the time frame for observing counts of election violence, or how to delineate organizers, participants, and targets, has important implications for the theories that scholars generate, the observable patterns that emerge, and the ability for scholars to make inferences across different datasets. For example, Hafner-Burton et al. (2013) limit their definition of election violence to "government-sponsored electoral violence" (Hafner-Burton et al. 2013). This conceptualization excludes cases of election violence where opposition leaders instigate violence (Collier & Vicente 2012) or where ordinary citizens rather than state officials participate in violence.

Many scholars define electoral violence as a subcategory of fraud (e.g. Mares & Young 2016), a type of political violence aimed at

---

[11] The crowdsourcing platform, "Ushahidi" monitored and collected data on incidents of hate speech during the US 2016 election (Kuo 2016).

[12] This statistic comes from the National Elections across Democracy and Autocracy (NELDA) dataset (NELDA33). "Significant violence" refers to at least one civilian death during, before, or after the election.

[13] A more conservative estimate, which uses a threshold of twenty-five deaths, finds that 23 percent of all elections between 1985 and 2005 have been violent (Arriola & Johnson 2012).

[14] These countries include Côte d'Ivoire, DRC, Ethiopia, Kenya, Nigeria, South Africa, Sudan, Togo, and Zimbabwe (Straus & Taylor 2012: 27).

[15] The survey was conducted by Afrobarometer (Round 5).

[16] According to the Electoral Contentious and Violence (ECAV) dataset, the highest number of election-related contentious events occurred in Asia (31 percent) followed by Africa (26 percent).

influencing the electoral process (e.g. Birch & Muchlinski 2017; Fjelde & Höglund 2016a; Höglund 2009; Wilkinson 2004), or more broadly, as any event where "the use of coercive force coincides with the electoral process" (Birch & Muchlinski 2017: 3). Yet there is considerable range in the type of events that could fall into this category of political violence. Fischer (2002), for example, includes hate speech and blackmail as well as the destruction of property and assassination. Recent datasets on election violence leave the concept equally broad. For instance, the Electoral Contention and Violence (ECAV) dataset uses the terms "electoral contention" rather than election violence, encompassing a broad range of violent and nonviolent events.[17]

The conceptual ambiguity of these definitions raises a number of important questions. For example, should counts of election violence encompass both intimidation (e.g. hate speech) and direct physical violence? If so, is there a need to distinguish levels or scales of violence? Who organizes and perpetrates violence and do they have to be "political actors"? And when do acts of violence become acts of election-related violence?

I define electoral violence as a form of political violence in which the dynamics of electoral competition shape the motives of perpetrators, the identification of targets, and the forms of physical violence.[18] Several studies also note the importance of timing, specifying a time frame whereby violent events are more likely to be associated with an upcoming or recent election.[19] And while violence does appear to increase in the months prior to or following an election (Harish & Little 2017; Straus & Taylor 2012), specifying a particular time period can become a somewhat arbitrary endeavor. Instead, I suggest the election violence is a political process that does not fit easily into a bounded time frame. Söderberg-Kovacs makes a similar argument, suggesting that it is nearly impossible to specify a precise time period, given that "the strategic electoral game is an ongoing process" (Söderberg Kovacs 2018: 6).

---

[17] ECAV authors define electoral contention as "public acts of mobilization, contestation, or coercion … used to affect the electoral process" (Daxecker et al. 2019).

[18] The definition draws on the conceptual work of Birch & Muchlinski (2017); Staniland (2014); Bekoe (2012) and Höglund (2009).

[19] For example, Straus and Taylor (2012) define the period for observing electoral violence as six months prior and three months following an election.

Using this broad definition, I identify three broad categories of electoral violence. The first is government or *state-sponsored violence*. By relying on state security forces (e.g. police or state militia), the incumbent party can use violence against key opposition members as a way to prevent opposition supporters from voting in competitive areas (Kasara 2016; Klopp 2001a) or as a way to suppress opposition protest. The key distinguishing feature here is that it is state security forces, rather than ordinary citizens, who carry out violence.

While state-sponsored violence accounts for the majority of violent events around elections, this book focuses primarily on joint violence. *Joint violence* describes violence that political or state elites organize – from either the incumbent or opposition party. In these scenarios, the main perpetrators are often ordinary citizens or members of non-state armed groups such as rebel groups, gangs, or vigilante groups. Unlike violence that relies primarily on state security forces, joint violence requires a process of mobilization and recruitment. Political leaders (national or local) must convince ordinary citizens to run the high risks of participation in violence on their behalf.[20] As I emphasize throughout this book, the perpetrators of joint violence can have multiple motives. Party leaders deploy or organize violence primarily as a way to alter the outcomes of the electoral process, either in the pre- or postelectoral period. Yet for individual participants or non-state actors, decisions to participate in violence are more varied, ranging from concerns about access to land, employment, status, physical security, desires to seek revenge, or group-level interests in gaining control of key resources, land, or territory (Staniland 2014; Straus & Taylor 2012; Kalyvas 2003).

A third and more ambiguous form of election-related violence is what I call *private violence,* which can escalate when a private altercation, such as a bar fight between individuals from opposing political sides, provides the trigger that sets political violence into motion. I categorize this type of violence as election-related if the trigger for the fight gains meaning in the context of broader narratives around electoral politics, or what Kalyvas (2003) calls the "master cleavage."

---

[20] Importantly, state actors must also recruit citizens to join state security forces. Yet in most cases, this recruitment is institutionalized and occurs prior to an episode of election-related violence.

The challenge for scholars is to identify acts of violence that may be linked to electoral politics and those acts that take a similar form (e.g. assassinations or arson) but are not linked directly to electoral politics. In many instances, however, acts of violence have multiple motives, where personal, territorial, and electoral motives intersect. This book aims to unpack these dynamics.

Election Violence in Kenya

Kenya is among the few countries in Africa that has experienced recurring and large-scale electoral violence. Figure 1.1 show the patterns of election violence since the reintroduction of multiparty elections in 1992 through the 2017 general elections.

Violence escalated before and after the reintroduction of multiparty elections in 1992 and again in 1997. In both elections, the incumbent party, the Kenya African National Union (KANU) used pre- and post-electoral violence to ensure electoral victory over opposition parties. National and local party leaders orchestrated violence in districts and constituencies where "ethnic outsiders" and those believed to favor

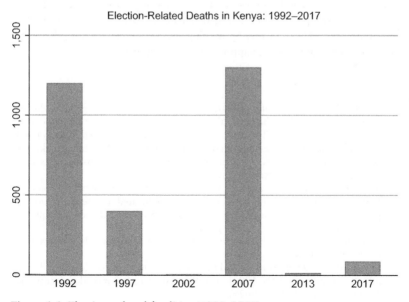

Figure 1.1 Election–related fatalities (1992–2017).

opposition parties threatened the electoral victories of KANU politicians (Klopp 2001a; Rutten et al. 2001; Throup & Hornsby 1998).[21] In
the pre and postelectoral periods throughout the 1990s, political entrepreneurs employed a dangerous set of anti-outsider narratives that
encouraged "natives" to remove "outsiders" from their lands.
Specifically, KANU elites revived and reinvented calls for *majimboism* –
a form of federalism based on exclusive ethno-territorial claims to each
region.[22] Kalenjin residents saw themselves as the indigenous, while
framing Kikuyu and other "migrants" as noncitizens who had to be
expelled or "cleansed" from the Rift Valley (Rutten et al. 2001: 75).
The targets of violence included the Kikuyu, but also other groups who
challenged KANU and the land rights of Rift Valley "natives," including Luos and Luhyas living in western Kenya.[23] Thousands of people
were killed and hundreds of thousands displaced from contested political territory.[24] The practice of violently displacing nonsupporters has
shaped expectations about the use of violence. An interview with
a resident living in the border zone between Nakuru and Narok
Counties (formerly districts) demonstrates the way that many citizens
interpret the logic of elite-led electoral violence:

Issues of land are connected with politics because the politician sees the
presence of other communities in a region as a threat to his [victory] in the
area since most people vote along tribal lines. So he will try his best to
eliminate them. He does this by inciting his community, telling them that
the other community is not supposed to be living there.[25]

---

[21] By "ethnic outsider" I refer primarily to the Kikuyu and other groups who are
viewed as "settlers" in the Rift Valley who have migrated from their ancestral
homes in other regions. The term "outsider" is widely deployed in Kenya and
much of Africa to denote a person or ethnic community who cannot make first-
comer claims to the land. Outsiders are distinguished from "insiders," or those
who see themselves as "sons of the soil."

[22] The idea of majimboism emerged in the early 1960s when the opposition party
KADU, comprised of minority ethnic groups, advocated for the devolution of
power to ethnically defined regions as a way to protect land and economic
interests from more power ethnic groups (i.e. the Kikuyu).

[23] Many Kalenjin communities in the Western Rift Valley were also targets of
retaliatory attacks.

[24] In the 1991–1993 electoral period there were 1,500 recorded deaths and
300,000 displaced (HRW 1993). In 1997 there were 100 recorded deaths and
10,000 displaced (HRW 2002b).

[25] Interview-Tipis-Nakuru County-Rift Valley, October 18, 2012 (14).

Despite the violence that marked elections in the 1990s, the 2002 election marked an important break from the past: the KANU regime was defeated by a significant margin and the election was mostly peaceful.[26] Yet only five years later, Kenya experienced its most violent election to date.

Violence escalated in 2007 when the Electoral Commission of Kenya (ECK) announced the incumbent candidate, Mwai Kibaki of the PNU, as the President reelect of Kenya. The main opposition party, the ODM, disputed the results, citing massive vote fraud. ODM party leaders, including the opposition candidate Raila Odinga, encouraged party members to mobilize *en masse*. Within minutes of the ECK announcement, violence had escalated across urban and rural regions of the country – from poor neighborhoods of Nairobi and Kisumu to farming communities across the Rift Valley. The violence followed a distinct pattern. It began with ODM members targeting PNU supporters or "outsiders" from contested or "electorally pivotal" areas (Kasara 2016). Coordinated reprisal attacks followed this first wave of violence.[27] The violence took several forms: evictions, killings, rape, looting, the destruction of homes and properties, and violent repression by the police. As I argue throughout this book, the primary trigger for the 2007–2008 postelection violence was anger over perceived electoral fraud committed by the incumbent regime (PNU). However, while this anger and frustration provided the key impetus for setting violence into motion, violence was possible because elites were able to draw on narratives of fear and opportunity around losing or gaining land and power. These historically rooted narratives provided a key script through which local and national elites mobilized and produced violent forms of collective action.

---

[26] In 2002, Mwai Kibaki, leader of the Democratic Party and the opposition coalition, National Alliance Rainbow Coalition (NARC), defeated Uhuru Kenyatta of KANU. Kibaki defeated Kenyatta by 61.3 percent to 31.6 percent of the popular vote (see Throup 2003 for details). The lack of violence was largely the result of the massive popular support for NARC, which represented a multiethnic coalition, alongside a severely weakened KANU.

[27] KNHRC 2008; Government of Kenya 2008; Author interviews (June 2012–February 2013, Rift Valley).

Existing Theories of Election Violence

A growing literature examines the relationship between electoral competition and political violence. These studies also engage with theories
of contentious politics (e.g. Tilly 2003), civil war (Balcells 2017; Arjona
2016; Kalyvas 2006), and ethnic conflict (e.g. Cederman, Gleditsch, &
Hug 2013; Lynch 2011; Oucho 2002). In the section below, I review
this broad literature and organize these studies into five broad, though
overlapping approaches that include institutionalist, rationalist (i.e.
elite-centered),   identity-based,   and   material   and   ideational
explanations.

Institutionalist Accounts

Institutionalist accounts view election violence as an outcome of
institutional weakness or breakdown. One of the dominant observations about election violence is that it follows a country's transition out of authoritarian rule, civil conflict, or war. Many scholars
thus claim that "democratization is often violent" (Berman 2007;
Carothers 2007; Snyder & Mansfield 2007) and further, that multiparty elections in weakly institutionalized democracies may provoke violence and instability associated with contestations over
power and political transition (Snyder 2000; Huntington 1991;
Dahl 1971). A range of studies echo the claim that state-organized
violence will follow political liberalization as political elites resort
to extreme measures to maintain the status quo or defeat rivals
(Mansfield & Snyder 2007; Chaturvedi 2005; Hegre et al. 2001;
Sambanis 2001).

These studies focus on the formal and informal institutions that
create a context for electoral violence – from weak property institutions
(Boone 2011; Kanyinga 2009; Onoma 2009; Klopp 2002), weak public security and rule of law (Mueller 2008), entrenched patronage and
clientelism (Boone & Kriger 2012; Reno 2007), an all-too powerful
executive (Branch & Cheeseman 2009), or majoritarian electoral institutions (Fjelde & Höglund 2016a).

Democratization scholars were among the first to theorize how
underdeveloped political institutions could facilitate rather than
restrain political violence in unconsolidated democracies. These scholars debated whether and how certain conditions were necessary before

a stable democracy could take shape.[28] Snyder (2002) and Mansfield and Snyder (2007) argued that states that democratize prematurely are much more likely to experience civil or interstate war in part because these "institutions are too weak to manage the upsurge in the political power of newly enfranchised masses" (2007: 4). While a curvilinear relationship between the onset of democratization and the risk of violence may describe some regions, the levels of election-time violence in Africa have been, on average, consistent over the first twenty years of multiparty electoral processes. Drawing on the African Electoral and Violence Dataset (AEVD) from 1990 to 2008, Straus & Taylor (2012) note that both the onset and deepening of democratization does not seem to correlate with patterns of violence. Kenya's history of electoral violence illustrates the need for more fine-grained theories. The first episodes of violence occurred during Kenya's first multiparty election in 1991–1992. Yet when violence erupted after the 2007 election, Kenya was regarded as among the most democratic countries in the region.

Other scholars examine how majoritarian or "winner-take-all" electoral institutions can increase incentives for electoral violence (Fjelde & Höglund 2016a; Boone 2009). Specifically, the insights of Przeworski (1991) and Boix (2003) suggest that incentives for violence should be greater when property rights or other distributive goods are not insulated from the outcome of a majoritarian election. In such cases, the electoral "losers" or minority groups have strong incentives to opt out of the democratic game, relying on violence as a way to subvert the process (Boone 2009).

Other institutionalist approaches have instead emphasized the role that patronage and corruption play in shaping the likelihood for violence (Boone & Kriger 2012; Reno 2011). Where patronage and corruption are most entrenched, citizens or "clients" must secure patronage relationships to access public goods and services such as security, jobs, contracts, housing, or land. Hence, elections create the opportunity to secure these goods if the "patron" or party wins, as well the prospect of losing access to these goods if the patron loses. Many of these studies suggest that in the absence of inclusive democratic institutions, electoral violence is more likely where political supporters link

[28] Dahl 1971.

the outcomes of elections with their exclusion from state resources (van de Walle 2007; Diamond et al. 1995).

In the Kenya context, scholars emphasize that electoral violence was possible in large part due to entrenched patronage practices and corruption alongside highly centralized state power. These features enabled national executives to use state resources for personal gain. Equally, they allowed the state to use state-sponsored security forces as a repressive tool to retain power while ignoring legal institutions meant to safeguard political and human rights (Branch & Cheeseman 2009). Importantly, some scholars point to the stabilizing potential of patronage politics (Lemarchard 1972; Scott 1969). Relatedly, in a cross-national study of African countries, Arriola and Johnson (2012) find corruption associated with patronage politics actually mitigates the likelihood for electoral violence.

While these institutional or structural accounts are an important part of explaining why electoral violence is possible, one shortcoming is that they provide retrospective accounts. The occurrence of violence is not a puzzle, but an inevitable event. For example, Susanne Mueller argues that in the lead up to the 2007–2008 election violence "Kenya was precariously perched and *poised to implode* even prior to the election" (Mueller 2008: 186). Further, many of these accounts focus on identifying the institutional features that help explain the escalation of violence nationally. Yet many of these theories are unable to explain the micro-level patterns and dynamics of escalation and non-escalation.[29]

This book pays particular attention to a set of scholars who theorize the links between land tenure institutions and violent conflict, including electoral violence (e.g. Kapstein 2017; Albertus 2015; Boone 2014; Branch 2009; Kanyinga 2009; Onoma 2009). A key insight from this scholarship is that where property rights in land are weak, political elites can use land as a patronage tool, distributing land or tenure security to loyal supporters while revoking rights or violently evicting opponents. Catherine Boone's work on rural land tenure regimes and land conflict in Africa has been at the forefront of this research agenda. Many other studies have outlined similar dynamics, analyzing cases such as Zimbabwe (Boone & Kriger 2012), Côte

---

[29] An important exception includes scholars who focus on land institutions, namely, Catherine Boone (2014, 2011). Other scholars who take a micro-level approach to election violence include Agbiboa (2018); Mitchell (2018); and Gutiérrez-Romero (2014).

d'Ivoire (Bassett 2011; Straus 2011), Colombia (Steele 2011), Venezuela (Albertus 2017), and the Democratic Republic of the Congo (DRC) (Autesserre 2009).

Yet to date, there are few studies that combine qualitative and quantitative evidence to examine systematically the micro-foundations of electoral violence – in Kenya or elsewhere. While scholars have noted the importance of land as a factor in electoral violence, few studies theorize and test the conditions under which factors relating to land compel ordinary citizens to use violence during an electoral period. Why, for example, might appeals to land provide an effective strategy to organize violence in one community, but not another similar community? Why and when does land provide a compelling reason for ordinary citizens to fight? As Giuliano (2011) observes, "People will not necessarily respond to an [elite appeal] unless those issues map onto some aspect of their lived experiences" (2011: 18). I build on the insight that certain institutional arrangements increase the likelihood for electoral violence (Daxecker 2019; Boone 2014, 2011; Klopp 2001a). The book's focus, however, is on identifying the role of land narratives in electoral violence, focusing on how these narratives act as a key mechanism linking institutional effects with the mobilization of electoral violence. This approach enables me to specify why violence is a thinkable and feasible strategy for elites and ordinary citizens in one local context, but unthinkable in the next.

Instrumentalist Accounts

One of the dominant theories of electoral violence argues that electoral violence is an elite strategy to alter the electoral or political process (Fjelde & Höglund 2016a; Höglund 2009). This approach builds on the democratic transition debate, but focuses on explaining when and why elites choose to incorporate violence into electoral campaigns. Broadly, these studies find that political actors have the greatest incentive to employ violence where vote margins are narrow (Wilkinson 2004) or where one side is uncertain about their probability of winning (Hafner-Burton et al. 2013). Violence provides a strategy of suppressing the turnout of nonsupporters through coercion or intimidation, changing voter preferences, or by displacing opposition voters as a way of altering the political terrain (Kasara 2016; Boone 2011; Klopp & Zuern 2007; Klopp 2001a). In his study of ethnic riots in

India for example, Wilkinson (2004) demonstrates how the degree of electoral competition at the local level helps explain whether the regional-level government would leverage security forces to prevent or foment ethnic riots. Harish and Little (2017) add to this debate, arguing that elections themselves do not create more violent politics. Rather, elections "affect the incentives to use violence to further political objectives not only leading up to and directly after the voting, but at all times" (2017: 238).

Many scholars taking a rationalist approach also consider which political party actor – the incumbent or opposition – is most likely to use violence. Most studies find that the incumbent is more likely to use violence because they are best able to exploit state resources to deploy violence and also have greater incentives to maintain power (Taylor et al. 2017; Hafner-Burton et al. 2014; Straus & Taylor 2012). Chaturvedi (2005) claims that political parties with lower levels of initial support are more likely to use violence. Similarly, Collier and Vicente (2012) find that opposition candidates are more likely to use violence to influence vote outcomes because they do not have the same comparative advantage as the governing party to use vote buying and electoral fraud.

In the Kenya context, several studies have documented how zones of political competition have overlapped with political violence, particularly during the first decade of multiparty politics under the regime of Daniel arap Moi. During these elections (1991–1992 and 1997–1998), the KANU government deployed violence as a way to displace presumed opposition supporters ("outsiders") in politically competitive regions. There is less evidence to show how political calculations shaped the patterns of violence in the postelectoral violence of 2007.[30]

This book builds on the insight that the electoral calculations of elites shape decisions to organize violent mobilization. These theories, however, make two assumptions that conceal many of the local dynamics that both foment and restrain violence. The first assumption is that political entrepreneurs use violence solely as a way to win their own political races. I suggest, however, that the possibility of winning an election is one among several motivations to

---

[30] Kasara (2016) suggests that election violence was greater in administrative locations that were "pivotal" to electoral outcomes of the 2002 parliamentary election.

use violence. For example, at the ward-level, the benefits of winning are rarely large enough for local councilors to run the high costs of engaging in violence. Instead, many local councilors facilitated violence to move up in the political party, win favors, and gain status and recognition as "big men" within their own community and larger political party. Second, these theories assume that the interests and motivations of citizens are homogeneous and unchanging, without explaining why certain people might be more or less compelled to fight for a particular political party or candidate. Political elites must have the incentives to use violence, yet violence is only feasible and thinkable when the motives for using violence resonate with citizens and local political actors on the ground. These motivations and logics may vary both spatially and temporally. Third, elite-level explanations tend to assume that civilians are willing to fight on behalf of their leaders, or that leaders will be able to mobilize followers when they have the incentive to do so, without specifying why a select group of civilians might be willing do to so and why most civilians are not. Instead of assuming that elites are able to mobilize citizens to fight or that particular institutional settings will inevitably give rise to violence, this project examines the local-level conditions that restrain or enable the organization of violent collective action in the context of elections.

Identity-based Explanations

The role of ethnic diversity or ethnic polarization is perhaps the most enduring explanation for violent conflict and war. Early scholarship on elections in democratizing societies viewed ethnicity as a threat to political stability. Ethnic diversity, scholars argued, would encourage ethnic outbidding, polarizing voters and undermining democracy (Weiner 1978; Rabushka & Shepsle 1972; Dahl 1971). These early theories were followed by cross-national econometric analyses that measured the relationship between ethnic diversity or fragmentation and the propensity for war or civil conflict (e.g. Sambanis 2001; Easterly & Levine 1997).[31] Despite

---

[31] Ethnic fractionalization is measured by the ethno-linguistic fractionalization index (ELF). This is calculated as the likelihood that two randomly drawn individuals speak a different language.

numerous pitfalls and critiques associated with measuring ethnic fractionalization, many scholars continue to rely on measures of ethnic polarization or fractionalization as predictors of war or civil conflict.

Many other studies focus instead on the mechanisms linking ethnicity and conflict, and in particular, on the role of ethnicity as a tool for mobilizing political support and building minimum winning coalitions (Eifert et al. 2010; Wilkinson 2004; Horowitz 1985; Bates 1983). These studies suggest that voters may use ethnicity as a shortcut to predict how leaders will distribute patronage goods or clientelistic benefits, ranging from land, jobs, infrastructure projects, or cultural rights and protections (Carlson 2015; Ferree 2011; Wilkinson 2004; Chandra 2005; Posner 2005; Bates 1983). Elections in these environments can become a zero-sum game where the loss of power means the loss of access to the "national cake" or the "democratic dividend" (Boone 2009; Snyder 2000). A general assumption or observation is that the use of ethnic-based appeals during elections increases ethnic polarization and, hence, increases the likelihood for ethnic violence. This link, however, is not well specified.

Kasara (2013) argues that the spatial segregation of ethnic groups, rather than ethnic diversity, can exacerbate interethnic mistrust, increasing the likelihood for electoral violence. Other studies meanwhile, focus less on polarization or fractionalization, and instead, on the cultural or institutional features of particular ethnic groups that make different groups more or less likely to engage in conflict (e.g. Wig & Kromney 2018; Laitin 1986).

An additional approach in thinking about the relationship between ethnic identity and violence comes from scholars taking a constructivist approach. This line of thought pushes back against the primordialist assumption underlying many existing studies: that ethnic groups and the meaning attached to these identities are singular and unchanging (Chandra 2012). The key insights are that (1) individuals hold multiple and changing identities and (2) the meanings and function attached to ethnic identities are an outcome of institutional arrangements or social and political processes (Boone & Nyeme 2015; Lynch 2011; Chandra 2005). There is a long literature in particular that demonstrates how both competitive elections (Posner 2005; Chandra 2004) and violence (Kalyvas 2003) can transform ethnic identities and alliance.[32]

Few people would deny the role that ethnic identity plays in Kenyan politics. The dynamics of violence are often cast in ethnic terms: Kalenjin chasing out Kikuyu or the Kikuyu taking revenge on Kalenjin or Luo. The challenge for scholars is to separate the act of ethnic targeting during an episode of violence from the conditions that explain why certain ethnic groups become the perpetrators or targets of violence, and why these identities are significant at certain times but not others. Building on recent constructivist theories of conflict, I argue that in contexts where rights in land or property are not secure, group members may be more likely to see a neighboring group as a threat to their own tenure security. In these settings, narratives of land access and security are infused with narratives of ethnic identification and belonging. These highly contentious narratives, which delineate ethnic insiders and outsiders, provide an easy and volatile discourse for politicians to exploit during elections. Key, however, is that the salience and meaning of ethnic identification is endogenous to the property rights environment in which these narratives take shape. This book demonstrates how one feature of state institutions – land rights – can shape the political salience of ethnic identification (Lieberman & Singh 2012).[33]

Material and Ideational Accounts: Theories of "Greed" and Grievance

I turn now to two prominent and contending explanations for ethnic conflict and civil war – between scholars who emphasize the role of "grievance" and those who instead emphasize the role of "greed" (i.e. material incentives). Grievance-based theories have focused on how political exclusion or inequalities in wealth between groups can generate contentious claim-making or violent forms of collective action

---

[32] For example, Fearon and Laitin (2000: 846) claim, "violence has the effect ... of constructing group identities in more antagonistic and rigid ways. These new constructed (or reconstructed) ethnic identities serve to increase support for elites who provoked the violence while favoring the continuation or escalation of violence." Lynch (2011) makes a similar argument about the construction of ethnic identity, focusing on the construction of the Kalenjin identity.

[33] Boone and Nyeme (2015) make a similar argument with reference to Tanzania.

(Cederman et al. 2017; Cederman et al. 2010; Stewart 2008; Gurr 1993; Horowitz 1985; Scott 1976).[34] Scholars have conceptualized grievances in terms of resentment among indigenous populations (Laitin 2007), ethno-nationalist grievances (Cederman et al. 2010), perceptions of "state or societal discrimination" (Fearon & Laitin 2003), and competition for state resources (Cederman & Giardin 2007). For many scholars, ethnicity establishes the boundaries around which inequalities and grievances emerge. Cederman and Wucherpfennig (2017) and Cederman, Gleditsch, and Buhaug (2013) pay particular attention to the role that inequalities in political and economic resources between ethnic groups play in inducing grievance that can foster violent conflict.[35] One of the main observations is that groups who experience marginalization, political exclusion, or socioeconomic inequalities are more likely to violently rebel or protest than groups who benefit from political inclusion (Cederman et al. 2010; Stewart 2008; Gurr 1993).

Critics of classical grievance theory note that while grievances play a role in fomenting violence, conventional measures of grievance cannot explain why some grievances provide sources of violent mobilization while the majority remain latent (Fearon & Laitin 2003). Cederman, Gleditsch, and Buhaug refer to this as the "ubiquity-of-grievances claim" (2013: 19). Proponents of grievance-based theories also struggle to prove that exclusion-based grievance is indeed exogenous and not a consequence of a government's initial decision about which groups to exclude.[36]

Despite measurement and conceptual challenges, there is renewed interest in the explanatory power of grievances, as well as efforts to demonstrate the causal effect that grievances have on conflict outcomes (e.g. Wucherpfennig et al. 2016).

Simmons (2014: 514) argues that by understanding the meaning that grievances acquire, scholars can better explain, "how and why social movements emerge, develop, strengthen, and fade." One of the main shortcomings of grievance-based scholarship has been the failure to

---

[34] Gurr launched a dataset, the Minorities at Risk (MAR) dataset that has become one of the main sources available for evaluating theories about ethnic groups (1993).

[35] See Lars-Erik Cederman's related studies (e.g. Cederman, Gleditsch, & Buhaug 2013; Wucherpfennig et al. 2012).

[36] Blattman and Miguel 2010 and Fearon and Laitin 2000 argue that political exclusion is endogenous to regime decision making and hence cannot be treated as an exogenous treatment or a variable with causal power.

take the meanings of grievance seriously, often by relying on proxies such as income or education level that measure material inequality, but rarely providing meaningful measures of grievance (Cederman, Gleditsch, and Buhaug 2013). Grievances are often rooted in a sense of injustice that cannot be captured by material measures alone.

A second approach suggests that grievances or ideology alone cannot sufficiently explain an individual's participation in political violence. Drawing on Mancur Olson's theory of collective action (1965), these scholars underline a key puzzle: if a successful revolution, protest, or social movement produces public goods that nonparticipants enjoy (e.g. new leadership or land redistribution), why would any rational individual take on the high costs of participation? (Humphreys & Weinstein 2006; Olson 1965). This approach suggests that individuals will participate in violence if the perceived benefits of doing so outweigh the costs. Armed groups can alter this cost calculation by offering recruits particular "selective incentives" such as wages, land, employment, or the opportunity to loot (e.g. Collier & Hoeffler 2004). Accordingly, individuals may choose to fight when their opportunity costs of participation are sufficiently low. Conventional "greed" models thus predict that poor and unemployed individuals, with little to no education, would be more likely to participate in violence, given that their opportunity costs are lower than individuals who could derive greater material benefit from nonparticipation (e.g. through formal employment, farming, or attending university). Kalyvas and Kocher (2007) intervene in this debate, pushing back against the assumption that nonparticipation is costless. Armed groups, they argue, can also recruit individuals by raising the risks of nonparticipation, directing violence toward bystanders and offering protection or security in exchange for participation. In the context of election-related violence, politicians can provide followers with selective incentives to fight, such as cash rewards, plots of land, title deeds, or the bounty from looting homes and business in exchange for a "day's work" of fighting.[37]

---

[37] According to interviews, the Commission of Inquiry into Post Election Violence (CIPEV) Waki Report (Republic of Kenya 2008) and Kenya National Human Rights Commission (KNCHR) (2008), participants were rewarded in cash and kind for each house they burned/destroyed or in some cases, for the number of people they "removed."

With regard to Kenya, many explanations of electoral violence focus on how historical or ethnic grievances provide a basis for elites to mobilize "natives of the Rift Valley" against "non-natives" (Kanyinga 2009; Anderson & Lochery 2008; Lynch 2008). One short-coming of these discussions in Kenya (and elsewhere) is the tendency to assume that because historical or land grievances exist, elites will be able to mobilize them. There is little theorization about how these grievances evolve and vary, and why elites might succeed in appealing to grievances in some contexts but not others.

Many recent studies of participation in political violence push back against the bifurcation of "greed" and "grievance," acknowledging that a range of motives interact to shape the logic of participation in violence. Sambanis, for example, writes that greed and grievance are "usually shades of the same problem" (2004: 263). More so, these two approaches do not account for the full range of possible motives. Participation in violence for example, may also be related to emo-tional factors, including anger, resentment, or the desire for revenge (Wood 2003; Petersen 2002). And as Gates (2002) and Humphreys and Weinstein (2006) demonstrate, coercion may often play a decisive role, for example, when rebel groups forcibly recruit child soldiers. In such cases, individuals have little agency over the decision to fight.

Rather than treat material and ideational incentives as theoreti-cally distinct, I argue that land grievances (what I term "land narratives") have material and ideational elements. Beliefs about the illegitimacy of land allocation can provide a powerful form of grievance. People may join in a violent protest or engage in acts of violence because they see their participation as necessary to advance a particular agenda – whether it is about reclaiming stolen territory or "righting wrongs." But equally, people may run the risk of participation in violence because they seek opportunities for perso-nal gain. In other words, the mobilization of land grievances encompasses multiple logics: feelings of economic and political powerlessness, such as the inability to secure land tenure, alongside the hope that participation in fighting will yield private, materials payoffs such as a plot of land, a title deed, or livestock. Narratives about reclaiming land or defending one's territory can justify and lend credibility to individual motives.

Land and Violence

Many scholars debate the causal relationship between land and political violence (Scott 1976; Sansom 1970 in Kapstein 2017). The rural-based uprisings of the Soviet era helped inspire a wave of scholarship focused on measuring the link between land inequality and rural unrest (Brockett 1992; Midlarsky 1988). Much of this scholarship suggests that because land is a livelihood resource, land deprivation would motivate collection action (Østby 2008; Brockett 1992; Muller et al. 1989; Midlarsky 1988). Other scholars, meanwhile, have focused on whether land reform can diminish or preempt insurgency (Albertus 2015; Wood 2003; Paige 1975).[38] Yet there is little consistent evidence linking land distribution or inequality with political violence.

One shortcoming of existing approaches is that scholars focus primarily on the material dimensions of land (e.g. land as plots that can be redistributed) while overlooking the multiple pathways through which land can shape political action.[39] By contrast, I suggest that land shapes the dynamics of political action through four broad and interconnected mechanisms: it serves as a livelihood asset, shapes parameters of territory, establishes belonging, and provides a key dimension of state-building. I explain each of these briefly.

First, as existing studies observe, land serves as a critical material asset and livelihood source.[40] When I ask respondents to explain what land means to them, a prevailing theme is that land "is life itself." Understanding the material value of land, its ability to sustain life and endow future generations is important for understanding why barriers to land access can become a source of grievance and collective action. This material dimension of land frames land politics as a distributional question about how land is divided among individuals or groups within society and whether the status

---

[38] Several recent studies suggest that land reform can have the unintended effect of inducing rather than curbing rebellion (e.g. Finkel et al. 2015; Albertus & Kaplan 2013; Skocpol 1979; Scott 1976).

[39] "Null findings" in many analyses of land inequality and violent conflict also relate to measurement problems or discrepancies in how scholars conceptualize and measure land inequality and conflict (see Thompson 2016).

[40] According to the World Bank, 70 percent of people living in "least-developed countries" live in rural areas, the majority of whom rely on agriculture. 73 percent of Kenya's population is classified as rural. http://data .worldbank.org/topic/agriculture-and-rural-development

quo distribution of land threatens or maintains the political order (Acemoğlu & Robinson 2006).

Thinking about land as a livelihood source also helps explain how changes in land quality and access, hastened by urbanization, population growth, and environmental change, can place significant pressure on communities that rely on land for survival. A growing literature in conflict studies focuses on how climate and environmental changes affect the occurrence and patterns of communal conflict – particularly between pastoralists and farmers. While scholars debate the causal role of environmental change,[41] most agree that there is a rise in communal conflict, pointing to cases across the Sahel and Horn of Africa. The general argument suggests that climate change alters the productive capacity of the land, bringing communities into conflict with one another. Yet while climate may affect the availability and quality of land, several scholars argue that the likelihood of communal conflict is more so a function of a group's political and economic marginalization (Buhaug et al. 2015; Raleigh 2010) and the capacity of political institutions to mediate the effects of climate change.

A second way that land shapes contentious politics and violence is by establishing the parameters of territory. Thinking about land as territory allows us to think about land as more than soil, but as political space that can be claimed, controlled, or challenged (Toft 2003). Competing claims over land or territory can arise between different groups (e.g. ethnic groups or political parties) or between non-state groups and the state. In the context of multiparty Kenya for example, political parties have transformed land into political territory by using violence to assert dominance over their respective territories, displacing or disenfranchising people who "do not belong" on the land. Analyzing land as territory also helps expand theories of land to urban areas where it is not necessarily acres of arable land that people challenge. Rather, competing groups may assert claims over a section of a city such as a marketplace or informal settlement that "belongs" to those who "settled first" (Klaus & Paller 2017). Hence, by focusing only on the material value of land or its productive capacity, scholars miss a key dimension that can help explain why people feel both a sense of

---

[41] On this debate see, for example, von Uexkull et al. (2016); Buhaug et al. (2015); and Raleigh and Urdal (2007).

threat – of losing land, property, and power – and a motive to claim or expand territorial control on behalf the group.

Third, land provides a way of claiming belonging: to a family, clan, or larger community. Similarly, it provides a way of self-identifying: as a member of a community or "ancestral home," the offspring of a prominent community member, or as a landed or landless member of society. Across many settings, the most salient and powerful identity is whether a person can claim to be a "son of the soil" or is instead cast as a "foreigner" (Weiner 1978).[42] These lines of identification affect how individuals or group members make claims to the land and the rights they can expect to receive – formally or informally. In this way, identification and belonging are an important part of contentious claim-making and the violent politics that can arise from these competing claims.

Finally, as Catherine Boone and others have argued, the allocation and control of land links citizens with the state, providing a key dimension of state-building (Boone 2014).[43] These institutions establish a "political relationship" between citizens making claims to land, and the state, which has the power to enforce, allocate, and revoke land rights from citizens.[44] This relationship brings citizens under the jurisdiction of the state and thus provides one way for the state to expand its authority over citizens and space (Boone 2014, 2007; Herbst 2000). Similarly, political elites can use land reform to consolidate power, especially under more authoritarian regimes, expropriating land from political opponents (Albertus 2015). States can also use land settlement policies to expand territory and "engineer" particular ethnic or racial visions of the nation-state (Frymer 2014).

Kenya provides a particularly good case to examine the relationship between land and political violence. Land provides a critical livelihood source, an investment opportunity, and means of identification. Yet the formal and informal rules that mediate access to land rights are arbitrary and exclusive. Rather than strengthening formal institutions, Kenyan leaders have used land as a source of political patronage, allocating land rights to followers while removing rights from opposition members. During election periods, leaders use land narratives to

---

[42] See also: Geschiere (2009); Lund (2008).
[43] See for example: Lund and Boone (2013); Boone (2007).
[44] Boone (2014) and Joireman (2011) make this point with respect to property regimes in Africa.

establish targets of violence. Political opponents are cast as "outsiders" who must be removed from the contested districts or blocked from voting. In this way, land has become synonymous with contested political territory. Equally, the provision of land rights has provided a way for the state to exert its authority over citizens.

Outline of the Book

I develop and test the argument I have outlined here through seven main chapters. Through these chapters, I aim to explain how land underlies the process of violence, from the political and institutional factors that shape land access and security, the land narratives that emerge from these institutions, and the ways in which these land narratives contribute to the mobilization of electoral violence.

Chapter 2 presents the book's main theory, which links contests over land with the local-level dynamics and escalation of electoral violence. I argue that the escalation of electoral violence is part of an historically rooted process that includes inequality in land rights between two identity-based groups, the formation of contentious land narratives between these groups, and the mobilization of these land narratives to organize and produce electoral violence. The chapter explains each of these "stages" in the process of violence. I begin by theorizing how inequality in land rights between groups can shape a distinct set of contentious narratives around land. I then explain how land narratives work to shape political action, enabling or restraining the production of violence. The chapter also explains the research design and methodology that provides the evidentiary basis for this theory of electoral violence.

Chapter 3 provides readers with the historical context in which to understand land and political violence in Kenya. It does so by comparing the histories of land ownership and distribution between Kenya's highlands and the Coast region. The main research question examines how and why practices of land allocation vary between regions. In explaining this variation, the chapter draws on patterns of land allocation within settlement schemes, archival data from the colonial and postcolonial period, and in-depth interviews. The chapter argues that two styles of political leadership – the vote-seeking land patron and rent-seeking landlord – reflect different modes and logics of land accumulation and distribution that have developed over different political periods in each region. I explain how these different modes of land distribution and the broader politics of land play out under three phases of Kenya: colonial rule and the Mau Mau civil war (1900–1962), the single party rule of Jomo Kenyatta (1962–1978), and the *de facto* single party rule of Daniel arap Moi (1978–2002).

Chapter 4 asks why contentious land narratives form between some communities, but not others. The chapter presents a large qualitative dataset collected through case comparisons of settlement schemes and LBCs in the Rift Valley and Coast regions. The chapter provides brief summaries of each of these eight case studies to demonstrate how inequality in land rights manifests in different contexts. Leveraging comparisons between neighboring communities, the chapter argues that the degree of land rights inequality plays an important role in the formation of contentious land narratives.

Chapter 5 turns to a case comparison between two sets of farming communities in Nakuru County to explain why contentious land narratives emerge between ethnically distinct communities in one area, but not another. I use the case of Mauche and Likia to show that where two neighboring ethnic groups gain access to land through distinct processes, both groups are likely to challenge the legitimacy of the other's land claims. I contrast this with the case of Ogilgei and Kerma, where each ethnic community has acquired title deeds and land narratives are not contentious. The chapter demonstrates that contentious land narratives between ethnic groups are not the inevitable outcomes of ethnic rivalry but are instead, endogenous to the local institutional context that shapes the way that residents access and secure rights to land.

Chapter 6 analyzes the escalation and production of electoral violence, with a focus on Kenya's 2007–2008 postelection violence. The chapter's central question asks how land narratives shape the actual escalation and occurrence of violence. Using a process-tracing approach based on qualitative evidence from three communities in Nakuru County, the chapter demonstrates how land narratives contribute to the production of election violence. I take the reader through four stages in the escalation of electoral violence. These stages include: 1) the mobilization of land narratives, 2) the trigger event, 3) local escalation, and 4) scale-shift. As part of this analysis, I explain how different logics of violence – from preemption, opportunities to alter the status quo, revenge, and desire for material gain – play out at these different stages. Broadly, the chapter shows how local land narratives can provide a key discursive tool through which elites and ordinary civilians establish motives for organizing and engaging in violence.

Chapter 7 examines why contentious land narratives are not sufficient predictors of electoral violence. In contrast to the previous chapter, which demonstrates how elites use narratives to organize violence, this chapter draws on evidence from counties in the Coast region where there are salient contentious land narratives yet electoral violence is rare. The chapter argues that land narratives work differently along the Coast because residents do not link their land rights with electoral outcomes. Hence, residents have few motives to participate in electoral violence and politicians have far less power to use land narratives to organize violence. To account for this regional difference, the chapter brings the reader back to the theory of "landlord" and "land patron," which I discuss in terms of patronage strength. It also explains the importance of group size: the proportion of ethnic insiders relative to outsiders at the local level.

In Chapter 8, I shift from the more inductive approach that guide preceding chapters to a deductive one, using survey data to test existing theories about the causes and consequences of electoral violence. In doing so, I also shift the unit of analysis from the region and group-level, to the individual. The chapter has two main parts. The first examines the predictors of electoral violence, focusing specifically on the role of divisive land appeals in increasing an individual's likelihood of experiencing violence. The second part focuses on the effects of violence, asking how the experience of election violence shapes openness toward ethnic outgroups, trust in political leadership, and engagement across ethnic lines. Broadly, I show that the experience of election violence has an enduring effect on how an individual perceives and engages with her political and social world. Further, examining the effects of electoral violence helps unpack the potential endogeneity of violence, enabling scholars to better specify the mechanisms through which election violence increases or diminishes the prospects for democratic consolidation and durable peace.

Chapter 9, the conclusion, provides a brief summary of the book's main argument and discusses its generalizability. To do so, it draws on examples that illustrate how the book's theory might generalize to other cases such as Burundi, Côte d'Ivoire, and the DRC, as well as cases such as Colombia, and Bangladesh. The chapter then discusses how the main argument can inform broader theorizing about the relationship between democratization, political violence, and postconflict politics. Finally, it reflects on potential lessons learned from a close study of land rights, group narratives, and violence.

2 | A Theory of Land and Electoral Violence

"The most painful thing is that the people who did this to us were our neighbors from the beginning. And during attacks they would tell us that this is not the time of knowing each other."

Resident of Shalom Resettlement Farm, Rongai
(Author's interviews, July 2012)

This book is a study of land and the process of electoral violence. It analyzes how the distribution and control of land and property shape the patterns, logics, and organization of violence. As existing studies have emphasized, politicians must have the incentive and capacity to select violence over or in addition to other electoral strategies.[1] Yet violence is only possible where a select group of supporters come to believe that their participation in violence may advance their interests or well-being. This view of violence shifts the focus from one that is a primarily elite-driven process to one in which elites must organize, collaborate with, or coerce local supporters.

The main question of this book then is not "why do elites use violence?" Rather, it asks how the political objectives of elites interact with the motives and fears of ordinary citizens to shape the *process of mobilization* and *spaces of violent escalation*. Where political leaders coordinate with local actors to produce violence, election violence represents what Kalyvas (2003) terms, the "joint production of action."

Existing studies of electoral violence tend to attribute the occurrence of electoral violence to institutional features of the state, ethnic polarization across society, or the rationalist calculations of political elites. Despite this growing literature, we still know very little about how the

---

[1] Several scholars examine the use of electoral violence as one extreme "tool" among other options available to politicians for altering electoral outcomes that can include vote rigging, vote buying, voter intimidation, etc. (See for example Mares & Young 2016; Norris 2015; Dunning 2011.)

process of political and social mobilization occurs: how political entrepreneurs compel ordinary citizens to fight on their behalf. Understanding this process of coordination and mobilization requires an analysis of how political leaders engage and communicate with citizens and voters: what narratives are most powerful and why? What are the origins of these narratives and how do they change during electoral periods? And why might particular narratives – around land, territory, identity, or jobs – provide more effective tools for mobilizing violence than others?

I argue that in contexts where land shapes livelihood and identification, and where tenure institutions are weak, land narratives can serve as a key device around which elites and citizens coordinate the use of violence. A key premise is that the occurrence of electoral violence is far less common than the spaces where contentious land narratives are salient. Therefore, I do not claim that contentious land narratives cause or predict violence. Rather, I treat land narratives as a key mechanism through which distributional land inequalities shape the occurrence and dynamics of local-level violence.[2] My main interest is in explaining why these land narratives enable elites to organize violence in some cases but not others.

In the Kenya context, I find that electoral violence is most likely to escalate in areas where elites have incentives to organize violence, but equally, where a subset of citizens link the outcome of elections with their ability to access or secure land. Individuals may participate in violence if they believe that elections present either an opportunity to strengthen or reclaim land rights, or where the electoral process presents a threat to status quo claims. In these cases, violence can become a means of ensuring one's preferred candidate at all costs, or a mechanism to preempt the abrogation of one's land rights.

Argument: Land Narratives and the Process of Violence

This book draws on recent microlevel studies of civil war and contentious politics that emphasize civilian agency, inequality, and grievance

---

[2] Drawing on existing definitions, I define causal mechanism as "the pathway or process by which an effect is produced" (Falleti & Lynch 2009 in Checkel, 2017: 596).

Figure 2.1 The process of election violence: summary view.

to develop a theory about how access and rights to land structure the process and organization of violence at the local level.[3]

I argue that the escalation of electoral violence is part of an historically rooted process that I analyze in two main stages. In the first, I analyze how the parity in land rights between two groups affects the formation of contentious land narratives. In the second, I analyze how these land narratives enable or restrain the ability of local and national elites to organize and mobilize election-time violence. Figure 2.1 provides a summary view of this process of violence.

Stage 1: The Formation of Contentious Land Narratives

Defining Land Narratives

I begin by theorizing the determinants of contentious land narratives: the particular institutional or political factors or events that help explain why contentious land narratives become salient between certain groups. In the sections below, I argue that a key source of variation is the degree of parity in land rights between two proximate groups.

I define narratives as the stories people tell to make sense of their social or political realities (Cramer 2012; Patterson & Monroe 1998). They are interpretations of historical and ongoing events as well as everyday rules and norms.[4] Drawing on Bedford and Snow (2000) and Simmons (2016), I suggest that narratives act like "frames"; they enable individuals to make meaning out of events and in so doing, these narratives help to "organize experience and guide action" (Bedford & Snow 2000: 614).

---

[3] These microlevel studies include: Arjona (2016); Autesserre (2009); Fujii (2009); Kalyvas (2006); Straus (2006); Weinstein (2006); Wood (2003).

[4] This concept of narrative is very similar to the concept of frames used first by Goffman (1974) and now commonly used in the social movements literature and specifically, work on collective action frames. (See Tarrow 2011; Gamson 1992; Snow & Bedford 1992.)

I use the term "land narrative" to describe how members of a subnational group explain their experience of land acquisition or land loss, claim rights to land, and interpret threat to land access or land security.[5] Land narratives have several important features. First, as Tilly has remarked, land narratives can provide shared stories about the boundaries between "us" and "them," delineating between ethno-political communities, or between members of the in-group and out-group. Second, land narratives specify the land rights to which group members – claimants – believe they are entitled. Third, they specify a set of goals and a program of action for protecting or promoting land claims of the group. Fourth, land narratives are practices of meaning-making: they create and affirm the value of land within the community or larger cultural sphere. These narratives can shape beliefs about how land or property contributes to livelihoods, wealth, development, and group identification. Land narratives convey why land matters and hint at the possible forms of political action that people might take to protect or assert rights to land at a future point. As Simmons writes, "by paying attention to meaning, we improve our ability to explain and analyze the dynamics of contention" (2014: 514). Examining the meaning that people attach to land thus helps explain why certain claims might be more likely to generate political protest or violence compared to other claims (Simmons 2014; Wedeen 2002).

Contentious Land Narratives
Narratives around land become contentious when a group's claim to land or territory competes with the rights and claims of another group or set of individuals. Specifically, contentious land narratives are those that: (1) assert rights to land based on membership in a group; (2) describe other groups in terms that denote nonbelonging (e.g. "foreigners," "invaders"); (3) blame other groups or leaders for land injustices endured in the past (e.g. unfair land allocation, loss of property rights, or forced eviction); (4) express fears of losing land to a competing claimant; and (5) articulate a plan of action for reclaiming or protecting land.

---

[5] By subnational group, I refer to a group of people who commonly identify along ethnicity, race, religion, or place/region or residence.

In Kenya, people tend to craft narratives of land around particular themes: the metaphor of the insider–outsider,[6] the political leader who favors his own group, the sanctity of the title deed as proof of ownership,[7] or the belief that "first-comers" have the legitimate claim to the land. Individuals – as members of ethnically or regionally defined groups – narrate these beliefs and outlooks to their families and broader social and political networks. Such narratives – in Kenya or elsewhere – often recall a past in which land was plentiful and accessible until outsiders invaded or grabbed land. The most ubiquitous land narrative in Kenya draws on the metaphor of the "visitor/outsider" and the "native." In the excerpt below, a Kalenjin interviewee from Mauche (Nakuru County) illustrates one side of this insider–outsider narrative:

There are people who consider themselves natives while the others are viewed as visitors. [The visitors] have reached a point where they have acquired more land than the natives who wonder how their counterparts managed this. Yet they, the natives, are the ones who should own land. But the visitor – having seen the benefit of this land – cannot relinquish it. Yet the native is insisting on his departure ... For example, in Nakuru most people are Kikuyu. And the natives question how the Kikuyu acquired land. But [Kikuyu] would respond and say that they bought the land, which makes them the legal owners too. And this causes chaos.[8]

The narrative is partly about a more powerful and land-hungry migrant group who acquires the land of natives, pushing them off their ancestral land. The second story emphasizes the method through which "visitors" acquire land – purchasing the land and following legal procedure – and the feelings of powerlessness that this process evokes in the storyteller.

Importantly, narratives are distinct from grievances in that they not only express group-level resentment over perceived inequality or marginalization. Rather, they are dynamic stories that help to define or reinforce a group's mode of identification and sense of entitlement, while serving as a strategic discourse for claiming or securing land. The assertions, "this is my family land because ... " or "we have

---

[6] Sarah Jenkins refers to this as the "Immigrant-Guest" metaphor (2012).
[7] See Ndungu's note on the "myth of the sanctity of the title deed," pp. 16–17 of the Ndungu Report, Government of Kenya (2004).
[8] Interview-Mauche Settlement-Nakuru County-Rift Valley, July 21, 2012 (16).

the right to this land because ... " can become group narratives about how property rights are constituted and equally, the methods that people can use to claim or defend these rights. As I detail in later parts of the book, these land narratives emerge locally within the group but are also shaped by broader regional and national political narratives.

By contrast, noncontentious land narratives are group-level practices of meaning-making around land. Such narratives imbue land with both symbolic and material value, but unlike contentious narratives, they do not emphasize imminent threats to the tenure security of group members. Further, these more "neutral" narratives emphasize stability rather than changes to status quo claims.

Narrative Themes

I identify two broad narrative themes that emerge from local environments defined by relative land inequality: narratives that contest past allocation (*injustice narratives*) and narratives that emphasize tenure and territorial threats (*insecurity narratives*). Injustice narratives are retrospective: they are based on a group's shared history about wrongdoings in the recent or distant past, and center around beliefs about illegitimate or unjust land allocations, evictions, or land seizures. The result is a set of competing land claims where each side challenges the tenure or territorial rights of the other. For example, members of one group might accuse the other of acquiring land illegitimately through networks of political patronage or outright theft. The injustice narrative might also emphasize how migrants have stolen or invaded the ancestral land of "natives." Key here is that members of each group believe they are the rightful inhabitants of a particular piece of land or territory. In many cases, these narratives manifest as debates over which group has the more legitimate claim to the land: "sons-of-the soil" or migrants who have worked the land or have obtained formal title deeds.[9] A key question, which I detail later, is identifying how and why particular events or actors activate or mobilize these narratives, which often remain latent for years or decades.

---

[9] There is a growing scholarship on sons-of-the-soil conflict. See for example, Cote & Mitchell (2017); Bhavnani & Lacina (2015); Lentz (2014); Fearon and Laitin (2011); Marshall-Fratani (2006).

Insecurity narratives by contrast, are collective stories that convey threat: fears of eviction, expropriation, or territorial loss. These narratives most often emerge when members of at least one group fear that rival claimants will use their superior political or coercive power to displace group members from their land. Fears of displacement are more likely when group members draw on personal or group stories of eviction by the state or a rival group. These varying narrative themes do not necessarily shape different forms of electoral violence. Yet making the distinction is important because each narrative helps explain a distinct logic of violent political action, or why ordinary people become willing to take on the high costs of violent collective action. Each narrative, in other words, provides a different script that legitimizes previously unthinkable actions (Autesserre 2012; Schatzberg 2001).

Inequality and Land Narratives

I return now to the first of two research questions motivating this book: what explains the formation of salient and contentious land narratives between two groups? In answering this question, I draw on a large body of scholarship that considers the relationship between inequality and violent conflict, including revolution, protests, and armed uprisings (e.g. Albertus et al. 2018; Finkel et al. 2015; Cederman et al. 2013; Wood 2003; Brockett 1992; Paige 1975). I focus on three features of this debate. The first considers the relevant cleavage lines around which scholars should conceptualize or measure inequality: whether the relevant distinction is between inequality among *individuals* in society, or between relevant social, ethnic, or class *groups*. A second debate concerns the *type* of inequality that is most likely to generate contentious politics and violence. Notably, while most studies have focused on inequality in income, there is also a long tradition focusing more explicitly on inequality in land ownership and its relationship to rural unrest (e.g. Albertus 2015; Wood 2003; Brockett 1992; Russett 1964). Finally, a third set of debates, which I discuss in a later section, aim to identify the particular causal mechanisms linking inequality and violent conflict.

Among the first to theorize the effects of inequality was Tedd Gurr (1970), who focused primarily on individual-level inequality. His theory of relative deprivation attributed violence to an individual's frustration and anger over a perceived discrepancy between one's social or economic situation and another's. Structuralists, by contrast, focused on the role of distributional inequalities in land or income across society (e.g. Scott 1976). The main claim was that the majority poor or landless would inevitably turn to violence as a means of redistributing resources in their favor.

Both approaches have received considerable pushback. One set of critiques has come from social movement scholars, who emphasize the need to specify changes in political opportunity that equip actors with the organizational structure and resources required for overcoming the collective action problem (Tilly 1978; Snyder & Tilly 1972). Many civil war scholars, by contrast, have built on Gurr's individual-level theory of inequality and conflict. These studies rely on measures of vertical inequality: inequality between individuals rather than groups (e.g. Collier & Hoeffler 2004; Fearon & Laitin 2003; Alesina & Perotti 1996; Muller & Seligson 1987). Yet these scholars find little evidence that inequality affects conflict.

Yet because these studies rely on measures of vertical inequality, they overlook key conflict-inducing effects of inequality, specifically, that most internal conflicts are organized along group lines (Cederman, Gleditsch, & Buhaug. 2013; Østby 2008; Stewart 2008: 11). These observations reflect a recent turn in many studies of inequality and violence away from individual-level measures to a focus on inequality *between groups*.[10] Many of these studies draw on the theoretical insights of Donald Horowitz (1985), who applied theories of social psychology to link group inequality and ethnic conflict through mechanisms related to group comparisons, collective self-esteem, and concerns over group status.[11] A key focus now is on what Stewart terms, "horizontal inequality" or inequities in economic, social, or political dimensions or cultural status between culturally defined groups (2008: 3).[12]

---

[10] Many scholars working on questions of inequality and collective action emphasized the explanatory power of the group or collective over the individual. Tilly (1998) argued for example, that "durable inequalities" in social systems emerge along categorical distinctions such as gender, ethnicity, or citizenship, rather than individual-level differences.

[11] Early theories of social psychology, from which Horowitz borrowed, included Tajfel (1982); Tajfel & Turner (1979).

[12] For an overview of existing measures of intergroup inequality including potential drawbacks, see Jayadev and Reddy (2011).

Recent analyses focusing on inequality between groups provide a useful way to conceptualize and measure inequality and its potential effects on contentious politics and violence. One risk, however, is that in treating the ethnic group as a unit of analysis, scholars make potentially problematic assumptions about ethnic groups as stable, bounded, and cohesive units. Yet as constructivist scholars have argued, ethnic group identification and group boundaries are dynamic and far from stable. These changes are often endogenous to political and social processes or institutions. Group boundaries can become more or less inclusive or exclusive in response to state policies, war, or state collapse (e.g. Lieberman & Singh 2012; Herrera 2005; Kalyvas 2003; Laitin 1986; Young 1979). The political salience or meaning that a given ethnic identity acquires also changes, often with shifts in political representation or political cleavage lines (Posner 2005).

Further, by taking the group as the unit of analysis, scholars attribute motive to the group. Yet groups do not act. Rather, individual group members, with varying beliefs, preferences, and motives, choose or are compelled to participate in different forms of political action. Relatedly, studies that focus on the group-level risk assuming that all individuals place equal meaning on their group identity. Yet as Chandra (2012) writes, individuals may have multiple ethnic options and may choose to activate certain ethnic identities over others, depending on the context. Hence, accounting for the fact that individuals hold multiple identities at any given time is crucial in thinking about when and why group-level inequalities or perceived injustices might motivate an individual group member to participate in violent politics.

An additional shortcoming in recent analyses is that they do little to theorize the *type* of inequality that might best predict the emergence of contentious claim-making or the escalation of violent collective action. Amartya Sen (1992) underlines this point, encouraging scholars to begin by asking, "equality of what?" Conventional studies tend to analyze economic inequality using measures such as the Gini coefficient.[13] Recent studies rely on more specific dimensions of individual and group-level inequality such as inequality in infant mortality (Østby

---

[13] As Cederman et al. (2017) note, the Gini coefficient is an explicit measure of inequality between individuals in society and hence "does not correspond to any well-known theory of ethnic conflict" (2017: 24).

et al. 2011), luminosity (Alesina et al. 2016), or education (e.g. Hillesund 2015). Yet these studies say little about how or why distributional inequalities in healthcare, infrastructure, or education might provoke violent or nonviolent collective action more than inequalities in some other right or resource.

I argue that intergroup inequality is itself not sufficient to explain contentious politics or violence. Rather, group inequality becomes a relevant category of analysis when that inequality acquires particular social or political significance, heightening a group's sense of threat to identity and status, as well as livelihood and well-being.

Between-Group Inequality in Land Rights

My analysis focuses on inequality in land rights. The evidence for my theory comes from Kenya, where land serves as a key livelihood good, source of wealth accumulation, and form of identification for the majority of the population. I draw on recent scholarship focusing on how intergroup inequality can shape grievances.[14] Notably, Cederman et al. (2017) specify a causal path whereby grievances form among a disadvantaged or excluded group who engage in intergroup comparisons, or as they term, "evaluations of injustice," and "framing and blaming" of a target group (2017: 22). For Tilly (2003), a key mechanism is what he describes as "opportunity hoarding": when members of a "categorically bounded network" acquire access to a valuable resource, thus strengthening the political salience of the categorically bounded network (i.e. group identity).

I build on the insight that inequality can shape grievances where one or more groups feels excluded or disadvantaged. Yet there are many scenarios where groups feel aggrieved, but violent forms of contentious politics do not emerge. I outline a causal process that helps account for this variation. Broadly, I argue that the degree of land inequality has important implications for political mobilization and violence. Yet counter to many existing theories (Wood 2003; Wickham-Crowley 1992; Scott 1976; Gurr 1970), I argue that contexts of *moderate*, rather than significant land inequality, are most conducive to violent political mobilization. As I outline below, I suggest that this is because the

---

[14] This recent set of studies includes, for example: Cederman & Wucherpfennig (2017); Higashijima & Houle (2017); Cederman et al. (2013); Jayadev and Reddy (2011); Houle (2009); Østby (2008); Stewart (2008).

degree of inequality tends to correspond to specific political orders and cleavage lines.

In spaces of extreme inequality, the political order and cleavage line that emerge tend to mitigate the potential for violence. Yet in spaces of moderate inequality, the corresponding political order (based on patronage) and cleavage line (based on ethnic identity) tend to exacerbate such potential. In the section that follows, I begin by describing three scenarios of intergroup inequality around access to land. I then outline a few potential pathways through which these different scenarios affect the type of land narrative that emerges, beginning with the origins of elite land accumulation. Figure 2.2 illustrates this process. Importantly, I do not aim to prove a causal relationship between each of the factors I outline below. Doing so is beyond the scope of this book. Rather, my claim is that there is often a close association between each factor. Understanding how each of these factors interacts can provide important insights in the narrative that emerges, and in turn, the possibilities for political violence.

Land equality: In the first scenario, two nearby groups from a similar socioeconomic class both benefit from similar levels of land tenure rights. In rural or agrarian spaces, these two groups will often comprise smallholder farmers. In more urban spaces, they might include two groups of market-vendors or traders. I refer to this scenario as "*relative land equality.*" The main potential cleavage line is around ethnic identity rather than class, given that group members are from similar economic backgrounds. This relative equality in tenure rights between two groups may exist or emerge when members from both groups hold title deeds to their land and both benefit from state recognition of these titles. Alternatively, members from both groups may derive similar rights from customary authorities. Importantly, equality in land rights between two groups does not mean that members necessarily benefit from secure land tenure, but rather, that the strength or weakness of each group's tenure rights are more or less equal.

Moderate land inequality: In the second scenario, there are two identity-based groups from the same economic class. Yet in this case, members of one group benefit from stronger land tenure rights than the other. I refer to this as "moderate land inequality." There are several common observable implications of moderate land inequality. For example, land inequality can emerge where members of one group

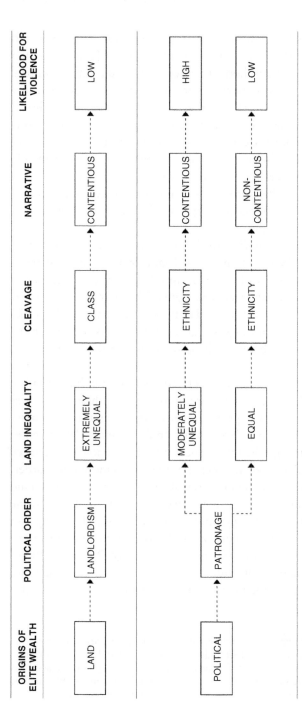

Figure 2.2 The process of election violence: detailed view.

have title deeds to their land while members of the other group do not. Informal factors may also skew the distribution of land rights. For example, a politician may choose to enforce the land rights of political supporters, leaving nonsupporters with much higher levels of tenure insecurity (Boone 2014). The qualifier of "moderate" inequality is important in this scenario because group members on both sides belong to a similar socioeconomic class. The size of each group's landholdings may also differ, but by a matter of 2–5 hectares rather than 50–1,000 hectares. Hence, the degree of inequality between groups is relatively small. Equally, with shifts in political power, each group's land holding or tenure rights are subject to change, shifting the advantage from one group to the other.

Significant land inequality: In the third scenario, there is *significant inequality* between an entrenched landowning elite that owns and controls the majority of the area's arable land and a large majority who access land as squatters or tenants. The main cleavage line is not ethnic identity, but class (i.e. landlords vs. tenants). While the social or ethnic identities of each group may be distinct, the most salient cleavage line is between those who own land and those who work the land.[15]

As I indicate in Figure 2.2, one key factor in understanding variation in intergroup land inequality is the origins of elite wealth: whether elites have acquired wealth through the inheritance of land and property (landed elite) or through political office (political elite). Where elites acquire wealth through the inheritance of large landholdings, I argue that "landlordism" is likely to emerge as the dominant political order. Where landlord–tenant dynamics prevail, elites will tend to resist land redistribution efforts, seeking to preserve their land holdings while ensuring a supply of cheap agricultural labor. Landed elites may also rely on private means of coercion and violence to undermine the potential for collective mobilization (Acemoğlu & Robinson 2006). Further, where there is an entrenched landed elite, these families often constrain the capacity of local politicians to act as effective

---

[15]   In Kenya's Coast region for example, the landowning minority primarily comprises people (families) of Arab descent, as well as families of Indian and European origin. In recent decades, people from "upcountry" Kenya have also acquired large tracts of land (notably, Kenyatta and Moi families), blurring the line between "entrenched landlord" and the national-level political class.

patrons, co-opting them as brokers. The distributional arrangement that emerges or persists is often one of significant land inequality.[16]

By contrast, where the main source of elite power is political – acquired through political networks, followers, and proximity to persons in power – "land patronage" is more likely to emerge as the dominant political order. By "land patronage," I mean that in these spaces, elites have the incentive or capacity to redistribute land as a way to consolidate political support or build a clientele. That is, because these leaders typically require popular support to gain or maintain power, they will be more responsive to redistributive demands from below. Hence, in these spaces we are more likely to see land distribution that is relatively equal or only moderately unequal between identity-based groups. In the Kenya context, politicians have been able to use land as a patronage good by allocating plots or title deeds, assisting with land finance, resettling the landless, or promising to protect *de facto* land rights in exchange for political loyalty (Boone 2011; Onoma 2009). In sum, while landlords are primarily "rent-seeking," land patrons are "vote-seeking."

The question remains: how does the degree of inequality and type of political order explain narrative formation? My main argument is that contentious land narratives are most likely to emerge in contexts where land patronage is the dominant political order and where there is land inequality between groups. More so, in spaces of moderate land inequality, contentious land narratives are more conducive to the formation of electoral violence. My claim is not that contentious land narratives only emerge in contexts of intergroup land inequality, but rather, that land inequality between nearby groups is a particularly powerful source of such narratives.

There are several reasons why moderate intergroup land inequality has such effects. First, where patronage politics is the dominant mode through which citizens and groups acquire and secure land, tenure rights are not stable, but instead, can change depending on electoral outcomes and political alliances. Many citizens are thus likely to believe that having a co-ethnic patron in power (or close to power) is imperative for acquiring or securing land rights. Inequality in land rights exacerbates this instability by calling into question both the

---

[16] In the Kenya context and elsewhere, these landed elites have historically been a class separate from the political elites in these same regions.

source of inequality and its implications for political representation. Inequality thus raises questions of past injustice such as: "how did that group over there get more than us?" or "With whom did they conspire to steal so much land or acquire so many titles?" Inequality can also heighten the perception of threat. For example, residents may see their eviction as imminent, believing that "if they have gained so much land already, they will certainly be able to evict us in the coming elections." In contexts of land inequality, a strong land patron – a figure who can credibly commit to redistributing land rights or protecting the rights of supporters – can heighten the salience and credibility of contentious land narratives.

By contrast, where there is relative *equality in land rights* between two groups of ethnically distinct smallholders, contentious land narratives are not likely to form, even where land patronage is the dominant form of political leadership.[17] A few factors help explain this absence of contention. First, equality in land rights can create a state of political equilibrium that neither group seeks to challenge or disrupt. More so, where both sides feel equally land secure, they are less likely to view a nearby group as the cause of their tenure insecurity or land shortage. Hence, while group members may make claims against the state, they are not likely to challenge the land claims of the neighboring group. The absence of contentious claim-making reinforces the tenure security of both groups. Second, where tenure rights are equal, a narrative based on past injustice – in which one group has been favored over another – has less legitimacy and resonance. Third, where both sides benefit from formal land rights (i.e. title deeds) both sides may prefer formal tenure rights while placing less priority on customary or informal tenure rights.

Finally, in contexts of significant land inequality (i.e. between land-lords and tenants), contentious land narratives are also likely to form. Landless or land insecure tenants or squatters may articulate grievances or assert claims to land occupied by landlords. Yet in contrast to spaces of moderate land inequality, it is far *less* likely that these narratives will serve as a tool for elites to organize election violence. One key reason for this, I suggest, is that where there is extreme land inequality, leaders tend not to act as strong land patrons, but rather,

---

[17] Measures of inequality in land rights can include the type of tenure security, size of plot, and quality of land.

as landlords or weak land patrons constrained by the interests of local landlords. Hence, citizens are likely to see their leaders as landlords who lack the incentive or political will to advocate on their behalf or as weak patrons who have been co-opted by more powerful elites. As a result, elite efforts to appeal to land narratives are rarely sufficient for organizing violence, given that most people will be unwilling to run the high costs of participation for a leader or political cause which is unlikely to produce either selective material benefits or broader group-level gains.

In sum, the section outlines the process through which group land inequality affects the formation of contentious narratives. Importantly, I see each of the factors that I've outlined as *conditioning* rather than causal or determinative. For instance, we can imagine spaces where patronage politics prevails alongside significant inequality. Similarly, ethnic identity might be the more salient cleavage line where landlord–tenant dynamics prevail. The key point, however, is that the degree of land inequality and the political significance that such inequality acquires is bound-up in particular histories of wealth accumulation and production, and the political orders that these political economies create or perpetuate.

Looking ahead, I argue that a key distinction between land narratives that emerge in contexts of moderate land inequality compared to significant inequality is the way that the narrative frames the logic of violence. Specifically, I argue that in contexts of multiparty elections, citizens living in extreme land inequality are less likely to associate elections with either threat to their land security or opportunity to gain land. They are thus far less likely to run the high risk of participating in violence. By contrast, where there is moderate inequality and patronage politics, citizens are more likely to link elections with threats to their land or opportunities to secure or reclaim land rights. With an effective land patron, these citizens have greater incentive to run the high costs of participation in electoral violence.

Stage 2: The Mobilization of Election Violence

The second stage of the book examines the causal pathway between contentious land narratives and the organization and escalation of electoral violence. I start by explaining how land narratives "work" – or how they shape political action. I then specify how particular narratives can provide the discursive tools that enable elites to organize electoral violence. As I argue throughout this book, however, land narratives alone do not cause violence. Rather, in certain contexts, they provide an important tool for organizing violent action. There must also be some shift in the political opportunity structure, often a trigger event such as a disputed election or an assassination of a high-profile leader that sets violence into motion (Tilly 2003).

How Do Land Narratives Work?

Broadly, narratives guide political action. They provide a set of frames that make certain actions thinkable or logical (Schatzberg 2001). Polletta (2006) writes that familiar narratives "make some courses of action seem reasonable, fitting, even possible, and others seem ineffectual, ill-considered, or impossible" (2006: 4).[18] Similarly, Autesserre writes that narratives provide the frames that shape "our views on what counts as a problem" (2012: 206). By this account, narratives alone do not have causal power, but "they make action possible; they authorize, enable, and justify specific practices" (ibid). In his theory of genocide, Straus (2015) conceives of narratives as "akin to a political grammar or cognitive map that guide decision-making in conscious and un-conscious ways" (2015: 63).[19] Narratives can thus act as a "cognitive mechanism," working to "alter individual and collective perceptions" (Tilly 2003: 20).

In the context of land and electoral violence, land narratives can become a discursive tool or "script" through which elites and ordinary citizens coordinate the use of violence. Land narratives in this sense serve as a coordination device that lowers the barriers to violent collective action. These narratives are far less effective sources for mobilizing violence when the narrative script does not resonate widely across the group, and in particular, when residents do not link threats to land or opportunities to gain with electoral outcomes.[20]

I suggest three mechanisms through which narratives work to shape violent action. First, land narratives provide a mechanism for

---

[18] For more on socialization and violence, see Checkel (2017).
[19] Here Straus refers specifically to "founding narratives," which are narratives constructed by elites that tell a "fundamental story about the character and purpose of a state" (2015: x).
[20] I expand on this argument in Chapter 7.

socializing group members.[21] As narratives form through bottom-up and top-down processes, they provide the frames that shape people's views of "the land problem." These frames are often cast in stark terms of threat, opportunity, and justice, whereby group members portray themselves as the victims of past injustices perpetrated by an out-group, or emphasize their vulnerability to future attacks on their land, livelihood, and political power by an increasingly powerful out-group. Further, as particular land narratives become more widely shared and resonant across the group, they encode and solidify a common ideology: a set of beliefs, preferences, and ideas about "who belongs," "what is rightfully ours," "what has been taken away from us" and "who threatens us."[22] Engaging in these narratives solidifies group membership or belonging.

Second, and relatedly, land narratives provide a strategic discourse for group members to articulate claims to land or territory. A salient and enduring narrative among residents might be: "we are landless today because Group A has stolen our lands" and "therefore, we have the right to evict Group A from the land that they illegally occupy." In this hypothetical, land narratives provide a discursive "script" for individuals and groups to assert claims to land or territory.

Third, existing narratives provide a way for leaders to bargain with their followers. The mobilization process becomes a form of bargaining where leaders (i.e. electoral candidates) use land narratives to persuade or coerce potential recruits in exchange for their political support. In each "discursive exchange" (e.g. rallies, pamphlets, secret meetings, and text messages) leaders draw on the fears, anxieties, and frustrations embedded in land narratives. These exchanges emerge from existing patron–client relationships. The following examples, which I've extrapolated from my interviews, illustrate common mobilization strategies that typify this type of patron–client exchange.

Example 1: "If you vote for me, I will protect you from eviction."
Example 2: "If you support Party A, we will kick Group B off these lands."

---

[21] Here I use Jeffrey Checkel's (2017: 592) definition of socialization as "the process through which actors adopt the norms and rules of a given community."
[22] See Sanin and Wood (2013).

Example 3: "If I am voted in, I will ensure the eviction of the other tribe."

Example 4: "If you fight [for me] you will earn land titles, jobs, property and cash."

These political exchanges help explain how land narratives shift from beliefs about rights to land, and methods of making claims, to mechanisms for violent political mobilization. As Tilly observes, elites are better able to bargain with followers over the use of violence as they gain greater control over "rewards and punishments" (2003: 51). This means that where elites can credibly commit to punishing opponents (e.g. evictions, targeted killings), or rewarding participants (e.g. plots of land, employment, or cash), they will have greater control over land narratives as a tool to organize violence.

Fourth, in addition to justifying or authorizing acts of violence that might otherwise be unthinkable, land narratives equip elites with a language for justifying and specifying the *form* of violence or program of action. For example, the belief that "outsiders" have invaded ancestral land can justify a campaign to "uproot the weeds" through violent evictions.[23] Recruits carry out these evictions by burning and destroying homes, businesses and fields, stealing property and livestock, and killing members of the target group.

Importantly, elite efforts to tap into existing land narratives often fail. Even where certain polarizing narratives exist, group members can challenge a dominant narrative or the politicization of a particular narrative. More so, even among the many ordinary people for whom a particular narrative resonates, the vast majority will not willingly participate in individual or collective acts of political violence.

The specific argument that I make here is that contentious land narratives heighten the saliency of threats to land rights and opportunities to expand or reclaim previously "stolen" lands. This increased saliency of threat and opportunity creates distinct logics for participation in collective violence. Figure 2.3 outlines this process, which links the particular narrative theme, the logic of violence that the narrative

---

[23] The phrase "uprooting the weeds" typically refers to evicting Kikuyu and other "outsiders" from the homes. According to Kalenjin respondents, Kikuyu leaders also use the phrase, referring to Kalenjin as "weeds" that must be uprooted from the land.

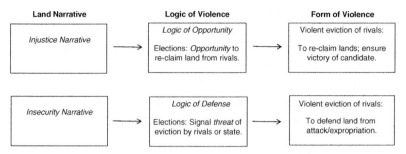

Figure 2.3 Land narratives, logic of violence, and form of violence.

invokes, and the form of violence that the narrative helps to establish or justify.

Injustice narratives are likely to shape a logic of opportunity: the belief that elections present a narrow window of opportunity for group members to strengthen or reclaim land rights. Political elites build or strengthen this perceived opportunity by drawing on existing narratives about the rights of the group members to reclaim, or formally secure contested lands.

Insecurity narratives, by contrast, are based on the idea that the land rights of group members are insecure or unstable because a rival group benefits from better tenure security, economic prosperity, or political representation. Participants in the narrative draw on memories of past land acquisition, which can fuel fears of losing land to state or nonstate actors. In the context of electoral competition, politicians can tap into this narrative to establish *a logic of defense*, a belief that: "we must attack or evict them before they can evict us." This threat gains credibility as rumors of planned attacks circulate during elections. Group members have incentives to fight as a way of defending their land or the well-being of their families and communities.

Yet there are many contexts where at least one of these narratives is a salient feature of intergroup relations, but violence does not escalate during an electoral period. A central aim of this book is to theorize why contentious land narratives help facilitate the organization of violence in certain contexts but not others.

Broadly, I argue that violence is only possible when citizens come to believe that their access and rights to land hinge on the outcome of an election.

When, then, are citizens likely to make this connection? The first key factor, as I've outlined above, is the capacity of a political candidate to act as a "land patron."[24] Elections represent opportunities to strengthen land rights when political elites have the capacity to distribute land or protect the tenure security of supporters. Yet where citizens view their politicians as weak, constrained, or unwilling to advocate for their land rights, they are far less likely to see elections as moments of opportunity to alter the distribution of land.

In settings where political patrons lack the capacity or political incentive to distribute land to ordinary citizens, "landlordism" may shape the norm of land distribution. Landlords have the power to provide temporary land access and collect rent, but they lack the political legitimacy or moral authority to mobilize political action, and even more so, violent political action.

A second factor that can work to enable or restrain the organizational power of a particular narrative is the size of the two largest ethnic groups at the local level. In many cases, the relevant cleavage line is between an ethnic group whose members see themselves as "natives" or indigenous and another group framed as "outsiders" or settlers. Elections are more likely to signal threats to the land security of one group when outsiders vote as a block and are relatively equal in number to insiders. In this scenario, insiders and outsiders each provide viable bases for mobilization and competition (Posner 2004). Further, where political competition closely aligns with a salient insider–outsider cleavage, electoral politics becomes a zero-sum game where outsiders compete over political power and resources with insiders. In this scenario, each side has the political incentive and power to use coercion and violence, including eviction, to alter electoral outcomes in the pre- and postelectoral periods. As a result, each side is more likely to associate elections with violence, including the use violent land expropriation (e.g. burning the homes and fields of opponents).

Yet when either the insider or outsider group makes up only a small minority, the insider–outsider distinction rarely provides a viable cleavage around which elites can mobilize support. Specifically, the smaller group is far less likely to pose a threat to the political power of the

---

[24] By land patron, I refer to a regional political leader, typically elected (e.g. Member of Parliament).

majority group in that region. As a result, there are few incentives for either side to use violent evictions to ensure electoral victory. Neither group, therefore, is likely to anticipate attacks from the other side, diminishing the threat that group members might otherwise associate with elections.

Elite Logics of Violence

So far, I've outlined how land narratives can provide a tool or "script" that enables political elites to organize violence. Land narratives work to: (1) strengthen group boundaries; (2) strengthen the urgency and legitimacy of land claims; and (3) provide a "program of action" that offers both symbolic and material benefits at the individual and group level. Taken together, these narratives have the power to mobilize violent forms of collective action when they succeed in convincing a group of citizens that elections present a threat to land rights or an opportunity to acquire land. As I explain above, this hinges partly on how ethnic cleavages overlap with political cleavages, and whether ethnic outsiders represent a credible threat to land and power.

A key question remains: if narratives can serve as a device to organize violence, when will elites seek to organize or deploy violence? In theorizing elite motives, I build on the large and growing scholarship on electoral violence, which suggests that political elites are strategic actors who, under certain circumstances, have incentives to resort to electoral violence as a means of altering electoral outcomes in their favor (Collier & Vicente 2012; Ellman & Wantchekon 2000). These studies suggest that all else equal, incumbent and opposition candidates have stronger incentives to use violence in spaces where they think they might lose or where vote margins are narrow (Hafner-Burton et al. 2014; Wilkinson 2004). For example, Bangura and Söderberg Kovacs (2018) use evidence from Sierra Leone to demonstrate that candidates are more likely to deploy violence in politically contested "swing districts."

One of the main strategies available for altering elections is the use of violence and intimidation to suppress the vote of opponents or to increase turnout among supporters (Bekoe 2012; Wilkinson 2004). In the preelectoral period, elites may select among several strategies of voter suppression (Norris et al. 2015). At one end, this could include efforts to manipulate voter registration laws seeking to exclude "out-siders" from voting in a particular district or constituency. Politicians can also use the threat of violence to convince opponents to stay at home on voting day. Yet if these strategies are deemed cumbersome or ineffective in achieving political goals, elites may opt for more extreme and violent methods of "suppressing" the rival vote. One such strategy that political entrepreneurs have deployed is the eviction of political opponents.

Current research provides important insights into the incentives shaping elite decisions to use electoral manipulation and violence in the pre- and postelectoral periods. While I draw on many of these insights, I depart from existing research by suggesting that elite-level decisions to organize violence often have multiple logics, sometimes relating only indirectly to elections. I outline a few of these alternative logics. First, organizing and deploying violence can provide a way for local or regional party elites to demonstrate their commitment to defend and protect the rights and livelihood of supporters from political threat. In political primaries, for example, the promise or use of actual violence can become a mechanism for co-ethnic outbidding. In such cases, leaders from the same party or ethnic community resort to increasingly extreme policies in an effort to prove who is best suited to protect the land, territory, or security of co-ethnic followers. In contexts where candidates exploit perceptions of insecurity during elections, citizens may seek out candidates who present themselves as "big men" who can defend the interests of the community. The ability to orchestrate violence, or to displace the opposing group can be a sign of political power that is requisite to winning – even if a politician never acts on this capacity. Hence, while the use of violence can be part of a campaign strategy to prove one's political credentials, it can also be part of a broader strategy to prove or assert one's political power and status – both within and outside the formal realm of electoral politics.

Second and relatedly, politicians may organize violence as a way to gain status in their political party. For example, they may help organize violence outside their own constituencies, directing their own followers to disrupt elections in a nearby constituency or electoral zone. In such cases these "violence volunteers" are able to demonstrate their commitment to larger party objectives, their capacity to organize and mobilize followers, as well as their ruthless resolve.

Third, the use of violence during elections, as with other forms of political violence, can generate valuable material resources that leaders rely on to reward political supporters and expand patronage networks (Collier & Hoeffler 2004). Such resources can include the homes, land, and livestock of people who have been violently evicted or killed, as well as the seizure of businesses, and other property. Where gains are significant, such theft can help fund future political campaigns.

An important caveat in this discussion, however, is that electoral violence, including coordinated evictions, is costly to organize and deploy. In most cases, elites make calculated decisions about where and whom to target, even if they underestimate these costs (Rosenzweig 2016). Specifically, politicians risk losing legitimacy among supporters while facing potential punishment and sanctioning from domestic and international audiences (Asunka et al. 2017; Van Ham & Lindberg 2015; Daxecker 2014; Bekoe 2012). Costs apply to opposition candidates as well. For instance, opposition candidates who use violence risk undermining their own "democratic credentials" (Taylor et al. 2017: 398). Further, and as Hafner-Burton et al. (2014) observe, the ability of a leader to use election violence depends on the strength of institutionalized constraints, notably, the ability of accountability groups (e.g. courts, legislatures, or the party) to prevent or impose consequences for the use of violence (Hafner-Burton et al. 2014: 157).

The Joint Production of Violence

As I mention previously, this book makes a basic claim about the process and dynamics of electoral violence: that successfully mobilizing individuals to participate in violent collective action is, to borrow Kalyvas's term (2006, 2003), a "joint production." In doing so, I argue that electoral violence is a process of social mobilization whereby political elites must coordinate with ordinary citizens whose motives and incentives for participating in violent action are often distinct from elites who are organizing violence. Analyzing election violence as a joint production is distinct from many existing studies that examine election violence as an event based solely on the strategic interests of elite actors (e.g. Denny & Walter 2014; Gutiérrez-Romero 2014; Hafner-Burton et al. 2013; Wilkinson 2004; Snyder 2000).[25]

For Kalyvas, collaboration is more likely when violence is selective; when armed actors require the knowledge of local collaborators to identify or gain information about potential targets or target communities. In such cases, elite or national-level actors rely on "resources and symbols" to ally with local-level supporters, establishing the "joint production of action" (Kalyvas 2003: 476). While the dynamics of civil war are distinct from election violence, theories of collaboration between armed actors and local civilians provide relevant insight into the dynamics of electoral violence in a number of ways.

First, most violence that escalates around an election is selective. While the targets may include high-ranking political elites, election officials, or political activists, the targets are more often ordinary citizens. In these cases, citizens are often targeted based on their political, ethnic, religious, or racial identities. In many cases of election violence, the incumbent regime directs violence toward opposition members, either as a way to intimidate or remove opposition support in the preelectoral period or to suppress protest in the postelectoral period (e.g. Zimbabwe in 2008 and 2018).

Further, in nonauthoritarian settings, parties seeking to deploy selective violence rarely rely explicitly on state security forces. While incumbent party leaders may be able to use the state security apparatus, institutional constraints and reputational concerns tend to restrain the overt use of state security to deploy significant violence against citizens.[26] The implication is not necessarily less violence, but rather, violence that is more diffuse across a broader set of actors within society. The key point is that because most candidates have limited

---

[25] Several scholars working on the organization of violence in civil war theorize collaboration between armed groups and local civilians (e.g. Balcells 2017; Justino 2009; Wood 2003) and civilian resistance to collaboration or co-optation (e.g. Finkel et al. 2015; Fujii 2009).

[26] Importantly, I do not imply that incumbent regimes do not use state security forces against their own populations. Rather, I make the distinction between authoritarian vs. democratic (or semidemocratic) regimes. While there are many examples of authoritarian regimes relying explicitly on the military or police to subdue or kill opponents (e.g. Kenya under Daniel arap Moi, Zimbabwe under Mugabe), elites in democratic regimes may use state security to "bring law and order" but rarely resort to state security to enact large-scale violence.

ability to rely on the state security apparatus, they must instead rely on local supporters to carry out violence.

This collaboration between political elites and local supporters helps overcome a few key challenges. First, because electoral violence is selective, based primarily on presumed political and ethnic identities, ethnically and politically mixed communities present elites with an information problem in that they may not be able to distinguish supporters from opponents. However, because local collaborators often know the ethnic identities, political affiliations, and social networks of their neighbors, they are able to fill in this information gap, identifying and perpetrating violence against targeted individuals or households.

Hence, rather than targeting all members of the opposition or rival ethnic community, more selective forms may be preferable for candidates who seek to reduce the "costs" of violence. By costs of violence, I refer both to the costs of organizing and producing violence, which include the costs of recruiting local participants, financing weapons, or transporting fighters, as well as reputational and political costs that I mention above. In light of these significant logistical and political costs, an additional benefit of local collaboration is that it can shift the burden of these costs onto local communities. As the primary perpetrators of violence, accountability and blame more often fall to ordinary citizens rather than higher-ranking political candidates and elites. While domestic groups often suspect or know the role that a political leader or party played in deploying violence, domestic courts often fail to prosecute political officials due to conflict of interest and corruption (Brown & Sriram 2012).

Methodology and Research Design

My research design and case selection are intended to answer two questions that are central to the book: (1) how do contentious land narratives form, and (2) how do contentious land narratives shape the production and escalation of electoral violence? The evidence that I use for analyzing these two broad questions draws from fifteen months of multimethod research that I conducted in Kenya.[27] I rely on two main research strategies to develop and evaluate hypotheses linking land

---

[27] I conducted preliminary research from May to August 2010. The research design that I describe here is based on twelve consecutive months of fieldwork, May 2012–2013.

rights and violence: a comparative case study and a household-level
survey. Additionally, I also conducted key informant interviews with
political officials and human rights activists, and reviewed transcripts
from parliamentary proceedings, court cases, as well as archived data
on land governance and administration.[28]

Comparative Case Study

The comparative case study follows a most-similar case selection
strategy across farming communities in Kenya's Rift Valley and
Coast regions.[29] Map 2.4 shows the four counties where I conducted research: Nakuru and Uasin Gishu, located in the Rift
Valley region, and Kwale and Kilifi, located in the Coast region.

I limit my universe of cases to settlement schemes and land-
buying companies (LBCs): two categories of rural land tenure
where political elites have *de jure* or *de facto* control over the
distribution of land rights.[30] In total, I conducted interviews with
230 people, most of whom were farmers living on these settlement
schemes and LBCs. Additionally, I conducted focus groups with
youth and elders from each case-study location.[31] I also include
cases where claimants hold land rights through either freehold or
leasehold tenure.[32]

The individual interviews and focus group discussions that I conducted across Nakuru, Kilifi, and Kwale counties help me develop and
examine my theory of election violence and the mechanisms and logics

---

[28] I accessed these documents at the Kenya National Archives (Nairobi). In
addition, respondents provided me with nonclassified land documents.

[29] For more on using comparative case studies for causal inference, see Gerring &
Seawright (2008) and Mahoney & Goertz (2004).

[30] Settlement schemes refer to farms (consisting of individual plots) that the
government creates to resettle portions of the population. Land-buying
company refer to land that is purchased by a company or cooperative.
Individuals purchase plots as shareholders.

[31] Appendix A details how I conducted these interviews and provides a list of
selected interview questions. Appendix B provides a list of all respondents.

[32] These cases include KISCOL, a sugar plantation in Kwale County, and Hell's
Gate, an administrative location in Naivasha District (Nakuru County), where
households own or rent privately held land (freehold and leasehold) in the
vicinity of commercial flower farms.

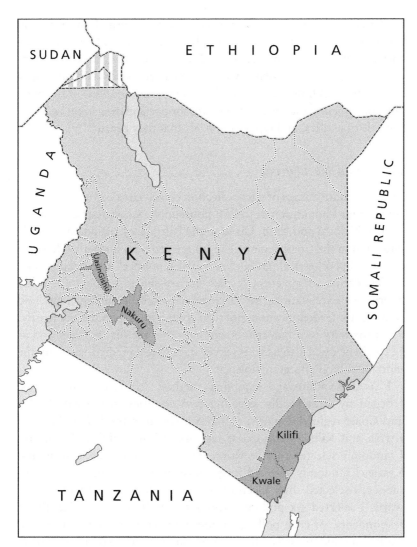

Map 2.4 Fieldwork sites.

shaping citizen participation in such violence.[33] The first round of interviews in each case study asked respondents about their history of land acquisition, the strength of their land rights, their beliefs about the

---

[33] The county is the largest electoral and geographical unit at the subnational level. Kenya has forty-seven counties.

land rights of other groups, and their views of formal and informal institutions governing land rights. The second round of interviews focused on election violence. In each case-study site, I asked respondents about their experience with the postelection violence and their recollections of how events unfolded, their interpretations of the postelection violence, their view on motives for participating in the fighting, the role of leaders, and types of appeals that they heard.[34]

Household-level Survey

The quantitative stage of data collection consisted of a household-level survey that I administered to 750 households across four counties of Kenya: Nakuru and Uasin Gishu in the Rift Valley region, and Kwale and Kilifi in the Coast region. The survey provides further evidence to examine hypotheses about land narratives, political mobilization, and the escalation of violence. It also enables me to account for other alternative explanations for electoral violence, including household wealth, ethnic identification, political competition, population density, and proximity to urban spaces, among other factors. Further, and as I explain below, I also use this survey data to test predictions about the individual-level effects of violence.

I used a multistage sampling method to select respondents. I began by strategically selecting two counties in the Rift Valley and Coast regions (Nakuru and Uasin Gishu in the Rift Valley and Kwale and Kilifi in the Coast region). Within Kilifi and Nakuru, I randomly selected four constituencies and within Uasin Gishu and Kwale, I randomly selected three constituencies. Within the constituency, I selected three electoral wards randomly. And within each ward, I selected six polling stations to randomize the selection of respondents. At each polling station, enumerators used a "random-walk" method to select three households (one respondent within each household). The survey sampled 210 respondents in Nakuru,

---

[34] In conducting interviews dealing with interpretations of election violence, we never asked respondents to identify their role in the electoral violence. I followed the same interview protocol as I used during other stages of the qualitative research. Village escorts were never present during the actual interview. To protect the privacy of the respondent, escorts stood beyond earshot during the interview. See appendix for further details on the questionnaires and more details of interview methodology.

216 respondents in Kilifi, and 162 respondents in Uasin Gishu and Kwale counties.

I conducted the survey in January and February of 2013, in the two months preceding the March 2013 general election. This enabled me to measure individual attitudes at the height of a particularly high stakes election – the first since the post-election violence of 2007-08, the first under a new constitution, and one in which the politics of the International Criminal Court significantly shaped political and ethnic alliances. While the timing could reduce external validity and generalizability, it also provided a unique opportunity to measure the effects of intense political mobilization on beliefs about land rights and identity. I provide further details on the sampling and methodology in the appendix.

The survey is innovative in part, because I developed the questionnaire directly from my in-depth qualitative work, which enabled me to design context-relevant questions to measure and test concepts derived from theories of land rights, inequality, and political violence. More so, by interviewing ordinary citizens rather than experts or political elites, the voices and experiences of ordinary people are at the center of analysis. This is a departure from many existing studies that rely either on crossnational event datasets or government-commissioned reports aggregated at the subregion. The survey is particularly important in Kenya, which lacks a reliable source of data on violence or displacement related to the 2007–08 postelection violence or past episodes of election violence. Existing sources available to scholars include Kenya's Commission of Inquiry into the Post-Election Violence (CIPEV) and datasets based on media reports of the postelection violence.[35] While these sources provide an important baseline, they do not reflect a systematic and politically neutral data collection process (see Chapter 8 for further discussion).[36]

---

[35] Existing datasets that count reports of election violence include the Uppsala Conflict Data Program Geo-referenced Event Dataset (UCDP GED), the Armed Conflict Location and Event Data Project (ACLED), the Electoral Contention and Violence Dataset (ECAV), and the Social Conflict Analysis Database (SCAD).

[36] Some scholars have relied on satellite images of fires as a proxy for violent events (Kasara 2016).

Research Design and Case Selection

Taken together, the evidence that I gather enables me to examine a set of hypotheses about the stages of electoral violence, including the determinants of contentious land narratives (stage 1), and the determinants of electoral violence (stage 2). Table 2.1 outlines my research design, specifying the research question, unit of analysis, and specific research strategy guiding each chapter.

I begin by proving an historical analysis of land allocation and settlement in the Rift Valley and Coast regions (Chapter 3). The main question asks why and how the practice of land distribution

Table 2.1 *Summary of research design*

Chapter	Research question	Unit of analysis	Research design
Stage 1: Determinants of contentious land narratives			
Chapter 3	Why and how does the practice of land allocation vary?	Region	Process-tracing
Chapter 4	Why do contentious land narratives form in some cases but not others?	Neighboring communities (all pairs)	Most-similar case comparison
Chapter 5	Why do contentious land narratives form in some cases but not others?	Neighboring communities (Two pairs)	Most-similar case comparison
Stage 2: Determinants of election violence			
Chapter 6	How do narratives translate into actual violence?	Neighboring communities (Two pairs)	Process-tracing
Chapter 7	Why do contentious land narratives foment electoral violence in one context but not another?	Regions	Most-similar case comparison
Stage 3: Consequences of election violence			
Chapter 8	What are the effects of election violence?	Individual	Clustered sampling

varies between the Rift Valley and Coast regions. I select these two regions for comparison because they share important similarities along key independent variables, but vary in significant ways along others. Across both regions, there is marked land inequality between groups, contentious land narratives between these groups, and the politicization of these narratives during electoral campaigns. Yet broadly speaking, the two regions are distinct in terms of the origins and degree of land inequality and the salience of ethnic divisions. On this latter point, in the Rift Valley counties of Nakuru and Uasin Gishu, the largest ethnic community comprises a small majority, with 52 percent of Nakuru's population identifying as Kikuyu, and 58 percent of Uasin Gishu's population identifying as Kalenjin. Yet in Kilifi and Kwale, the largest ethnic community – the Mijikenda – are a large majority, comprising 86 percent of the population in Kwale and 83 percent in Kilifi.[37] Relatedly, the Kikuyu and Kalenjin are among the largest ethnic communities nationally, and hence, each group has significant power in determining the outcome of a national election. By contrast, Mijikenda residents from the Coast have had far less power on the national electoral stage, owing both to political configurations and the fact that Mijikenda comprise little more than 5 percent of the national population.

More so, there is also important variation in the main dependent variable: the occurrence of election violence during the 2007–2008 postelectoral period. This selection strategy thus enables me to compare a region heavily affected by electoral violence (Rift Valley), with a region where electoral violence has been rare and relatively isolated (Coast).

Stage 1 asks why contentious land narratives emerge between some groups and not others. The dependent variable is the degree of contention that defines the salient land narrative.[38] I analyze this question in Chapters 4 and 5. In both chapters, I draw primarily from interview data based on comparative case studies. The main unit of analysis is a location where two different ethnic groups border or live near one another. This does not imply that each community is ethnically homogeneous, but rather, that the majority of residents within a

---

[37] Data comes from Kenya's 2009 Census and from Burbidge (2015).
[38] See Chapter 4 for coding and measurement details.

given community identify along a common line of identification. Each case, then, is a pair of groups (e.g. a Kikuyu land-buying company bordering a Kalenjin settlement scheme). I select cases based on variation in two explanatory variables. The first is the parity in land rights between each community. I categorize each case as having equal, moderate, or significant land inequality based on the degree of land inequality between the two groups. The second source of variation is the type of cleavage line that distinguishes the boundaries of two groups, and specifically, whether I observe class or ethnic identity as the more salient cleavage. In total, I present evidence based on eight pairs. Table 2.2 summarizes this case selection strategy. Table 4.1 in Chapter 4 provides further details on each of these cases.

Drawing on evidence from these case comparisons, supplemented with survey results, Chapters 4 and 5 aim to evaluate the following hypothesis:

Hypothesis 1: Contentious land narratives are more likely to form where there is a salient cleavage line between two distinct ethnic communities who are relatively equal in size and where there is inequality in the strength of land rights between these two groups.

In Chapter 4, I analyze empirical patterns that emerge from the interviews and focus groups that I conducted across each pair of case studies. In Chapter 5, the research question remains the same: why do contentious land narratives emerge in some spaces, but not other, seemingly similar spaces? I use this chapter to provide an in-depth analysis of two paired cases: one where contentious land narratives emerge (Mauche and Likia) and another nearby set of communities where I do not observe contentious land narratives (Ogilgei and Kerma). As with Chapter 4, I use a most-similar research design. And while both paired cases have a salient ethnic cleavage line, the key source of variation is the degree of land inequality.

Stage 2 asks why electoral violence escalates in some cases but not others. I analyze this question in Chapters 6 and 7, and part of Chapter 8. My dependent variable becomes variation in the escalation of violence during the 2007–2008 electoral period. I select cases based on two main sources of variation: (1) whether there is a contentious land narrative and (2) whether local and regional leaders act as strong

Table 2.2 Summary of case studies

	Region: county, constituency	Case comparison	Cleavage line	Land rights: degree unequal	Contentious narrative	Postelection violence (2007–2008)
1	Rift Valley: Nakuru Rongai	Ogilgei Kerma	Ethnic	Equal	NO	NO
2	Rift Valley: Nakuru Rongai	Umoja Belbar	Ethnic	Equal	NO	NO
3	Rift Valley: Nakuru Njoro	Likia Mauche	Ethnic	Moderate	YES	YES
4	Rift Valley: Nakuru Njoro	Mwisho wa Lami Tipis[1]	Ethnic	Moderate	YES	NO
5	Rift Valley: Nakuru Naivasha	Oljorai Nyakinyua	Ethnic	Moderate	YES	YES
6	Rift Valley: Nakuru Naivasha	Hell's Gate[2]	Ethnic[3]	Moderate	NO	YES
7	Coast: Kilifi Kilifi South	Kijipwa REA Vipingo	Class	Significant	YES	NO
8	Coast: Kwale Msambweni	Ramisi KISCOL	Class	Significant	YES	NO

Notes: SS= Settlement Scheme, LBC= land-buying company

[1] The LBC in Tipis is a disputed, *de facto* LBC, but not recognized officially.

[2] Hell's Gate is an adjudication scheme and administration location that surrounds commercial flower farms. The majority of residents are workers inside these flower farms.

[3] Main cleavage line is between Kikuyu/Luo, yet location is diverse due to flower farms that recruit labor nationally.

"land patrons."[39] Drawing on evidence from both the qualitative case studies and survey results, this stage evaluates the following hypothesis:

Hypothesis 2: Electoral violence is most likely to escalate where there are: (1) salient and contentious land narratives between two distinct, but similarly sized ethnic groups, and (2) where there is moderate inequality in land rights between these two groups; and (3) where local or regional leaders act as strong land patrons.

In Chapter 6, the specific research question asks how contentious land narratives translate into actual violence. The main unit of analysis is two sets of neighboring communities. In contrast to preceding chapters that exploit variation in a key explanatory variable, this chapter uses process-tracing to demonstrate how contentious land narratives can shape the escalation of violence. In Chapter 7, the research question is about regional-level variation in the escalation of electoral violence. Specifically, it asks why contentious land narratives provide a viable tool for the mobilization of violence in parts of the Rift Valley, but not the Coast. The chapter uses a most-similar research design, with variation along several of the key explanatory variables, including strength of the land patron and ethnic group size. The main unit of analysis is the region.

The final stage of analysis, which I present in Chapter 8, shifts from analyzing the sources of electoral violence to focus instead on its effects. Specifically, I ask how direct or indirect exposure to election violence affects openness to ethnic outsiders, political trust, and interethnic engagement. The chapter draws primarily on survey data, but includes qualitative evidence as well.

In sum, this book explores the ways that group-level land inequality can shape a set of narratives that leaders can use to organize violence. Importantly, there are many countries with high land inequality yet relative political stability. This suggests that land inequality alone does not predict or explain violence. What also matters is the way that local actors and political elites interpret and politicize land inequality, giving rise to "land narratives." These narratives are the stories, beliefs, and ideas about distributional justice, and the threats and opportunity to claim

---

[39] I explain this concept in greater detail in Chapters 3 and 7.

rights. Narratives in this sense provide a key mechanism linking a set of institutional variables with the onset and dynamics of violence. One aim of this book is to understand when and why inequalities in land give rise to a particular set of narratives that can, in rare instances, provide a tool for elites to produce electoral violence.

3 | Historical Origins of Electoral Violence

One week after the March 4, 2013, elections the newly elected president Uhuru Kenyatta had acquired a nickname along the Coast. "We call him our landlord," explained a community activist from Kilifi. "He owns most of the land here on the Coast, so this is just the way people see him."[1] Despite the Kenyatta family's significant land holdings across the Coast region, Uhuru Kenyatta's newly formed coalition, the Jubilee Alliance, had polled only 35 percent of the vote across the six counties that comprise the Coast region. Kenyatta's control over much of the region's land, however, did not translate into his ability to control or leverage votes.

By contrast, in the fertile and more populated inland regions including parts of Rift Valley, Central, and Nyanza, land ownership has shaped political loyalty in very different ways.[2] Owning large tracts of land has been one of the political requisites to securing political office: it signals the ability of a leader to distribute land and other development goods to political supporters. Equally, securing office has provided one of the main mechanisms for elites to secure and acquire land. In these regions, political elites have had the ability and incentive to use land as a source of patronage to build political support among their mostly poor and rural constituents. One implication, I suggest, is that many residents in the Rift Valley and Central region have come to view their leaders as "land patrons." As patrons or ethnic "big men," citizens expect their leaders to protect or provide basic land rights.

Yet on the Coast, many citizens have come to view their political leaders as landlords. This image of political leadership extends back to the caricature of the Arab landlord or master and the African squatter or slave

---

[1] Phone conversation with R.M., community activist and resident, Kijipwa SS, Kilifi County, March 12, 2013.
[2] "Inland" distinguishes landlocked regions of the country (e.g. Nairobi, Central, and Rift Valley) from the Coastal region.

(Brennan 2008). The term "landlord" is also part of a broader national narrative about an outsider who leverages power and coercion to extract from the local population. The identity of this outsider has varied by place and time. It was once the Arab slave trader, then the colonial official or European landowner, and later, the "upcountry" Kenyan with powerful ties to the central state. Importantly, the landlord has few incentives to protect the tenant. Landlords seek rents, whereas land patrons seek political supporters. These two images of political leadership – the vote-seeking land patron and rent-seeking landlord – reflect different logics of elite land accumulation and redistribution that have developed within inland and coastal Kenya since the early twentieth century.

One aim of this chapter is to explain the different practices of land politics between Kenya's inland and coastal regions. I do not aim to make any causal claims. Rather, I suggest that the distinct political economies of each region can help explain the regional distinctions in land patronage that have emerged. Broadly, I argue that politicians act as strong land patrons in much of inland Kenya because an early source of elite power was political: postcolonial elites gained land and wealth through their political connections and proximity to the central state. This contrasts with the Coast region, where most of the elite were members of an entrenched landed (or business) class. Many of these landed elites were members of Arab families who had owned land since the late nineteenth century.[3]

Hence, in inland Kenya elites had incentives to use land as a political tool. They acquired land through political connections. Likewise, they could promise land or tenure security to build a political following. Along the Coast, however, elites were members of a landed rather than political elite; they derived their wealth and status from family-owned land or businesses rather than political networks with postcolonial elites. Further, most coastal elites were among a privileged ethnic minority – typically Arab or Indian – who benefited historically from rights to land, but were seen as outsiders or aliens by the majority population.[4] As a result, landed elites from the Coast have had few

[3] The category of Arab on the Swahili coast typically refers to descendants of migrants from the Oman Peninsula since the seventeenth century (Willis & Gona 2013).

[4] The Mijikenda comprise linguistically related coastal groups previously referred to as the "nine towns." They include the Giriama, Rabai, Duruma, Chonyi, and Digo. Mijikenda became a unifying term of identification in the 1940s with the formation of the Mijikenda Union (Prestholdt 2014; Brennan 2008).

incentives to use land as a patronage tool; they have acted as landlords but not land patrons. Further, because this landowning class has controlled so much of the region's arable land, there have been few opportunities for local (i.e. Mijikenda) leaders to control or accumulate land, and hence to act as strong land patrons. For the first several decades after independence, these individuals more often acted as "brokers" to coastal elites or politicians from upcountry. I thus characterize them as "weak" patrons compared to their counterparts in inland Kenya (i.e. Rift Valley and Central regions). As I argue throughout this book, identifying where leaders act as strong land patrons is important in understanding the process of electoral violence. Specifically, I argue that where elites act as strong land patrons they are better able to use land narratives to organize violence compared to leaders who act as landlords.

In this chapter, I explain how land politics has played out under three phases of Kenya: colonial rule and the Mau Mau civil war (1900–1962), the single party rule of Jomo Kenyatta (1962–1978), and the single party rule of Daniel arap Moi (1978–1992). In doing so, the chapter aims both to present a descriptive story of land politics in Kenya while providing the reader with the historical context in which to understand sources of regional and temporal variation in land politics and contentious claim-making.

Losing Land to the Colonial State

When the British came here they asked to whom the land belonged. Our forefathers told them the land belonged to God. The British lied to them. They said that they wanted to find out the size of God's land. So they put beacons on our land and stayed here as settlers ... Unknowingly, the locals leased this land to these foreigners. And that's where the lease system started.[5]

The ability for elites to act either as land patrons, who supply land access in exchange for social or political support, or landlords, who rent their land in exchange for cash or kind, hinges on a population of landless people. There must be a sufficient number of people seeking access to land but who cannot secure individual tenure rights due to

---

[5] Interview-Ramisi SS-Kwale County, November 13, 2012.

barriers to ownership or land shortages. Along Kenya's Swahili coast and in its interior highlands, landless groups have existed well before European colonial rule – as slaves, captives from war, tenants, or unmarried young men. Further inland, within the patron–client system that had defined Kikuyu societies until the 1930s, landless young men could work the lands of their elder land patrons until they had acquired sufficient wealth to begin a household (Berman & Lonsdale 1992).[6] Meanwhile, Mijikenda who migrated to the coastal belt were able to negotiate somewhat favorable terms with Swahili and Arab land-owners facing labor shortages on their plantations (Cooper 1980: 220). While the flexibility of land arrangements between landless and landowners has varied, British colonial rule did the most to institutio-nalize and formalize a system that protected the property rights of a narrow and racially based elite while ensuring the persistence of a landless or land insecure majority. As Kanyinga writes, "The creation of a people without rights to land – the squatters – and the pre-eminence of land in the political process began with the incorporation of Kenya into the British colonial empire during the late nineteenth century" (2000: 34).

I begin by looking at the adjudication of land rights around the highly contested and strategically important "Ten-Mile Strip," or *Mwambao*: a strip of coastal land extending from the border of Tanzania to the Tana River in Kenya.[7] In the late nineteenth century, Britain was interested in gaining territorial control of the Ten-Mile Strip as part of its plan to build a railway linking Uganda to the Coast. Yet because the entire Swahili coast was under the control of the Zanzibari Sultanate,[8] the British government negotiated an agree-ment to lease the land *Mwambao* from the sultan of Zanzibar.[9] The

---

[6] These landless were referred to as *ahoi*.

[7] It spreads "to a distance of ten miles from the high water mark into the interior" (Kanyinga 2000: 34).

[8] The Arab-Swahili slave trade, which provided the economic base of the Zanzibari Sultanate, was one of the catalysts for Mijikenda land dispossession. Mijikenda who had been cultivating along the Kenya coast fled into less arable hinterlands to avoid slave capture (Kanyinga 2000:11; Cooper 1980). Arab and Swahili leaders moved onto vacated lands and used slave labor to establish plantation economies. Slavery was officially abolished along the Swahili coast in 1888, though the practice continued informally.

[9] The lease was part of the Anglo-German Agreement of 1886.

agreement, however, failed to acknowledge the land claims of indigenous African residents within and outside *Mwambao,* rendering the interior of the Coast "ownerless," and enabling Germany and Britain to compete over land and territorial rights (Kanyinga 2000; Ghai & McAuslan 1970).

In the early twentieth century, Britain turned to agricultural settlement schemes as a longer-term strategy to generate taxable revenue, in particular, to pay for its plans for a railway. An editor of the *Kenya Weekly News* later explains (in 1960):

> The deficits on the Protectorate and the railway had to be borne by the British taxpayers ... The only way whereby both Protectorate and railway could be set on a sound economic basis was by the development of the raw and almost empty lands on either side of the railway. If that task had been left to the Africans there would have been little chance of the railway paying its way within 20 years. (Hill 1960)

Between 1902 and 1915, Britain passed several pieces of legislation that made the colonial state the *de facto* landlord, empowering the British Crown to seize African land and re-lease or sell these lands as freehold titles to European settlers (or in the case of the Coast, to Arab and Swahili landlords). These policies initiated, deepened, and formalized the squatter economy in the highlands and across the coastal belt.

The Crowns Lands Ordinance of 1902 designated that the Crown "had original title to land," facilitating the sales of land and leases to European settlers, and initiating European settlement in the interior of the county (Kanyinga 2000; Okoth-Ogendo 1991). Further, the ordinance declared all land that was not occupied by Africans, as "waste and unoccupied land," and reverted it to Crown land. The Crown then redistributed this land to European settlers.

A similar ordinance, the Land Title Ordinance of 1908, was specific to the Coast region. Under the ordinance, the British colonial government created a mechanism for race-based land rights whereby titleholders had to be subjects of the sultan of Zanzibar (Prestholdt 2014). Freehold titles were thus only issued to a few powerful Arab, Swahili, and Indian families who had the power and pedigree to stake individual claims to the land. Cooper (1980) remarks, "European settlers and Indian businessmen had no desire to get involved in an intricate web of economic and social ties; they wanted titles" (1980: 195). The process thus largely bolstered individuals whom "[British] officials could accept in the role of landlord" (Cooper 1980: 192). Prominent Arab and Swahili families succeeded in registering their claims in part because the process of claim-making was controlled through Arab administrators.

The ordinance, however, marginalized the claims of Mijikenda and other communities who made family or community-based claims to land. Mijikenda residents were largely excluded from the mosques, could not locate witnesses to verify their claims, and could not use the Arabic documents that many Arab landowners used to track land inheritance and allocations (Kanyinga 2000: 58). Families along the Coast continue to tell stories of losing land to this highly exclusive process. In an interview with a family from Kijipwa (Kilifi County), the 1908 ordinance remains central to their story of land dispossession:

When the land tenure came from Zanzibar, this place belonged to the sultan of Zanzibar. And the sultan of Zanzibar in 1908 started land tenure for the 10-mile strip and therefore it reached here about 1912. The reason we have no land is that [the sultan] was a Muslim and we are Christian and this land tenure was preached in Mosques ... So those Arabs and non-Arabs who were attending the mosques came out and started claiming [land]. They got hold of us, telling us that we were going to be portioned some land for the natives to stay. But eventually they were just portioning [the] land for themselves .... Afterwards we came to realize that the land had been registered under their names. And we were squatters and we had to pay some fees for staying in that land.[10]

All land that was not registered by Arab or Swahili families reverted to Crown land. As happened across the country, the majority who could not make formal claims were pushed onto communal native reserves – mostly in far less arable hinterlands of the Coast. The only way that Mijikenda residents could access arable land was by squatting on the land of Arab and Swahili landlords.[11] This moment remains the focal point for articulating a coastal land narrative of dispossession. The same family I mention above explains further:

The injustice that has been done to us is that the land that should have been given to us has been given to other people. That is the injustice. Our ancestral

---

[10] Interview-Kijipwa SS-Kilfi County, December 1, 2012 (1).
[11] The economic decline of many Arab and Swahili landlords relative to European farmers, particularly after the abolition of slavery, meant that they had less power to evict squatters and more so, that they needed the farm labor that squatters provided.

land, which had no papers, had been grabbed by people. They got it while we were still there and they came and got the title deed and claimed the land. That is the injustice.[12]

The Crown Lands Ordinance of 1915, revised from previous land ordinances, transformed property rights in Kenya. It expanded British Crown land to include all land occupied by natives while formally establishing the native reserve system.[13] These reserves provided the colonial government with an effective though ruthless mechanism to extract labor and tax agricultural production (Boone 2014).

In the postcolonial period, the function of this ordinance changed very little. While the wording shifted from "Crown land" to "government land," the postindependence government maintained a property-rights system that vested the president with full powers to lease and grant land (Onoma 2009). These laws fully established formal English property law in Kenya, but along racially exclusive and class-based lines.

Land, Work, and War: the Escalation and Defeat of Mau Mau

In the decades preceding the Mau Mau civil war, European colonization and settlement dramatically transformed the land and labor market.[14] Land shortage was most profound in the densely populated Kikuyu reserves in Central Province, most of which were clustered around settler plantations. Kikuyus migrated into the Rift Valley seeking wage labor and tenancy arrangements on white-owned farms.[15] As Schatzberg writes, "by 1950 there were over 250,000 squatters working on white-settled farms with virtually no rights in land" (1987: 18). These transformations in land, labor, and the movement of people help explain the origins of the war between the Land and Freedom Army ("Mau Mau") and the colonial state. As a way of identifying the historical context in

[12] Interview-Kijipwa SS-Kilfi County, December 1, 2012 (1).
[13] The reserve system pushed Africans onto ethnically segregated land set apart from the more fertile lands designated for European settlement.
[14] By 1920 Kenya was an official colony of Britain, though it had been part of the East Africa Protectorate since 1895.
[15] Many also traveled to Nairobi, where many joined or started businesses in the informal sector, given that black Africans were excluded from participating in the formal sector.

which land became a strategic tool, this section focuses on how the colonial government used land to suppress the Mau Mau insurgency while building a loyal political coalition among Kenyan elites.

The Mau Mau civil war lasted from 1952 to 1960 and resulted in the deaths of approximately 25,000 Kenyan Africans (Branch 2009: 5).[16] The insurgency arose in part due to a breakdown in the patron–client relations that had once provided young men with a way of accessing land and accumulating wealth. By the 1940s extreme land shortage in the Kikuyu reserves undermined the patronage capacity of Kikuyu elders who might otherwise have provided land to young men. Poorer Kikuyu "were thus forced off their holdings and cut adrift by Kikuyu elites" (Branch 2009: 6). Branch writes:

Those who became insurgents critiqued the action and words of their self-proclaimed leaders ... [Kikuyu elites] failed to protect the poor's access to land and forced their clients off the land ... Mau Mau thus represented ... the "repudiation of clientage" by a society that felt "betrayed by their patrons," white and black. (Branch 2009: 131)[17]

The formation of the Mau Mau movement was a rejection of two forms of authority that had "failed to provide": the colonial state that had undermined rights to land and modes of entering adulthood, and the Kikuyu leadership that many young people viewed as negligent.

Mau Mau fighters promised their supporters *ithaka na wiathi* – "land and freedom." At the outset of the movement, this slogan held legitimacy. Many supporters believed that the "Land and Freedom Army" would liberate the poor and landless from colonial and Kikuyu oppressors. Yet the colonial state and its collaborators co-opted this message by outbidding Mau Mau promises of land redistribution, rewarding loyalists with land while revoking or withholding the land rights of Mau Mau fighters and supporters (Branch 2009; Njonjo 1977). This strategy created incentives to defect from Mau Mau and to inform on friends and family. The use of land to reward supporters and punish dissenters would continue well into the

[16] Approximately 1,800 of these 25,000 deaths were loyalists (i.e. home guards) who fought on behalf of the British. Thirty-two Europeans were killed (Branch 2009: 5).
[17] Branch (2009) is here drawing on John Lonsdale (1992), "Wealth, Poverty, and Civic Virtue."

postindependence period, particularly with the reintroduction of multi-party elections in the 1990s (Boone 2011; Klopp 2001b).

As a second mechanism to undermine the Mau Mau movement, the colonial government implemented a land privatization program known as the Swynnerton Plan. In 1954, J.M. Swynnerton, Kenya's Assistant Director of Agriculture, advocated for a model of land reform that:

Focused on the African progressive farmer ... who must be provided with such security of tenure through an independent title as will encourage him to invest his labor and profits into the development of his farm and as will enable him to order it as security against such financial credits. (Swynnerton 1954: 9)

The Swynnerton Plan, however, was hardly revolutionary. It promoted a form of agrarian development that would encourage the consolidation of land in the hands of a capable or entitled few while maintaining a landless class.[18] Swynnerton writes: "In future, these able, energetic or rich Africans will be able to acquire more land and bad or poor farmers less, creating a landed and landless class. This is the normal step in the evolution of a country" (Swynnerton 1954: 10). These statements signaled a vision of land reform that would perpetuate an elite landholding class. Further, the plan provided a language for singling out the "good, hard working, farmer" from the "bad, lazy, poor" farmer. This language would be useful in discriminating between the hardworking loyalist that received land, and the "lazy" Mau Mau supporter who expected land for free.

Beyond any development objectives that Swynnerton envisioned, the plan was also an explicit tool to quell rebellion. Swynnerton writes: "In the long run the greatest gain from participation of the African community in running its own agricultural industries will be a politically contented and stable community" (Swynnerton cited in Shipton 2009: 144). The Swynnerton Plan unfolded as a large-scale land reform project that gave the provincial administration – the state's main bureaucratic and highly coercive apparatus – full powers over land titling and consolidation, allocation of plots, access to credit and land financing, farm planning, cash crops, and cooperatives (Branch 2009:

[18] See Shipton 2009; Klopp 2001a; Okoth Ogendo 1991; Haugeraud 1989.

121).[19] Other laws were passed in the early 1950s that gave farming incentives to loyalists.[20]

Officials, including chiefs and their local collaborators (e.g. village headman and local elders), allocated these resources to loyalists while Mau Mau supporters – many of whom were in detention camps – were excluded from the benefits of the land reform process. An elderly Kikuyu farmer recounts this process: "The way the official land administration used to divide land was not satisfactory. The people who had important jobs or authority like the chiefs, the home guards and forest guards were allocated chunks of land."[21]

The British colonial state also used land reform (i.e. Swynnerton) to create clientelist networks with local leaders. This relationship provided an effective counterinsurgency strategy on the ground, while establishing allies with whom the colonial state could rely on as it brokered independence. In 1954, a colonial official wrote, "Elite loyalists ... [were to] become the anchor of the tribe, the solid yeoman farmer, the land owner who knows that he has too much to lose if he flirts, however lightly, with the passions of his nationalistic friends." (Branch 2009: 120). This move was critical in undermining the influence of Mau Mau fighters who, "at first threatened to supplant incumbent elites patrons and create new networks of clients across Central Province" (Branch 2009: 146). The colonial administration's strategy of co-opting leaders thus had the long-term effect of reordering of patron–client relationships that had organized many facets of Kenyan society, and Kikuyu society in particular (Branch 2009). The new postwar patronage system reaffirmed the legitimacy of the colonial state and their collaborators, which comprised the burgeoning Kenyan elite, while further marginalizing many younger and land-poor Kikuyu. These logics of land distribution and reform would continue into the postcolonial period.

Along much of the Coast by contrast, elites did not fear mass rebellion and thus had little need to embark on large-scale land reforms.[22]

---

[19] For more on the coercive capacity of the provincial administration, see Hassan 2017 and 2020.

[20] For example, loyalists in Kiambu were allowed to grow the highly profitable leaf crops, coffee and tea (Kanyinga et al. 1994: 74).

[21] Interview-Likia LBC-Nakuru County, June 27, 2012 (3).

[22] There were mass rebellions along the Coast (e.g. the *Mwambao* movement and Giriama uprising) but nothing on the magnitude of Mau Mau rebellion.

And because the landless public did not present a significant political threat at independence, land reform was relegated to an issue of economic development rather than national security. Equally, few elites at the national-level would see the value in distributing state land, both because the Mijikenda population was not valued politically and because there was little case for using land reform to prevent an uprising. Squatters on the Coast were not, until very recently, seen as a threat to political stability.

Land Politics at Independence

There is a tribe that got colonized (Kikuyu) while the other tribes did not get colonized. The Kikuyu know the importance of independence more than the other [tribes]. The others don't know the price of freedom.[23]

The Mau Mau War ended officially in January 1960, leaving significant divisions within the Kikuyu community and between different subgroups of Kenyan society. It also affirmed a political logic of using land as a tool for state building and expanding patronage. Strong patron–client relationships would emerge in regions where elites could profit from the land, but equally, where elites needed to assert control over the population, either to consolidate political support or to prevent rebellion. By contrast, these political imperatives of building political support or quieting dissent were mostly absent from the Coast region.

In the years surrounding independence in 1964, political alliances and constitutional design hinged largely on the issue of land. The Kenya Africa National Union (KANU), led by the newly elected President Jomo Kenyatta, represented an elite, Kikuyu-led party. Kikuyu elites had strong connections with the former colonial government and consequently had the political and financial means to accumulate much of the land left by departing white settlers. By contrast, the opposition party, Kenya African Democratic Union (KADU), pressed for an ethnoregionalist constitution, known as *majimboism*.[24] This agenda, led

---

[23] Interview-Likia LBC-Nakuru County, June 28, 2012 (5).

[24] Many local parties merged to form KADU. These include Moi's Kalenjin Political Association and the Maasai United Front. (This alliance would become KAMATUSA: Kalenjin, Maasai, Turkana and Samburu.) KADU support also came from the Coastal Africa People Union headed by Ronald Ngala, the Somali National Union, and the white settlers party, the New Kenya Party.

by Daniel arap Moi, was largely an effort by smaller ethnic communities to protect local land interests.[25] Majimbo advocates rallied supporters around fears of Kikuyu invasions on the "ancestral lands" of KADU supporters. KADU leaders "made it clear that they wanted a constitutional provision that guaranteed their ethnic groups fair compensation for land that had already been effectively expropriated" (Kanyinga 2000: 47). Appeals to *majimboism* provoked a politics of claim-making based on ideas of historical precedent, indigeneity, and the political authority of borders. By contrast, KANU members rejected ethnoregionalist claims to land and political governance and promoted a party based on national unity.

By September 1963, KANU had eroded many of the powers of KADU and Kenyatta called on opposition members to join KANU in a "government of national unity."[26] All but the most ardent KADU supporters crossed the aisle. Formal independence was declared in December 1963. A year later, in November 1964, KADU's formal demise came when Ronald Ngala, the party's last holdout and elected leader of the Coast Assembly, crossed the aisle.

The defeat of majimboism in the Coast Province was described as "a bitter moment." Willis and Gona (2012) remark that majimboism had united Arabs and Mijikenda, but that "[t]he demise of KADU left no space for a formal politics of coastal identity" (Willis & Gona 2012: 61). With the dissolution of KADU and the defection of its members into KANU, Kenya became a *de facto* one-party state by the end of 1964. But KADU's agenda did not disappear. Instead, *majimboism* would reemerge as one of the most polarizing issues in the multiparty era of the 1990s.

Hakuna cha Bure – *"Nothing Is for Free"*

Another major debate that framed the early independence years revolved around the highly contentious land purchase program intended to foster agrarian development and resettle the country's landless population. Two debates polarized KANU leaders: 1) the

[25] Prominent KADU leaders also included Ronald Ngala, one of the few Mijikenda Coast politicians.

[26] In the June 1963 elections, KANU gained a majority of votes in the House of Representatives and Senate. The Regional Assembly was split between the two parties.

terms of acquiring the lands of former white settlers, and 2) the terms
for reallocating former Crown land to the country's landless. KANU
liberals advocated for a free market in land while more populist "radi-
cals" argued for the redistribution of lands expropriated by the British
Crown (Kanyinga 2000: 47).[27] Specifically, Jomo Kenyatta and many
of his elite inner circle favored a conservative plan that would enable
the newly independent Kenyan government to "buy back" the white
highlands from the departing white settlers on "willing seller–willing
buyer terms."

Kenyatta's market-based view of land reform prevailed, marginalizing more redistributive visions.[28] A state-led ideology of land
settlement accompanied these reforms. President Kenyatta tapped
into existing Kikuyu narratives about hard work, land ownership,
and wealth accumulation to legitimize his famous slogan, *hakuna
cha bure* – "nothing is for free." The narrative was also
a reinvention of colonial state discourse, which framed Mau
Mau's demands for land distribution as lazy and immoral. The
statement became central to the regime's narrative: that landless
squatters should not expect land for free but must acquire it
through their own toil and sweat. It required that smallholders
had the sufficient resources or networks to finance a plot of land.
The narrative thus worked to counter the claims of political rivals,
and equally, was a way for elites and ordinary Kenyans to delineate between those "who worked for their land" and "those who
wanted land for free."

This narrative also altered the way through which land acquired
value. Beyond any family or community attachment, land came to
acquire value through the market transaction. The land purchase,
marked by gaining a title deed or plot allotment letter, signified the
work and labor that a household poured into the land (Lonsdale 2008).
This claim to land through labor provided a legal and moral basis for
claim-makers to elevate their claim above all others, particularly those
making ancestral or first-comer claims to the land. An interviewee from

---

[27] Bildad Kaggia and Oginga Odinga led the radical movement arguing that land
should be free for landless citizens because it had been stolen by the British.

[28] Kaggia and Odinga were forced out of KANU and formed the Kenya People's
Union (KPU). However, KANU ensured that the KPU never evolved into
anything more than a regional party marginalized to the Luo-dominated area of
Nyanza (see Mueller 1984: 424; Bates 1983:108).

Likia, an LBC in Njoro Constituency, emphasizes the enduring importance of purchased land, illustrating the belief that tenure rights only
accrue to those who have purchased their land.

After Independence, when I was a young woman, I never heard of anything
for free. You had to buy land. People had to form societies and bought the
land … If my land was given to me for free, then the government has a right
to take it away. That's also the main reason why we always fight bitterly to
defend our land in Likia: it's because of the value we have for it: we bought it
with cash.[29]

An elderly man in this same community of Likia provides similar
remarks. He also hints at the ways in which the narrative of resettlement, framed by the slogan of '*hakuna cha bure*' has shaped the
language of land politics in the region.

After independence it was announced that the Whites were leaving the
country and you could buy their property. But some other tribes didn't
heed the call. These tribes thought that they would be given land for free.
Those who were eager to buy got the land but those who wanted free things
started complaining when the land was finished. And now they complain that
the Rift Valley is their ancestral land. Complaining never helps. The president
[Kenyatta] said for you to work hard and to get your own property and that
nothing is for free.[30]

Kenyatta's call to purchase land served as a way to validate particular claims to land in the Rift Valley while undermining the
claims of other poor and landless Kenyans. We see this in the
above remarks. For both respondents, land went to those who
worked hard. From this perspective, there was no injustice done
to families who remained without land. Rather, these landless
families were entitled: they expected free land but were not willing
to work for it.

By institutionalizing this narrative of hard work, Kenyatta altered
the possibilities for a more populist, class-based discourse. Because
there was "no free land," those who were able to purchase their land
were also those who deserved the land. This silenced dissent and
demand for redistribution. Equally, it legitimized elite accumulation
of land in full view of the public.

[29] Interview-Likia LBC-Nakuru County, July 4, 2012(12).
[30] Interview-Likia LBC-Nakuru County, June 28, 2012 (5).

As another Likia interviewee explains:

After independence, the government was not able to allocate land equally to all Kenyans. The first President Kenyatta said *hakuna cha bure* ... thus everyone had to buy land and people bought according to their capability. Those who were not able to raise enough money did not get land ... The rich benefited because they used their money to buy big pieces of land ... Even President Kenyatta allocated himself big pieces of land and when he saw that whatever he got wasn't enough, that's when he said "nothing is for free."[31]

As the respondent describes, the wealthy amassed large swaths of land, while most Kenyans, Kikuyus included, were left without any. This market-based narrative of land acquisition was effective in part, because it framed land claims that were not based on a market transaction as immoral or illegal, rendering ancestral or customary claims as legally and morally dubious. It also exacerbated reactionary land narratives among ethnic and regional communities who saw themselves on the losing end of the land settlement process. As the state became more dogmatic about land registration and the sanctity of title deeds above other claims, there was a hardening of identity-based claims, particularly those making ancestral land claims.

The Politics of Settlement Schemes

The creation of government settlement schemes was and remains among the most powerful, though contentious mechanisms for redistributing land and settling large segments of the population. In Kenya, a settlement scheme refers to land that the government purchases and then subdivides into plots for farming or residential purposes, with each scheme typically ranging from 100 to 20,000 acres.[32] The government subdivides each settlement scheme into individual plots. The size of these plots, and the targeted set of recipients vary from scheme to scheme, depending on the political and economic objectives of the government. Many settlement schemes were drawn over the boundaries of the colonial-era native reserves. Thus, over time, these schemes have created or reaffirmed ethnic claims over territory that was

---

[31]   Interview-Likia LBC-Nakuru County, July 3, 2012 (9).
[32]   The largest recorded settlement scheme was Lake Jipe Scheme (24,000 acres with 1,438 settlers) in Taveta, Coast region. The smallest was Gazi Scheme, Kwale County with only 2.5 acres with eight settlers (Lukalo & Odari 2016).

previously more diverse or more open (Anderson & Lochery 2008; Leo 1981: 111).

The government has subdivided most schemes into small plots for subsistence farming purposes. These schemes referred to as "high-density schemes" typically range from one to ten acres. While on paper, high-density schemes were designed for landless farmers, many of the beneficiaries of these plots went to middle-class farmers instead: those who could convince the Land Development and Settlement Board (LDSB) that they had the sufficient skill and capital to meet the loan and interest payments on a plot of land.[33]

The government also created low-density plots to maintain or encourage consolidated land holdings among a class of "progressive African farmers." These plots ranged from 20 to 100 acres. In practice, the political class used these plots as a source of elite accumulation and patronage, often acquiring far more than 100 acres. These schemes provided a key source for elites in power to buy the political support of key members by distributing plots within these schemes or supplying "credit and extension support" within schemes (Klopp 2001b: 78).

Importantly, the state does not allocate plots of land on settlement schemes for free. Instead, allottees must finance the cost of their plot, often on prohibitive terms. It is only after an individual or household meets the debt obligations on their allotment that they receive the title deed. Yet because loan repayment is so challenging, many households remain without titles to their land, even decades after the initial allocation. As several scholars have observed, settlement schemes have shaped a dynamic whereby the state acts as the landlord, and allottees as the tenants (Boone 2014; Harbeson 1973).

The first major land resettlement program, known as the Million-Acre-Scheme (MAS) rolled out in 1962 in the wake of Kenya's independence. The MAS program aimed to settle approximately 35,000 African families on 1.7 million acres of land that the Kenyan government had purchased from departing whites settlers (about 4 percent of the total area of the country).[34] It became the first and largest of many land resettlement programs that transferred lands from European to African ownership on "free-market" terms: the state would act only as

---

[33] Interest payments were 6.5 percent for the first thirty years. Most farmers struggled to meet these interest payments and there was very weak enforcement. The LDSB was the body designed to manage the transfer of land.

[34] Leo (1981: 201).

a mediating institution to place households on the land while providing loans to smallholder and large-scale farmers (Leo 1981).[35]

The Million-Acre Scheme provided a financing plan for the Kenyan state to "buy back" the white highlands from outgoing European settlers. The Kenyan government purchased the land through international aid loans from the World Bank and the Colonial Development Corporation, but assumed the loans at highly inflated prices.[36] Yet it was the smallholder farmer who was ultimately responsible for interest and loan repayment (Leys 1975 in Klopp 2001b: 77). The program thus appealed to white settlers who worried about having their farms seized or nationalized upon independence while ensuring that a land market would remain intact (Leo 1981: 210). Equally, many members of the Kenyan elite – particularly within KANU – saw settlement schemes as a way to resettle a landless population without jeopardizing the prospects for economic growth based on large-scale agriculture.

The Million-Acre Scheme ended up creating approximately 123 settlement schemes in the 1960s and facilitated the settlement of about 500,000 people on government land by 1970 (Boone 2011: 14).[37] And while the MAS was the most expansive settlement scheme program, many other schemes followed, each with varying objectives and levels of success and permanence.

Over the course of the first three presidential administrations (1962–2012), settlement schemes became a useful tool for managing land demands and building a political clientele. Figure 3.1 illustrates the patterns of settlement over the fifty-year period from 1962 to 2012. It shows the intensity of land settlement under President Jomo Kenyatta, the decline in the mid-1980s under President Moi, and the continued rise under President Kibaki in the era of competitive multiparty politics. Over

---

[35] The loans and grants received for the purchase of the resettlement program were credited by Parliament and managed by the Settlement Fund Trustees (SFT). SFT was established under the Agriculture Act (cap. 318, Laws of Kenya) and mandated to manage and purchase any land for resale purposes (Republic of Kenya 2004: 123).

[36] Development Finance Institution that was part of the British Government. The name changed to the Commonwealth Development Corporation in 1963. Hornsby (2013: 75) states that funders provided one-third of the land purchase as a grant, while two-thirds were given as a loan that had to be re-paid by Kenyan settlers.

[37] Anderson and Lochery (2008) cite that the government settled nearly 70,000 families across 250 settlement schemes by 1975.

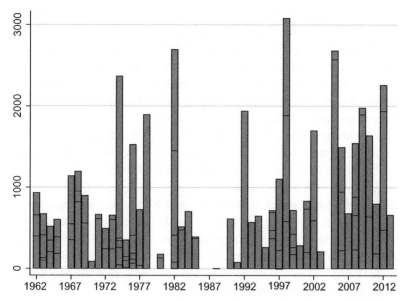

Figure 3.1 Total number of households settled on settlements schemes during first three postcolonial regimes: Kenyatta (1962–1978), Moi (1978–2002), and Kibaki (2002–2012).

a forty-year period, records from the Ministry of Lands indicate that the government created 480 settlement schemes, accommodating approximately 275,713 households on 1,248,267 hectares of land.[38] Importantly, however, settlement schemes comprise a relatively small proportion of all arable land. And while the state created settlement schemes in five of the country's original eight provinces (the Rift Valley, Eastern, Central, Western, Nyanza, and the Coast), most settlements – at least in the first decades after independence – were concentrated in the Rift Valley, Eastern, and Central provinces.

A few provincial and temporal-level trends are worth noting. First, most settlement schemes were created in the first decades after independence, primarily under Jomo Kenyatta. This is not surprising, given that settlement schemes were a key tool for promoting economic growth and resettling Kenyans after the departure of white Europeans. Kenyatta's administration created 236 settlement

[38] The average plot size across all settlement schemes over time (1962–2012) is 4.5 hectares.

schemes, settling 76,802 households over a total of 584, 295 hectares of land. The government created the majority of these schemes in the highly fertile districts of the Rift Valley, Central, and Eastern Provinces. The government targeted these areas in part because they encompassed the former white highlands – the fertile farming regions vacated by European farmers. Yet as I'll discuss below, there were important political calculations as well.

In the first few years of President Moi's tenure in office, plot allocations within settlement schemes remained a key tool for managing land demands. Yet by the mid- to late 1980s, settlement had all but ceased – due partly to an economic downtown, but also as a result of strategically weakened land tenure institutions (Onoma 2009), and dwindling reserves of public land from which to legally resettle households. I discuss these factors in greater detail in the sections below. During Moi's twenty-four years in office (1978–2002), 166 recorded settlement schemes were created. These schemes totaled 426,351 hectares and settled 105,603 households (see Appendix for details).

The creation of new settlement schemes and the allocation of plots slowed under the Kibaki Administration (2002–2012). Yet as Figure 3.2 indicates, settlement schemes remained an important policy and political tool in select regions. In total, the Kibaki regime created 78 settlement schemes, and settled 93,308 households on 237, 621 hectares of land. Figure 3.2 shows provincial-level variation in the mean plot size over the 1962–2012 time period.

Two key political logics help account for some of the regional and temporal variation in the creation and allocation of settlement scheme land. The first was a logic based on preempting or preventing rebellion. In the aftermath of the Mau Mau civil war, colonial and Kenyan elites were well aware of the need to settle portions of the population, particularly the Kikuyu, in order "to secure an orderly transition to independence without destroying the large farm sector and foreign aid opportunities, and to avoid a land grab or new emergency" (Hornsby 2013: 74). Distribution to the poor and landless could temper more radical demands and political action and provide poor farmers with incentives to join the modern agricultural economy (Harbeson 1973: 134). The priority of settling Kikuyu over other groups culminated in efforts for an "Accelerated Kikuyu Settlement Program" (see Wasserman 1973).

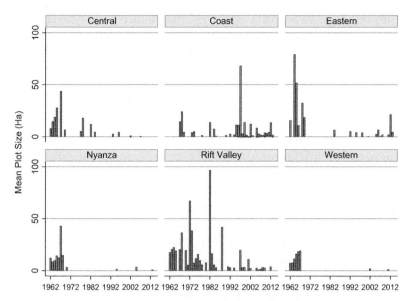

Figure 3.2 Annual allocations of settlement scheme land by province. The figure shows the mean size of plots allocated in a given year in each province (mean plot is the total number of households settled/total settlement scheme land).

Yet while fears of insurgency account for some of the broader patterns in land reform and resettlement across much of the former white highlands, there was nonetheless significant variation in resettlement within ethnic groups, particularly among Kikuyu. Many former Mau Mau supporters received the lowest priority during resettlement or were excluded altogether from the resettlement process. A Kikuyu farmer living in Mau Narok, whose father lost his land because he was a "freedom fighter," remarks on this policy: "My parents moved from Central Province because my dad was a freedom fighter and the colonial chiefs always detained him. They also destroyed his properties, so he sought refuge here in the Rift Valley."[39] To this day, many households or communities who supported Mau Mau still have no legal rights to land.[40] Hence, while land resettlement often fell along ethnic lines, the enduring identities of

---

[39] Interview-Tipis-Nakuru County, October 16, 2012. A "freedom fighter" refers to a member of the Mau Mau, aka, the "Land and Freedom Army."
[40] See for example: Weru 2016.

"loyalist" and "Mau Mau insurgent" determined those who received
or lost land. The state was thus able to keep alleged Mau Mau fighters
off settlement schemes signaling the power of the state to use land as
both a patronage good and punitive tool.

In addition to security concerns, political elites also created
and lobbied for settlement schemes in order to create "patronage
banks." The ability of rising elites to access plots of land on govern-
ment-controlled settlements schemes provided a critical opportunity
for personal enrichment, and equally, an opportunity for elites to use
the reallocation of these plots to build patronage networks. Land
could be used to develop and secure political and business networks
among the growing professional and political class. Equally, individuals with political ambitions could use land resettlement to develop
a political support base.[41] And because elites had so much to gain
in the creation of patronage networks, the allocation of plots was
selective and political. Plots tended to go to households from particular ethnic communities, notably the Kikuyu, who could leverage
the financial or political connections to secure a plot (Kanyinga
2000: 50).

Land patronage has worked in two main ways. The first is
between elites: when elites with connections to executive office or
relevant ministries allocate settlement scheme plots to one another.
According to the findings of the Ndung'u Commission Report
(Republic of Kenya 2004), the main mechanism that facilitated this
process was the use of a "presidential directive to the provincial administration to settle specific groups of people in designated areas" (2004:
132).[42] These plots were often between 20 and 100 acres or more. In
such exchanges, land was not typically given explicitly as a gift, though
this would commonly occur under President Moi. Instead, the government would extend generous loans to help finance these farms (Leys
1975), with the understanding that these loans would never be repaid
(Leo 1981).[43]

---

[41] The President transferred large parcels of land to elites using a "presidential
directive to the provincial administration to settle specific groups of people in
designated areas" (Republic of Kenya 2004: 132)

[42] Report of the Commission of Inquiry into the Illegal/ Irregular Allocation of
Public land, V1 (aka "Ndung'u Report") (Republic of Kenya 2004).

[43] From 1963 to 1964 these loans came from the Land and Agricultural Bank of
Kenya, which was the primary lending institution under the colonial
government. Loans were available to both Kenyans and Europeans (Leo 1981).

Land patronage has also worked to build patron–client relationships between political elites and ordinary citizens (i.e. smallholders). Settlement schemes serve as a patronage good for aspiring or acting political elites when they can distribute plots, title deed, or land financing to build or expand bases of support among a group of smallholders, landless farmers, or urban squatters.

Land-Buying Companies

Land-Buying Companies (LBCs) provided an alternative and often more efficient method for aspiring political elites to develop an ethnically aligned clientele of smallholder farmers. Unlike settlement schemes, LBCs allowed the political patron to have more direct control over the management and allocation of land to clients (i.e. shareholders) as the process bypassed the more bureaucratic institutions that governed land rights within the settlement schemes.

LBCs involve a group of individuals (i.e. shareholders) who purchase a tract of land. In many cases, the Settlement Funds Trustees or the Agricultural Finance Corporation facilitate this purchase (Boone 2011). The director of the company divides the land into individual plots and then makes the land available for sale to individual shareholders. In well-managed LBCs, shareholders can acquire title deeds. Yet in many cases, companies were mismanaged or corrupt and farmers who purchased shares never gained title to their land. Hence, they remained as shareholders but never as complete owners of their land (Boone 2011: 16). By 1973, there were over 1,000 LBCs in Kenya, most of which were managed by "influential individuals from Central Province and a few from the Rift Valley" (Republic of Kenya 2013a).

One of the starkest examples of the LBC as a vehicle of political patronage is the case of Kihika Kimani, whose rise to political prominence was largely the result of the 55,000-member Ngawataniro Land Buying Company that he founded and chaired. Using this position, he became Member of Parliament for Nakuru North, a seat that he held until 1979.[44] He was also the director of the extremely influential GEMA Holding Corporation, a powerful and ethnically exclusive

---

[44] In 1979, Kimani was defeated by Koigi wa Wamere – in large part due to President Moi's successful efforts to expose Kimani's mismanagement of the LBC in Nakuru (Onoma 2009).

political interest group and LBC that guarded the interests and assets of the Kikuyu, Embu, and Meru communities.[45]

Kihika Kimani and many other elites who organized LBCs attained their political stature in large part by creating loyal followers who relied on the LBC for land access and security. This shaped the belief that elites had the capacity and political will to protect the land rights of their constituents. A respondent in Naivasha constituency illustrates the enduring narrative of the Parliamentarian as "land patron":

Some MPs who were concerned about the welfare of their people helped them acquire land after the white settlers left. They included Kihika Kimani who assisted people in Nakuru region and G.G. Kariuki who established land in Laikipia. Offices were established so that those who were interested could register themselves with a small amount of money. This is how I got land.[46]

Yet these LBCs also amassed tremendous wealth by collecting shares from smallholders without allocating titles in return. A resident of Likia, a land-buying company, also located in Nakuru County explains that many settlement schemes and LBCs were not successful because "some people like me who were members of a land buying company led by Kihika [Kimani] contributed money for buying shares of land yet we did not get land."

The ethnically exclusive practices of these schemes exacerbated land grievances among smaller or marginalized groups, furthering the belief that only Kikuyu and other well-connected individuals benefited from land reform programs. Kalenjin youth from Mauche Settlement Scheme discuss how these companies favored land accumulation along class lines:[47]

---

[45] GEMA started as a social welfare association in 1971 but quickly evolved into a political organization with an explicit agenda to keep Moi from becoming the Vice President of the country. It also functioned as a club that enabled acquisition and speculative trading of land within an ethnically exclusive inner circle. By 1977 the membership of GEMA was 3 million and by 1979 its total assets were worth about 50 million (Onoma 2010).

[46] Interview-Oljorai-Nakuru County, September 7, 2012 (3).

[47] Focus group with youths - Mauche SS-Nakuru County, Mauche, July 9, 2012.

Participant 6: Most of the owners of the LBCs had influence in the government and they are the ones who benefited. But the common *mwananchi* (citizen) did not. So LBCs did not succeed because they only benefited family members and people with connections, not the ordinary person.

Participant 1: Land-buying companies only benefited a few enlightened ones. Even me, I don't know how I would have approached a land-buying company.

These comments illustrate the way that many ordinary Kenyans, particularly in the agricultural zones of the Rift Valley, relied on a political patron to help them secure land access. Leaders had so much power precisely because the process was so chaotic, arbitrary, and corrupt. Citizens relied on land patrons to link them to the land. In areas where such patronage did not exist, many people remained landless.

From Land Patronage to Land Grabbing: Land Politics Under Moi

When Daniel arap Moi, a Kalenjin, assumed office following the death of Jomo Kenyatta, he declared that he would follow in the footsteps of Kenyatta – "*fuata nyayo.*" In part, the declaration was meant to assure Kenyatta supporters that he would not depart from the status quo, easing Moi's transition and enhancing his political legitimacy (Haugerud 1995: 82). But the slogan would soon take on a life of its own. Whether by intention or not, many ethnic communities across Kenya have come to understand the idea of "*fuata nyayo*" in terms of land. It has come to encompass the idea that the political leader in power will take land and distribute it among his community. So while many Kalenjin interpreted "footsteps" as a promise of land distribution, many others heard it as a threat that the game was changing. As a respondent in Likoni (Mombasa County) remarks, "Moi's slogan was 'fuata nyao!' [Kenyatta] was a land grabber, so Moi just continued grabbing [land]."[48] A Kalenjin respondent in Rongai (Nakuru County) provides a similar view: "The Kikuyu feel that they are the ones who fought for the country's independence, so they had to reward themselves by acquiring land. So when Moi came to power he followed

---

[48] Focus Group-Likoni - Mombasa County, December 3, 2012.

[Kenyatta's] footsteps."[49] Key here is the belief that Kenyatta had rewarded his followers with land and hence, Moi would follow in the same tradition.

While there were certain continuities in the practices and logics of land distribution between Kenyatta and Moi, there were key distinctions as well. First, there was a shift from a highly centralized and formal system of land distribution to a much more overt practice of "illegal or irregular" land allocation. Notably, the Ndung'u Report found that among the 200,000 title deeds that were illegally allocated between 1962 and 2002, 96 percent were created under President Moi between 1986 and 2002 (Manji 2015: 7). Second, there was a shift toward a much more coercive use of land as a political tool. Whereas Kenyatta's regime had relied on the distribution of land to build both elite and grassroots supporters, Moi used the abrogation of land rights as a punitive tool to punish or displace opponents (Onoma 2009; Boone 2011).

Moi continued Kenyatta's practice of using state-owned land to build support among individual elites and broad-based coalitions. The key difference, however, was that Moi strategically subverted the property-rights institutions that had previously protected and enabled the accumulation of land wealth under the Kenyatta regime. As Onoma (2009) argues, the Kenyatta regime had much stronger incentives to strengthen and protect the land-based assets that the state inherited at independence. Moi and his Kalenjin network, however, had been largely excluded from the gains that Kenyatta and the GEMA elite had reaped through the transfer of lands at independence. Rather than strengthen institutions that guarded property rights in land, Moi subverted property-rights institutions as a way to seek gains from land "unmediated by its productive use" (Onoma 2009). The allocation of land, in other words, became a purely political strategy absent any concern for economic or development objectives. Strong or functional land institutions, such as registries or other mechanisms of enforcement or adjudication, would have hindered Moi's ability to produce fake title deeds and carry out fraudulent land "grabs" that transferred public land into private hands (Onoma 2009, Republic of Kenya 2004). Specifically, by undermining property-rights institutions, Moi was able to target the institutions that had facilitated Kikuyu wealth

---

[49] Focus Group-Ogilgei - Nakuru County, August 15, 2012.

accumulation, creating new rules for generating land wealth and political power. In particular, Moi and KANU elites aimed to undermine the legitimacy of formal property-rights institutions and the title deed itself, which had come to symbolize the power of Kikuyu land claims.

During the 1980s, Moi used several strategies to dismantle the land rights of his opposition, most of whom were Kikuyu living in the Rift Valley. He began by cutting back on the capacity and reach of the main institutions that had facilitated the development and management of settlement schemes (e.g. the Department of Land Adjudication and Settlement under the Ministry of Land). He further undermined oversight of land titling and settlement by transferring authority to local arms of the provincial administration, where there was little possibility for oversight or accountability (Republic of Kenya 2004: 126). Accurate record keeping fell by the wayside (Onoma 2009: 149), making it much easier to produce and use fake title deeds. Onoma explains how "flawed registers also increased the flexibility that politicians had in deciding which rights to enforce" (2009: 165). Moi also starved the Lands Ministry of the capacity to create reliable settlement scheme maps. This meant that many land transfers within schemes were never officially recorded (i.e. mapped onto the settlement scheme), enabling multiple allocations to the same plot of land and exacerbating conflicts over disputed land.

Moi also relied on the private distribution of public lands. With much of the best agricultural land already alienated, Moi carved settlement schemes from forestlands, national parks, and public lands set aside for urban development, schools, hospitals, and cemeteries. While Moi settled some smallholder communities on these settlement schemes, many beneficiaries were political elites with connections to Moi's inner circle.[50] Individuals included "district officials, their relatives, members of parliament, councilors and prominent politicians from the area, Ministry of Lands and Settlement officials, and other civil servants and the so called 'politically correct' . . . at the expense of the deserving poor."[51]

Relatedly, Moi also relied on the illegal allocation of land belonging to state corporations (parastatals), including land assigned to the

---

[50] Most of the smallholder recipients of plots within settlement schemes never received a genuine title deed to their allotted plot (Republic of Kenya 2004; Author interviews).

[51] Republic of Kenya 2004, VI: 126–127.

Agricultural Development Corporation (ADC). ADC farms were designed to provide the country with agricultural inputs to sustain food security. Because these farms were located across the country, they were easy targets for land grabbing. Moi allocated many of these farms to close allies while using other ADC farms as *de facto* settlement schemes. In other instances, particularly along the valuable coastline and in productize zones of the Rift Valley, parastatal land was sold for speculative purposes. According to the Ndung'u Report, "the manner and speed with which the transactions were effected leave no doubt that the allocation of land was aimed at enabling the allottees to speculate with corporation land" (Republic of Kenya 2004: 86). As the country headed toward multiparty elections in 1990s, these parastatals, many of which were headed by Kalenjin, served as valuable "cash cows" for funding political campaigns (Lynch 2011: 134).[52]

Several scholars have argued that the illegal allocation of state land under Moi was a response to declining state revenues in the mid-1980s, including declining aid for land reform, plummeting coffee prices, and rising oil prices.[53] Kanyinga (2000), for example, writes that with the economic downturn "Moi turned to resource-rich parastatals, especially those in the agricultural sector, where he placed his own people in managerial positions to act as political gatekeepers, to tap resources for patronage purposes" (2000: 52). Figure 3.3 shows the notable decrease in the number of households settled on settlement scheme land in the Rift Valley under Moi. The figure also indicates that allocations increased considerably after Moi was voted out of office in 2002. At this time, the promise of land – rather than the threat to revoke land – became a prominent strategy for political parties seeking to gain and maintain support.

Land politics under Moi was also defined by coercion and violence. This is not to say that ruthless acts of violence did not occur under Kenyatta's regime. Indeed, Kenyatta used selective violence to silence individuals who he viewed as threats to political or economic power.[54] Moi's government differed in that it strategically incorporated targeted

---

[52] By September 1991, Kalenjin headed forty out of eighty-five parastatals (Lynch 2011: 134). Kalenjin accounted for about 12 percent of the population.

[53] Scholars that have made this argument include Mueller (2008); Throup and Horsby (1998); Boone (2011); Kanyinga (2000).

[54] Kenyatta targeted assassinations against a number of political figures, including former allies. These include Tom Mboya, J.M Kariuki, and Ronald Ngala.

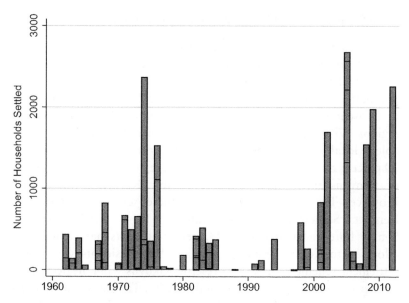

Figure 3.3 Total number of households allocated on settlement scheme land annually in the Rift Valley Province (1962–2012).

coercion and violence into its land politics. In the 1980s, Moi relied on the state security apparatus to seize lands belonging to LBC managers and smallholder farmers.[55] And in the multiparty context of the 1990s, KANU used violent evictions to alter the political landscape. As Kenya was set to hold its first multiparty election in 1992, one of KANU's most powerful and notorious politicians warned famously: "the title deed is nothing but a piece of paper."[56] This statement would take on particular meaning throughout the first decade of multiparty elections in the 1990s, which was marked by significant violence. With the subversion of formal property rights, the title deed had indeed become little more than a piece of paper. Enforcement of land rights hinged on being loyal to the KANU security forces. And without protection from KANU security forces, many Kenyans found their rights withheld or seized by the state or individuals.

---

[55] In 1981 Moi issued an edict to break apart the LBCs in the Rift Valley and Central Province, undermining one of the main economic and political sources of Kikuyu power (Boone 2014).

[56] William Ole Ntimama was a powerful member of the KANU. He was MP for Narok North for twenty-five years.

Land Politics at the Coast: What Was Different?

I turn now to highlight some of the ways that land reform and resettlement policies along the coast have played out in ways that are notably distinct from inland regions. First, when accounting for population density, there is not a significant disparity in the number of households settled along the coast compared to other inland regions. What differs, however, is the proportion of land made available to local residents. Specifically, the government designated nearly 30 percent of settlement schemes in Coast region for the resettlement of Kenyans from other regions, notably Kikuyu from Central Province. The most contentious of these schemes is the Lake Kenyatta Settlement Scheme, located in Lamu district near the Somali border. Created in 1973, nearly all plots have since been allocated to Kikuyu residents.[57] Many local residents viewed the settlement scheme as a way to resettle Kikuyus while neglecting or further undermining their own land security. The Kenyatta administration also initiated several *Haraka* schemes in Kwale and Kilifi, which were designed to ease the squatter problem along coastal areas.[58] Yet because "outsiders" could also apply for plots, "upcountry people" who worked as laborers or in administrative offices often obtained plots over local residents (Kanyinga 2000).[59]

Second, a far greater proportion of settlement schemes on the Coast are categorized as *squatter* settlement schemes rather than *conventional* settlement schemes. The distinction is important, as the designation of squatter settlement schemes indicates that residents have no formal tenure rights (Lukalo & Odari 2016). As of May 2012, the government categorized 64 percent of settlement schemes in the Coast Province as "squatter schemes," compared to only 36 percent of

---

[57] At its creation in 1973, the state allocated 3,562 plots over 14,224 hectares. Analysts have attributed the salient anti-outsider narrative with the infamous attack in Mpeketoni in June 2014 that killed sixty people. Al-Shabaab claimed responsibility.

[58] *Haraka* schemes were created from abandoned European farms. Most were located in the Coast province.

[59] The government also created settlement schemes to accommodate government officials or private companies. For example, it created the Vipingo Settlement Scheme to accommodate the expansion of the Vipingo Sisal Plantation, removing squatters who were impeding the expansion of the plantation (see Kanyinga 2000).

schemes in the Rift Valley and 24 percent in Central Province (Lukalo & Odari 2016).[60]

Third, central state elites had few political incentives to implement extensive land reform along the Coast compared to inland regions. As I've mentioned, this is partly because the central government was less concerned about rebellion along the Coast than they were in zones previously affected by the Mau Mau uprising. Further, the KANU regime derived greater benefit from using coastal land to reward local officials than it did from building a loyal coastal electorate. Relatedly, the largest ethnic group on the Coast, the Mijikenda, comprises less than 5 percent of the national population. Hence, even with the advent of multiparty politics, the region did not figure prominently into electoral calculations.

Fourth, land reform along the Coast differed from other regions of the country in part, because a large proportion of arable coast land remained in the hands of Arab families (e.g. the Mazrui family). Many of these landowners, referred to as "absentee landlords," owned the land on paper, but did not occupy, invest in, or cultivate the land. Further, the majority of arable land along the Coast was under freehold title under the names of Arab families. In addition, while Arab lands were privately held, many estates continued to allow squatters to occupy or cultivate land into the postcolonial period, providing an informal pressure valve (Kanyinga 2000: 66). As a result, the government had less land at its disposal that it could convert into settlement schemes. More so, the government had neither the ability nor motive to "buy back" these lands from Arab families as they did with outgoing European settlers in the former "white highlands." The belief that Arab landholdings were a barrier to resettlement shaped the development strategies of coastal administrators in the early 1960s. In 1965, the Coast Provincial Commissioner wrote a letter regarding the "the problem of freehold farms":

Most of the old 10-mile Coastal strip which is not Government Land is Arab owned freehold. Much of the land is underdeveloped and some completely undeveloped. There is a large African population on this land who demand

---

[60] For a more detailed account of why the government formally registers some settlement schemes sooner than others, see Hassan and Klaus (2019).

that they should own the undeveloped portions . . . We require funds and staff to do this. This is a very large and very urgent problem – covering a good proportion of the productive arable land of the district. The problem would probably be solved if Arabs were bought out, as was done with Europeans in the Highlands.[61]

But the government never "bought out" Arab lands to redistribute to coast residents. In conversations with Kilifi residents about land access, the government's failure to purchase Arab lands remains a focal point. Two residents of Kijipwa Settlement Scheme explain:

Money was lent to the Kenyan government from the U.K. They were compensating those Europeans who had big farms. [British loans] were used to buy the white highlands but not the land on the Coast . . . Had they used that money, they would have bought the land from the Arabs as well so that the land could be given back to the people. But they left the Arabs with the land, so the Arabs sold the same pieces of land to the big farms.[62]

It's impossible to know whether the government would have succeeded in purchasing land from Arab families along the Coast. What's key, however, is the state's apparent ambivalence toward land reform along the Coast compared to other regions (e.g. Rift Valley and Central Province). This attitude is evident in the remarks of Isaiah Mathenge, who was the Provincial Commissioner for Agriculture, and who would later become the Provincial Commissioner for the Rift Valley:

With regard to the mismanaged farms I suggest we leave them for the time being as I do not consider the Government has funds to buy out the owners of these farms . . . most of these so-called mismanaged farms . . . have never at any time been properly managed or developed and in my view these farms can hardly justify consideration similar to the ones given to the mismanaged farms in the former White Highlands.[63]

The Commissioner's remarks reveal the attitude of many high-ranking government officials who had little interest in resettling indigenous people along the Coast. As a result, there were fewer settlement

---

[61] SETT/3/ii/114 (12 April 1965)/ Coast Provincial Commissioner, Mombasa, "Potential Settlement Schemes: Coast Province." Retrieved at the Kenya National Archives (Nairobi).
[62] Interview-Kijipwa SS-Kilifi County-Coast, January 1, 2012 (father and son).
[63] SETT/3/ii/144 of 12.4.64 / Mombasa. (I. Mathenge, Provincial Commissioner of Agriculture). Retrieved at the Kenya National Archives (Nairobi).

scheme initiatives. And the schemes that were established tended to benefit people from other regions of the county.

Lastly, central state elites have, for the most part, controlled and managed land on the Coast through a process that Kanyinga (2000) describes as "re-distribution from above" or "grants from above."[64] Kanyinga (2000) describes how many coastal settlement scheme plots went to members of the inner-circle national elite, bypassing both local residents and local leaders. Hence, by allocating coast land in ways that excluded local leaders along with the majority of the population, successive regimes undercut a source of patronage that could have linked local leaders to their coastal supporters.

In the 1980s, the Moi government created many settlement schemes with the stated intention of settling squatters who were indigenous to the Coast. While some locals were able to secure a plot of land, most never obtained a genuine title deed. More so, many plots were illegally allocated to elites and political officials as "grants from above." Plots near the coastline were particularly vulnerable to illegal allocation, as they were in highest demand among hotel developers. A respondent in the Kijipwa Settlement Scheme (established in 1982) in Kilifi talks about the multiple titles issued in the scheme:

There is a [double allocation] next to the Paradise Hotel. During Moi's government everyone in government would allocate their cronies land. Imagine somebody coming in all the way from Narok with a title deed while the locals don't have one . . ..[65]

One consequence of Moi's ambivalence toward property-rights institutions was a new set of informal rules where individuals or companies could leverage their political ties to make claims to prime coastland. While there is nothing particularly unique about "big money" influencing the land acquisition process, there was an important change in how these dynamics played out along Kenya's Swahili coast. Notably, while the land market excluded many ordinary citizens, it did create opportunities for "entrepreneurial" middlemen or brokers who were

---

[64] Specifically, they tended to be either high-ranking national-level elites or officers within the provincial administration. Recipients would often use these lands for speculative rather than developmental purposes.
[65] Interview-Kijipwa SS-Kilifi County, November 20, 2012(7).

less central under the more formal process of land allocation under Kenyatta. This new environment created a set of incentives that rewarded local leaders who could facilitate the illegal transfer of land from their own communities into the hands of private individuals or companies. Chiefs, local councilors, or MPs were rewarded with plots of land, cash, or political positions by "selling out" their own communities. This further undermined the ability of local political leaders to act as "land patrons" who had the capacity or will to distribute to the community.

Over time, citizens would come to see their own leaders as brokers to more powerful business or upcountry elites, selling out the communities that they claimed to represent.[66] Instead of looking to political leaders to provide land, coastal residents have continued to secure land informally through old and new forms of landlord–tenant relationships, squatting as "tenants" on the land of absentee (or mostly absent) landlords or on the land of private companies.[67]

An additional implication of settlement policy along the Coast is that even where land allocations occurred, many Mijikenda or Swahili residents have struggled to gain secure tenure rights to plots of land on these schemes. Further, the ethnic, political, and class exclusivity of these plots has exacerbated land insecurity and landlessness among most of the coastal population, working to deepen an anti-outsider land narrative.

Conclusion

This chapter examines the historical origins of land access and distribution between inland Kenya and the Coast region. I suggest that leaders in inland Kenya have been able to use their land wealth to signal their ability or willingness to distribute land to followers, acting as *land patrons*. Yet along the Coast, there has been little precedent for politicians distributing or providing land to ordinary citizens. Instead,

---

[66] This assertion is based partly on my interviews with residents in Kwale and Kilifi who talk about leaders (district officials and elected officials) using positions of power to sell land to "outsiders" – upcountry politicians, Arabs, or foreigners. See Chapter 7 for further details.

[67] On the Coast, many of these companies include sisal, sugar, or cashew plantations or titanium or salt mines.

coast leaders – most of whom are ethnic minorities in the region – fall into the role of the *landlord*: a figure who extracts rents in exchange for land access but who cannot be expected to protect or provide rights. Very few Mijikenda leaders from the Coast have acquired the level of land wealth needed to signal redistributive objectives or capabilities required of "land patrons."

The chapter has outlines how the origins of elite wealth and whether state elites view the region as a potential site of insurgency help explain different patterns and strategies of land resettlement between the coast and inland regions.

I suggest that coast residents did not present the same political threat to the state as did residents living in or near zones of the Mau Mau civil war. Equally, the relatively small size of the Mijikenda population, the homogeneity of the population, and the lack of shared ethnicity between the landed elite and the broader public meant that elites had few incentives to build a political clientele through land reform.

The logics of land distribution that I analyze in this chapter are key for understanding the distinct ways that citizens access and make claims to land in each region at different historical moments. In regions characterized by strong land patrons, more contentious claim-making between local groups is likely to emerge. In such cases, land access is linked to having a co-ethnic patron in power. As a result, changes in political power can signal threats to land rights or opportunities to challenge the status quo distribution of rights. Hence, while individuals and groups in these environments have more opportunities to access rights through patronage relationships, these environments are also more politically unstable and vulnerable to election-related violence. By contrast, in regions characterized by the landlord–tenant dynamic, access to land does not hinge on having a powerful co-ethnic patron in office. And so, with the onset of competitive elections citizens are less likely to associate electoral outcomes with their ability to gain land or their risk or losing land. With little to gain or lose, citizen participation in electoral violence in these areas is less likely. In Chapter 7, I return to a comparison of the Rift Valley and Coast regions, where I ask why elites have succeeded in organizing election violence in parts of the Rift Valley, but less so in the Coast.

PART I

Determinants of Contentious Land Narratives

4 | *Land Inequality and Land Narratives: Theory and Evidence*

This chapter examines the first stage in the process of electoral violence: Why do contentious land narratives form in some cases but not others? I argue that the degree of land rights inequality between two neighboring, but ethnically distinct groups can have a significant effect on how and where contentious land narratives form: shaping the discourse that citizens use to assert rights to land.[1] To evaluate this argument, I draw primarily on a large qualitative dataset comprising hundreds of interviews that I conducted across communities in Nakuru, Kwale, and Kilifi counties.[2] I also draw on original household-level survey data to show broader, descriptive patterns in both land security and belief in contentious land narratives.

Two main findings emerge. First, I find that where there is land *equality* between groups, contentious land narratives are far less likely to form. In the cases that I analyze here, land equality exists when the majority of group members from both sides have title deeds. Noncontentious narratives are also possible where both groups are equally land insecure.[3] While there are many measures of land tenure security, such as plot size and perceived risk of eviction, I focus primarily on whether a household holds a title deed to their land. I focus on the presence or absence of a legitimate title deed in part because it provides a relatively objective and consistent measure of formal land rights. More so, it is the primary metric that Kenyans use to think about their own rights and the rights of others. Discussion around the title deed is always contentious, with politicians at times, reducing it to a "mere pieces of paper."[4] Indeed, in spaces where the

---

[1] By "neighboring" I mean here that two distinct social groups (ethnic, class, religious) live within close proximity to one another, but they need not necessarily border one another.

[2] See appendix for more details on this dataset.

[3] I explain these scenarios in greater depth in the next chapter.

[4] For instance, the powerful KANU politician, William Ole Ntimama, declared in 1993 that "land titles were nothing but pieces of paper" ("The Indigenous and the Natives," *Weekly Review* (Nairobi), July 9, 1993).

state lacks the will or capacity to evenly and consistently protect property rights, the title deed may in fact represent little more than a piece of paper. Yet for many title deed holders, the title is sacrosanct: proof of one's ownership and hard work. A respondent in Likia captures this view: "Whenever you have a title deed, it gives you power. Wherever you go, everyone takes you seriously because you have a title deed. Your title deed is your sweat . . . who can chase me away from my land while I have a title deed? No one can."[5] The almost mythic value that the title deed has come to acquire provides a key campaign tool, as it has since independence. This strategy was on full display during the 2013 and 2017 presidential elections, with Uhuru Kenyatta's Jubilee Party promising to distribute millions of title deeds across the country.[6] Among sampled respondents in the Rift Valley and Coast region, 45 percent claim to have formal and legitimate title deeds.

Second, the data show that contentious land narratives often, though not always, correlate with spaces of electoral violence (see last column in Table 4.1). Contentious land narratives can provide a key mechanism linking land tenure inequality between groups and the escalation of violence. Yet as Table 4.1 shows, land inequality and contentious land narratives correlate with election-time violence among cases in the Rift Valley, but not the Coast. In Chapter 7, I explain that while there are contentious land narratives between insider and outsider groups in Kwale and Kilifi, the absence of political leaders who can act as strong and credible land patrons mitigates the violent potential of such narratives. Specifically, in environments shaped by a political logic of "landlordism" rather than land patronage, political elites have less moral authority and political legitimacy and thus have less power to mobilize election violence.

I organize the chapter as follows. I begin by explaining how I measure and observe contentious land narratives. Second, I present my concept and measure of local land inequality, specifying how it contributes to existing studies of inequality and conflict. In the next chapter (Chapter 5) I specify the precise mechanisms linking land inequality and narrative formation. The third and main section of the chapter presents evidence for my argument – a qualitative dataset containing eight case comparisons across the Rift Valley and Coast region.

[5] Interview-Likia LBC- Nakuru County, July 4, 2012 (16).
[6] The Jubilee government promised to distribute three million title deeds by the August 2017 election. See for example: *Daily Nation*, "The Land Question: the Elephant in the Room." February 14, 2017.

Defining and Measuring Land Narratives

Broadly, land narratives can provide group members with a discourse for constructing meaning around land in everyday life: around themes of survival, inheritance, burial rights, investment opportunities, and identity. A collective land narrative becomes contentious when the narrative challenges the land or territorial claims of another group. Perhaps the most universal and contentious land narrative consists of the proclamation, "*this is our land.*" The narrative – whether deployed by Palestinians in the West Bank, Kalenjins in the Rift Valley, or Navajo in the American West – almost always contains a longer story about a collective "we" who are entitled to land based on place or birth, lineage, race, or ethnicity, and an out-group (e.g. "migrants" or "settlers") who have taken lands or threaten to take land or territory.

I rely on individual-level interviews and focus group discussions to determine whether a contentious or noncontentious narrative best characterizes a given case study community. Where the majority of interviews in a given community fit at least one of the five following criteria, I categorize the case study as having contentious land narratives. These criteria are as follows:

1. articulates collective claims to land or territory based on shared group identity;
2. blames another group for the land insecurity or general suffering of group members;
3. articulates fear or anxiety of losing land to nearby out-group;
4. articulates plan of action for reclaiming land;
5. describes other groups in terms that denote nonbelonging (e.g. "foreigners," "invaders").

Stepping back, the defining feature of these narratives is their emphasis on *threat* to land rights or *opportunities* to reclaim land. As I emphasize through this book, the salience of threat and opportunity often increase as elections approach.

In several of my case studies, respondents do not articulate contentious land narratives. Where land narratives are noncontentious, group members avoid framing out-groups as threats or invaders, do not challenge past or current allocation of land rights, emphasize a preference for order and stability, and articulate land rights in accordance with liberal views of national citizenship rather than sub-national or ethnic citizenship.

In the Kenya context, noncontentious narratives that articulate these "liberal" views of land ownership convey an idea about a "right to live anywhere," a central tenet of national or liberal forms of citizenship (Ndegwa 1997). There is a long history of Kenyans debating national versus subnational forms of citizenship. At the formal level, Kenyans have disagreed about the type of con-stitution that would provide the most effective form of governance. The constitutional model that prevailed after 1963 was based on the idea of national citizenship. An alternate model, referred to as *majim-boism,* was based on ethnic citizenship and promoted the devolution of power to ethnically defined regions. Smaller ethnic groups believed that this model would better protect their land and economic interests from the "tyranny of the majority." These constitutional debates continue to influence views about the right of citizens to live, own land, and accumulate wealth anywhere within the borders of the nation-state beyond one's imagined ethnic homeland.[7] The tension between national and ethnic citizenship is evident in the following focus group conversation among Kalenjin youth in Mauche (Nakuru County):[8]

Participant 2: The entire land belongs to the Ogiek but now we have so many tribes living here.

Participant 4: The Constitution says you have a right to live anywhere you want in Kenya, so whoever has land here and has a title deed has the right.

Participant 6: The constitution was passed and so many opposed it like me because it was not addressing land issues accordingly. But we think of ourselves as the owners of Njoro district.

Participant 1: In short [we] say that [we] should own Njoro. But because of the law [we] will allow anyone to live here.

Before turning to the chapter's main argument, I provide results from my household-level survey that illustrate county-level patterns in agree-ment with a set of contentious land narratives. I measure two common narratives. The first, which I call the "invader narrative" measures

---

[7] See Chapter 2 for historical background on this debate.
[8] Interviews-Mauche SS-Nakuru County, July 9, 2012 (Youth Focus Group).

whether a respondent agrees with the following statement, "Our community is landless today because other tribes have invaded and taken land that belongs to us." The question aims to measure a person's belief that people from other regions of the country have unjustly "invaded" the land or territorial space of one's own group, thus undermining the land rights of the so-called native group. The second is an "anti-outsider" narrative, which I measure using a survey question that probes a respondent's agreement with the following statement: "Outsiders do not deserve to own land in this area. The problem is that they use corrupt means to buy land from indigenous people." The narrative has two main elements. The first is based on the idea that members of a given ethnic community can only make legitimate claims to land within the boundaries of their ancestral homeland. The implication, therefore, is that people living outside their ancestral home do not have the same rights to land as the "native" or "son of the soil."[9] The idea here is similar to the narrative theme above, where Kenyans debate the primacy of ethnic versus national citizenship. The narrative also implies that non-natives who have acquired land outside their ancestral home must have done so using corrupt or illegitimate means.

Figure 4.1 illustrates two key points. First, the patterns here suggest that belief in divisive and contentious land narratives are widely shared among a cross-sections of rural society. Secondly, the figure reveals notable regional and county-level variation. For instance, while only 20 percent of respondents in Kilifi agree with the anti-outsider narrative, 70 percent in Nakuru and 82 percent in Uasin Gishu agree.

The ubiquity of these narratives raises an important challenge in identifying the causal role of contentious narratives in the process of violence. Namely, if belief in these narratives is so widespread, yet violence is rare, what, if any predictive power do they have? As I'll argue throughout this book, these contentious narratives are often necessary, but not sufficient conditions in explaining the escalation of violence. Other factors also must come into play.

Further, while these narratives appear common when I aggregate results at the county-level, there is in fact, important local-level

---

[9] There is a long literature examining conflict related to the indigene/migrant divide; see for example, Lentz (2013); Fearon and Laitin (2011); Geschiere (2009); and Weiner (1978).

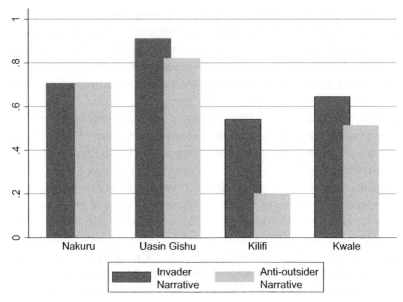

Figure 4.1 Mean agreement with contentious land narratives (by county).

variation. Specifically, when looking at mean responses to the anti-outsider narrative at the ward level, the proportion of respondents who agree ranges from 40 to 100 percent among wards in the Rift Valley, and between 10 to 90 percent across wards in the Coast.[10]

I'll argue that much of this variation can be explained by underlying land inequalities between groups, and further, that this local-level variation in contentious narratives can indeed be a powerful factor in explaining the organization of electoral violence (see Chapter 6). I document this local-level variation in contentious narratives in the sections below, providing a more in-depth analysis of this variation in Chapter 5.

Argument: Inequality in Land Rights

This chapter argues that inequality in land rights between two distinct and locally based groups is a key factor in explaining where contentious

---

[10]   In the Rift Valley, the ward with the lowest level of agreement with the anti-outsider narrative was Kiptagich (Nakuru County), while the highest mean was in Racecourse (Uasin Gishu County). In the Coast, the lowest level of agreement was in Tezo ward (Kilifi), while the highest was in Kubo South (Kwale).

land narratives form. This argument contributes to existing studies of inequality in a few specific ways. First, most studies of group inequality analyze inequality at the national level.[11] Hijashijima and Houle (2017) for example, draw on Afrobarometer data to analyze how between- and within-group inequalities nationally affect ethnic identification. Their study draws on the earlier work by Baldwin and Huber (2010), which examines the link between group inequality and public goods provision. Relatedly, Alesina et al. (2016) examine the link between ethnic inequality and development. Østby (2008) meanwhile constructs a measure of horizontal inequality by focusing on the two largest ethnic groups in each country as a way to explain civil war onset cross-nationally. And recently, datasets such as the Ethnic Power Relations dataset (Cederman et al. 2010), Geo-Referencing Ethnic Groups (Weidmann et al. 2010), and Nordhaus's (2006) Geographically based Economic Data (G-Econ),[12] enable scholars to calculate economic inequality between groups within a country (Cederman & Wucherpfennig 2017).[13] These studies have made important contributions to understanding how group-level inequalities can help explain the emergence of group grievances, voting behavior, and civil conflict. Yet nearly all these studies do so by comparing the relative wealth of groups at the national level.

By contrast, I argue that local-level inequality can provide a more precise and potentially more powerful explanatory variable. First, by shifting the lens to the subnational or local level, scholars can better account for subnational variation in the outcome of interest (e.g. violent protests). More so, however, discrepancies between groups at the local level often matter more than discrepancies between groups nationally. Imagine, for example, that Group A and Group B are the largest and second largest ethnic groups nationally, with Group A controlling a disproportionate share of legislative seats and national wealth. One expectation is that grievances should form among members of Group B, given that these

---

[11] For example, Gurr's (2000) "Minorities at Risk" (MAR) dataset, Hijashijima and Houle (2017), who rely on Afrobarometer, studies by Cederman and co-authors that rely on the Ethnic Power Relations (EPR) dataset, and Østby (2008) who constructs a measure of horizontal inequality by comparing national surveys (DHS data) across countries.

[12] https://gecon.yale.edu/

[13] Further, G-Econ data rely heavily on official statistics whose quality and reliability is questionable in many countries (see for example Jerven 2015).

members are more likely to feel politically and economically excluded. This grievance may indeed exist nationally. Yet the salience or importance of national-level inequality does not always map onto the local. Locally, Group B may be the largest and more powerful, while Group A is a small minority and economically marginal. The key point is that while the ranking of groups nationally may figure into the narratives that group members and their leaders deploy, they may not be as meaningful as the inequalities that are most visible to people in their everyday lives – the inequalities between the north and south side of an urban slum, the market sellers on the right and left side of the road, the landed elite with mansions on the ridgeline, and squatters living down below, or the village with titled land next to the village without title deeds. Further, people tend to imagine their political worlds – their rights and obligations – locally. No doubt, national politics matters because political power is often highly centralized, especially in countries transitioning from authoritarian rule. But national politics can also feel distant or abstract for many ordinary citizens, particularly rural-based citizens living far from centers of power. In sum, I argue here that inequalities at the local, rather than national level, can powerfully shape local-level land narratives – contentious or otherwise.

As a way to illustrate this concept of inequality in land rights at the local level, I begin by drawing on survey data to show local-level variation in land inequality. Specifically, Figure 4.2 shows the proportion of Kalenjin and Kikuyu residents who hold title deeds, measured at the ward level, which is the smallest electoral unit. This figure shows results from Nakuru County (Rift Valley region). While these figures are an imperfect measure of land rights inequality, they provide one illustration of how inequality in land rights might manifest at the local level. In particular, we should expect contentious land narratives to be most salient where nearly all members of a given group has title deeds yet very few members of the other group have title.[14]

---

[14] One drawback to this figure is that it conceals the base ethnic composition within each ward. I do not, in other words, provide title ownership as a proportion of each group's true population, as data on ethnic demography (at any level) is unavailable.

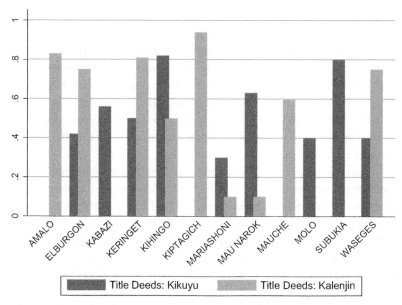

Figure 4.2 Land rights inequality between Kikuyu and Kalenjin residents in Nakuru County.

A Qualitative Measure of Intergroup Land Inequality

I measure the degree of land rights inequality between two neighboring or nearby groups though a series of case comparisons. Specifically, I use individual in-depth interviews and focus group discussions with residents of settlement schemes and LBCs in Nakuru, Kwale, and Kilifi counties. The interviews with residents provide data on the level and forms of subjective and objective land tenure security of group members, the history of these tenure rights, how respondents view and navigate land tenure institutions, and their views of competing land claimants. Yet for the purposes of constructing a measure of land inequality at the group level, I focus on a set of questions that ask respondents how and whether they can access land.[15]

My key explanatory variable is the degree of inequality in land tenure rights between members of two groups. The degree of inequality can fall into three broad categories: (1) relative equality, (2) moderate inequality, and (3) significant inequality. In the set of

[15] See appendix for details on these questions and their wording.

case studies that I present, I characterize groups as being relatively equal if members of both groups have title deeds to their land. Yet land rights equality may also exist in the absence of title deeds. For example, if both sides only have allotment letters to their land, then here too land rights are likely to be equal between groups. Alternatively, if neither group has formal tenure rights but both benefit from the same level of customary rights or informal protection, then in theory, members from each group have similar levels of land rights.

I code two respective communities as "moderately unequal" when members from one group benefit from title deeds while members of the neighboring group have a less secure form of land documentation (e.g. allotment letter). There may also be moderate inequality when one group benefits from the *de facto* recognition of a chief or local government, while a second group (e.g. ethnic outsiders) lack such recognition. These discrepancies, however, can be more difficult to discern than, for instance, discrepancies in title deeds.

I aggregate individual responses to generalize the main form of tenure security at the group level. While this method of aggregating up or generalizing from the individual up to the group may be inappropriate in some contexts, it is generally appropriate when analyzing settlement schemes and LBCs in Kenya because there is very little variation in the type of tenure rights within a given settlement scheme or LBC. Most households, as settlers or LBC stakeholders, receive the same size plot at a given point in time.

Finally, analyzing group-level land inequality, I aim to identify disparities that were salient or emerged prior to the 2007 general election. This enables me to make a more compelling argument about the effect of group land inequality on narrative formation, and in turn, the role that contentious narratives may have played in facilitating the 2007–2008 electoral violence.

Evidence: Paired Case Comparisons

The table below summarizes each of the eight case comparisons that I analyze. In the first six cases, all located in Nakuru County, the relevant cleavage line is ethnic identity, though this ethnic difference does not imply polarization or conflict. The latter two case studies are located in Kilifi and Kwale counties, in the Coast region. These cases are distinct from those in the Rift Valley in that the degree of land inequality between groups is significant. For this reason, the most salient cleavage line is not based on ethnic identity, but instead on class: between an entrenched landowning elite ("landlords") and majority population who have few, if any, tenure rights ("squatters"). In the section that follows, I provide brief descriptions of these case studies to demonstrate variation in group-level land inequality, with a focus on how inequality (or lack thereof) can provoke or moderate contentious land narratives between groups. Specifically, I use these case comparisons as evidence that where there is local-level inequality in land rights between ethnically distinct groups, contentious land narratives between these groups are more likely to form. In later chapters, I explore the second part of the process of electoral violence, focusing on the link between contentious land narratives and the organization and escalation of violence. The next chapter focuses on two paired cases to explore the specific mechanisms through which land inequality affects narrative formation.

Case 1: Ogilgei and Kerma (Rongai Constituency, Nakuru County)

In the first case comparison, I analyze a Kalenjin LBC (Ogilgei) that borders a Kikuyu settlement scheme (Kerma). I find that residents of both Kerma and Ogilgei can regularly access land for small-holder farming, and more so, that the majority of households have title deeds to their individual plots. While Kalenjin plots are larger than Kikuyu plots, I focus on inequality in terms of formal tenure rights (i.e. title deeds). As I explain, where both sides have been able to secure tenure rights, each side is less likely to question the claims of the other group and more likely to promote the status quo distribution of rights. I describe this paired case in greater detail in the next chapter (Chapter 5).

Case 2: Umoja and Belbar (Rongai Constituency, Nakuru County)

Most residents of Belbar and Umoja – two bordering villages in Ronagi constituency – have title deeds. Hence, I code these cases as having relative equality. Umoja, which means unity in Swahili, is a multiethnic

Table 4.1 *Qualitative case comparisons*

	Region: county, constituency	Case comparison	Land documents	Groups	Land rights: degree unequal	Contentious narrative (DV)
1	Rift Valley: Nakuru Rongai	Ogilgei Kerma	Title deeds Title deeds	Kalenjin/ Kikuyu	Equal	NO
2	Rift Valley: Nakuru Rongai	Umoja Belbar	Title deeds Title deeds	Mixed/ Kalenjin	Equal	NO
3	Rift Valley: Nakuru Njoro	Likia Mauche	Title deeds Allotment letters	Kikuyu/ Kalenjin	Moderate	YES
4	Rift Valley: Nakuru Njoro	Mwisho wa Lami Tipis	Title deeds Allotment letters	Kikuyu/ Maasai	Moderate	YES
5	Rift Valley: Nakuru Naivasha	Oljorai Nyakinyua	Allotment letters Title deeds	Mixed/ Kikuyu	Moderate	YES
6	Rift Valley: Nakuru Naivasha	Hell's Gate[1] Flower Farms	Title deed Lease	Kikuyu2/ Mixed	Moderate	YES
7	Coast: Kilifi Kilifi South	Kijipwa REA Vipingo	No documents Title deed	Squatters/ Landlords	Significant	YES
8	Coast: Kwale Msambweni	Ramisi KISCOL	No documents Title deed	Squatters/ Landlords	Significant	YES

Notes:

[1] Hell's Gate is an adjudication scheme and administration location that surrounds commercial flower farms. The majority of residents are workers inside these flower farms.

[2] Main cleavage line is between Kikuyu/Luo, yet the location is diverse due to flower farms that attract citizens from nationwide.

farming community that formed when former tenants of a white settler farm jointly purchased the farm, forming the LBC in 1967.[16] According to residents, the farm's founders selected the name "umoja" to signal the founding mission of the farm, which was to bring different ethnic communities together. Shareholders shared a common title deed until recently, when they received individual titles to their plots of land.[17] Yet while all shareholders in the LBC have title deeds, the size of their plot varies depending on the "total contributions [a shareholder has] paid by the time the lands were issued."[18]

Belbar farm borders Umoja. While the plots of land in Belbar are far smaller than Umoja, most residents have title deeds (though some still hold allotment letters). And like Umoja, the community is ethnically diverse by comparison to many other farming communities in the central Rift Valley. The largest groups include households from different Kalenjin subgroups, followed by pastoralist groups from the North Rift, and Kikuyu families.

An older Turkana man explained how he had bought his land in 1969 after deciding to invest in land rather than cattle, which he viewed as a wiser and less risky investment. Like other residents of Belbar, he was issued with three letters upon acquiring land: one from the village elder, one from the chief, and one from the government – the title deed.[19] His experience reflects that of many other community members. While a few still remain with plot allotment letters, many have managed to gain title deeds.

The case of Belbar and Umoja provides evidence for my argument that where two distinct and local groups benefit from relatively equal land rights, the land narratives within and between these groups should be less contentious. The majority of residents recognize and respect the land rights of the neighboring group. More so, most residents do not see neighboring groups as a threat to their livelihood or land security.[20] What I observe instead is a more liberal, market-oriented view of land rights which does not place emphasis on one's ethnic identity or place

[16] Interview-Umoja-Nakuru County, August 8, 2012(1).
[17] Interview-Umoja-Nakuru County, August 8, 2012 (2).
[18] Interview-Umoja-Nakuru County, August 8, 2012 (1).
[19] Interview-Belbar-Nakuru County, August 9, 2012 (3).
[20] Notably, because large commercial estates owned by wealthy politicians surround resident of Umoja and Belbar, there is a heightened awareness of class inequality. But these grievances do not fall along ethnic or communal lines as they do in other areas.

or origin, but instead, on one's title-based claim to land. The elder Turkana remarks:

There is no harm if someone from a different community buys land around here because according to the new constitution everybody has the right to live anywhere within the boundaries of the nation. Again, when people originate from different areas they bring varying ideas that help in developing the region.

He continues:

Despite the fact that there are some tribes that inhabited land in the Rift Valley before the coming of the colonialist – which were the Kalenjins, Maasai, Turkana, and Samburu – I don't think they have more rights of ownership to land than other tribes. This is because they must have sold the land to the others. So if they didn't want [outsiders] to own land they could have not sold it. Also, they [the newcomers] are now in possession of legal documents – the title deed.

Several respondents did, however, articulate a narrative that is common among "natives" of the Rift Valley. This narrative tells a story in which the first President Kenyatta, a Kikuyu, settled his "tribesmen" in the Rift Valley while displacing or neglecting Kalenjin and other "sons of the soil." Yet while some respondents recount this history, I do not code this community as having a contentious narrative because residents here are not using this narrative to actively undermine the rights of a neighboring group, nor do residents frame a nearby community as a specific or imminent threat.

The liberal, market-centric, and national view of citizenship and belonging goes against a more exclusive narrative that frames the rights of migrants (outsiders) as subordinate to the claims of natives or first-comers. While numerous factors may help account for this respondent's worldview, I suggest that because members of both communities feel equally land secure, contentious land narratives are not a salient feature of local discourse. As a result, even as elections approach, neither side perceives an imminent threat to their land security.[21]

---

[21] One caveat to note when analyzing Belbar and Umjoa is that these communities are not as ethnically distinct from one as the other Rift Valley cases that I analyze. Hence, when thinking about the key factor working to moderate both contentious land narratives and the escalation of violence, it is difficult to distinguish between the absence of land inequality and clear ethnic difference.

Case 3: Likia and Mauche (Njoro Constituency, Nakuru County)

In contrast to the cases I've sketched out above, there are many cases where members of one group benefit from stronger tenure security relative to a nearby group. In these scenarios, contentious land narratives are much more likely to emerge. The neighboring farming villages of Likia and Mauche illustrate such a dynamic. In Likia, nearly all Kikuyu residents have title deeds to their 1.25-acre plots of land. Yet in the neighboring farming community of Mauche, Kalenjin farmers lack title deeds to their five-acre plots – either because the government canceled their title deeds or because they were never allocated in the first place. As Table 4.1 indicates, contentious land narratives are salient and highly divisive. Further, electoral violence has escalated in the 1990s and 2007–2008. I detail this case study in the next chapter.

Case 4: Tipis & Mwisho wa Lami (Njoro Constituency, Nakuru County)

Mwisho wa Lami – "end of the road" in Swahili – is aptly named. Where the pavement ends, Mwisho wa Lami becomes Tipis, named after Justus Ole Tipis, a powerful Maasai politician and advocate for Maasai land rights.[22] Both communities sit near the edge of the current Nakuru–Narok county border, along the edge of the Mau forest. Mwisho wa Lami was formed as a mostly Kikuyu LBC in the mid-1970s in the final years of the Kenyatta administration.[23] In 1984, Kihika Kimani, who was then MP for Nakuru North District and a powerful Kikuyu land patron, issued residents (i.e. shareholders) with title deeds to their plots of land. These plots, according to residents, averaged two acres each.[24] Many of the original shareholders have since left the community for more stable regions, selling

[22] Ole Tipis was a KANU cabinet secretary for Narok North from 1982 to 1988. In 1962, he was part of a Maasai delegation to the Kenya Constitutional Conference at Lancaster House in the UK asking for land relinquished to the British in the early 1900s be returned to the Maasai (Lotte 2005).

[23] The LBC was formed through the purchase of land belonging to a departing white settler.

[24] Kimani's 30,000-member LBC was the largest in Kenya. His land wealth facilitated his rise to politics, using shareholder funds to fund political campaigns. He served as MP for Nakuru North (1974–1979), Laikipia West (1992–1997), and Molo (1997–2002).

their property to so-called strangers or leaving their land to children or in-laws. Yet while the demographics of the community have shifted over the decades, Mwisho wa Lami remains a primarily Kikuyu community whose residents cling to their title deeds in the face of Maasai land claims.

In Tipis by contrast, the forms of land tenure are largely informal, mixed, and ambiguous. This ambiguity emerges in part from the multiple and powerful land claims in the area, including a land dispute over a 4,000-acre commercial estate belonging to the late Mbiu Koinage,[25] a dispute over a large parastatal (1,440 acres), and the longer-standing dispute over the return of Maasai lands taken during British rule (Lotte 2005).

Maasai residents, who comprise the majority of the Tipis community, describe two main modes of land access. Historically, Maasai have gained access to land through user rights on group ranches.[26] Over the years, however, Maasai elders have subdivided these group ranches into smaller *shambas* or farms. While some households have obtained title deeds to these subdivided land parcels, many others have not. A respondent explains the informality of these agreements: "there was no legal document issued. The only thing that people have is an agreement letter indicating that you have bought land from somebody and there are about three witnesses."[27]

The second and more problematic mode of land access is the acquisition of land on the now defunct Agricultural Development Corporation (ADC), a government parastatal.[28] While the government still claims to own the land, an informal LBC emerged when the ADC leased the land to a private estate, which then subleased plots to individuals.[29] Many local Maasai leaders asserted control over these plots, leasing or selling plots to land-poor Maasai and Kikuyu families.

---

[25] Mbiyu Koinange served as Minister of State under the Kenyatta Administration, and as Minister of Environment and Natural Resources under Moi.

[26] Group ranch: "livestock production system where a group of people jointly own freehold title to land, maintain agreed stocking levels and herd their livestock collectively which they own individually" (Ministry of Agriculture 1968). Group Ranches fell under Trust Lands (Cap 288, 1963 Constitution).

[27] Interview-Tipis-Nakuru County, October 18, 2012 (10).

[28] The Kenyan Parliament designated the ADC in 1965 as a parastatal to support and develop Kenya's agricultural production and enterprise, including the development and management of seed production and livestock genetics and technology transfer (Mwakale 2015).

[29] Residents and media reports suggest that this intermediary actor was Scoff Estates.

Yet because the ADC still holds the official title deed to the land, none of the "shareholders" have genuine title deeds to their individual parcels. Residents note, however, that it is possible to acquire fake or counterfeit title deeds through bribery.[30]

Inequality in land rights in the area takes two main forms. The first is the inequality between Mwisho wa Lami and Tipis. Nearly all Kikuyu households in Mwisho wa Lami have title deeds to their two-acre plots. In Tipis however, the situation is much more varied. While some Maasai families have managed to obtain title deeds to subdivided ranch lands, many others have not. These are the "landless Maasai" that motivate the group's defensive stance against the "invasion" of new groups. A Maasai respondent explains:

My land rights are not protected because I don't have the title deed. Also, we hear that the rich and powerful people are planning on how to acquire the disputed lands. This will definitely cause chaos because most of the youths are unemployed, have no land, and will not let the land go.[31]

The ability for Kikuyu to secure land and title in Mwisho wa Lami and the inability of the Maasai in Tipis to secure formal state recognition of their land claims contributes to a longer-standing set of contentious narratives between Maasai and Kikuyu. The salience and particularity of these claims change, especially as elections approach. Yet the enduring Maasai narrative emphasizes two main themes: 1) the alienation of Maasai land by the British and later, a Kikuyu-led government; and 2) fear that Kikuyus would come to dominate and control the "ancestral lands" of the Maasai. This narrative is summed up succinctly by one respondent: "the Maasai were the owners of the land before the colonialists came and the agreement was that after [the British] left, the land would be given back to the Maasai. But the government gave the lands to other people."[32] In interviews, Maasai respondents explain how the British colonialists dispossessed the Maasai of their land, breaking an agreement that would have restored their lands. For many group members, this colonial-era expropriation has fueled both a tremendous sense of injustice and has heightened fears of any large-scale land acquisition or development project led by the state or ethnic strangers. The ADC land and the Mbiyu Koinange estate are so contested because the Maasai

---

[30] Interview-Tipis-Nakuru County, October 16, 2012 (1).
[31] Interview-Tipis-Nakuru County, October 18, 2012 (8).
[32] Interview-Tipis-Nakuru County, October 18, 2012 (8).

believe that these lands should be returned to the Maasai community. Anything short of the return of these lands represents both the growing power of outsiders and the strategic dismantling of Maasai political and territorial land claims.

The narrative of the Maasai, as reinterpreted through their Kikuyu neighbors, is vehemently anti-outsider. A Kikuyu resident in Mwisho wa Lami explains that postelection violence in 1993 escalated between the Kikuyu and Maasai, "because [Maasai] were claiming that the lands we occupy are theirs." The respondent continues: "there are times that we feel unsafe with our rights of land ownership. [The Maasai] around here will often be heard saying that one day we shall have to leave because we are occupying their land."[33]

A second discrepancy is between Maasai who benefit from title or customary rights to the land and Kikuyu residents who lack title deeds and ethnic entitlements to group land rights. This discrepancy can embolden Maasai claims while also heightening fears among some Maasai that Kikuyu politicians may seek to resettle "landless" or land insecure Kikuyu in Maasai territory. Among Kikuyu who have weaker land tenure rights than their Maasai neighbors, this discrepancy shapes a narrative of insecurity and fear that Maasai will, in a matter of time, evict Kikuyus. For two Kikuyu respondents in Tipis, it was their lack of a title deed that made them feel most vulnerable:

What brings tension . . . is people lacking title deeds, a situation which makes [us] feel that if the [Maasai community] realize that [we] don't have this legal and vital document of proof, they might start disturbing [us] and even at times wanting to evict [us] . . . They believe that if they fight, they may win the land simply because they got a hint that around here people don't have title deeds.[34]

In sum, I suggest that the two cases of Mwisho wa Lami and Tipis provide evidence for my broader argument that contentious land narratives are more likely to form where two ethnically distinct communities live near one another but benefit from different levels of land tenure security. The case of Mwisho wa Lami and Tipis complicate the simplicity of this theory in that there are members of each group who have title, while others do not. These narratives provide insight into how and when local and regional elites are able to organize violence.

[33] Interview-Mwisho wa Lami-Nakuru County, October 15, 2012 (2).
[34] Interview-Tipis-Nakuru County, October 18, 2012 (6).

Specifically, the Maasai land narrative in Tipis and Mwisho wa Lami, which frames Kikuyus as invaders on Maasai ancestral land, has contributed to the use of political violence. However, while there were a few isolated incidents of violence in 2007–2008 (e.g. windows of businesses broken, cows stolen), violence did not escalate between the two communities.

Case 5: Oljorai Settlers vs. Nyakinyua Shareholders (Naivasha Constituency, Nakuru County)

Oljorai is a highly contentious settlement scheme carved from 24,000 acres of land that once belonged to the ADC: a parastatal designed to promote agricultural development for the county. The settlement scheme is situated in Naivasha constituency in the southern part of Nakuru County. Many of the lands surrounding the scheme have contentious histories of their own: tens of thousands of acres of agricultural and grazing lands are still owned by the Delemere family, one of the first and most powerful white settlers in Kenya. In the early 1970s, the ADC established a farm in Oljorai by purchasing land from departing white settlers.[35] From its inception, ADC land and the labor and housing it offered became a patronage tool for both local and high-ranking politicians.

Two main groups shape the dynamics of group claim-making in and around the settlement scheme. The first group consists of Kalenjin households, along with Turkana and Kikuyu households who were displaced in earlier waves of election violence in the 1990s or state violence in the 1970-1980s. Kalenjin respondents describe how the Moi government issued land in Oljorai to thousands of families who had been evicted from their homes in the mid-1970s by P.C. Isaiah Mathenge,[36] the Provincial Commission of the Rift Valley under Jomo Kenyatta. Respondents also recount the large in-migration of families in the 1980s from across the Rift Valley, Central, and Nyanza Province. While most families were Kalenjin, many were also Kikuyu or Kisii

[35] As a parastatal, the ADC had the power to acquire land and dispose of land as it needed.
[36] Specifically, the respondent explains that about 6,000 families were violently evicted under the order of P.C. Mathenge between the years 1973 and 1980. Interview-Oljorai-Nakuru County, September 8, 2012 (7).

farmers who had purchased their land through a Kalenjin or local Kikuyu politician.

The Moi regime resettled these households in Oljorai, but did so by allowing the ADC to become the *de facto* landlord of the Oljorai settlement scheme. By 1988, the Government of Kenya had dissolved the ADC. The dissolution coincided with a shift in supervisory authority over the ADC from the Ministry of Agriculture to the Office of the President.[37] These changes gave President Moi virtual free-range over how – and to whom – he could allocate former ADC lands.[38] Unlike many other ADC farms that were disbanded and sold for parts to private companies, organizations, and politically connected individuals, the government preserved most of the Oljorai ADC farm to serve as a settlement scheme. Importantly, at no point during this process and rebranding did the ADC have the legal authority to issue plot allotment letters. As residents would discover decades later, the allotment letters they received from the ADC were invalid.[39] Residents explain how this process has enabled land grabbing and the double allocation of land. Nearly every plot has been allocated to more than one person, and each person has received multiple letters from the ADC. Several younger members of the community describe their frustration: "The allotment letters are just like a cartel where each officer who gets to office allocates to his [ethnic] type and even reshuffles to the people around just to make money, which renders the letters futile."[40]

The second and more powerful group is the Nyakinyua Cooperative Society (Ltd), a Kikuyu LBC claiming to have purchased 8,000 acres of land in Oljorai in 1983. The LBC is part of the larger Nyakinyua Investments Company Limited, now one of the largest and most well-organized LBCs in Kenya. It has thousands of shareholders.[41] The LBC formed when Jomo Kenyatta rewarded groups of Kikuyu female

---

[37] See Report, "Unjust Enrichment" (KNCHR) and Republic of Kenya (2004).

[38] The Kenya National Human Rights Commission has created a list of ADC farm beneficiaries – all of whom were companies and elites rather than landless groups.

[39] In 2005–2006, the High Court cancelled the letters of allotment on the grounds that the ADC had no authority to issue them.

[40] Focus Group with youth-Oljorai-Nakuru County, September 11, 2012.

[41] Nyakinyua Chairman, Issak Nderitu said in 2013 that 5,470 company members were women (Njenga 2013).

singers with small parcels of land.[42] Women combined their land and investments to form the cooperative. Like many LBCs, Nyakinyua branches formed through the Rift Valley and Central Province. In 1982, a Nyakinyua branch purchased the 8,000-acre plot that overlaps with part of the Oljorai settlement scheme.[43] Yet rather than set aside the 8,000 acres that the Solai-Nyakinyua group had purchased, President Moi allocated the land to the Maasai and Kalenjin. So when members of the Nyakinyua group arrived in the mid-1980s to begin building homes and setting up their farms, they discovered that other families occupied their land. The Nyakinyua fought these occupations, yet with KANU's victory in the 1992 election, and the regime's stronghold over land offices, state security, and the courts, the Nyakinyua group were at a significant disadvantage.

This all changed when Moi's KANU party lost power in 2002, ending twenty-four years in power. As Mwai Kibaki's National Rainbow Coalition (NARC) stepped in, the patronage base shifted back to ethnic communities from Central and Eastern Province, notably the Kikuyu.[44] The Nyakinyua group in Oljorai, sidelined under Moi, could now begin reclaiming their 8,000 acres. In the final years leading up to the 2007 election, local administrative officials and land officers launched an even more aggressive effort to evict households settled during the Moi era in order to free up land for Nyakinyua claimants.

There are many ways to measure variation in rights between the two main groups – by the number of eviction notices that many Oljorai settlers have received, by the multiple plot allotment letters on a given parcel of land, or whether an individual's name has been erased from the list of land allottees in the local district office. Yet the clearest way to delineate and rank tenure rights between the mostly Kalenjin

---

[42] Nyakinyua were originally female traditional dancers who sang praise to President Jomo Kenyatta.

[43] The full name of this group is the Nyakinyua Solai-Ruiyobei Company, denoting the village (Ruiyobei) within Solai ward, where most of the members originate.

[44] Kenyans rallied around Mwai Kibaki in part because he promised to bring in a new era of multiethnic politics. It was soon clear that he was following the same path of his predecessors – where one set of ethnic groups dominated the Office of the President. The "GEMA" group or the "Mount Kenya mafia" refers to the close circle of Kikuyu, Embu, Meru and Kamba politicians who dominated the set of political institutions under Kibaki.

residents of Oljorai and the shareholders of the Nyakinyua LBC is that Nyakinyua members have title deeds and the support of the state. By contrast, Oljorai residents have allotment letters at best, most of which the state refuses to recognize. In the eyes of the state, they are squatters. Residents remark on how, especially as elections approach, political leaders make promises of title deeds. According to a Turkana resident of Oljorai: "With every politician who comes here they say that 'if you vote for me I will ensure that you will get land tenure.' But in a real sense those are empty promises. And we can't really trust any of that."[45]

As inequality in land rights between the two group increases, contentious land narratives have become stronger and more divisive in tone. Residents of Oljorai describe Kikuyu claims using a well-rehearsed insider–outsider narrative that tells the story of a wealthy outside group who benefits from state support, undermining the ancestral or first-comer rights of locals. While most residents of Oljorai are settlers themselves, they see themselves as having more legitimate claims to the Rift Valley, referencing their ancestral claims to the entire Rift Valley region. A respondent illustrates this anti-Kikuyu narrative, linking Kikuyu land claims with the escalation of violence. He remarks, "the clashes were a result of Kikuyu relocating to the Rift Valley from the Central Province to occupy the land of other communities. Yet [these other communities] didn't shift to the Kikuyu land. So people want [the Kikuyu] to move back to their ancestral land."[46]

Participants in a youth focus group provide similar views. One participant explains that land disputes in Oljorai are the result of government favoritism in the issuance of land: "Rather than giving land to the squatters who have lived in the land for ages, they opt to give it to others from other regions." Another participant explains how this favoritism leads to fear of eviction, emphasizing a narrative that is as much about land insecurity as it is about injustice.

The administration – from the Minister of Lands down to the area sub-chief – are the causes of the land insecurity that the residents feel. This is because they collude with those people who have money and give them land that

[45] Focus Group with Turkana residents-Oljorai-Nakuru County, September 6, 2012.
[46] Interview-Oljorai-Nakuru County, September 8, 2012 (2).

belongs to other people. For example, I was born in this area. The ADC had given my father a letter and later when the whites left he was issued with an allotment letter though he still doesn't have a title deed. So it angers me to see or hear people say that we are meant to leave this place or worse still, when we witness other people from elsewhere being given land and even being issued with title deeds. We feel that any time we may be evicted. And this will definitely result in clashes.[47]

As residents fear their impending eviction in the face of Nyakinyua land claims, the anti-outsider narrative has also allowed so-called "natives" to target "outsiders" living in Oljorai – many of whom are also poor and land insecure farmers who fled violence in earlier decades. This is largely because residents and local politicians have constructed a narrative whereby threats to land security come not only from Nyakinyua but also from a more ubiquitous "outsider."

In sum, inequality in land rights between Kikuyu shareholders and the mostly Kalenjin residents of Oljorai have shaped a set of highly contentious land narratives that emphasize themes of insecurity and threat posed by "the outsider" and a negligent government that colludes with land speculators.[48] As elections near, local and national politicians can exploit these narratives of injustice, resentment, and fear of losing land to organize political support and even violence. Parts of Oljorai experienced significant violence during the postelection violence in 2007–2008. Violence did not escalate in 2013, but there have been intermittent land clashes between newcomers and the original residents of the ADC farm. I explain the dynamics of election violence in Oljorai in Chapter 6.

Case 6: *Kikuyu and Luo Laborers in Naivasha's Flower Farms*

Hell's Gate is an administrative location and electoral ward located just a few miles outside Naivasha town – a bustling town at the southern end of Nakuru County. As its name indicates, it sits not far from the entrance to one of Kenya's more famous national parks.[49] The case of Hell's Gate is unique from the paired cases I've outlined above. Here, the lives of nearly every resident revolve around the many large

---

[47] Focus group with youths, Nakuru County, September 9, 2012.
[48] Interview-Oljorai-Nakuru County, September 11, 2012 (2).
[49] Hell's Gate National Park.

horticultural farms. Very few residents identify as "sons of the soil." Instead, people describe the area as defined and shaped by the people – from every region of Kenya – who come to work on the flower farms.

There are two ways that area residents think about the distribution of land rights. The first emphasizes the difference between the foreign-owned farms who have leaseholder rights to hundreds, and in some cases, thousands of acres (e.g. Delamere), and everyone else. Remarking on the landholdings of the Delamere family, one respondent captures this disparity: "People like Delamere have the biggest land. Even if it were divided among all the people of Naivasha, they would not exhaust it."[50] Yet the distinction that most residents emphasize is the line between renter and landowner. Most households here rent land, about 80 percent by one account. Yet among the few who have purchased plots of their own, most are Kikuyu. Tenants, meanwhile, tend to identify as Luhya, Luo, and Kisii from the western part of the country. According to one respondent, this distinction exists because "the other tribes do not see a need to buy here because they might have enough back home, while the Kikuyu don't have much land in Central region. Hence, they have decided to buy here."[51] According to several other respondents, people rent because they don't earn enough on the flower farms. As one respondent explains, you may have to save for ten years to buy a plot of land . . . so you many never buy."[52]

The local political economy of the region complicates a simple categorization of land rights inequality. Commercial farms – most foreign-owned – do indeed control a significant proportion of arable land. Yet in thinking about the tenure rights that shape people's daily access to land, I argue that the more meaningful form of inequality is between Kikuyu residents who own property (land, housing, and market space) and the broader cross-section of laborers who rent from these households. Nonetheless, the difference between the rights and landholding is not profound. Kikuyu who own land must in many cases work alongside renters. Hence, I suggest that "moderate land inequality" best characterizes the tenure discrepancy in the area. I apply this categorization with the caveat that other land dynamics apply as

---

[50] Interview-Hells Gate-Nakuru County, October 13, 2012 (5).
[51] Interview-Hells Gate-Nakuru County-Rift Valley, October 20, 2012 (12).
[52] Focus Group-Hells Gate-Nakuru County, October 20, 2012.

well. In many ways, the area might best be defined as having relative
land equality because the majority of area residents – Kikuyu included –
rent plots of land that are barley large enough to accommodate a house
and small garden. Yet the area could also be defined by the significant
land inequality that exists between the large-scale landowners and its
workers.

It is this ambiguity perhaps – the inability to define clear winners and
losers – that moderates land narratives. Hence, while the area has the
potential for contentious narratives – as was evident in the preelectoral
period of 2007 – the more common land is not contentious. Instead,
most respondents emphasize the area's openness – a space for anyone
to earn a living. Illustrating an ambivalence toward belonging,
a respondent remarks, "In Naivasha, there are no outsiders."[53]
Another respondent explains, "The presence of flower farms in
Naivasha has enabled many tribes to live together in peace because
you have workmates from different tribes and we have a good working
relationship. Also, we live well together unlike other areas like Eldoret
where it is mostly one tribe."[54]

Yet while residents describe a sense of shared solidarity through the
workplace, many other residents are quick to point out the persistence
of ethnic politics in daily life, particularly as it pertains to hiring
practices within the flower farms. For instance, several respondents
described how general managers tend only to hire their co-ethnics. As
the 2007 election approached, narratives on both sides shifted. Luo
residents taunted that they would seize Kikuyu properties if Raila
Odinga were elected. A Kikuyu resident recounts the rising tension
during the preelectoral period:

The Luo were saying that if Raila takes power they will take all our land and
property by force ... They used to throw insults at us, saying all the wealth
we have will belong to them ... If Raila had taken power then they would
have pounced on us. They even passed outside my house and said they will
burn this house down ... it is the Luo who started it all.[55]

Hence, by the time elections rolled around, Kikuyu and Luo communities each articulated contentious land narratives that were rooted in

---

[53] Interview-Hells Gate-Nakuru County, October 20, 2012 (13).
[54] Interview-Hells Gate-Nakuru County, October 20, 2012 (12).
[55] Interview-Hells Gate-Nakuru County, October 13, 2012 (10).

fears of losing land or hopes of claiming land and property from the opposing side.

In the end, electoral violence did escalate in Hell's Gate. Yet the dynamics of violence were distinct from many of the other cases I analyze. In Hell's Gate, the main perpetrators were not local residents, but Kikuyu communities fleeing violence in the western city of Kisumu and surrounding areas. Respondents are quick to point out how violence was different here: "These Kikuyu [from Kisumu] were angry because they had been evicted from other areas, so they were the people who continued with the violence. It was never people from this area."[56] Displaced Kikuyu did indeed instigate much of the violence that escalated in and around Hell's Gate. Yet the scale of the violence against Luo residents was possible in large part because some local Kikuyu residents decided to join the violence. Local participants likely empathized with the pain and horror witnessed by co-ethnics from Kisumu. Yet participation in violence was "thinkable" because local land narratives had framed Luo residents as an imminent threat to the land and property of Kikuyu residents. As I explain in subsequent chapters, the violence thus had multiple logics: driven by a desire to extract revenge, but for local residents, a desire to defend land and property.

Case 7: Kijipwa Squatters vs. "Landlords" (Kilifi South Constituency, Kilifi County)

Kijipwa is a government sponsored settlement scheme located approximately 20 miles north of Mombasa along the Indian Ocean.[57] The scheme covers approximately 1,600 acres, encompassing highly coveted beachfront. In 1974, the Provincial Commissioner of the Coast Province wrote a letter to a group of local residents promising that he would adjudicate and subdivide the area to local occupants. The government allocated the land in 1978 and officially registered the scheme five years later in 1983. Yet almost fifty years later the residents of Kijipwa settlement scheme reside as squatters on their own land.[58]

---

[56] Ibid.
[57] Kijipwa settlement scheme falls within Kikambala Division in Kilifi South constituency.
[58] During the data collection period (2012–2013) the government had not issued residents with title deeds. Title deeds were finally issued, however, in 2018/2019.

Most residents do not have title deeds or plot allotment letters. Many families have been forcibly evicted, often without any compensation. Residents tell stories and show documents of thirty-year court battles with no resolution, and the letters they have filed to nearly every level of the Ministry of Lands, most with no reply. They talk about their houses that have burned under the watchful eye of the police, and of the many arrests and detentions they have endured as "squatters."

Land inequality in Kijipwa is significant. And in contrast to the cases I've described in the Rift Valley, where moderate levels of inequality sharpen ethnic boundaries, the salient cleavage here is class. This is not to say that ethnic identities do not matter, but that ethnicity is not the most relevant category in delineating those who own and control land from those who do not. I focus my analysis on two groups of claimants. The first comprise the residents of Kijipwa settlement scheme, who define themselves as "locals" or "ordinary coastal people" but also as "squatters." As a Kijipwa respondents explains: "People at the Coast are squatters not out of choice but neglect by the government. People are evicted left right and center with nowhere to go."[59] Most residents further identify as Mijikenda, specifying their ethnic subgroup as Giriama or Chonyi.[60]

The second is an elite group of landowners that includes foreigners, investors, absentee landlords, and political elites from across the county. Importantly, and with some exceptions, these elites are largely absent in the everyday lives of locals. They live and conduct business in Mombasa, Nairobi, Nakuru, or cities abroad. Their presence is felt primarily in their attempts to keep local residents ("squatters") off their land – through eviction orders, the use of private and informal security, and the Kenyan Police. The lands that these landowners or "landlords" seek to protect include thousands of acres of sisal plantations,[61] golf and beach resorts, and luxury beachfront apartments.[62] For example,

[59] Interview-Kijipwa SS-Nakuru County, November 20, 2012 (11).
[60] Kijipwa, like much of Kilifi, is religiously mixed, with a small majority of people identifying as Christian and a large minority identifying as Muslim.
[61] Sisal is one of the main cash crops along the Kenyan coast. The two main sisal estates are Kilifi Planation Ltd (established in 1920), which has 3,000 acres in Kilfi and Rea Vipingo (established in 1995), which has 4,279 acres devoted to sisal in Kilifi (Rea Vipingo Annual Report 2013).
[62] Sultan Palace is a gated luxury beach resort owned by a Chinese real estate company. The development occupies forty-three acres of land that fell within the boundaries of Kijipwa. In addition to losing land, residents complain that Sultan

only seven miles up the road from Kijipwa sits the 2,500-acre Vipingo Ridge, one of the country's most exclusive luxury golf resorts and playground for national and international elite. Yet much of the land to which this second group holds title or claims ownership is left undeveloped, often for speculative purposes (Kanyinga 2000).

While the Coast region has a long history of land inequality, the history of land allocation within the Kijipwa settlement scheme has further exacerbated these inequalities. In theory, government settlement schemes facilitate the distribution of land to otherwise landless households while providing a path to tenure security. Yet as was the case with many mismanaged settlement schemes across Kenya, this did not happen in Kijipwa. Instead, district administrative officials took control of the plot allotment process in order to allocate to themselves and other "higher ups" in the KANU administrative large plots of land.[63]

Local administrators and political elites use several strategies to misappropriate settlement schemes lands. They can alter the lists of intended recipients, manipulate the settlement schemes maps (altering the boundaries of specific plots), or block access to title deeds for settlement scheme allottees. Notably, the allottee lists that district officers compiled for Kijipwa included friends and patrons of the district and provincial officers.[64] The belief that the government allocated an unfair percentage of plots to outsiders, including government appointees and the well-connected, has fueled a narrative that the government actively undermines the land rights of Coastal people.

I analyze the contentious narrative that has formed in Kilifi in greater detail in Chapter 7, much of which draws on specific evidence from Kijipwa. Key, however, is that narratives here are contentious. Residents have crafted a set of land narratives that emphasize *injustice* of past land allocations and expropriations as well as the *threat* of future evictions. Yet they are distinct from the narratives that many of the communities in the Rift Valley articulate. First, they do not make an explicit link between electoral outcomes and the possibilities of losing

---

Palace and other hotels have blocked their access to the beach, which is public land and a critical source of livelihood for the fisher-folk in the community.
[63] According to Kanyinga, some of the largest plots in Kijipwa were allocated to cabinet ministers and permanent secretaries, senior officers in the Ministry of Lands and Settlement, a judge, a member of the national choir group, and a District Officer, among others (2000: 76).
[64] Interviews (various)-Kijipwa SS, November–December 2012; Kanyinga (2000).

or gaining land rights (see Chapter 7 for details). Second, the dominant narrative does not frame perpetrators of land injustice as an ethnically distinct neighboring group. Rather, this competing group consists of varied members of an elite and landholding class. A Kilifi resident, telling his story of eviction, provides one version of this land narrative:

The rich people own more land in the coastal areas than anybody else. We have Arabs, Europeans, Indians and fellow Africans. When they buy the land they use company names, so when you go to court you don't know who you are fighting. These people can even kill you because of land. There is nobody who is safe here regarding land. I live by the grace of God.[65]

The emphasis here is not on a specific ethnic community, but on "the rich people." The respondent refers to their identities in terms of race or nationality: as "Arabs, Europeans, Indians, fellow Africans." Yet for the respondent, it is the ability of these elites to hide behind their "company names" that weakens his own sense of agency in the land dispute process.

As I argue in Chapter 7, understanding the structural and political origins of these land narratives in Kilifi (as well as Kwale) helps explain why they are contentious, yet remain relatively ineffective tools for mobilizing election violence. These narratives emerge in a context of significant land inequality between landless or land insecure "squatters," and "landlords" who leverage tremendous control over the allocation of land and provision of tenure. Without a clear or easily identifiable "ethnic other," and an ambiguous link between elections and land tenure, these narratives do not have the same potential for mobilizing election violence as I observe in part of the Rift Valley.

Ramisi Squatters vs. Ramisi Sugar (Msambweni Constituency, Kwale County)

The case studies that I examine in Kwale County are similar to Kijipwa settlement scheme. In both counties, there is significant inequality between a landless majority and class of "landlords." I focus on the land rights of two main groups. The first is the residents of the Ramisi settlement scheme – a sprawling and partly informal settlement on

---

[65] Interview-Kijipwa SS-Kilifi County, November 20, 2012 (7).

which an estimated 4,174 households reside over an area of 6,500 acres.[66] The scheme is located approximately 40 miles south of Mombasa near the border with Tanzania, its eastern plots nearly reaching the Indian Ocean. Like most communities in Kwale, residents of Ramisi identify as Mijikenda and practice Islam.[67] Further, nearly all residents lack title deeds to their plots of land.[68]

A second set of actors includes the business and political elites involved in large-scale commercial agriculture and mining in the area. These industries include sugar, sisal, cashew farms, as well as titanium mining. I focus my discussion on sugar plantations, as this industry has played the most prominent role in shaping the land security and everyday life of Ramisi residents over the last century.

The sugar industry has a double-edged history in Kwale: it has provided employment and land access through tenancy and share-cropping agreements. Yet the industry has also undermined the land tenure rights of residents over the decades. The history of sugar in Ramisi dates back to 1927, when a privately owned and managed Indian company established the first sugar mill (Wanyande 2001).[69] This sugar mill became Ramisi Sugar Factory, which at its height employed over 3,000 workers and cultivated 45,000 acres of cane sugar.[70] Despite opportunities to enter contract agreements with the company, residents talk about evictions and losing their ancestral land to the Ramisi Sugar Factory. One family explains:

> We went to court about Ramisi Sugar. The government had paid the owner of that land and then the Indian was still declared the valid owner. The local people are at the mercy of the courts. These people (Ramisi Sugar) are buying justice.[71]

The factory collapsed in 1988 due to alleged mismanagement.[72] For the next three decades, the land and its facilities sat empty. During this time, area residents began "re-claiming" sections of this land, moving

---

[66] Source: unpublished dataset on settlement schemes provided by the Ministry of Lands (2013).
[67] Most residents of Ramisi further identify as Digo, a subtribe of the Mijikenda.
[68] The figure of 22 percent is based on "Kwale County Annual Development Report FY 2017/2018." Kwale County Economic Planning Division (p. 43).
[69] The sugar mill was managed by the Madhvani Group International of India.
[70] Oyuke 2012.   [71] Interview-Kinondo-Kwale County, November 13, 2012 (3).
[72] At independence, the Kenyan state participated directly in the ownership and management of the sugar industry. However, all these state-owned enterprises were located in Nyanza Province in Western Kenya (Wanyande 2001).

onto the abandoned sugar plantations and starting small farms. In the months before Kenya's 2007 election however, President Mwai Kibaki signed a lease agreement with the Kwale International Sugar Company (KISCOL) to take over the assets of Ramisi Sugar Factory and reinvigorate the sugar industry in Kwale.[73] This agreement granted KISCOL 15,000 acres of land for sugar cultivation, specifying that the remaining 12,000 acres be converted into settlement scheme land for area residents. While KISCOL made some land available to residents, many more residents were evicted as part of the company's efforts to clear squatters from former Ramisi Sugar land and expand the company's acreage. An elderly man, whose land and coconut grove had been bulldozed by KISCOL only days before our 2012 interview, remarks on the 2007 lease agreement to the sugar company:

We don't understand why we were evicted ... We thought that [the government] was going to bring development. We were told it was the government that sold the land ... I told [local leaders] it was President Moi who gave us the land and we were not going to move even if Kibaki said so. I was given a few days' notice and was finally evicted, and my crops uprooted.[74]

The opening of KISCOL signaled employment and economic growth for some residents, but for many others, particularly older members of the community, it revived memories of coercive evictions, land loss, and exploitative labor arrangements – both with sugar and other plantations. As a respondent remarks: "People have been here since time immemorial. But the sisal people chased away locals from this land. And now we are going through the same thing with [KISCOL]."[75]

The inequality in land rights between residents of the Ramisi settlement scheme and agro-industry elites has shaped a highly contentious set of land narratives. As with the narratives in Kijipwa, the dominant themes of these narratives emphasize past injustices, ongoing land grabs, and coercive evictions. Yet as with Kijipwa, these contentious narratives are distinct from the contentious narratives that I observe in parts of the Rift Valley, where residents attribute their land insecurity to another nearby ethnic group. In Kwale, the culprit is not an ethnically distinct neighboring group, but a more formidable and less clearly defined entity. At times, residents frame this "other" as the national

[73] Government of Kenya 2007.
[74] Interview-Ramisi SS-Kwale County, November 12, 2012 (2).
[75] Interview-Ramisi SS-Kwale County, November 12, 2012 (3).

government. And very often, this "other" group is at once the foreign company, the national government, entrenched landlords, and Kenyans from "upcountry:" people who are not local, who take from the community rather than support. A respondent explains:

> It's the government that's not fair! How come somebody from upcountry comes with a title while I don't have any? How does this happen in [the government's] presence? ... The whole of the coastal strip, from Lunga Lunga to Lamu, has the same issues – evictions are all over. And the people who have title deeds are upcountry people.[76]

Here, the respondent frames his community's lack of land rights as the result of unjust decisions by the government to favor the tenure rights of upcountry people (e.g. Kikuyu and Kamba) over locals. Importantly, this type of narrative may help explain certain forms of political violence. But as I argue in this book, this version of the anti-outsider narrative that I describe in Kwale and Kilifi is rarely a sufficient rhetorical tool for organizing electoral violence. What's missing is a clear and visible target group (i.e. ethnically distinct neighboring group) that presents both a viable threat to land and political power, and a strong "land patron" who can use and reformulate existing land narrative to organize violence.

Conclusion

In this chapter, I've aimed to examine this first stage in the process of electoral violence: the formation of contentious land narratives. Specifically, I asked why and how contentious land narratives form between two groups. I answer this question by drawing on a large dataset consisting of hundreds of qualitative interviews across eight paired case studies (twelve case study sites). My main finding is that contentious land narratives are most likely to form between two ethnically distinct and proximate communities, where residents of one community have stronger tenure rights than the other.

In contexts of moderate and significant land inequality, collective land narratives tend to emphasize the injustice of past land allocations or evictions, in addition to the threat of future evictions. A key

---

[76] Interview-Ramisi SS-Kwale County, November 12, 2012 (3).

difference, however, is that in contexts where the main cleavage line is class-based and land inequality is significant, residents rarely connect beliefs about land injustice or fears of losing land to an impending election. In contrast, people living in spaces defined by moderate inequality in land rights are much more likely to associate opportunity or threat with elections. As I explain in greater detail in Chapter 7, this difference is partly because where there is both land inequality and a salient ethnic cleavage (i.e. two group of a similar size), political mobilizers are better able to frame elections as threats to land and opportunities to claim or reclaim land from ethnic rivals. Yet where class is the main cleavage, the landless (or land insecure) comprise the electoral majority. Hence, while they struggle to secure land rights, residents in such spaces are not likely to see election periods heightening their threat of eviction any more than nonelectoral periods.

In thinking about the link between inter- or between-group inequality and conflict, I suggest that future research would benefit from paying greater attention to inequalities between groups at the local level. This is not to say that national-level inequalities do not affect grievances and violent conflict. Rather, because local- or regional-level disparities are often the most visible in daily life – and often have more concrete implications in people's everyday lives – such inequalities are also more likely to generate contentious narratives or grievances. These narrative in turn, are more likely to help explain the dynamics and production of violent conflict.

5 | Narrative Formation in the Central Rift Valley

The problem here is that our neighbors have never accepted and recognized us as legal owners of the land ... The Kikuyu demand their forest back ... which we consider a great disregard to the Kalenjin community.

Mauche resident[1]

In Ogilgei we have never witnessed land clashes because the community has lived peacefully with our neighbors the Kikuyu, and the elders from the two communities are respected by both sides and their decisions are final.

Ogilgei resident[2]

Mauche and Ogilgei are farming communities only 20 km apart along a road that runs through Nakuru County. In both farming communities, most residents are Kalenjin. Both border Kikuyu farming communities. Yet as the contrasting comments above suggest, residents in Mauche view their rights to land through a much more contested lens than residents in Ogilgei, despite similar ethnic arrangements. In Mauche, residents view the strength of their tenure security relative to the strength of their Kikuyu neighbors. As the rights of their Kikuyu neighbors strengthen, many Kalenjin residents in Mauche see their own land security and political power diminish. Most residents of Ogilgei, by contrast, do not see their Kikuyu neighbors as a threat: either to their land security or livelihood.

In this chapter, I aim to analyze why contentious land narratives emerge between two neighboring and ethnically distinct communities in one context, but not another. In other words, why do local narratives that emphasize land injustice, insecurity, and fear become salient and resonate widely in one setting, yet in a seemingly similar and nearby set of communities, these same narratives do not?

---

[1] Focus group with elders-Mauche SS-Nakuru County, July 21, 2012.
[2] Interview-Ogilgei LBC-Nakuru County, September 3, 2012 (3).

Drawing on two paired case comparisons in Nakuru County, the chapter identifies a set of factors that works to restrain or enable what I term broadly, "contentious land narratives."[3] The main argument is that the degree of inequality in land rights strongly affects the type of narrative that emerges between two nearby (or neighboring) groups. As the case of Mauche and Likia demonstrates, where there is *moderate inequality* in land rights, contentious land narratives are likely to form. Yet as the case of Ogilgei and Kerma demonstrates, where there is relative *equality* between two neighboring groups, land narratives are far less likely to be contentious.

Land narratives are contentious where they emphasize themes of land injustice or insecurity. Both narrative themes heighten the delineation between in-group and out-group: between rightful claimants and invaders or aggressors. By contrast, I describe land narratives as "noncontentious" when the dominant narrative does not emphasize threats to tenure security or blame neighboring groups for land shortage or insecurity. Further, individuals who engage in noncontentious narrative seek order and stability rather than changes to *status quo* claims.

This chapter demonstrates that contentious land narratives between groups are not the inevitable outcomes of ethnic rivalry (Kaufmann 1998; Horowitz 1985). Building on constructivist insights of ethnic conflict (Chandra & Wilkinson 2008; Kalyvas 2008), I show that they are instead endogenous to local institutional contexts that have shaped – for better or worse – the way that residents acquire land and livelihood security.

Methodology and Case Selection

I compare two paired cases where the arrangement of ethnic groups does not vary. In both case studies, a Kalenjin farming community neighbors a Kikuyu farming community. This selection strategy enables me to control for ethnic composition. Yet the main outcome of interest, a salient and contentious set of land narratives, is only evident in the case of Mauche and Likia. A key distinction between

---

[3] As I define elsewhere, land narratives are the stories that groups use to talk about histories of land acquisition and loss, fears of losing land to the state or rival groups, and rights to claim or contest land and territory.

each pair of communities is the method through which each community acquired land and the relative equality in land rights that has emerged as a result. Table 5.1 summarizes the paired-case selection between Ogilgei and Kerma (Case 1) and Mauche and Likia (Case 2).[4] Importantly, while there are other modes of acquiring and securing land in Kenya, particularly within customary lands, this chapter focuses on LBCs and government settlement schemes: the two methods of land acquisition that are most common in the Central Rift Valley.

Ogilgei (Case 1) is an LBC whose residents are primarily Kalenjin. It borders Kerma, a settlement scheme where most residents are Kikuyu. Ogilgei and Kerma are located a few kilometers from the bustling commercial center of Njoro town, where farmers from throughout the Central Rift Valley come to trade and conduct business. Both communities are situated at the border of Rongai and Njoro Constituencies, the fault line between Kikuyu and Kalenjin centers of power. Yet when electoral violence rippled throughout the region during the 1992, 1997, and 2007 elections, violence never escalated between Kalenjins living in Ogilgei and Kikuyus living in the adjacent settlement scheme of Kerma.[5] The dominant land narrative between these two communities is not contentious. Residents do not feel threatened by their neighbors, nor do state authorities or surrounding neighbors challenge the property rights of Ogilgei residents. Residents of Kerma and Ogilgei have title deeds to their plots of land. One important implication, as I demonstrate in later chapters, is that divisive campaign appeals, particularly around land, do not resonate with most residents of either Kerma or Ogilgei.

The second paired case is a sharp contrast. Mauche is a Kalenjin settlement scheme created between 1994 and 1997 under the regime of Daniel arap Moi. The Moi government carved the scheme out of the edge of the Eastern Mau Forest as a way of resettling the landless Ogiek

---

[4] Counties were referred to as districts prior to the implementation of the new 2010 constitution. Nakuru County is composed of twelve electoral constituencies. In 2007, Mauche and Likia were located in Molo constituency, but currently fall within Njoro constituency. Ogilgei and Kerma are located at the border of the Njoro constituency (Kikuyu dominated) and the Rongai constituency (Kalenjin dominated). In general, Kikuyu politicians have exerted greater influence over Nakuru politics since independence.

[5] The Kerma settlement scheme shares a border with Ogilgei Farm (LBC). Njoro town, which is both ethnically diverse and a site of past violence, is less than a kilometer down the road from certain parts of the company farm.

Table 5.1 *Summary of paired-case design*

Community	Land tenure type	Method of land acquisition	Equality of land rights	Land narrative
Case 1 **Ogilgei** (Kalenjin)	Land-buying company	Purchased	Relative equality	Not contentious
Kerma (Kikuyu)	Settlement scheme	Purchased		
Case 2 **Mauche** (Kalenjin)	Settlement scheme	No purchase	Moderate inequality	Contentious
Likia (Kikuyu)	Land-buying company	Purchased		

people – a subtribe of the Kalenjin – living in the Western Mau Forest.[6] The previous Kenyatta administration had rendered many Ogiek landless when it forced them out of government forestlands in the Western Mau Forest.[7] As the KANU regime headed into its first multiparty election in 1991–1992, the scheme signaled the regime's commitment to settling the landless, particularly landless Kalenjin, helping to consolidate a Kalenjin voter base in an otherwise Kikuyu-dominated district.[8] The government allocated each household five acres of land within the scheme, accompanied by a plot allotment letter. Many residents claim that their plot allotment letters were replaced with title deeds sometime between 1997 and 2005.[9] Yet early in the Kibaki administration, the government issued a caveat on all Mauche

[6] The Ogiek now consider themselves a subtribe of the Kalenjin ethnic group. Until the last few decades, they lived as forest-dwellers and have been fighting for their rights as an indigenous people to live in the forests. The government has treated Ogiek as illegal squatters and have, since 1977, used coercive tactics to remove them from the lands they occupy in and around the Mau Forest (Barume 2005).

[7] The majority of the original residents in Mauche come from Tinet Forest, a government forest in Western Mau Forest. The government won a High Court battle to evict Ogieks from their ancestral home in the forests in the March 2000 Case, Tinet Ogiek (S/Western Mau) vs. the Republic of Kenya (HCCA 228/99). High Court of Kenya, Nairobi.

[8] Mauche was formerly part of Molo district. Due to border changes over the years, it is now located within Njoro district.

[9] Ndungu Report (Government of Kenya 2004: Vol. II, Annex 14, Nakuru/Likia Forest Excision); Interviews with Mauche residents.

title deeds, rendering all title deeds "null and void."[10] In the absence of formal state recognition of their land rights, Mauche residents lack a critical dimension of tenure security.

Mauche borders Likia, a Kikuyu LBC. Kikuyus in Likia are poor rural farmers. Nonetheless, most residents hold genuine title deeds to plots they acquired after independence. Beginning in the early 1960s, Kikuyu farmers began purchasing small 1.25-acre plots of land as shareholders in the Rare LBC or what is now called Likia Farm. The once powerful Kikuyu politician, Kihika Kimani purchased the 800-acre farm from outgoing white settlers and distributed the land among relatively poor but well-connected Kikuyu farmers.[11] Yet while Likia residents have formal land security, they face land threats from Kalenjins in Mauche who claim that Kikuyus in Likia are occupying Kalenjin "ancestral land."

Argument

This chapter draws on individual interviews and focus-groups with residents of each case study in order to examine one of the book's main questions: how and why do contentious land narratives form? As the previous chapter asserts, my main argument is that contentious land narratives are most likely to form where there is *moderate* inequality in the form or strength of land tenure rights between two neighboring ethnically distinct communities.

Yet in this assertion, a key question remains: Why does inequality in rights provoke contention? I suggest that what often matters is not inequality *per se*, but the source of such inequality, or how members from each group have acquired (or failed to acquire) land. Specifically, contentious land narratives are more likely where the process of land acquisition varies between two groups, enabling members from one group to acquire formal land tenure, while members of the other groups must depend on the patronage of political leaders.

---

[10] According to Mauche residents, the Kenyan government issued title deeds in 2005 and in the same year placed a caveat on these titles. The laws defining a caveat are outlined in the Land Titles Act, Cap 282, Article 72 (Revised ed. 2010).

[11] Kimani served as MP for Nakuru North (1974–1979), Laikipia West (1992–1997), and Molo (1997–2002).

These distinct processes of land acquisition become the main subject of contentious narratives. In general, the group with weaker tenure rights will challenge the legitimacy through which a neighboring group has acquired land rights. These narratives pose the question: "did rivals acquire land by stealing it, getting it for free, displacing others, settling on protected land, or benefiting from ethnic favoritism?" If one group believes another has acquired land illegitimately – through fraud, theft, or unfair advantage – this group is likely to contest the land rights of the other.[12] An interviewee from Tipis explains why the process of land acquisition is key in shaping intercommunity relations: "If one community has more land than the other and *yet both got the land in a fair way* then I think there can be no dispute, the two will be satisfied with the land they received."[13] Key here is that inequality in land size matters less than the process of land acquisition, and specifically, whether members from each group see these processes as "fair" or legitimate.

I specify two modes of land acquisition that can shape how each group views the legitimacy of the other. The first is a process of land acquisition whereby group members have *purchased* land on the private market, through LBCs, or through settlement schemes. Where group members purchase land, residents should have the opportunity to purchase their individual parcels (i.e. on the settlement scheme, LBC, or adjudication scheme) and acquire formal title to their land and property.

A second method of access is by acquiring land "for free" as part of a special resettlement program or mode of political patronage (i.e. land grant). This can happen when the government settles residents onto a section of land without requiring immediate payment. In Kenya, this method of settlement occurred most frequently under President Moi (1978–2002), who would use illegal or "irregular" means to allocate public land such as national parks, cemetery land, or parastatal land to settle co-ethnics or other political supporters (Government of Kenya 2004). This form of settlement can also occur when the state resettles communities displaced by violent conflict, evictions, or natural disaster.

This process becomes particularly problematic, however, when the government settles residents without creating the political or legal

---

[12] The term "group" can refer to the ethnic, religious, regional, and political categories of identification and belonging.

[13] Interview-Tipis-Nakuru County, October 18, 2012 (13).

| | **Group B** | |
	Purchased	Grant
Group A Purchased	No contentious narrative	Contentious narratives
Group A Grant	Contentious narratives	Both narratives possible

Figure 5.1 Land acquisition and narrative formation.

mechanisms for residents to acquire formal tenure rights (i.e. title deeds). The absence of such channels is often because land allocations are illegal or unsanctioned. Thus, residents cannot make formal claims to land because they remain officially, "illegal squatters." The absence of tenure rights can solidify patron–client relationships as residents depend on political or state elites to protect their informal or "illegal" land claims.

A key factor in tracing narrative formation, however, is how the land acquisition experience of one community compares to another nearby community. To illustrate how the land acquisition process shapes different outcomes, I delineate three scenarios. In these hypothetical scenarios, I assume there are two different ethnic groups (Group A and B) living in close proximity to one another (i.e. they share borders). Figure 5.1 illustrates each of these scenarios.

In the first scenario, members from Group A and Group B both purchase their land. When two groups have opportunities to purchase land on relatively equal terms, they are more likely to view the other's land acquisition process as fair and legitimate. The second scenario can occur when one group receives land through private purchase and the other receives land through a government settlement scheme or on land managed by the state.[14] Key here is that where two groups access land through two different methods (i.e. "purchased" and "granted"), one group is more likely to have stronger formal rights than the other. In addition, they are each likely to question the credibility of each other's claims.

---

[14] Many settlers on government land did pay, especially during the Kenyatta era. But in general it was easier for politicians (especially in the Moi era) to resettle people (i.e. political clients) on land "for free."

The third scenario can arise if both groups receive land as beneficiaries on government land. If both groups are equally land insecure, claim-making may be directed toward the state rather than a nearby group. Yet group members will also be quick to interpret any changes in the *status quo* with changes in the local power arrangement and, hence, as potential threats to the land security of their group.

In the analysis that follows, I aim to trace the process of narrative formation, beginning with the historical moment when each community acquires land. I also theorize the role of two intermediary factors that can shape narrative formation: 1) the type of land security that a group acquires and maintains and 2) the role of local leaders (e.g. village elders). I show that where group members receive land "for free" as part of a government grant, tenure rights are generally weak and local leaders have less autonomy from political and state officials. In these scenarios, local leaders are also more likely to promote narratives that challenge the status quo distribution of land rights.

By contrast, where group members from both communities are able to purchase their land, I expect residents to have stronger land tenure security. Further, I show that local leaders have greater autonomy from political elites who promise land security in exchange for political loyalty. Further, community leaders have stronger incentives to protect rather than disrupt the *status quo* distribution of rights. The dominant narrative that emerges is thus one that emphasizes stability and intergroup cooperation, while de-emphasizing threats from rivals.

Type of Tenure Security

I conceptualize land tenure security along two dimensions: 1) formal recognition by the state, and 2) informal or tacit recognition that members receive from a neighboring group. This is what I refer to as "relational land security." The Kenyan state does not enforce formal property rights evenly and consistently. Hence, even with a title deed, a household's tenure security depends partly on the informal recognition of its neighbors and surrounding groups.

Let us assume two hypothetical groups: Group A and Group B. The government guarantees the title deeds of Group A, but revokes the title deeds of Group B. Group B will have little incentive to recognize the title deeds of Group A because the state is seen as a biased allocator of land rights. As a result, Group B may seek to undermine the land rights

Table 5.2 *Relational land security*

Group	Formal land rights	Informal land rights	Actual land security
A	Title deed	Threat from Group B	Not secure
B	No title deed	Threat of eviction by state	Not secure

of Group A. In this scenario, the title deed is not a "matter of fact" but a political good that can be challenged. Table 5.2 illustrates this relational theory of property rights.

Group members are most likely to challenge the land rights of another group when they question the legitimacy of the land acquisition. Perceptions of legitimacy hinge on whether new residents have displaced old residents, occupy contested land against the will of other groups, or have worked and paid for the land.

Local Leadership

Several studies examine the role that local leaders play as "brokers," or intermediaries in influencing the vote choice of civilians (e.g. Thachil 2014; Koter 2013; Stokes et al. 2013; Posner 2005). In this chapter, I focus on the role that unelected local leaders play in influencing local narratives around land. I argue that the form of land allocation matters in part because it shapes the power and autonomy that community leaders maintain from political elites. When community leaders such as village elders and chiefs are able to play an active and beneficial role in the settlement of a community – by organizing groups to purchase land and obtain individual title – they acquire greater political and moral authority over group members. In addition, if group members are able to bargain for larger land plots and title deeds during the land acquisition or allocation process, the likelihood for stronger land security and economic well-being is greater for all members. This bolsters the social standing and authority of local leaders.

In many cases however, the process of land acquisition is more top-down, particularly within government allocated settlement schemes. In these cases, local leaders (i.e. chiefs, village elders) become enmeshed in the politics of the land allocation (Boone 2014; Shipton 2009; Berry

1993). They may have a role in creating the lists of land recipients; determining who acquires land rights and who is excluded. In many cases, however, local leaders (e.g. village elders) do not actively shape the politics of land settlement. In areas where the government allocates land, leaders and ordinary residents alike depend on higher-up political leaders to act as land patrons. These "land patrons" can offer promises of land security or title deeds in exchange for political loyalty or support. Community leaders can act as brokers for higher-level elites, but there are few sources of status and authority that are independent of these patron–client relationships.

In much of Kenya as well as other parts Africa, elders derive their authority from their ability to manage or distribute land or property to members of the community. Leaders are also expected to have enough land to provide for future generations. The elder generation loses influence and authority over younger generations when they are neither able to secure land rights nor pass on land to the next generation. In the case of Ogilgei, elders are land secure and hence derive political authority independent from politicians. In Mauche, elders lack land security and hence are beholden to politicians to ensure the security of their land.

These distinctions have important implications for the ways that local leaders construct, restrain, or foment contentious land narratives. Where leaders have benefited from an environment where most members have formal property rights, they are more likely to promote narratives that advocate law and order and emphasize the sanctity of the title deeds. Importantly, they will also have the moral authority to shape a narrative that promotes stability and interethnic cooperation. Yet where local leaders or elders have had little control over the tenure security of group members, or where group members remain land insecure, these leaders are more likely to promote narratives that challenge the status quo distribution of rights.

Ogilgei and Kerma: Land Equality and Noncontentious Narratives

Noncontentious Narrative in Ogilgei

Land narratives in Ogilgei are explanations of land security rather than insecurity. They are stories of pride and success: "this is why our land rights are secure" rather than strategies of reclaiming the land they have lost to another group. Narratives focus on the centrality of the title deed, hard work, and peaceful coexistence.

Most residents of Ogilgei do not view their neighbors as a threat to their land security. Instead, they assume their land rights are secure due to their title deeds and the amicable relationships with their Kikuyu neighbors. Residents highlight the positive interactions with their Kikuyu neighbors. A respondent describes how residents of Ogilgei have fostered this relationship through trade, business, marriage, and socializing. He explains:

Because of the time we came here we have built strong bonds with the Kikuyus; bonds that go way back to the 1960s. As a result, intermarriages have sprung up. We can say we know each other. We know each other's weaknesses, aggressiveness and everything about them. We don't fear them even during clashes. We have beer together. And a good thing about the Kikuyu is that they don't hold grudges.[15]

Key here is that residents feel like they know and trust their neighbors – *"we do not fear them."* In the excerpt below, the respondent talks about the in-migration of Kikuyus into the region. In contrast to many Mauche residents who feel overwhelmed by the proportion of Kikuyu entering the Rift Valley, the respondent here provides a very different view of Rift Valley demographics. He explains:

I would say that the percentage of outsiders in Rift Valley is not that high. Kikuyus dominate Nakuru but that is not because of the first president [Kenyatta]. The second president [Moi] opened the doors for Kikuyus to come to Rift Valley. The Kikuyus are very entrepreneurial but they don't take up big land. [Rather] they retain their one-acre humbly unlike the Kalenjin who have their ten acres and above. [The Kikuyu] are many but they don't have that much land in acreage.[16]

In contrast to many Kalenjin views of Kikuyu in-migration, the respondent does not see Kikuyu settlement as a numeric threat. Further, he does not view the dominance of Kikuyu as a result of political bias under President Kenyatta. Rather, he attributes it to the "entrepreneurial spirit" of Kikuyu along with the opportunities that President Moi afforded them. Countering the common narrative that Kikuyus are land greedy, he compares the humble one-acre plots of the Kikuyu to the larger ten-acre plots of his Kalenjin community. The narrative is far

---

[15] Interview-Ogilgei LBC-Nakuru County, September 4, 2012 (3).   [16] Ibid.

more nuanced than the one that has formed in Mauche. It reflects a more class- rather than ethnic-based view of the world. Another respondent illustrates this more open worldview, emphasizing the impracticality of ancestral claims to land:

We, as the people of the Rift Valley, allow outsiders to come in. We voluntarily sell the land to them. We should not base [our] claim along the ancestral line because [we] are the same people who sold the land in the first place. And in the later years [we] come to say that we have no land because of the invaders.[17]

Because they have title deeds, relatively large plots of land, and good relations with their Kikuyu neighbors that go back to the first decade under Kenyatta, residents do not frame their everyday land security in relation to neighboring groups.

The primary mode through which residents make claims to land is through the title deed, not ancestral belonging. The government has not challenged the titles, nor have their neighbors questioned their legitimacy. The title deed provides residents with a feeling of belonging to a nation-state rather than an ethnic community. As respondents explain, the title deed is the prize that residents have earned after years of hard work: proof that Kenyans must earn their way into the club of national citizenship. As one respondent explains, "The title deed is of [so] much importance to the people who own the land. As for my father's case, he truly treasures his. In fact, I can term it as his heartbeat."[18] In describing the superiority of the title deed over ancestral claims to land, another respondent explains:

The title deed owner knows that s/he is following the law and the constitution ... I don't acknowledge ancestral land rights because my Kikuyu friends have no idea where their ancestral land is and they can never go back to where they lived in Central Province. The fact remains that the land is theirs but they have nothing to show for it.[19]

The respondent's comments reflect a wider narrative in Ogilgei whereby ancestral land claims lack legitimacy because they are exclusive; not all Kenyans can make such claims. Yet the purchase of land – symbolized by the title deed – enables any Kenyan to access land in any part of the country. From this perspective, it is one's level of wealth

---

[17] Ibid.   [18] Interview-Ogilgei LBC-Nakuru County, September 3, 2012 (4).
[19] Interview-Ogilgei LBC-Nakuru County, September 4, 2012 (1).

rather than one's ethnic identification that limits or enables mobility and land acquisition. For the respondent above, the title deed also provides the foundation for a more open and democratic society. He emphasizes that for the many Kikuyu who no longer have land access in their ancestral home, they deserve a way of claiming land in another part of the country. In the sections below, I outline three factors that help explain the formation of this "noncontentious" or outward-oriented land narrative.

The Process of Land Acquisition in Ogilgei

In the first decade after Kenya's independence, the state redistributed a majority of land previously owned by white Europeans to landless and wealthy Kikuyus in the central part of the Rift Valley. Kikuyu elites dominated the land markets and organized ethnically exclusive land-buying schemes.[20] In this context, the case of Ogilgei is unique because it was a group of Kalenjin farmers, rather than Kikuyu, who succeeded in purchasing the farm from a departing white farmer.[21] The farm would become the Ogilgei Society, one of the few successful Kalenjin LBCs in the Central Rift. Members succeeded in acquiring the farm in part because they had the assistance of an ambitious and competitive local elite, a man named Kibowen Komen. Komen had been a manager on the Egerton estate and was a local councilor from Baringo North constituency. In addition, the land purchase, which was part of Komen's "Kalenjin Enterprise," received the support of President Kenyatta and Vice President Moi.[22]

The enterprise played a critical role in opening up parts of the Rift Valley to Kalenjin land ownership. In forming Ogilegi, Komen informed people of the land sale, led negotiations between the land-owners and society members, and facilitated financing.[23] A respondent describes the Komen's Kalenjin Enterprise as a company that could rival the Kikuyu-dominated LBCs:

---

[20] I explain this history in detail in Chapter 2.
[21] The group purchased the land from Lord Egerton, who was among the first white settlers to purchase and develop land in the Rift Valley.
[22] Gabrielle Lynch (2011); Interviews (various)-Ogilgei LBC, August–September 2012.
[23] Interviews (various)-Ogilgei LBC, August–September 2012.

[Komen] formed an even larger society to buy land in Rift Valley through a society called the Kalenjin Enterprise with the help of the first president Mr. Kenyatta. His job was to approach the whites and ask them to sell their land. Back then it was competitive because the Kikuyu had their own land-buying company called Nakuru-Guatanero Company (part of GEMA) so the two [land-buying companies] were competing for land acquisition in the Rift. The Kalenjin Enterprise won this battle and that was because the first president wanted to settle everybody without discrimination because he was a nationalist in ideology. So he gave Kikuyus one side – Ngecha and Ndeffo – and the Kalenjin were set aside to live in Ogilgei.[24]

The way the respondent interprets this process is important. Despite growing land competition from Kikuyus, he credits the success of the Kalenjin Enterprise to Kenyatta's nationalist ideology and his desire to settle Kenyans "without discrimination." This contrasts with a more common narrative among many Kalenjin, which depicts Kenyatta as favoring his co-ethnics at the expense of Kalenjins and other minority tribes. This interpretation also provides insight into why anti-outsider narratives develop or, in this case, do not develop. Ogilgei residents received land and title and saw the process as an outcome of multi-ethnic cooperation between the president (a Kikuyu) and their Kalenjin representatives.

The respondent's comments above also point to the key organizational role that Komen played in Kalenjin land acquisition. At a time when the Kikuyu elite dominated the land market, middlemen such as Komen enabled Kalenjins to become key stakeholders in the land acquisition process. Local leaders such as chiefs, village elders, and local brokers played an important role in organizing members and managing the company. This organizational structure was more inclusive than other settlement schemes and land-buying companies. It enabled members to feel like they had a common interest in the success of the company. The structure was unique from many other settlement schemes and LBCs where powerful politicians led the farms but had few incentives in ensuring that poorer members received land or title. One elder in Ogilgei attributes higher levels of corruption on other farms to the fact that most settlement schemes were allocated to individuals holding political power. Another respondent adds:

[24] Interview-Ogilgei LBC-Nakuru County, September 4, 2012 (3).

The success of the settlement schemes was dependent on the management of the office holders. Some schemes like Kihingo, managed under Kihika Kimani[25] experienced chaos because other people who were not supposed to benefit received the land instead of the intended beneficiaries.[26]

In Ogilgei, politicians did not take over the land acquisition process for purely political gain. Komen did not have any known political ambitions (Lynch 2011), nor was he able to leverage the Kalenjin Enterprise to gain a foothold into KANU party politics.[27]

Kalenjin members of Ogilgei succeeded in maintaining their plot of land in large part because they had access to loans that were usually not available to smaller ethnic groups or the very poor. Ogilgei farmers jointly purchased the Egerton farm through individual contributions and group loans. "People from different communities joined hands and contributed 1,200 shilling each to enable us buy the land because it was quite hard for an individual to raise the required amount alone."[28] Members also took out Guarantee Minimum Return (GMR) loans to finance the initial costs of settlement and cultivations. After receiving the loans, "we would settle in the farm, cultivate the land, sell the produce, and pay back the loans."[29]

Individual contributions were not sufficient to meet the total costs of the land, so members took out a loan from the ADC.[30] People "grouped themselves in partitions of fifty to acquire the loan and after loan repayment was over, the groups were issued with a common certificate."[31] In 1983, fifteen years after the company's

---

[25] MP and one of the most powerful politicians in Nakuru, he was also the national organizing secretary of the Gikuyu, Embu, and Meru Association (GEMA) and chairman of Ngwataniro group, a land-buying company whose membership reached over 30,000.

[26] Focus group with elders-Ogilgei LBC-Nakuru County, August 15, 2012.

[27] Gabrielle Lynch suggests that President Moi undermined the land acquisition efforts of Komen and his Kalenjin enterprise because it threatened or interfered with Moi's personal land enterprise. Moi wanted to reap any benefits for development initiatives and did not want credit to go to someone else (Lynch 2011: 100).

[28] Interview-Ogilgei LBC-Nakuru County, September 3, 2012 (2).

[29] Interview-Ogilgei LBC-Nakuru County, September 4, 2012 (3).

[30] The Kenyan parliament designated the ADC in 1965 as a parastatal (state corporation) to support and develop Kenya's agricultural production and enterprise. It was among primary institutions that provided loans to wealthy and middle-class farmers to purchase land.

[31] Interview-Ogilgei LBC-Nakuru County, August 15, 2012 (3).

formation, members finally received individual title deeds to their ten-acre plots of land.

Ogilgei's acquisition and management model succeeded in part because they were able to cultivate collectively in the early stages before they acquired individual titles. This enabled them to pay off loans, save money, and purchase more lands elsewhere to relieve the growing land pressure.[32]

In sum then, the land acquisition process in Ogilgei succeeded for a few important reasons. First, the company purchased the farm in 1969 when Jomo Kenyatta – a Kikuyu – was still in power. Kenyatta's indirect support of the purchase was an important signal to neighboring Kikuyus that Kalenjin land ownership in the area was legitimate. The purchase of land by a Kalenjin land-buying society during a Kikuyu presidency provided the company greater legitimacy in the eyes of surrounding groups. In contrast to Kikuyu LBCs or the settlement schemes the Moi sponsored in the 1980s and 1990s, few could argue that the purchase of the farm was the result of ethnic patronage alone. Second, Kalenjin farmers were able to access the critical land financing that remained out of reach for many other smaller ethnic groups. This financing included GMR loans and financing from the ADC. With access to finance, members were able to make the investments in their farms that enabled them to reap crop yields that they could use to pay off loans. Third, the process of acquisition encouraged an organizational structure whereby each member played an active role in the company. Ogilgei was able to access the ADC loan in large part because they applied for the loan as a collective. Members drew on this organizational power and sense of community to advocate for the provision of title deeds for each stakeholder. While the process would take about fifteen years, the end result provided them with much higher levels of land security than many Kalenjins and even Kikuyus would acquire – most of whom could not overcome the financial and institutional barriers to transform their plot allotment letters into title deeds. As I will explain, this process helped endow the community with higher levels of social capital and trust than many other communities in the Rift Valley.

---

[32] According to the focus group with community leaders (August 15, 2012), the Subukia Farm was 1,500 acres.

Land Security in Ogilgei

Ogilgei's land acquisition process was key in enabling members to organize and demand title deeds for all shareholders. Pioneering members of Ogilgei emphasize that "the allocation of land [which] was accompanied by the title deed has enabled us to live peacefully without any conflicts."[33] Every original shareholder received a ten-acre plot of land and after a period of waiting – a title deed.[34] This process contrasts with many settlement schemes and LBCs where people never received their title deeds, or hold fraudulent titles acquired through "illegal or irregular" means.[35] Yet most Ogilgei residents express complete confidence in the title deeds. In talking about the strength of their land security, many acknowledge how important it is that each household received the same ten acres of land: "everybody received land that was equal to the number of shares."[36] According to respondents, this equal distribution matters, because it prevents jealousy and resentment. As one interviewee explains, "when a person doesn't have any [land], chances are high that he is likely to start eyeing his neighbor's property."[37] Yet because each resident has received a plot of land and title deed, "issues of land conflict are not common between people or between the people and the government."[38]

In addition, because there is a relatively equal distribution of rights within the community (and between surrounding communities) Ogilgei residents benefit from informal tenure rights. Residents are secure because other residents and surrounding groups recognize the legitimacy of each household's land rights. A Luhya resident emphasizes the security he feels living in Ogilgei, despite coming from Western Province.

I am Luhya by tribe and I was born in Western Province, but I live here with the Kalenjins and Kikuyus. This land belonged to the Kalenjins but we bought it from them. I bought my piece in 1990 and I have been living here for more than twenty years ... My land rights are secure here. My security

---

[33] Focus group with elders-Ogilgei LBC-Nakuru County, August 15, 2012.
[34] Residents explain that they were first issued with certificates to indicate their membership, but title deeds were issued in 1983. This period of waiting was about fourteen to fifteen years (1968/1969 to 1983).
[35] See the Ndung'u Report (Government of Kenya 2004).
[36] Interview-Ogilgei LBC-Nakuru County, September 4, 2012 (2).
[37] Interview-Ogilgei LBC-Nakuru County, September 3, 2012 (2).
[38] Focus group with elders-Ogilgei LBC-Nakuru County, August 15, 2012.

has never been threatened here. No one has ever pointed a finger at me telling me I took their ancestral home. I feel very safe when I live here with my neighbors.[39]

The mutual recognition of rights emerges in part from the fact that residents in and around Ogilgei view the original land acquisition process as legitimate. Residents did not displace other groups (it was purchased from outgoing white settlers). Further, they did not receive land "for free" as a form of political patronage. Instead, they see themselves as hardworking purchasers of the land. This history of ownership and hard work provides a source of pride and power. The chief of Ogilgei speaks to this history, suggesting that the "legal way" in which Kalenjin and Kikuyu groups have purchased the land has, among other factors, reduced the potential for land conflict:

I don't think land is the cause of conflict because we were born near the Kikuyus and we went to school with them, with Kikuyus from both Ngecha and Kerma. They bought the land in a legal way and therefore there has never been any conflict between us.[40]

Kenyans in the wider Njoro region draw similar conclusions when reflecting on Ogilgei's peaceful relations with Kikuyu neighbors. Respondents emphasize the fact that both Kalenjin and Kikuyu have purchased the land. A respondent living in the far more contentious region of Likia (opposite Mauche) explains:

Even though the inhabitants are Kikuyu and the Kalenjins, there have never been clashes in places like Kerma and Ogilgei because the two tribes both acquired land through buying at the same time. And they understand the history of this region very well. A politician cannot incite [the Kalenjin] about the land occupied by the Kikuyu by saying it is their ancestor's land. This has sustained the harmonious living between them.[41]

This mutual recognition of land ownership emerges in part because Kikuyus living in Kerma settlement scheme also have title deeds to their 2.5-acre plots of land. Each community has an incentive to recognize and respect the rights of the other group. As I have argued throughout this study, when two neighboring groups have relatively equal levels of land security, they are far less likely to see the other as a potential threat

---

[39] Interview-Ogilgei LBC-Nakuru County, September 4, 2012 (5).
[40] Interview-Ogilgei LBC-Nakuru County, September 5, 2012 (Chief, 1).
[41] Interview-Likia LBC-Nakuru County, September 13, 2012 (4).

to their land security. It is this relatively equal degree of land tenure security between Ogilgei and Kerma that helps moderate contentious land narratives.

Leadership in Ogilgei: the Power of the Elders

Scholars have observed the role that local leaders – formal and informal – can play in restraining or mobilizing appeals or narratives that may lead to violence (Straus 2006; Weinstein 2006; Varshney 2002). In Ogilgei, chiefs and village elders play an important role in shaping local land narratives, restraining violence, promoting peace, and organizing community members.[42] Many members link the respect and authority of local leaders to the level of education that they have obtained, their organizing skills, and their moral authority. I suggest that residents' deference to the authority of their local elders rather than politicians emerges partly from the strong property rights environment of Ogilgei. Specifically, because residents are relatively land secure, they are less dependent on the willingness of politicians to distribute or protect land rights. An interviewee explains:

My rights to own land rights are protected by the government through the law and with the evidence provided to me as the legal owner of the land. This means that the politician has no bargaining power to defend my rights to own land. So there is no particular politician who can get my vote by promising that they will guard my land – unless I am not of sound mind.[43]

While residents still seek other goods from politicians, such as schools, roads, and cattle dips, none of these social goods has the same political implications as land. Hence, narratives around land do not become politicized at the local level during electoral periods.

Instead, residents look deferentially to leaders in Ogilgei, whom they credit with local unity and land tenure security. In particular, residents emphasize the ability of their leaders to impose their vision of peace. Residents speak of themselves as prone to jealously and suspicion, but

---

[42] Strong local leaders do not always have a peace-enhancing effect. Human rights reports in Kenya describe the role that Kalenjin elders played in encouraging Kalenjin youth to fight during electoral violence. See for example KNCHR 2008, "On the Brink of the Precipice: A Human Rights Account of Kenya's Post-2007 Election Violence."

[43] Interview-Ogilgei LBC-Nakuru County, September 3, 2012 (2).

with the guidance of their elders – much like the moral voice of religious authority – they live peacefully with their Kikuyu neighbors. A resident explains, "we live in peace with our neighbors and we don't have jealousy. I would also like to congratulate our leaders because their advice has been visionary. I don't want to say that everyone is learned in Ogilgei but the elders have a done a good job."[44]

Leaders promote peace by encouraging youth to avoid fighting and by engaging in peace meetings with Kikuyu elders. Residents attribute the absence of violence during the 2007–2008 electoral crisis to their local leaders. As one respondent explains: "The elders from both communities convened a meeting and agreed to urge the youths from their respective tribes not to engage in the fights." Another respondent claims, "The power of the Holy Spirit was upon the elders who requested the youths not to attack their neighbors."[45] In nearly every interview, respondents remarked on the power of local elders to prevent the escalation of violence between Kalenjins and neighboring Kikuyus – even as tension mounted and fighting escalated in surrounding areas.[46]

The ability of Ogilgei leaders to restrain violence is partly a function of their ability to control the local-level narrative. This power is most apparent during electoral periods, when land narratives are most contentious. Political candidates tap into local narratives to gain support, exploiting fears of land dispossession and hopes of gaining land to mobilize violence. In Ogilgei however, elders have been able to counter the mobilizing efforts of politicians by mitigating perceptions of threat and, equally, influencing how community members act on threats and fears in moments of violence. Many respondents referred to the impermeability of Ogilegi from the incendiary political messages that circulate during campaigns. A resident explains:

We have never had a politician come here and spread messages of hate against the other community but we know of other places where this happens. This is because people are well organized right from our elders' time.[47]

These divisive "hate" messages do not resonate with Ogilgei residents in part because village elders are in a position to offer an alternative

44 Interview-Ogilgei LBC-Nakuru County, September 4, 2012 (1).
45 Focus group with elders-Ogilgei-Nakuru County, August 15, 2012.
46 Interview-Ogilgei LBC-Nakuru County, August 15, 2012 (2).
47 Interview-Ogilgei LBC-Nakuru County, September 3, 2012 (3).

narrative: one that emphasizes the benefits of interethnic cooperation and the risks of potential violence. Because residents have much to lose on both sides – large plots of land with titles – this pro-stability message resonates across the group.

Mauche and Likia: Land Inequality and Contentious Narratives

Contentious Land Narratives in Mauche

Land narratives in Mauche emphasize injustice. These injustice narratives are about migrants who have invaded the ancestral lands of the Kalenjin, evicting them and undermining their land rights. A respondent from Mauche remarks: "Those who benefited more are the ones who have come [from outside the Rift Valley] because they have denied the real inhabitants their rights to own the land."[48] The comments reflect a widely held belief that migrants into the Rift Valley have displaced and taken land away from original occupants. Participants in a youth focus group in Mauche interrogate the process of land acquisition.

The people who say that they bought land from the whites are just telling a cover up story. When the whites came they did not buy this land from anybody. They chased away the natives. What was being sold when they left was barbed wire fence, the cows, and one farming tractor. So in essence, the whites did not buy any land in Kenya. The catch is that they invented the land-buying phenomenon just as a cover up.[49]

The excerpt is revealing in two ways. First, it demonstrates a belief about a more powerful group that has dispossessed rightful. More revealing perhaps, is a narrative about how the land market itself is the creation of Europeans – with the complicity of Kikuyus – designed to dispossess less powerful groups such as the Kalenjin. Such views may also help explain why Kalenjin and other smaller ethnic communities have historically been wary of participating in formal land markets.

Another respondent provides a similar narrative of land injustice. For him, *genuine owners* of the Rift Valley should have been

---

[48] Interview-Mauche SS-Nakuru County, July 18, 2012 (3).
[49] Interview-Mauche SS-Nakuru County, July 21, 2012 (Youth Focus Group).

empowered to purchase land from outgoing white farmers. His comments are part of a larger narrative whereby the outside group (i.e. the Kikuyu) has undermined the land rights of "natives" when they first migrated from the Central Province to the Rift Valley. The respondent adds the exception that "[o]ne could however be a genuine owner if he is a good person, if he is one who wouldn't think of evicting the Kalenjin community."[50] In other words, migrants can become legitimate landowners and residents in the Rift if they have purchased land without evicting or displacing natives of the Rift.

A second narrative theme is *land insecurity*, based on the threat of losing land to another group. Most Mauche residents see their land insecurity resulting from two specific sources: 1) the caveat on their title deeds and 2) the selective curtailment of land rights by the Kikuyu-led government. Referencing the caveat on his title deed, a Mauche resident talks about the threat he feels from his Kikuyus neighbors: "With a caveat on my title deed, I don't feel safe because anytime I may be chased out. And I think this is why the Kikuyu will want us to be moved from here."[51] The respondent views his own rights in relation to the formal rights of his Kikuyu neighbors: as his own land security weakens, his Kikuyu neighbors present an increasingly greater threat. Another respondent emphasizes the importance of having a genuine title deed. For him, the caveat on Mauche title deeds has weakened the competitive power of Kalenjin in the region, giving the Kikuyus an advantage in trade and development. This economic edge makes Mauche residents feel even more vulnerable:

The title deed is a very vital document in Kenya but the people from the Kalenjin community have no title deeds though the Kikuyu have [the title] and they are able to use it in the bank and secure a loan. But in our case, our titles have a caveat hanging on them. This allows the Kikuyu to develop very fast compared to us.[52]

Narratives in Mauche also emphasize the selective or arbitrary allocation of rights toward Kikuyu members at the expense of Kalenjin members. Residents interpret Kikuyus as a threat because they see

---

[50] Interview-Mauche SS-Nakuru County, July 21, 2012 (15).
[51] Interview-Mauche SS-Nakuru County, October 4, 2012 (3).
[52] Focus group with elders-Mauche SS-Nakuru, October 2, 2012.

them benefiting from government policies and patronage (Horowitz 1985).[53] Mauche elders point out the disparities:

The Kalenjin have land here, the same as the Kikuyu. But only the Kalenjin land is being termed a water catchment area. So they [Kikuyu] are planting wheat and barley with tractors and our people are being kicked out from the forest.[54]

Land narratives also contain strategies of claiming or asserting rights to land. Claim-making narratives in Mauche have developed out of an institutional environment framed by weak and uneven access to land. I highlight three salient themes of this claiming-making narrative. The first is a claim based on taking back "what belongs to us." In a focus group with Mauche elders, respondents reveal a narrative rooted in the idea of reclaiming ancestral land. Through this narrative, the Rift Valley provides an imagined territorial boundary through which identification is forged.

All the other tribes from outside have come to take away our land and that is why we have clashes. It's all because of land. Now we want our land back. Even with the counties, we still want *what belongs to us*.[55] These people have taken our land and it belonged to our forefathers, I can say this because I know the history of Rift Valley.[56]

The second feature is a desire to assert land claims using the title deed. The narrative emphasizes constraint due to the caveat on the title deed. It emphasizes potential power rather than actual power. Residents acknowledge the potential power of the title deed, seeing it as "a weapon" to defend their land against theft or land grabbing from others, particularly from people in more powerful positions. Yet because Mauche residents have a caveat on their title deed, the narrative highlights the injustice that the caveat creates for Mauche residents

---

[53] Interviews were conducted in 2012 at the end of the term of President Mwai Kibaki, a Kikuyu and leader of the PNU, who vis iewed by many non-Kikuyu as representing the narrow interests of Kikuyus and members of the GEMA alliance. The current president is also a Kikuyu (Uhuru Kenyatta) but has allied with William Ruto, a Kalenjin, forming a powerful Kikuyu–Kalenjin alliance.

[54] Focus group with elders-Mauche SS-Nakuru County, October 2, 2012.

[55] The participant is referring to the creation of counties, as part of the new devolved system of government, created by the new 2010 constitution. As of December 2019, there are forty-seven counties.

[56] Focus group with elders, Mauche SS-Nakuru County, July 21, 2012.

compared to Likia residents who enjoy the benefits of genuine title deeds. One resident explains:

The individual title deed ... is more powerful than the ancestral land, although now our titles are not powerful because of the caveat. I feel that if these titles were to have equal powers like those of our neighbors in Likia Farm, which is also part of Mau [Forest] then it would be better.[57]

The comment illustrates how narratives of injustice and insecurity emerge from assessments of *moderate* rather than significant inequality. Narratives in Mauche make little reference to the large landowners throughout the county and region. Rather, what matters for Kalenjin farmers in Mauche is the inequality in land rights between themselves and their neighbors: that Kikuyu in Likia have title deeds and they do not.

The Land Allocation Process in Mauche

Residents in Mauche describe the first Kenyatta regime pushing their community deeper into the forest to make space for landless Kikuyus coming from Central Province. "[The Kikuyu] benefited because their leader was [also] a Kikuyu." But twenty years later in the early 1990s, President Moi acted in the same capacity as Kenyatta, resettling Kalenjin (including Ogieks) in Mauche. Drawing on this history, participants explain, "So there are two ways of land acquisition, the president-assisted way, and our way, which is when the landless people are resettled."[58]

While both forms of land acquisition involve the central state, what matters more is how both sides have interpreted these two methods of settling Kikuyus and Kalenjins. A common refrain from other groups is that Kalenjin in Mauche (and elsewhere) have not purchased the land, but instead, have received the land "for free." The defense of Kalenjin in Mauche is that they earned the land through their many years of suffering as a landless people. They juxtapose their hardship with the Kikuyus, who they say have received land through the patronage of the first President Kenyatta. Mauche residents frame their struggle to access land through stories of eviction, state repression, and finally, relocation by a merciful leader. They see themselves as recipients of

[57] Interview-Mauche SS-Nakuru County, July 7, 2012 (7).
[58] Focus group with youths-Mauche SS-Nakuru County, July 21, 2012.

state patronage – a sharp contrast from the shareholders of the Ogilgei land-buying society. Rather than strategically organizing themselves, residents who received land within the scheme were the "lucky" recipients of land allocations.

Many older allottees in Mauche describe the brutal repression and evictions they endured under the previous Provincial Commissioner of the Rift Valley, Isaiah Mathenge.[59] One Mauche farmer emphasizes that "there was no other way of acquiring land" but to wait for government resettlement. He says that "we were so used to that place in the forest [Tinet Forest] that the government had to forcefully evict us ... so if we were not given this land, we would still be living there [in the forest]."[60] Another resident explains: "As the Ndorobo (Ogiek) people, we took the forest as our homes until the government evicted us. We used to go back and build makeshift houses [but then] the police would come and burn our houses. This continued for some time until the government gave us this land."[61]

A theme that emerges from interviews with residents is the belief that the Moi government rescued them from the forests. This narrative has developed in spite of the forced evictions they endured under the Moi government. According to a group of Ogiek elders, the government "saw it was fair for us to quit living in the forest since it was a water catchment area and [we] were lagging behind in development."[62]

Another feature of Mauche's land allocation concerns the legality of the process. The former Moi regime excised part of the Eastern Mau Forest to settle those who were ostensibly landless. To do so, the government used government forestland for settlement purposes before the forests had been formally opened for transfer or sale.[63] This is an example of the illegal allocation of government land (Government of Kenya 2004).[64]

---

[59] P.C. Isaiah Mathenge is infamous among the Kalenjin for stealing Kalenjin cattle, burning homes, and imprisoning people (beginning in 1977). These abuses, which targeted Kalenjin subtribes, remain a source of grievances today.

[60] Interview-Mauche SS-Nakuru County, July 21, 2012 (16).

[61] Interview-Mauche SS-Nakuru County, July 19, 2012 (7).

[62] Focus group with elders-Mauche SS-Nakuru County, July 21, 2012.

[63] The term "de-gazzetment" refers to a process whereby national newspapers declare the alienation of certain lands. Land alienation refers to the expropriation of customary or private lands by the government for either its own use or for private development requiring a mortgage or other various forms of guarantees.

[64] Government of Kenya 2004: 153.

The legal status of Mauche is under scrutiny in large part because it sits on the eastern edge of the Mau Forest Complex – the largest closed canopy ecosystem in Kenya.[65] The Mau Forest Complex has become a political and ecological focal point beginning with the 2005 Forest Act and culminating in the Mau Forest Task Force (launched by the Prime Minister, Raila Odinga, in July 2008). The government has launched a project to remove any settlers or squatters living within the boundaries of the Mau Forest, regardless of whether residents hold title deeds. Mauche residents occupy land that in all likelihood was allocated illegally by President Moi in the early 1990s. In addition, the Kenyan government seeks to restore the Mau Forest. The full restoration process would likely entail their eviction.

Land Insecurity in Mauche

Most Mauche residents say they do not feel land secure. While many residents claim to have received title deeds, these titles have been rendered meaningless since the government imposed the caveat in 2005. Residents know they live in politically and ecologically contested terrain. They face threats of evictions from the state and from their Kikuyu neighbors. And without genuine title deeds, residents rely on political patrons to provide land security.

The land security of Mauche residents is weak in part because their Kikuyu neighbors in Likia question their rights to occupy the eastern Mau. Likia residents accuse Mauche farmers of taking land for free without working or paying. Kikuyu residents in Likia also see Mauche residents as "forest invaders," particularly as ideas about the Mau Forest and environmental preservation become popular. One Kikuyu resident in Likia states, "They should not even occupy that land because it's government land and also because it's a forest." A former forest guard describes the forestland as a site of contestation between both sides:

When the forest was being set aside for settlement for the second time it was given to one tribe only [Kalenjin]. We tried to kick them out of the forest but we were defeated followed by an order [from] 'above' [Office of the President] to let the forest invaders be. We tried to talk to them but they

---

[65] Government of Kenya 2009.

defiantly denied and said that the Kikuyu had their turn during the Kenyatta era so now it was their turn.[66]

Linking the Mau Forest allocation with violence in the Rift, another Likia farmer claims, "if the government had not given out the Mau forestland, we would not have had any clashes in the whole Rift Valley." Likia residents draw on narratives rooted in ideas of land purchase, hard work, due process, and forest management. Yet underlying each of these narratives is a fear of Kalenjins in Mauche. This fear stems in part from the Kalenjin raids that occur during elections.

In sum, Mauche residents lack two critical dimensions of strong property rights in land. The caveat on the title signifies their lack of formal recognition from the state. In addition, they lack informal recognition from neighboring Kikuyus. In the absence of formal and informal property rights recognition, Mauche residents rely on a set of narratives in which their access to land is both threated and constrained by their Kikuyu neighbors and a Kikuyu-dominated state.

Leadership in Mauche

This history of land acquisition in Mauche and the levels of land security that have emerged from the process also affect the way that local leaders, and Kalenjin elders specifically, assert their authority over community members. Their voice, beliefs and views of the world play a large role in how narratives develop from within the community. The narratives they promote, however, emerge from their experience of everyday land insecurity. Elders draw on histories of land dispossession and promote strategies of reclaiming land and preempting future threats. Mauche elders thus have significant power in promoting contentious land narratives, but they have less ability to restrain or moderate these same narratives when they become rhetoric tools for organizing violence. As violence escalated in the aftermath of the 2007 election, Mauche elders had very little power to restrain younger residents from fighting. This contrasts with Ogilgei, where leaders could use their moral authority to convince younger people not to fight. A respondent explains, "The elders tried their best to calm the

[66] Interview-Likia LBC-Nakuru County, July 28, 2012 (4).

youth, urging them not to engage in war. But the youth didn't listen and sometimes they collided with the elders."[67]

This suggests that the narrative voice of Mauche elders is quite limited. Local leaders shape the contentious narratives that focus on past injustices or impending threats from rival groups. But they have less ability to constrain or moderate these same narratives. I point to three possible explanations for this limited "moral authority" and local legitimacy. First, most Mauche elders – particularly the Ogiek elders – did not have the opportunity to receive any formal education. In 1975 the provincial government destroyed nearly all primary schools accessible to Ogiek children. This was part of the violent campaign to evict Ogieks from the Western Mau Forest.[68] In a focus group with Mauche elders, participants refer to marginalization and harsh repression that the Ogiek community faced under the colonial government and the subsequent Kenyatta regime:

The government neglected us and I didn't go to school because of that ... the Ndorobo (Ogiek) don't have any educated people to represent us because we were sidelined. We have so many problems that can never end. The whites forgot us and the government forgot us.[69]

As a result, many elders remain illiterate. They must rely on younger members to write letters or read newspapers. As education has become increasingly important in Kalenjin communities, older members without education do not have the same status as educated leaders. Many older leaders therefore struggle to retain authority over younger members. This contrasts Ogilgei, where the founding leaders of the community had access to schooling, in large part because they were working in more densely populated areas – near commercial farms or in urban centers – rather than the forest.

Second, Mauche, like many agrarian-based communities across Kenya, faces a dwindling supply of land. Unlike many Ogilgei elders who have been able to invest in their ten-acre plots of land and can thus pass on the land to their kin, leaders in Mauche do not have sufficient

[67] Interview-Mauche SS-Nakuru County, October 4, 2012 (2).

[68] According to a report submitted to the Truth Justice and Reconciliation Commission (TJRC) by the Ogiek of the Sururu/Mauche SS (Njoro District), the government burned over ten primary schools, arrested residents, raped women and children, and stole cattle, sheep, and goats in large numbers which they subsequently sold at "throw away prices" to Kikuyus.

[69] Focus group with elders-Mauche SS-Nakuru County, July 21, 2012.

land or proper documentation to pass on land to the next generation. This works to undermine their authority and status in the eyes of the younger generation. Lastly, because elders face dwindling access to lands, insecure land rights, and reside within a constituency where they are the political minority (Njoro constituency), they rely on local-level politicians and officials to provide land security and basic goods. This patron–client relationship between Mauche leaders and local politicians can provide a source of power for village elders during election time. Yet it also erodes the autonomy of Mauche elders who become beholden to local politicians.

Conclusion

This chapter begins by asking why contentious land narratives develop between groups in one local context, but not in another, seemingly similar space. My main finding is that *moderate inequality* in land security between two neighboring groups strongly affects the contentious land narratives that emerge. Yet when members from both sides have relatively equal levels of land security, land narratives tend to be far less contentious, Yet equality in land rights – or the way that group members interpret this distribution – is a function of the process through which each side acquires land.

In the case of Ogilgei, there is relative equality in the level of land security between Ogilgei residents and their Kikuyu neighbors in Kerma. These equal levels of land rights are largely an outcome of a land allocation process whereby Kalenjin and Kikuyu residents each had opportunities to purchase their land. Yet in the case of Mauche, there is inequality in the level of land security between Mauche residents who lack valid title deeds, and their Kikuyu neighbors in Likia, most of whom have title deeds. This inequality is an outcome of the varying processes through which Kalenjins and Kikuyus acquired land. Kikuyus purchased land as shareholders through a land-buying company, while Kalenjins were resettled on government forestland in the 1990s "for free." Their land rights have thus been called into question both by their Kikuyu neighbors and subsequent government regimes.

The comparison provides an opportunity to interrogate scholarly assumptions about the sources of group conflict at the local level. The arguments presented here contrast studies of ethnic group conflict, which tend to assume that ethnicity is the lens through which people understand their relative status and security. Instead, the case studies of Mauche and Ogilgei demonstrate that the property rights environment shapes how people evaluate group entitlements and ethnic threat. In local institutional environments defined by uneven and insecure property rights such as Mauche, where group members struggle to secure tenure security, they are more likely to see a neighboring group from a different ethnic community as a threat to their tenure security. Relative land inequality between groups shapes the political salience of ethnic identification.

Ogilgei provides an important counter case. Kalenjin residents do not view their Kikuyu neighbors as a threat or impediment to their own land security or development. Equally, they do not make claims to land based on ethnic or regional-identification but instead rely on formal land claims. I argue that Ogilgei's land acquisition process has had enduring effects on the narrative that has emerged. Specifically, I demonstrate that the opportunity to acquire land and tenure security has strengthened formal and informal levels of land security, shaped the political preferences of local leaders, and bolstered their moral authority and legitimacy. In contrast to Mauche leaders who advocate for the redistribution of rights between the Kalenjin and Kikuyu communities, Kalenjin leaders in Ogilgei have strong incentives to maintain the *status quo* distribution of land rights. Local leaders seek to insulate Ogilgei from the instability of the surrounding region. Because Ogilgei residents have relatively strong land rights and because their leaders advocate narratives that emphasize stability over reform, politicians have less power to exploit issues of land and ethnic identity during electoral campaigns. The Ogilgei case is also important because it demonstrates the role that local actors (e.g. village leaders) can play in increasing perceptions of security, and mitigating the divisive effects of contentious land narratives and political mobilization.

Determinants of Election Violence

6 | Contentious Land Narratives and the Escalation of Violence

Hatred and provocation propagated by the Kikuyu continued daily to the extent of open confrontation, daring us to be ready to pack and leave Mauche when Kibaki won the elections. The loathing and ridicule were a lot for the Kalenjin to take. So when Kibaki was sworn in as president, violence ensued. This was all made worse by disputes over the ownership of this land.[1]

Kenyans provide layered accounts of the postelection violence. People fought because of anger over a "stolen election," fears of their eviction, opportunities to earn cash or land, or frustration borne from years of feeling marginalized and politically voiceless. In the excerpt above, the respondent's comments point to the challenge of isolating any single cause of electoral violence. Violence "ensues" when Mwai Kibaki is announced the winner. The respondent's comments, however, suggest other motives for Kalenjin participation in the clashes: *fear* that their Kikuyu neighbors would evict them if Kibaki claimed the presidency, as well *anger* or a sense of injured pride that residents had endured from the "loathing and ridicule."

In this chapter, I examine how land narratives shape the production of election violence. In doing so, I analyze a set of more specific questions: 1) How do land narratives affect participation in violence, 2) what role do elites play in shaping or appealing to particular narratives; and 3) how do land narratives play out at different stages in the escalation of violence? This chapter takes a process-tracing approach. Using qualitative evidence from two violence-afflicted cases in Nakuru County, it traces the mechanisms through which narratives around land shape the process of violence. Specifically, I analyze the violence that escalated between Mauche and Likia (Molo constituency), and the violence that "came from the outside" in Oljorai (Naivasha constituency).

---

[1] Interview-Mauche SS-Nakuru, October 9, 2012 (5).

Broadly, I argue that local land narratives provide a key discursive tool through which elites and ordinary civilians jointly establish a logic for organizing and engaging in violence. In many communities across Kenya, land narratives develop out of fears of losing land and property, desires to strengthen land rights, and beliefs about the legitimacy or injustice of the land distribution process. Where these narratives are most salient and where they already resonate with a majority of the community, leaders can draw on these narratives to establish different logics of violence.

Logics of Violence

There are many reasons why an individual chooses – or is compelled – to participate in violence. I focus on four logics of participation that gain particular power and resonance in the context of contentious land narratives. The first is the logic of preemption and insecurity: "evict them from the land before they evict us." Leaders exploit an environment of fear and insecurity, accentuated by the proximity of elections, to convince followers that the rival group could displace them if the rival side were to win elections.

The second is the logic of political opportunity. Political entrepreneurs convince followers that elections provide a "window of opportunity" to strengthen or reclaim land rights. Yet where there is high uncertainty around elections – linked partly to distrust in electoral institutions – group members may resort to violence to guarantee an outcome in their favor. In the preelectoral period or on polling day, violence can reduce the number of opposition voters. In the postelectoral period, violence can provide leaders and followers with a way to "bargain" for a particular outcome, be it an electoral recount, the resignation of an elected leader, or a ruling coalition. Violence can work to undermine the legitimacy and authority of the ruling government. It can also provide a bargaining card, whereby fighters only agree to relent if they receive a satisfactory settlement. Followers may thus be willing to engage in violence if they believe that their own ability to secure land and livelihood hinges on the election of their favored candidate.

The third logic of violence is revenge and defense. Political leaders draw on narratives of past injustice to convince followers that violence is a way of avenging for crimes committed by the rival group in the past or present. Revenge is also endogenous to the process of violence. As members of one group kill, displace, or destroy the properties of another, violence becomes a mechanism of retaliation and defense.

The fourth logic is personal or material gain. Leaders can recruit individuals to participate in violence by offering land, cash, jobs, or other private benefits in exchange for their participation (Collier & Hoeffler 2004). Further, acts of election violence such as evicting opposition supporters or destroying homes and looting can free-up land that a leader can distribute among loyal recruits (i.e. participants in organized violence). For example, a common refrain among many Kenyans is that the poor are more likely to fight because elites can easily entice them with promises of cash, land, or a job. I find however, that Kalenjin and Kikuyu respondents think about motive quite differently. When I ask whether politicians can convince youth to fight using material incentives, 42 percent of Kikuyu respondents say that such promises are "the only reason some youth decide to fight." Yet among Kalenjin respondents, only 17 percent see such incentives as the primary motivating factor.[2]

Taken alone, none of these logics can explain the escalation of violent collective action. Instead, I show how different logics of violence – from preemption, opportunities to alter the status quo, revenge, and desire for material gain – interact at different stages in the escalation of violence.

Stages of Violence

In addition to the four logics of participation in violence, I also theorize four stages in the process of violent escalation. These include: (1) the mobilization of land narratives, (2) the trigger event, (3) local escalation, and (4) scale shift. At each stage, existing land narratives make acts of violence thinkable, feasible, or necessary. At the first stage, political leaders tap into existing narratives to

[2] These results are based on question from the household survey I conducted where we ask respondents the following: "Many people say that politicians are able to convince youth to fight because they provide motivation. For example, they give them cash, they bring them to the bars, or they promise them land or small jobs. In this area, how much do these offers affect young people's involvement in the clashes or violent activities?" Respondents can answer on a five-point scale where 1=a lot, 4=no effect, and 0=can't say (n=371). See appendix for full results.

mobilize potential fighters. By emphasizing themes of injustice and insecurity, mobilizers use fear of losing land and desires to gain land to convince followers that violence is a way to hedge against potential electoral losses or to secure the distributive benefits of an electoral outcome.

The second stage is the "trigger" – a discrete event at the national or local level that sets violent action into motion. In the context of the 2007–2008 violence, the announcement of the disputed poll results provided this necessary trigger. Yet in some communities, the trigger was a much more localized event such as the assassination of a community member or a bar brawl that spiraled out of control. In these alternative scenarios, an assassination or bar fight triggers inter-group violence, but only in the context of disputed elections and larger land issues. I analyze how these "triggers" gain meaning in the context of already existing narratives.

The third stage – local escalation of violence – occurs at nearly the same time as the outbreak of violence. After the first group has launched an attack, in some cases crossing a real or invisible dividing line between two communities, the second group engages in defensive fighting. As the destruction and death toll mounts, fighting is both defensive and revenge-oriented.

The fourth stage of violent escalation is "scale shift." At this stage, fighting is no longer between two groups who know and interact with one another on a daily basis. Instead, leaders organize killing groups to seek revenge against groups whom they deem responsible for the atrocities committed against their co-ethnics. Violence at this stage is well organized, well financed, fast-moving, and more diffuse geographically.

The Correlation Between Land Narratives and Election Violence

Before analyzing the process through which land narratives shape the production of violence, I begin by examining whether – and to what extent – there is a correlation between spaces of contentious land narratives and spaces of violent escalation. I evaluate this question in two ways. First, using my survey data, I show the correlation between variables that proxy for the salience of contentious land narratives and the occurrence of violence. As a way of measuring belief in a contentious land narrative, I draw on two variables that measure a person's openness to the settlement of ethnic outsiders in their community. I then look at how these variables correlate with two measures for election violence: 1) whether an individual was a victim of election violence (i.e. direct exposure) or 2) whether an individual witnessed violence in her community (i.e. indirect exposure). I present a pairwise correlation matrix in the appendix. As the table indicates, there is a positive and statistically significant correlation between agreement with a contentious land narrative and the occurrence of violence. This correlation is strongest between the variable that measures a respondent's openness to the settlement of ethnic outsiders and the indirect exposure to election violence (where pairwise correlation is 0.31).[3]

As an additional way of establishing a correlation, I draw on my qualitative dataset, comprising eight case comparisons, that I presented in Chapter 4. I show a version of this table below (Table 6.1). Here however, I show how each of my key explanatory variables, including contentious land narratives, correlate with the occurrence of election violence. First, the table indicates that contentious land narratives may be a necessary, though not sufficient condition for the occurrence of violence. In the two cases where I do not observe contentious land narratives (Ogilgei/Kerma and Umoja/Belbar), violence does not escalate. Yet I also include cases where there are contentious land narratives yet no violence (Kijipwa and Ramisi). As I've argued, this suggests that other factors must be at play as well. Among these, I focus on the importance of having a leader who acts as a strong land patron. That is, leaders must be able to signal their ability and willingness to help followers secure or gain land rights (see Chapter 3 and 7 for further discussion). The table also indicates that in the case of Mwisho wa Lami and Tipis, where there were contentious land narratives and strong land patrons, violence did not escalate in 2007–2008. The area has, however, experienced violence in past elections (1992 and 1997). Hence, the absence of violence in 2007 does not undermine the important role of contentious land narratives, but indicates that other local and unobserved factors also work to restrain or mitigate violence in spaces that might otherwise be vulnerable to violence. Among these,

---

[3] These variables are labeled "Anti_Settlement" and "Indirect Violence" respectively. Further details are available in Chapter 8 and the appendix.

Table 6.1 *Correlation between land narratives and the escalation of electoral violence (2007–2008)*

	Region: county, constituency	Case comparison	Land rights: degree unequal	Contentious narrative	Strong land patron	Election violence (2007–2008)
1	Rift Valley: Nakuru, Rongai	Ogilgei Kerma	Equal	No	Yes	No
2	Rift Valley: Nakuru, Rongai	Umoja Belbar	Equal	No	Yes	No
3	Rift Valley: Nakuru, Njoro	Likia Mauche	Moderate	Yes	Yes	Yes
4	Rift Valley: Nakuru, Njoro	Mwisho wa Lami Tipis	Moderate	Yes	Yes	No[1]
5	Rift Valley: Nakuru, Naivasha	Oljorai Nyakinyua	Moderate	Yes	Yes	Yes
6	Rift Valley: Nakuru, Naivasha	Hell's Gate	Moderate	Yes	Yes	Yes
7	Coast: Kilifi Kilifi South	Kijipwa REA Vipingo	Significant	Yes	No	No
8	Coast: Kwale Msambweni	Ramisi KISCOL	Significant	Yes	No	No

Notes:

[1] While there was not significant violence in Mwisho wa Lami/Tipis in 2007–2008, there was violence in previous elections (1992 and 1997).

a politician may not have the incentive to use violence, either because he or she does not fear electoral defeat or because using violence provides no strategic advantage.

In sum, while these cases cannot confirm a causal relationship between contentious land narratives and violence, they do point to a correlation. Notably, in three of the four cases where contentious land narratives were present, violence escalated during the 2007–2008 period. Further, If I were to broaden the outcome of interest to include any incident of election violence since the reintroduction of multiparty elections, then all four cases with contentious land narratives and moderate land inequality have also experienced election violence. Further, I do not observe any cases where contentious land narratives were absent, yet election violence still occurred. This provides evidence for my argument that elites are far more likely to organize electoral violence where they can appeal to already existing contentious land narratives.

Methodology

In the previous chapter, I compared two pairs of farming communities with different land allocation arrangements as a way of explaining why contentious land narratives develop between some communities but not others. In this chapter, I draw primarily from a single case study between Mauche, a Kalenjin farming community and Likia, a Kikuyu farming community, both located at the edge of the Eastern Mau Forest in Nakuru County. As I show in the previous chapter, salient and contentious land narratives have existed between the two neighboring communities dating back to the early 1990s when the government settled Kalenjin in Mauche. Election violence escalated in 1992 and 1997, but residents explain that the level of violence – marked by deaths, destruction of homes, and displacement – was most intense during the 2007–2008 postelectoral period.

I use interviews with respondents to trace the process of violent mobilization during stage 1 (mobilization of land narratives), stage 2 (the trigger) and stage 3 (localized revenge and defense). I analyze stage 4 (scale shift) by drawing on interviews that I conducted in the Oljorai settlement scheme and Hell's Gate, both located in Naivasha constituency.[4]

---

[4] For a more detailed discussion of these cases, see Chapter 3.

The data that I use in this chapter draws primarily from a series of questions about how an individual experienced and interpreted the violence: their recollection of how events unfolded (e.g. warning signs, sites of fighting, methods of violence that each side used, responses from community members, targets, spread and diffusion of violence), why they think violence occurred, the motivations they attribute to participation, and how they think about the role of leaders in the mobilization process.[5] I never asked respondents to identify their role in the electoral violence, although some chose to volunteer this information. I also held focus groups in each community after completing individual interviews (grouped by youth and elders).

While I rely primarily on individual interviews and focus groups to demonstrate my theory of election violence, I acknowledge that there are potential pitfalls in asking people to recount or interpret a violent event experienced in the past. As Elisabeth Wood (2003) warns, "memories of political events, however well they are initially remembered, may be later reshaped by social and cultural processes that affect which memories were retained, which emphasized, and which forgotten" (2003: 34). Similarly, Lee Ann Fujii (2010) warns that researchers should be aware of the political contexts that may shape how people decide to tell their story. Noting these observations, I do not use interviews as sources of absolute truth or verifiable facts about the violence. Instead, I am interested in how people make sense of the violence: how and why it unfolded, the motives and power of its organizers and participants, and how respondents place themselves and their communities in the larger national drama. I also structure the questionnaire in a way that helps respondents organize or sort through their experience – facilitating a separation of historical events in the distant past, events in 2007–2008, and ongoing issues.

The timing of my research is also relevant. I conducted interviews in the Rift Valley region of Kenya between June and November 2012 in the months before Kikuyu and Kalenjin leaders had solidified a political

---

[5] In conducting interviews dealing with interpretations of election violence, I followed the same interview protocol as I used during other stages of the qualitative research. Village escorts were never present during the actual interview. To protect the privacy of the respondent, escorts stood beyond earshot (outside the home or at the edge of the property, or would go visit a neighbor) during the interview. See appendix for further details on the questionnaires and more details of interview methodology.

alliance under the banner of the Jubilee Alliance.[6] The timing of my research also preceded the more controversial debates surrounding the trials of Uhuru Kenyatta (Kikuyu) and William Ruto (Kalenjin) at the International Criminal Court (ICC).[7] These trials had the unintended effect of suppressing discussion surrounding the unresolved postelection violence. If I had carried out interviews as little as four months later, many respondents may have filtered their recollections through a new political lens, one shaped by fear and compliance, or perhaps, a genuine sense of interethnic unity.

Land Narratives and Violent Mobilization: Stage 1

In this section, I demonstrate how particular land narratives can help elites establish different logics for participation in election violence. As elections approach, leaders can draw on existing local narratives to strengthen beliefs about imminent threat to land security or opportunities to reclaim land rights. For a narrow section of the population, violence becomes a form a political participation that is thinkable and even necessary.

I document two narrative themes that have formed between the neighboring farming communities of Mauche (Kalenjin) and Likia (Kikuyu). Injustice narratives draw on histories of allocation and past crimes by state or nonstate actors, including eviction. Leaders can frame elections as an opportunity for one group to reassert their land rights over the other – through violence or coercive state policies. The narrative works to justify the removal of people seen as "illegal occupants" or "invaders."

By contrast, insecurity narratives consist of stories about a potential threat from a rival group or the state. The narrative becomes stronger and more salient when political entrepreneurs (e.g. politicians) convince group members that elections signal a threat to land security or political

---

[6] The Jubilee Alliance was the political coalition that formed between Kikuyu and Kalenjin candidates: Uhuru Kenyatta's The National Alliance party (TNA) and William Ruto's United Republican Party (URP).

[7] Uhuru Kenyatta (President of Kenya, 2013–present) and William Ruto (Deputy President, 2013–present and former MP for Eldoret North), were charged by the ICC in 2011 for their role in organizing crimes against humanity related to the 2007–2008 election violence. Charges against Kenyatta were dropped in 2015 due to insufficient evidence. Trial chamber judges at the ICC terminated the case against Ruto in April, 2016.

Table 6.2 *Relationship between land narrative, logic of violence, and method of violence*

Narrative ⟶	Logic of violence ⟶	Method of violence
Injustice narrative	*Logic of opportunity*	
Kikuyu	Increase land holdings	State-led eviction of Kalenjin
Kalenjin	Reclaim ancestral land	Violent eviction of Kikuyu
Insecurity narrative	*Logic of defense*	
Kikuyu	Protection from Kalenjin	Elect leader to evict Kalenjin
Kalenjin	Preempt eviction by Kikuyu	Violent eviction of Kikuyu

representation. The narrative can establish a motive for violence on the basis of defending one's land rights and preempting "imminent threats."

The motive for violence is thus two-fold: to preempt or manage an impending threat by "evicting them before they can evict us" or using violence as a means of "taking back" or expanding land rights by evicting rivals. Table 6.2 illustrates how these two land narratives can work among Kikuyu and Kalenjin communities, establishing both a motive and method for using violence. For Kikuyu, each narrative can shape a logic of violence based on expanding land holdings or protecting these lands from attacks or violent expropriation by Kalenjin (or another rival group). For Kalenjin, narratives of injustice and insecurity can shape a logic of violence based either on reclaiming ancestral land or preempting eviction by Kikuyu or a Kikuyu-led state. The logic of violence in turn, helps explain the main form of violence.

Mobilizing Narratives of Injustice

As I describe in the previous chapter, Mauche is a Kalenjin settlement scheme bordering Likia, a Kikuyu LBC. Kalenjin did not settle in the area until the early 1990s when President Moi carved out a portion of the Mau Forest and created the settlement scheme. Each family received five acres of land "free of charge." Households received plot allotment letters, some of which were replaced with actual title deeds.

Yet early in the Kibaki administration, the government issued a "caveat" on all Mauche title deeds. While the caveat did not revoke the title deeds explicitly, it rendered the documents "null and void" for an indeterminate period.[8] In the absence of formal land claims, Kalenjin have resorted to "sons-of-the-soil" claims; asserting that their rights as "natives" supersede the claims of Kikuyu "migrants." And while residents acknowledge the role of former President Moi in their settlement, they are careful not to frame such settlement as patronage. As one resident remarks, "former President Moi did not give us this land as a political incentive. He gave us this land because we deserved it."[9] Another respondent remarks: "Those who brought us here were telling us, 'this is your land'"[10] Hence, while many residents acknowledge that they did not purchase the land, they nonetheless feel entitled to it – not because they are true first-comers to Mauche, but because they endured years of suffering and neglect. According to most residents, land in Mauche is their reward for years of suffering.

The most salient injustice narrative in Mauche centers around the caveat on title deeds, a policy that has stripped residents of any formal land rights. The caveat is also a policy that many associate with the government's desire to undermine Kalenjin land rights. Residents argue that if the caveat on their title deeds was meant to protect the [Mau] forest – as the government claims – then caveats should also be placed on title deeds in Likia. Yet no government official had questioned the sanctity of title deeds in Likia. A respondent talks about the injustice of the caveat and its role in the electoral violence:

The Kalenjins fight over land because they see the Kikuyu as being favored or as being the source of their misery. The Kalenjin title deeds have been cancelled, yet the Kikuyu still have theirs intact. I wish the government could treat both communities equally in matters of land by withdrawing the caveat on the Kalenjins' title deeds. Then violence would be no more on this land.[11]

---

[8] The caveat was part of a wider state-led initiative to investigate land that had been improperly and illegally allocated under previous regimes or human settlements located in critical water catchment areas such as the Mau Forest. (See TJRC 2013: Vol. 2B, paragraphs 377–380 and 564–565.)

[9] Interview-Mauche SS-Nakuru County, July 5, 2012 (9).

[10] Interview-Mauche SS-Nakuru County, July 18, 2012 (2).

[11] Interview-Mauche SS-Nakuru County, October 8, 2012 (2).

A key theme in these injustice narratives is the perceived injustice of unfair treatment, and in this case, unequal enforcement of tenure rights. The remarks highlight the particular power of moderate land inequality, in this case, where the government has granted one group of smallholders tenure rights, but has denied it to another group of smallholders. Another respondent conveys a similar narrative of injustice whereby a Kikuyu-dominated state arbitrarily revokes Kalenjin land rights while leaving Kikuyu rights intact. He explains:

> There is a time when the government established a land commission ... and it said that Moi gave the Mau Forest to people illegally. So the Kalenjins were left wondering why the land given by Kenyatta was not also illegal. This is an issue that leads to war.[12]

Narratives of injustice facilitate a mobilization strategy based on removing rival group members from a disputed political territory ("reclaiming land"). In the context of elections, this narrative frames Kikuyu and other non-natives as intruders who have rendered Kalenjin landless and politically impotent. It specifies and justifies a form of violent politics whereby the removal of "intruders" becomes synonymous with the restoration of land rights to the original or legitimate occupants. Leaders used subtle and overt methods to signal that electoral victory would result in the eviction of political opponents: from public speeches, radio, pamphlets, secret meetings, text messages, and metaphors in the vernacular. For example, a leaflet circulating in Narok District warned, "We cannot share the same space any longer with thieves who stole our votes and rights. We shall fight for our rights to the last. No peace" (CIPEV, Republic of Kenya 2008: 131).[13]

Promises to evict and fears of being evicted became central to the narratives and appeals that circulated locally. Respondents provide evidence for such strategies. As one Mauche respondent remarks, "Political leaders proliferated hatred between the two communities. For instance, during the political rallies, aspirants promised to remove the outsiders, the *madoadoa* (spots or stains), referring symbolically to

---

[12] Interview-Mauche SS-Nakuru County, October 4, 2012 (2). The respondent refers here to the Ndungu Commission to investigate illegal/irregular allocations of land (2002) (Government of Kenya 2004).

[13] The National Intelligence Service of Kenya found the leaflet on February 16, 2008.

the members of a particular community."[14] Similarly, participants in a focus group describe a common exchange between political candidates and supporters: "the politician uses his speeches to incite people against one another other by saying that if he is elected he will ensure that the eviction of the other tribe is a success ... This makes his supporters fight against those of his opponent."[15] Mauche elders, reflecting on the 1997 electoral violence, describe the ways that politicians would promise their respective communities that "if voted in, they would ensure that the [opposing group] would have to leave" thus enabling "[the politician's] community to take over the land."[16] By 'ensuring eviction' of the other group, politicians signal to their followers that they are willing and able to support violence. The signal emboldens followers while provoking the opposition. It instills fear and anger, but more importantly, it can encourage members of the rival group to prepare for a violent attack. Both sides may begin organizing themselves for potential "clashes" with one another because they have imperfect information about the intentions of the other side. Rumors of Kikuyus arming themselves can also create a "spiral effect," whereby Kalenjin attack Kikuyu communities preemptively, fearing that Kikuyus are also preparing to attack (Jervis 1978).[17]

Kikuyu residents in Likia provide their own interpretations of these anti-outsider narratives. In a focus group discussion with Likia youth, they talk about electoral violence erupting because candidates can easily manipulate Kalenjin but not Kikuyu. One participant explains, "Kalenjins have the issue of land injustices being planted in their hearts." According to Kikuyu participants, Kalenjin understandings of injustice are simply "misconception[s] that need to be cleared."[18] One Kikuyu participant provides his interpretation of the postelection violence:[19]

---

[14] Interview-Mauche SS-Nakuru County, October 8, 2012 (7).
[15] Interview-Mauche SS-Nakuru County, October 8, 2012 (2).
[16] Focus group with elders-Mauche SS-Nakuru County, October 2, 2012 (3).
[17] Some residents talked about politicians dropping letters and pamphlets, indicating that their community had vowed to fight the other. They would spread these letters through their "agents" along the road. Source: Interview-Mauche SS-Nakuru County, October 4, 2012 (3).
[18] Focus group with youth-Likia LBC-Nakuru County, October 3, 2012 (Q1).
[19] Ibid. The opening question (Q1) asked the participants to share their own experiences during the 2007–2008 post-electoral violence.

The reason the Kalenjins fought the Kikuyu is because the [Kalenjin] claim that the Kikuyu in the Rift Valley were given this land by the Kenyatta regime. Therefore, they made the Kalenjins landless. So [the Kikuyu] must be evicted. Politicians send these ill-intended messages when they want to gain political [power]. It's also seen that they fight the Kikuyu to instill fear [in the Kikuyu], forcing them to support a candidate of their choice … the clashes erupt because in most cases, the candidates whom the Kalenjins support rarely win, even for the position of the MP, so the [Kalenjin] view us as the cause of their failure.

This interpretation of events provides insights into how ordinary group members understand the relationship between land and the process of violence. In the excerpt above, the respondent begins by citing the role of the *land narrative*, that "Kalenjin claim Kenyatta gave Kikuyus this land." This narrative provides leaders with the *method of political mobilization*: "politicians only use the message when they want political power (i.e. to win elections)." He then specifies the *elite motive*: "to coerce Kikuyu into voting with the Kalenjin (by instilling fear)." Finally, he explains the motive of ordinary Kalenjins: their failure to gain seats in electoral contests triggers actual violence when they unleash their frustrations upon Kikuyu, "whom they blame for their failure."

Importantly, the use of injustice narratives to mobilize violence extends beyond the case of Mauche and Likia. In several of the case studies where violence occurred, respondents remark on how politicians encouraged the eviction of rivals or stoked fears of eviction. For example, a respondent in Hell's Gate (Naivasha constituency) explains:

Such terms as removing outsiders or "*madoadoa*" cannot be said in public. Instead, they call a meeting among a select group of people and tell them. For example, a leader can mobilize people from the Kikuyu community and tell them that the Luo have occupied their land and should be evicted … This happened in closed door meetings and some leaders used agents, like councilors.[20]

In this example, the hypothetical candidate exploits a narrative of land and injustice by suggesting that Luo's have taken the land that rightly belongs to Kikuyu. Using the narrative, the politician can justify a program of action – the eviction of Luos. The respondent's remarks

---

[20] Interview-Hell's Gate-Nakuru County, October 13, 2012 (1).

also provide clues into how these mobilization strategies work – in secret, behind closed doors with select community members, often brokered by low-level politicians, and rarely uttered publicly.

Mobilizing Narratives of Land Insecurity

Kalenjin narratives of land insecurity became particularly salient as the balance of power shifted to Kikuyus after the 2002 general election. President Moi accepted defeat and Mwai Kibaki, a Kikuyu, ascended to the presidency. Many Kalenjin believe that because Kikuyus dominate politics at both the local and national level, they have prevented Kalenjin from securing land ownership. Gaining political representation became a political imperative to gaining land security. Kalenjin anxieties were confirmed in 2003 when the Kibaki regime placed a "caveat" on all title deeds held by Mauche residents. With the caveat on land rights, the narrative became a story of Kalenjin persecution under a powerful Kikuyu state. Without a valid title deed, Mauche farmers could not access the bank loans that had enabled them to survive as smallholder farmers. These loans also provided a source of cash for school fees, hospital fees, funerals, and other emergencies. In their view, the Kibaki regime was not only undermining their land rights and economic competitiveness relative to Kikuyu, but was threatening their very right to survival in the Eastern Mau. One respondent explains how the fear and anger surrounding the caveat was an important driver of electoral violence in Mauche:

The postelection violence in Mauche erupted due to a lack of right to possess title deeds ... Meanwhile in the Kikuyu areas, they were spreading rumors to the Kalenjin community, saying that we don't have land and that we should be vacated out of Mauche area. All of these kinds of insults lead to the outbreak of the clashes.[21]

Another respondent in Mauche points to the rising land inequality between Kalenjin and Kikuyus as a source of insecurity and a motive to "see that Kikuyu vacate the land." He explains:

Land is the cause of violence because the Kalenjins see the Kikuyu as intruders from Central Province into the Rift Valley and in situations where

---

[21] Interview-Mauche SS-Nakuru-October 9, 2012 (2).

a slight difference arises between the members of the two communities the Kalenjins will take advantage to see to it that the Kikuyu vacate the land.[22]

This inequality – between Kikuyus with title deeds and Kalenjin without such titles – heightened feelings of land insecurity as much as it fueled a narrative of injustice. It also provided a valuable narrative device for leaders from both sides. Specifically, by building on fears of displacement, elites could frame the rival group as an imminent threat (i.e. to land security and safety).

This construction of threat, while not explicitly tied to land rights, is evident in the national campaign rallies that the opposition ODM held in the weeks and months before the December 27 general election. At one ODM rally in Eldoret Town, held a week before the election, William Ruto warned his supporters about the incumbent candidate, Mwai Kibaki. To a crowd of thousands, he stated:

I want to tell you Kalenjin people, let's get each other right. Kibaki is going home this time round, that I am sure. He won't escape [*Applause*]. Let me tell you, us and Kibaki, there is no relation at all. He is an enemy to us ... He stopped our people from work, burnt our houses, now he wants to take Moi to jail. Now he is employing his people in the army ... while ours remain pulling carts and riding [motorbikes]. He is an enemy and anybody who campaigns for him is a witch.[23]

The comments are notable for a few reasons. First, they are ethnically divisive, delineating between "us" (Kalenjin) and "them" (Kikuyu). Second, he frames PNU presidential candidate Mwai Kibaki as the enemy to the Kalenjin community; destroying Kalenjin homes, excluding members from lucrative employment, and jailing their ethnic patron (Daniel arap Moi). There is also the suggestion that by employing only "his people" in the army, that Kalenjins should not trust the army. Most powerfully perhaps, Ruto refers to Kibaki's supporters as "witches." In Kenya and many other African contexts, the accusation of "witch" is a powerful and dangerous one; implying evil, connection with the devil or dark magic, and the power to do great harm (Ashforth 2005; Geschiere 1997). Most importantly perhaps, witches are perceived as not fully human; they must be banished from

---

[22] Interview-Mauche SS-Nakuru-October 8, 2012 (2).
[23] William Ruto speaking at ODM Rally, Eldoret Town, December 20, 2007. This recording was made and generously shared by Jeremy Horowitz.

the community or killed. By transforming Kibaki and his supporters into "witches" – even metaphorically so – Ruto engages with a narrative that legitimizes violence.

In these contexts, politicians can present followers with a set of strategies for mitigating threat. These strategies range from more moderate promises to advocate for title deeds and expand land rights, to more extreme strategies such as state-ordered evictions and organized violence. According to ICC witness testimony, for example, the then-MP for Eldoret North, William Ruto, claimed that if the ODM won the 2007 election they would "uproot the tree stumps that are among the people" (referring to PNU supporters) and would "get rid of and send back to where they came from" all the people who had taken over local farms and businesses."[24] While the ICC never confirmed the veracity of these statements, interviews with respondents suggest that these types of remarks were quite common in the lead-up to the 2007 election and in previous elections in the 1990s.

Narratives of land insecurity provided a key mechanism through which elites and ordinary citizens established the logic for violence, one based on preempting future evictions while avenging for forced evictions endured in the past. In the lead-up to elections, candidates may seek to outbid one another, each proving that s/he has the capacity and resolve to protect followers from election-related threats, both from violence and loss of land. Politicians have the opportunity to present themselves as more than aspirants but also as "big men" who can defend the interests of the group in exchange for political loyalty. The ability and willingness to displace the opposing group is a sign of political power that can be requisite to winning – even if a politician never acts on this capacity.

A respondent in Mauche describes his impressions of this tactic as he sees it playing out among Kikuyu politicians: "Any MP who is voted in must promise to evict the Kalenjins from the land. And if he fails to deliver his promise then rest assured, he cannot go back into office."[25] Using the threat of violence – regardless of the election outcome thus provides an effective strategy for expanding a network of loyal followers.

---

[24] ICC pre-trial brief, September 9, 2013, ICC-January 9–11.The ICC charged William Ruto (now Deputy President of Kenya) for his role in organizing the 2007–2008 postelection violence. The charges were vacated in April 2016.

[25] Interview, Mauche SS-Nakuru County, October 4, 2012 (3).

Tenure insecurity in Mauche provided a particularly salient issue around which elites made political promises and sought to mobilize support. Another respondent explained how candidates promised that when elected, "they will ensure that the caveat on title deeds is withdrawn."[26] And despite the ubiquity of these promises, appeals to land security work when supporters believe that candidates recognize their claims. A respondent in Mauche explains:

When those vying for presidential seats make these promises, we tend to believe them and we feel that the government is on the verge of recognizing us as the legal owners of the land and we feel that our rights of land ownership are secure.[27]

By contrast, residents in Likia claim that because their title deeds are genuine and their land rights are secure, politicians cannot use the appeal of "land titles in exchange for votes." A Likia farmer explains how these mobilization strategies vary between the two communities:

In Likia the politicians don't use issues of land to woo voters because everybody has a title deed. But for Kalenjin politicians this becomes a tool for winning votes because they know that the Kalenjins are in Mauche illegally and need the protection. The lands are illegal because they don't pay land rates to the county council, which means the land is still under the custody of the government.[28]

Rather than promise title deeds as a form of land security, some Kikuyu leaders offer to "remove" or manage the Kalenjin threat. They do so by invoking fears of Kalenjin attacks, drawing on collective anxieties and memories of attacks in the past. A Likia resident explains the origins of his own fear, rooted in the electoral violence during the 1990s:

At one time, Mr. Ntimama ... who was a powerful political leader in Moi's government declared in public that Kikuyu men will become dog food during their eviction from the Rift Valley ...[29] I was forced to leave. Ever since the year 1997 we always felt and still feel that we were not safe at any time we hold general elections.[30]

---

[26] Interview-Mauche SS-Nakuru County, October 8, 2012 (2).   [27] Ibid.
[28] Interview-Likia LBC-Nakuru County, October 1, 2012 (2).
[29] William Ole Ntimama was a powerful member of the KANU and later, the ODM party. He was MP for Narok North (South Rift Valley) for twenty-five years. He is famous for declaring that the Kikuyu in the Rift Valley should "lay low like envelopes."
[30] Interview-Likia LBC-Nakuru County, November 29, 2012 (1).

Another respondent in Likia describes the day of the election announcement:

Before we voted there was tension in the land and we knew anything could happen at any time if [Mwai Kibaki] lost. After we voted and waited for the results the media would air news of the tally as the votes streamed in. And we could hear that Raila was up and this made us register fear in our hearts. We knew that the Kalenjins could now attack us fearlessly since the guy they were supporting was now headed to power.[31]

Stepping outside of the Mauche and Likia, respondents elsewhere also describe the fearmongering that defined the 2007–2008 pre- and post-electoral period. For example, a Kikuyu respondent living in Hell's Gate describes how William Ruto – then a high-ranking ODM leader and now the deputy president – invoked fear of eviction and land insecurity among Kikuyu residents by calling their title deeds into question. The respondent comments on the effects of such statements:

There was a time Mr. Ruto said that the titles here are just papers. I didn't like when he said that. This means that that we do not legally own this land and we should leave with our papers. This in essence meant that the Kikuyu were not supposed to be here.[32]

Many Kikuyu residents believed that they were only safe if another Kikuyu remained in power. Group members interpreted an ODM victory as a license for Kalenjin to kill or evict Kikuyus from contested zones.

   Kikuyu campaign strategies also heightened anxiety of eviction among Kalenjins. For example, Mauche residents describe how Kikuyu politicians used the issue of eviction to solidify support among Kikuyu. As one respondent comments: "We have heard of [Kikuyu] politicians ... saying that the Kalenjins will have to leave these lands especially during political campaigns."[33] Another Mauche respondent, who was among the few Kalenjins to campaign for the PNU in 2007, describes the campaign strategies of the previous parliamentary candidates, noting how both campaigned on their ability or willingness to remove Kalenjins using legal or violent means:

---

[31] Interview-Likia LBC-Nakuru County, October 1, 2012 (4)
[32] Interview-Hell's Gate-Nakuru, October 13, 2012 (11).
[33] Interview-Mauche SS-Nakuru County, October 8, 2012 (2).

In 2002, the [Kikuyu] elected a lawyer called Mukiri. He told them in one of their tribal meetings that he would use all legal means to [evict the Kalenjin from the forestland] so that the Kikuyu could occupy the lands. In 2007, [Kikuyu] elected Mr. Kiuna, a retired army officer who is said to have been involved in the 1997/1998 massacre of fifty-nine Kalenjins in Naishi-Lare. During his campaigns he used to tell them that if he were elected, he would "do to the Kalenjins in Mau Forest what he did to those in in Naishi." And so he was elected. When the Kalenjins heard of this they declared that they were ready to die but not leave the land. And after their man Raila didn't win in the polls, they knew the next thing was their eviction so they resorted to fighting.[34]

The respondent's account provides important insights into the construction of Kikuyu threat and how this threat shapes the logic of violence. According to the respondent, Kalenjins believed that their Kikuyu neighbors were electing leaders based on their promises to evict Kalenjin. This perception hardened people's resolve: "we are ready to die (to fight), but we will not leave our land." It also strengthened the need for a strongman or patron who could counter Kikuyu threats and protect Kalenjin interests. Many Kalenjins hoped that Raila Odinga could act as this protective leader at the national level. As one Mauche respondent explains:

Kalenjin were supporting the ODM candidate Raila for two main reasons, the impending threats of eviction. Also [there were] rumors that the MP of this region (Kiuna) said that when he was voted in, he would uproot the *visiki* – tree stumps that referred to the Kalenjin in this region.[35]

Raila Odinga's defeat then, provided the crucial tipping point, heightening fear among residents that their eviction was imminent. Many Kalenjin interpreted these campaign messages as grounds for preemptive war: they would evict the Kikuyu before the Kikuyu they could evict them. Elites were able to convince followers to evict PNU supporters in part because supporters in Mauche believed Kikuyu leaders were mobilizing along the same lines – waiting and ready to undermine the already precarious rights of Mauche residents.

In sum, the preelectoral period of 2007 strengthened and crystallized narratives of land injustice and land insecurity. Narratives of injustice shaped a logic of violence based on the idea of "reclaiming" lost land

[34] Interview-Mauche SS-Nakuru County, October 4, 2012 (3).
[35] Interview-Mauche SS-Nakuru County, October 8, 2012 (8).

and territory from a rival group. Elections created a key moment for Kalenjin and Kikuyu to reclaim land rights through eviction – violent or otherwise. Narratives of insecurity created a rationale for violence based on preempting one's own eviction. Kalenjin leaders could exploit the fears and frustrations of the caveat on title deeds and the fear of eviction that the caveat signaled. Leaders promised to *defend* the community from the possibility of evictions under a Kikuyu-led state, while encouraging citizens to ensure the victory of ODM at all costs.

Triggers of Electoral Violence: Stage 2

My family and I were staying in Tinet forest when the violence erupted spontaneously. It spread from Olenguruone and nearer it came to Kamwaura and faster was the spread to Mauche. An evil spirit, the spirit of war, found its place in the hearts of men.[36]

In this section, I examine when and how the idea of violence shifts to actual violence. What types of events provide the "trigger" that motivates people to pick up their guns or machetes, or prompts them to pour petrol over the houses of their neighbors? When and why does fighting begin? So far, I have focused on how land narratives help elites convince supporters that violence is the best or only strategy for avoiding losses or seizing opportunities during an election period. The next task is to identify the particular events that set violence into motion. I define a trigger for violence as a discrete event at either the local or national level that provokes violence.

Across much of Kenya, violence first escalated after the Electoral Commission of Kenya (ECK) declared Mwai Kibaki the president-elect. The timing of violence, however, varied across communities. While many respondents view the election results as the trigger that prompted fighting, others identify more local-level acts of violence such as a single murder or a bar fight as the event that pulled their own communities into the larger national drama. Several scholars, too, suggest that perceptions of electoral fraud provided the main trigger of the 2007–2008 violence (Norris et al. 2015; Dercon & Gutierrez-Romero 2012). In this section, I consider how different trigger events acquire meaning in the context of existing narratives of injustice and insecurity.

[36] Interview-Mauche SS-Nakuru County, October 9, 2012 (6).

Trigger Event 1: the Electoral Announcements

On the evening of December 30, 2007, residents in Mauche and Likia gathered around television screens and radios to listen to the ECK announce the results from the Kenyatta International Conference Centre in Nairobi (KICC). Amidst the chaos of that evening, one scene in particular captured the attention of Kalenjin viewers. The ECK chairman, Mr. Kivuitu was reading the final results for Molo constituency. As he read, The MP-elect for Eldoret North, William Ruto interjected to challenge the legitimacy of the results. A young man from Mauche describes his impressions:

> As the political leaders argued about who had won, Ruto was dragged by the General Service Unit. When we saw this we knew the whole of the Kalenjin community didn't have anyone to champion for their rights. The youths from the Kalenjin community proceeded to attack the Kikuyu.[37]

Many respondents in Mauche describe this moment as the beginning of the clashes.[38] Across the Rift Valley, images from the KICC triggered fears that the PNU was trying to rig the election. In Kalenjin farming communities across the Rift Valley, Raila Odinga's defeat provoked a set of emotions encompassing anger, frustration, and fear. One respondent recalls how "people were carried away by a spirit of violence."[39] Another claims that people "became emotional" because they believed Raila Odinga was in the lead.[40] Odinga's defeat prompted people to "protest by blocking the roads and attacking Kibaki supporters." According to another Mauche farmer, Kibaki's fraudulent victory signaled that the Kikuyu would never accept a leader "who did not originate from their community."[41] This refusal, marked by the delay in the results, "made the Kalenjin impatient, and so they attacked the Kikuyu."[42]

The disputed general elections established different logics for violence. First, the election results triggered underlying fears and anxieties rooted in Kalenjin narratives of land insecurity. Many residents equated Kibaki's victory with eviction, greater land insecurity, and further political marginalization. Residents "engaged themselves in fights ...

---

[37] Interview-Mauche SS-Nakuru County, October 8, 2012 (1); Shimoli 2007.
[38] Interviews (various)-Mauche.
[39] Interview-Mauche SS-Nakuru County, October 9, 2012 (5).
[40] Interview-Mauche SS-Nakuru County, October 4, 2012 (3)
[41] Interview-Mauche SS-Nakuru County, October 8, 2012 (1).   [42] Ibid.

due to fear that they would be denied the rights to own land."[43]
A group of Mauche elders suggest that because Kikuyus were encouraged to attack the Kalenjin, Kalenjin were "forced to respond to Kikuyu attacks [which were] aimed at forcing us off the land so that they could become the owners of these lands."[44] Another respondent explains: "In 2007, the clashes came because the Kikuyu didn't want the Kalenjins to live in their *shambas* located in Mau Forest ... The Kikuyu planned that once Kibaki won the election the Kalenjins would be forced to leave the forestland."[45] Another respondent who participated in the election violence describes how Kalenjin leaders and businessmen "were all claiming that outsiders came and grabbed land in the Rift Valley ... and so they decided to chase them away ... they said they wanted the Rift Valley to be clean of *madoadoa*."[46] These types of remarks describe Kalenjin attacks against Kikuyu as a means of defense: a way of preempting one's own displacement under a second Kikuyu-led government.

Second, the electoral results triggered violence by provoking a collective sense of betrayal by the political process and by extension, the Kenyan government. Kalenjins viewed the victory of the PNU as an assertion of Kikuyu power; that Kikuyu were unwilling to play by the electoral rules, but more so, that the party had the power and capacity to break the rules. The sense of betrayal and outrage that many ODM supporters felt was likely stronger than it might have been otherwise because candidates and party activists primed supporters to anticipate vote rigging by the PNU. For example, at a rally in Eldoret North, William Ruto proclaimed, "I want to tell you that now they are planning to do what? Steal votes. And we are telling them that here they are not stealing votes." A few weeks later, on December 20 in Eldoret Town, William Ruto made the same warning, claiming, "Kibaki is headed for home, so the only thing they are depending on is to steal the vote."[47]

---

[43] Interview-Mauche SS-Nakuru County, October 9, 2012 (2),
[44] Focus group with elders-Mauche SS-Nakuru County, October 2, 2012.
[45] Interview-Mauche SS-Nakuru County, October 8, 2012 (1).
[46] Interview in Njogu 2009: 282.
[47] William Ruto speaking at ODM Rally, in Eldoret North (December 3, 2007) and Eldoret Town (December 20, 2007) respectively. These recordings were made and generously shared by Jeremy Horowitz.

Interviews with Mauche residents reveal the sense of powerlessness that people felt in being able to challenge the status quo through elections, a feeling that several people described as a violation of their democratic rights. One respondent, for example, describes the efforts of Kikuyu to "win at all costs" as a "violation of democratic rights," explaining that "a few [Kikuyu leaders] wanted to maintain the status quo and remain in leadership posts. And this angered the Kalenjin in our native land. It dawned on us that it was a violation of our democratic right and we were angered."[48] Another respondent explains how community members knew that Raila was going to win, "but Kibaki rigged the election and was sworn in as the president. And that is what made Raila supporters go mad."[49] These comments point to the important role of emotions in the process of violence: the outrage and frustration of being denied some fundamental right. In particular, residents believed they had been denied the opportunity to win. According to many Kalenjin, in Mauche and elsewhere, an entrenched Kikuyu elite was determined to deny the Kalenjin community the political opportunities they deserved. Violent collective action emerged out of a sense of frustration and resentment toward the Kikuyu, whom residents saw as blocking an ODM victory. An interviewee explains the violence:

People fought because they felt that they were being oppressed. But in 2007 the Kalenjins wanted Raila to be in power because they knew that one of their own, Ruto, was a close ally to the president-to-be. This would favor them in matters of governance. When the opposite happened, the Kalenjins were frustrated and resorted to fighting the Kikuyu who seemed to have blocked Raila from gaining power by not voting for him and also by rigging elections.[50]

Violent protest provided a way for Kalenjins to demonstrate a sense of outrage but equally to assert a sense of power and agency over an electoral process from which they felt excluded or powerless to change. This is similar to Elisabeth Wood's analysis of *campesino* participation in the El Salvadoran civil war. She argues that joining the insurgency created a "pleasure in agency . . . the positive effect associated with self-determination, autonomy, self-esteem and efficacy" (Wood 2003:

[48] Focus group with youth-Mauche SS-Nakuru County, October 10, 2012 (3).
[49] Focus group with elders, Mauche SS-Nakuru County, October 2, 2012 (3).
[50] Interview-Mauche SS-Nakuru County, October 4, 2012 (3).

235). An interviewee from Mauche describes how youth attempted to take control of the process: "youth just disrupted the peace after it was declared that Kibaki had won. They had the intention of forcing Kibaki to step down and then Raila would take over power."[51] Joining in the violent protests, in this sense, was partly a way for Kalenjins to "reclaim a sense of agency" that the electoral process had denied them, as much as it was about getting a candidate into power.

Importantly however, there is not always so much agency in whether or how one participates in violent political action. As my own interviews and other human rights reports document, Kenyans often participated out of fear – of being killed, losing land, or social exclusion. A participant in the violence explains: "Personally I was forced to participate in the violence because everyone was supposed to participate in the violence. If you didn't go, your property would be destroyed completely and they would warn you that you are going against them."[52] The interviewee's remarks hint at the zero-sum logic driving the dynamics of the PEV: people were either loyal supporters willing to kill for the cause or opponents who had to be violently expelled (or killed).

Alternative Triggers for Violence

While many Kenyans believe that the electoral results were the main trigger for violence, others identify more local triggers such as a bar fight or a public feud. The ability for local dramas to trigger violent collective action relates to Kalyvas's observation that violence on the ground may have more to do with a local or private conflict than with the larger national or "master cleavage" (2003: 476). I apply this insight to Kenya's electoral crisis and find that in certain communities it was a local or private dispute in the context of the larger national drama that triggered violence. In the case of the Oljorai settlement scheme in Naivasha, violence did not escalate after the electoral announcement. Instead, respondents point to a quarrel between a boss and employee as a key event that provoked violence:

In 2007, people voted peacefully until [Kibaki] was declared the victor ... In this area the fight was instigated by a quarrel between two people who used

[51] Interview-Mauche SS-Nakuru County, October 8, 2012 (3).
[52] Interviewee from Iten, Eldoret, in Njogu 2009: 288.

to work together. One was the boss, a Kikuyu man, and the other was the employee, a Kalenjin. They were fighting over pay. One day when the Kalenjin fellow was walking around the center of town, the Kikuyu boss told the youths from his tribe that the guy was ferrying arrows and he was killed. The following day we were all surrounded and we had to defend ourselves.[53]

The story underlies the important interaction between a national event – the disputed elections – and a local event. In the case here, it is only when a fight erupts between the Kikuyu boss and the Kalenjin employee that members from both sides join the fight.

A few respondents provide similar accounts of violence in Mauche. According to one interviewee, "Claims that the Kalenjins had been paid to carry out the attacks are misleading because we had not planned for the fight. We were only angered by the fact that an expectant Kalenjin woman had been butchered and the infant thrown along the road." In this case, it not the disputed elections alone, but a single and highly visible act of violence that sets violence into motion.

Another respondent from Mauche provides his impressions of how the 1997 electoral violence escalated between Mauche and Ndeffo residents. The story does not explain the 2007–2008 postelection violence, but illustrates the ways that community members understand the process of violence during a larger electoral crisis. The respondent explains how, back in 1997, he went to Ndeffo (a Kikuyu community next to Mauche) to drink *muratina* (local brew):

We had barely taken our second round of "muratina" when a young man walked right up to where we were seated. He queried about our identities and place of residence. Thinking he was up to good intentions we told him our residential area at Mauche. He called us names and how we were fools because we had settled on government land. Later that evening, the young man who insulted us earlier in the day walked into the bar that was then packed by men who were drinking their heads off. He walked straight in and chopped an old Kalenjin man seated at the counter. And then he fled.[54]

The respondent explains that the bar owner – a Kikuyu – was subsequently killed by an angry Kalenjin mob who were avenging the death of the Kalenjin elder. He continues: "A scene had been created. Attacks and counterattacks followed for two consecutive days. Ndeffu center

[53] Interview-Oljorai-Nakuru County, September 8, 2012 (1).
[54] Interview-Mauche SS-Nakuru County, October 9, 2012 (6).

was torched, reducing it to ashes. The aftermath reached us in Mauche on the second day. Police intervention rested the differences." The 1997 electoral clashes, the respondent concludes, "arose following the insults and the killing of the old Kalenjin man at Ndeffu by that young man ... [who had] sowed hatred by turning us against our neighbors."

These examples illustrate alternatives processes of violent escalation. The primary trigger at the national or even regional level – such as the disputed victory of a presidential or parliamentary candidate, may not be the event that provokes the first strike. Instead, a fight between two individuals or a murder can become the event that polarizes community members along national cleavage lines.

Local Escalation of Violence: Stage 3

The third stage of violence closely follows initial attacks. In contexts such as Mauche and Likia, where Kalenjin residents attacked their Kikuyu neighbors, this third stage of violence is often a series of "localized" or intimate battles between neighbors. Participants on both sides fight within a familiar space: along a shared border, market-place or trading center. This contrasts with the fourth stage of violence where organizers transport participants from outside regions to form *de facto* militias or gangs to fight against targeted ethnic groups. The primary logic of violence at this third stage is defense and revenge.

In Likia, mostly young men mobilized in response to Kalenjin attacks in the hours and days after the elections results. Recalling the history of election violence in the area, and noting the anti-Kikuyus pamphlets and rumors that circulated in the months before the December 2007 elections, many Likia residents say that they anticipated attacks from their Kalenjin neighbors.[55] And while some residents describe the violence as "coming out of nowhere," many remarked that unlike in past elections, they "were prepared to defend themselves," suggesting that Likia residents planned to retaliate if Kalenjins attacked.[56] The

---

[55] Pamphlets warned of Kikuyu evictions in the event of a Kibaki victory. See Republic of Kenya 2008 (i.e. CIPEV Report) or KNCHR Report 2008.

[56] Residents in Mauche state that Kikuyu were armed with machetes and guns, while they relied on arrows and arson. Two interviews explain that if Kikuyu had better knowledge of how to operate the guns, the Kalenjin "would not have

following responses illustrate how past electoral violence shaped Kikuyu strategies of defense:

Now that the Kikuyu had experienced frequent attacks from the neighboring tribes in the previous instances, they were tired and were prepared to fight once provoked again. The Kalenjins ambushed us and we responded quickly before much damage had been done.[57]

Previously we have had various clashes, about seven of them in all. The [Kalenjin] agenda is for those considered "foreigners" to go back to their land ... we were sure the same would be repeated since it often occurs during election eve. In all instances ... the only response we resort to is defense.[58]

In a focus group with Kikuyu youth, they explain how years of election time clashes have equipped Kikuyu with the skills and readiness to defend the community:

Likia was the first place where clashes started in the year 1992 between the Kikuyu and the Maasai. The people who were born [here] are now grown, and they have become used to clashes and know various types of screams like war cries, theft etc. And by now everybody knows what he or she should do if a certain type of cry is heard. People are always ready to defend.[59]

These accounts suggest that many Kikuyu residents in the region organized, or at the very least, anticipated the first round of attacks. A familiar narrative of "evicting Kikuyus" from the land prompted Kikuyu residents to mobilize defensively. And as many Kikuyu residents feared, Kalenjin residents from Mauche waged attacks on Likia throughout the first night after the election results. They dug trenches along the road that prevented Kikuyus from escaping or reaching hospitals. One farmer recalls: "Our neighbors, the Kalenjin, started torching our houses and we were unable to watch our hard-earned wealth go down. We engaged in defense and that's how the fighting came along." Another respondent adds, "Kikuyu engaged in the fight because we grieved seeing that our people were losing lives and properties."[60]

As the deaths and destruction mounted, defensive fighting became part of the strategy of war. Elders organized and advised young men to

stood a chance." However, the CIPEV Report attributes most gun deaths and injuries to police involvement (Republic of Kenya 2008).

[57] Interview-Likia LBC-Nakuru County, September 13, 2012 (4).
[58] Interview-Likia LBC-Nakuru County, September 13, 2012 (7).
[59] Focus group with youth-Likia LBC-Nakuru County, October 3, 2012.
[60] Interview-Likia LBC-Nakuru County, September 29, 2012 (3).

defend the borders of the community against the Kalenjin invasion. As one interviewee explains, "The youths defended the society while the elders guided them on the tactics they could use so as to best defend the community, while telling them not to attack."[61] Kikuyu men joined in defense of the community to protect against Kikuyu losses and equally, to prevent Kalenjin territorial gains. The borderland between the two communities became the main battleground. One respondent describes how the youth protected the borders: "The community used the youths to defend itself. They would guard along the borders to prevent the enemy's attack. With time the youths were able to learn how to make the arrows from the samples that were shot at them and this helped them to counter the attacks."[62] Community defense was also a way for men to perform the roles and duties expected of Kikuyu men during battle or war. As one Kikuyu farmers explains,

We were ambushed and so the only thing that we did was to defend ourselves, because as men, that is our role and duty ... As a family man I was so concerned for my family's security. And that's why I, together with other young men in the society, had to act and defend our property and lives – by not allowing the Kalenjin to extend their destruction.[63]

In sum, Kikuyus in Likia viewed their own participation in violence as reactive and defensive. They did not attack the Kalenjin but defended their properties and families from further harm. Residents also acted to fulfill a sense of duty and obligation that Kikuyu masculinity demanded during times of war.

Mauche residents, by contrast, provide much more layered under-standings of how revenge and defense shaped their participation in the violence. For Mauche residents, the victory of Mwai Kibaki signaled the Kikuyu community's ability and willingness to rig an election. Many Kalenjin farmers, in Mauche and elsewhere, believed that now more than ever, their eviction was imminent. The logic of violence was two-fold: Kalenjins had to defend their communities from Kikuyus. Yet their defense was also a way of avenging for the injustices and "crimes" committed by the Kikuyu: the rigged election, Kikuyu threats, and the death and destruction that Kikuyus were waging on Mauche residents.

---

[61] Interview-Likia LBC-Nakuru County, October 1, 2012 (2).
[62] Interview-Likia LBC-Nakuru County, September 13, 2012 (3).
[63] Interview-Likia LBC-Nakuru County, September 13, 2012 (1).

These twin logics of self-defense and revenge are similar to Scott Straus's account of the logic of violence in the Rwandan genocide. Emphasizing the centrality of security and revenge he writes, "Perpetrators frame the logic of violence and self-defense in war as retaliation for the death of the president. Tutsi civilians were killed, perpetrators say, because Tutsis killed the president and represented a dangerous threat (Straus 2006: 154)." The key point of comparison here is that those who participated in the election violence believed that Kikuyus were responsible for a moral and legal wrongdoing – blurring perceptions of election rigging and ongoing injustices committed by a Kikuyu-dominated state. And because of these perceived wrongdoings Kikuyus presented a very real threat to Kalenjin political and physical survival in the Rift Valley.

These logics of defense and retaliation interact in sometimes seemingly contradictory ways. In conversations with Mauche residents, they describe their own participation or that of fellow community members, as reactive. A farmer claims, "we never started the attacks. But the Kikuyu did. And so we decided to defend ourselves."[64] In a focus group, participants discuss why they, as youth, participated in the clashes. Their descriptions illustrate the use of violence as a retaliation mechanism against "the target group."[65]

Participant 1: The torching of houses and shops was a way of revenging for the killings. It is aimed at inflicting pain and causing damage or loss to the target individuals or group of people.

Participant 2: The intent of violence is to kill, raid, torch houses, loot, [do] damage to property, all in the name of expressing bitterness and anger toward the target group.

Participant 3: Our people were killed on the roads and as a way of avenging people engaged in violence. The torching of houses was in response to damage to our property.

A member of this same focus group describes the level of stress that characterized the immediate postelectoral period, which he said, "can

---

[64] Interview-Mauche SS-Nakuru County, October 8, 2012 (3).
[65] Focus group with youth-Mauche SS-Nakuru County, October 4, 2012. Answers were in reply to the following question: "After the election results were announced and the violence started to break out in certain places across the country, how did the youth here in Mauche respond?"

be ranked into various levels. The reaction stage is characterized by revenge."[66] In this case, "stress" is a way of talking about the levels of fear, insecurity and vulnerability that many Kalenjin experienced in the moments after the electoral results. Many Kalenjin and other ODM supporters had joined in the call for "mass action" to protest the results. These protests were not necessarily violent, but once protests began, many participants confronted state security forces. Participants soon realized that they were playing on an uneven playing field where Kikuyus, with the backing of the police and the incumbent-Kikuyu president, had far greater power.[67] The realization that they lacked the security advantage prompted residents to react defensively: they had to protect themselves because they could not rely on the state. When the police began shooting into crowds and killing protestors, Kalenjins retaliated against the police and Kikuyus. One Mauche respondent explains how, in his estimation, police bias provoked violence:

The moment that Kibaki was declared the winner, people were urged to go for mass action, which was meant to be peaceful. But the police came and disrupted the processions by pelting teargas canisters at the procession and so people resorted to retaliatory attacks at the police as well as those who had voted for Kibaki. This made the situation turn into clashes countrywide.[68]

Another Mauche respondent explains how police action shaped the motive and use of violence among Kalenjin youth:

The youths got more agitated because some of them were arrested when found around the trading center. They were taken to Likia police station where a few were killed. The police were seen to be protecting the Kikuyu. This made the youths block the road so that their people could be released and also to ensure that the police didn't have easy access into the Kikuyu land.[69]

Violence reached this third state of "intimate" or localized fighting when both sides believed they were fighting as matter of self- or collective-defense and by extension, revenge. Each side reacted to the threat posed by the rival group and, hence, claimed to be acting defensively.

---

[66] Focus group with youths-Mauche SS-Nakuru County, October 10, 2012.
[67] Kikuyu provide the opposite account: they think many police were biased toward Kalenjin.
[68] Interview-Mauche SS-Nakuru County, October 8, 2012 (2).
[69] Interview-Mauche SS-Nakuru County, October 4, 2012 (4).

But as casualties mounted, the line between defense and revenge blurred. Many Kikuyus in Likia believe that they were pulled involuntarily into the clashes. They had no choice but to defend the border of their community and to protect their lives and properties. Kalenjin residents in Mauche however, emphasize the importance of violence as a tool for retaliation. It was not only a mechanism of defense but also a method of inflicting pain and "expressing bitterness."

Scale Shift: "Importing Revenge" – Stage 4

The fourth and final stage of violence that I document in this chapter is what I refer to as "scale shift." Unlike the third stage, engagement between groups is not local or intimate. It is not confined to neighbors attacking or killing their neighbors. This stage relies less on "ordinary citizens" and instead on well-trained and well-financed vigilante groups, criminal gangs, paramilitary groups, or other violent organizations. In the case of Kenya's 2007–2008 election violence, political and business elites organized and financed the operations of such groups, for example, by providing vehicles to transport fighters. Importantly, while political leaders and individual recruits have their own motives for organizing or participating in this form of organized violence, organizers frame the logic of violence as collective revenge.

The wave of collective and "imported" revenge that I focus on here is a series of attacks that escalated in the middle of January 2008, around three weeks after the announcement of the electoral results on December 30, 2007. The Commission of Inquiry on Post-Election Violence (CIPEV report) describes these types of orchestrated revenge attacks as follows:

These were systematic attacks on Kenyans based on their ethnicity and their political leanings. Attackers organized along ethnic lines, assembled considerable logistical means and traveled long distances to burn houses, maim, kill and sexually assault their occupants because these were of particular ethnic groups and political persuasion. Guilty by association was the guiding force behind deadly "revenge" attacks, with victims being identified not for what they did but for their ethnic association to other perpetrators.[70]

---

[70] CIPEV Report (Republic of Kenya 2008: viii).

I narrow in on the violence that escalated in late January in two communities in Naivasha constituency (Nakuru County). The first is Oljorai, a settlement scheme and farming community located about 30 km north of Naivasha town off the Nakuru-Naivasha highway. In Oljorai, like much of rural Naivasha, residents farm and graze animals on contested land (see Chapter 3 for more details of the Oljorai scheme). Hell's Gate is an ethnically mixed area comprised composed primarily of Kikuyu and Luo who work in one of Naivasha's many commercial flower farms. Kikuyu residents are in the majority, and own many of towns rentals and plots of land, while Kikuyus portray Luos as "outsiders."

Residents in Naivasha recall two waves of violence. The first wave was characterized by stages 2 and 3 that I have already documented. Several testimonies mention a public fight between a Kikuyu boss and Kalenjin employee, others point to the murder of a Kalenjin boy. For others, violence escalated after Kikuyus "began celebrating and [Kalenjin individuals] got angry with them, and armed we advanced to challenge them."[71]

Yet the most significant damage to property and loss of life occurred in mid-January when "outsiders" came "to seek revenge for their tribesmen in other parts of Kenya."[72] Another respondent describes the area as relatively peaceful "until the media showed violence to have mushroomed in many other regions countrywide." These images he suggests, fueled the "immigrant's incitements" who "questioned [residents] right to a peaceful stay here in Oljorai."[73]

In Hell's Gate, respondents describe a similar process of violence, emphasizing that the area was relatively calm until Kikuyus entered Naivasha as internally displaced persons (IDPs). Stories spread quickly among the Kikuyu community about the atrocities that their co-ethnics had endured at the hands of ODM supporters (Luos, Luhyas, and Kalenjins). A respondent explains this stage of the electoral violence, emphasizing that outsiders instigated the violence:

In Naivasha, the violence was not started by the residents of Naivasha. It was started by those who had been evicted from other areas and were seeking

---

[71] Interview-Oljorai–Nakuru County, November 1, 2012 (3).
[72] Focus group with youths-Oljorai-Nakuru County, September 11, 2012.
[73] Interview-Oljorai-Nakuru County, November 1, 2012 (3).

refuge in this area. They then decided to seek revenge on the tribes that had evicted them.[74]

Another resident of Hell's Gate recalls the unique timing of the violence, emphasizing that area residents did not provoke the violence:

Those who came here were bitter that we [Kikuyu] were living with the same people that fought them back in Eldoret, Kapsabet, Kisumu and other places. So the people who fought were not the residents in Naivasha but those who came in later. Before that Naivasha was very calm and peaceful and there were no plans to start any chaos.[75]

In many interviews, respondents highlight the role of "outsiders" in shaping the violence.[76] As one respondent in Oljorai explains, "Here ... clashes erupted because the Kikuyu wanted to avenge the deaths of their brothers and sisters *elsewhere*."[77] Similarly, another respondent attributes the violence to outsiders, to "people not known to the locals, such as Mungiki."[78] He continues, "these people torched houses and pastures beginning from the wider stretch of the Oljorai and advancing to Kong'asis trading center ... There were rumors about armed strangers (Mungiki) who came via Kiptangwanyi, which reveals their intention and preparedness for attack."

Yet while respondents emphasize that violence here was reactionary – collective revenge for the deaths of co-ethnics in other parts of the county – there is evidence that elites had planned for revenge or defense attacks well before the December elections.[79] Kikuyu IDPs – and the violence they endured – provided the popular support that Kikuyu politicians needed to mobilize large-scale violence.[80]

An important component of this preelectoral organizing was the use of Mungiki, a vigilante group with Kikuyu affiliations.[81] Mungiki is

---

[74] Focus group with youths-Hell's Gate-Nakuru County, October 20, 2012.
[75] Ibid.   [76] Ibid.
[77] Focus group with youths-Oljorai-Nakuru County, September 11, 2012
[78] Interview-Oljorai-Nakuru County, November 1, 2012 (3). Kiptangwanyi is a land-buying company bordering Oljorai and is occupied primarily by Kikuyu.
[79] CIPEV Report (Republic of Kenya 2008: 102–103). The report cites Kenya's National Intelligence Services (NSIS) reports, which document that Mungiki leaders engaged in a recruitment drive aimed at 300 new members in the Nakuru region before the December 27, 2007, elections.
[80] KNCHR Report 2008: 76
[81] Mungiki is much more than a gang and is better described as a politico-religious grassroots movement. It gained its power as a youth movement in opposition to Moi's KANU regime. They self-identify as the Kikuyu poor

well known for hiring itself out to politicians during local and national elections. A Kikuyu youth in Likia explains how each of the main ethnic communities have their own youth group: "The Kikuyu have Mungiki, the Kisii have the *Chinkororo*, the Kalenjin have their warrior groups."[82] He emphasizes that these groups form primarily as ways of "defending their communities with the blessings from the elders," adding, "with time, their aim and activities change under the influence of politicians who use them to gain political power."[83] An elder Turkana man comments on the role of Mungiki: "the post-election started when we heard that there were cars being burnt in Kisumu. Then the Kikuyu in Naivasha said that they needed to avenge for what was done to their brothers in Kisumu. So *Mungiki* from other areas came here in Naivasha."[84] The use of Mungiki is likely one reason why Kikuyu elites were able to mobilize such large-scale retaliatory attacks against ODM supporters (i.e. Kalenjins, Luos, and Luhyas) with such efficiency and speed. A respondent from Oljorai comments on the elite-orchestrated nature of political violence in the region.

There are those politicians that incite people and these are the big politicians, not amateurs. And the tactic they use is transporting people from one place to another, promising that if elected they will chase a particular community – "black spots" – from their land, a land they consider ancestral land.[85]

The comments illustrate two key features of this fourth stage of the violence. First, the respondent emphasizes that the leaders who organize violence are "big politicians, not amateurs," underlining the importance of having powerful patrons – in addition to local leaders – who have the status and capacity to organize violence. Second, he hints at how leaders were able to recruit pre-formed "outside" groups that had already been trained, financed, and armed. In cases where politicians hired Mungiki members, attackers had their own ideological, material, or political motives for violence that required little independent ideological mobilization. A participant in a youth group from

and children of Mau Mau who have suffered due to historical injustices created by Jomo Kenyatta, who never distributed land to the freedom fighters (see Rasmussen 2010).

[82] Interview-Likia LBC-Nakuru County, September 13, 2012 (3).
[83] Ibid. For more on other violent vigilante groups in Kenya, see Anderson (2002).
[84] Interview-Oljorai-Nakuru County, October 13, 2012 (11).
[85] Interview-Oljorai-Nakuru County, September 11, 2012 (2).

Oljorai explains this fourth stage of violence, emphasizing the role of Mungiki:

People started fighting in this area as a result of Kikuyus wanting revenge for their tribesmen who had been killed in other regions of the country after the votes were allegedly said to be rigged. They sent the Mungiki to come and reinforce the mission in Naivasha and its environs and so we had to respond and defend ourselves and property. And in the end, there was a clash.[86]

The respondent's comments are illustrative in two ways. First, they highlight the perception that these rounds of attacks were not from their Kikuyu neighbors, but rather from "foreign" Kikuyus, and specifically, Mungiki.[87] These "foreign" fighters were well organized, and openly declared their primary objective: to revenge the deaths of their co-ethnics. Second, the respondent highlights how these attacks fueled counterattacks from ODM supports. Youth from Oljorai then mobilized to defend the welfare of the community.

This fourth stage in the process of violence is distinct from earlier stages in a number of important ways. First, it is well organized, financed and planned by political and business elites well in advance of the trigger event. While earlier stages of violence may also be premediated, this stage is distinct in its scale – a shift from more local confrontations at the neighborhood or village level to more systematic and intentional series of attacks against a target group. Second, this stage relies on paid or hired fighters. It's likely Kikuyu leaders relied heavily on the organization, networks, and expertise of Mungiki. Third, at this stage of violence, local-level factors become less important in explaining the escalation of violence. Instead, more regional or national-level narratives guide political action on the ground. Fourth, organizers tend to frame this stage of violence as being about both revenge (i.e. avenging for the deaths of Kikuyu in Kisumu), and defending "the community" against further attacks. Fifth, distinct incentives guide this stage of violence. For hired recruits, material incentives may play a larger role than they do for other "ordinary citizens." Equally,

---

[86] Focus group with youths-Oljorai-Nakuru County, September 11, 2012.
[87] When violence escalates and "comes out of nowhere" ODM-aligned respondents across Kenya often point to the use of Mungiki. There is strong evidence from the CIPEV report and KNCHR (2008) that suggests the use of Mungiki in Naivasha town and along the Nakuru-Naivasha highway. It is therefore quite plausible that Mungiki was deployed to fight Kalenjin residents in Oljorai.

for members of an armed group, concerns about rank and status within the organization (e.g. Mungiki) may also motivate participation in violence. Yet while hired recruits may constitute the majority of participants at this stage, residents on the ground also get pulled in the fighting. As one respondent in Hell's Gate remarks:

The 2007–2008 postelection violence was a tough one. I am a Kikuyu and live among the Kikuyu but still I had to leave my home. What I hated most is that young men were forced to take weapons and kill the other tribes like Luo. And if you refused, you'd be killed. This was a tough experience for some of us who cannot dare kill a soul, so I had to flee with my family"[88]

The respondent's comments serve as a reminder that in addition to the more strategic and material incentives of elites and members of armed groups, fear and coercion played an important role as well, with citizens having to decide between joining the fight or fleeing for their lives.

Conclusion

This chapter has documented the different logics and stages that guided the process of violent mobilization during Kenya's 2007–2008 electoral crisis. At each stage, certain logics of violence played a greater role in shaping participation in violence. At the first stage, citizens acted out of *fear* of their imminent eviction (logic of defense). At the second, desires to change the allocation of land rights (logic of opportunity) shaped participation, while at the third stage, anger, fear and desires to "right wrongs" (logic of revenge) motived action. And at the fourth stage – "scale shift" – people participated in the violence to secure private benefits (e.g. salary or safety) and to take revenge. While all four logics interacted at each point of escalation, particular motives prevailed as the violence unfolded.

One of the main arguments of the chapter is that political elites can more easily mobilize violence where there are already contentious land narratives in place, i.e. those where questions of land access, distribution, legitimacy, and justice are central themes. The first stage of violence is therefore about the mobilization of existing land narratives. In illustrating this first stage, I drew on evidence from Likia and

---

[88] Interview-Hell's Gate-Nakuru County, October 13, 2012 (1).

Mauche to demonstrate how narratives of injustice and insecurity affect different logics of violence. Specifically, I've aimed to show how these land narratives shaped logics of violence based on defense and opportunity.

The second stage of violence helps to explain the shift from the mobilization of beliefs (narratives) to violent collective action. I argue that for a set of ideas to legitimize or motivate violence, there needs to be a particular event that "triggers" violence into motion (stage 2). The main trigger event that I describe here is the official announcement of the vote tallies that declared Mwai Kibaki the president-elect. I also emphasize how local-level events such as a bar fight or a personal feud can polarize a community (or communities), pulling them into the larger national drama.

After the trigger event (stage 2), violence escalates to stage 3, which I have described as "local dynamics." The primary logics are about community defense and revenge. As deaths and damage mount, the line between revenge and defense is easily blurred. Kikuyus used violence to protect members of their community and territorial borders. Kalenjins in Mauche however, conceive of defensive and retaliatory violence in multiple ways: as *defense* against a "Kikuyu threat" or the fear that Kikuyu would displace them; *revenge* for Kikuyu crimes in the past and the present (e.g. electoral rigging); revenge for mounting deaths of Kalenjin members as the electoral crisis unfolded and defense against the police, whom they perceived as allied with the Kikuyu and the PNU-run state.

In the fourth stage of violence, electoral violence reaches the stage in which the death toll and displacement are often the greatest. The main objective is to avenge the deaths of co-ethnics who have been killed or displaced in other regions of the country. This stage is particularly deadly because revenge attacks are well organized and well financed and the target is any citizen associated with the ethnic group who has perpetrated the crime.

In sum, this chapter evaluates the different logics that drive the process and organization of electoral violence. My central claim is that contentious land narratives provide the set of frames that enable political organizers to shape different logics of violence. In direct and indirect ways, these narratives shape the motives for participation at each stage of violent escalation. The existence of these narratives is thus a necessary but not sufficient condition for the escalation of violence. In the next chapter, I draw on comparisons between counties in the Rift Valley and Coast regions to explore why contentious land narratives correlate with electoral violence in the Rift Valley, but less so in the Coast.

7 | A Puzzle of Nonescalation? Contentious Land Narratives and Stability on Kenya's Coast

Why do contentious land narratives foment electoral violence in one context but not another? In the preceding chapters, I argue that contentious narratives around land can shape the dynamics of political violence, affecting how elites organize violence and why ordinary people participate. Under certain conditions, political elites can use land narratives to convince supporters that their access and rights to land hinge on electoral outcomes. In such scenarios, individuals may have a motive to engage in violence, either to preempt their eviction by rivals or to ensure the victory of a leader who will protect their land security.

While the salience of contentious land narratives between groups can help explain electoral violence, there are also contexts where strong contentious land narratives between groups do not map onto the sites of electoral violence. In this chapter, I analyze why land narratives might foment violence in one region but not another. I focus my analysis on two counties in Kenya's Coast region where contentious land narratives between insiders and outsiders are a feature of political life yet electoral violence is rare. I contrast these cases with counties in the Rift Valley where seemingly similar land narratives correlate with election violence. In this chapter, I build on recent studies that focus on the factors that restrain or moderate the escalation of violence (Straus 2012).

One of the main arguments I make in this book is that under certain circumstances, where elites have incentives to organize violence and act as "strong land patrons," they can use land narratives as a mobilizing tool; tapping into collective fears of losing land or desires to reclaim land. In these cases, narratives work by establishing a logic for violence; by making violence not only thinkable, but a necessary means of defending or providing for one's family and community.

212

In this chapter, however, I argue that land narratives in much of the Coast region work differently than they do in the Rift Valley. While salient and contentious land narratives exist among many communities along the Coast, they rarely frame elections as moments of land loss or gain, and hence, land narratives along the Coast rarely establish a logic of violence.

I specify two factors that help account for this regional variation. First, I argue that because most coast leaders tend to act as weak land patrons (see Chapter 3), they rarely have the moral or political authority to use land narratives as a mechanism to organize violence. While local leaders do contribute to contentious or divisive narratives, most residents doubt their capacity and willingness to follow through on promises to defend or promote land claims. As a result, citizens are far less likely to take on the high costs of participation in violence. Second, I argue that because "ethnic outsiders" are a much smaller proportion of the population compared to part of the Rift Valley, elections do not signal the same level of threat to land or political power.

Comparing Election Violence in the Rift Valley and Coast Region

Kenya's 2007–2008 postelection violence left approximately 1,500 people dead and 600,000 people displaced (Mwiandi 2008). The majority of these deaths occurred in only seven of the country's forty-seven counties, with the highest incidence of violence occurring in Nakuru and Uasin Gishu counties.[1] By contrast, in the coastal counties of Kwale and Kilifi, there was tension, isolated cases of looting, and destruction of property, but not significant violence. This is not to diminish the election violence that occurred in parts of the Coast region. Notably, the CIPEV Report described wide-scale destruction of property across Mombasa and in surrounding suburbs (Republic of Kenya 2008). There were hundreds of reported injuries and between twenty-five and thirty-two people were killed. Even in Kwale County, there was damage to shops and properties. Yet for the most part, violence was contained to Mombasa, an urban and highly cosmopolitan city that is in many ways distinct from the rest of the Coast region. My main focus is on the more rural counties of Kilifi and

---

[1] The reported death ranges were as follows: Kisumu (81–154); Nairobi (125–209); Nakuru (263–431); Uasin Gishu (206–230).

Table 7.1 *County-level variation in intensity of election violence*

When you recall the time following the elections, how would you describe events here?

Counties	Nakuru	Uasin Gishu	Kilifi	Kwale
Calm	22.8%	22.8%	83.6%	66%
Tension only	25.8%	24.7%	15.5%	27.8%
Isolated violence	27.3%	16%	0%	5.6%
Violence "everywhere"	23.4%	36.4%	0.9%	0.6%

Total Observations. 747

Kwale, located just north and south of Mombasa (see Figure 2.4). Table 7.1 shows variation in exposure to election violence across counties, which relies on a survey question that asks respondents to describe the level of violence they experienced. The differences between the two regions are stark. In Nakuru and Uasin Gishu, 51 percent of respondents recall violence, while in Kwale and Kilifi, less than 1 percent of respondents recall violence of any kind.[2]

Overall, the Coast region has been relatively stable during each electoral period since 1992. The notable exception is the 1997 preelectoral violence in Likoni (Mombasa County), the 2012 communal clashes in Tana River County, and the 2014 attacks in Mpeketoni (Lamu County). I address these events in later sections of this chapter.

The Puzzle: Land Inequality, Land Narratives, and Mobilization

I begin with the premise that Kwale and Kilifi counties are possible spaces for violence because they share important characteristics with parts of the Rift Valley, where electoral violence has been more common and more intense. These similarities include inequality in land rights between insiders and outsiders, salient and contentious land narratives along this insider–outsider cleavage, and the use of contentious land narratives by political

[2] 191 out of 371 respondents in the Rift witnessed some form of violence, while only 9 out of 375 respondents in the coast witnessed violence. Results not weighted.

candidates to mobilize political support. While a number of factors differentiate the Coast from the Rift Valley, I highlight relevant similarities to demonstrate that while the Coast region has not experienced significant electoral violence, is it nonetheless a setting where we could reasonably expect violence to occur (Straus 2012; Mahoney & Goertz 2004).[3] I outline how each region compares along each of these three points.

First, and as I've shown in earlier chapters, land inequality is a feature of both regions. Land inequality along the Coast however is more profound. The majority of Coast residents, most of whom identify as Mijikenda, have no formal land tenure rights. According to government reports, approximately 60 percent of residents in Kilifi lack title deeds, while 76 percent lack title deeds in Kwale County (Republic of Kenya 2013b, 2013c). Without formal title or state-recognized customary rights, many residents reside as "squatters" or *de facto* tenants on the land of absentee landlords. Title deeds for the region's prime agricultural and commercial land belong to the region's elite: prominent Arab families, Indians, Swahilis, and residents from "upcountry" Kenya. While land insecurity along the Coast is more profound than the Rift Valley, many residents in both regions believe that migrants have gained stronger land rights than the regions' natives.

A second parallel between the two regions is the salience of contentious land narratives between insiders and outsiders. Along the coast, the struggle for Mijikenda residents to acquire secure land tenure rights has generated strong anti-outsider land narratives. These narratives, while in some ways unique to the Coast, echo the nativist claims of Kalenjin farmers in the Rift Valley. A common narrative theme describes a process in which outsiders – Arabs, Europeans, and Kenyans from upcountry – have "grabbed" or stolen ancestral land. A second theme emphasizes extreme land insecurity. Yet in contrast to many Rift Valley residents, Mijikenda residents fear their imminent eviction by a powerful individual, corporate entity, or the state rather than a particular ethnic community.

A third point of comparison is the use of divisive land appeals during electoral campaigns. Table 7.2 shows results from a survey question that asks respondents whether they have heard politicians

---

[3] There are numerous differences between the two regions that fall beyond the explanatory scope of this chapter. For example, certain counties within the coast have a Muslim majority whereas all counties in the Rift Valley are Christian.

Table 7.2 *Exposure to appeal: "If you kick out the other tribe, you will get their land"*

County	Proportion who have had heard appeal	Total Obs.
Nakuru	55%	209
Uasin Gishu	41%	162
Kilifi	39%	215
Kwale	51%	162

or party activists issue statements that encourage followers to "kick out the other tribe" in exchange for land.[4] The results suggest that candidates in both regions rely on polarizing land appeals that encourage or condone violence. In the next chapter, I show how exposure to such appeals – alongside other variables – helps to explain the communities and individuals most likely to experience violence.

Alternative Explanations: Varied Histories of Violence

Across all four counties, there is land inequality between groups, although inequalities are more extreme along the Coast. Equally, there are salient and contentious land narratives across each region. Yet people are more likely to agree with anti-outsider land narratives in Rift Valley counties. And while the varied belief in particular land narratives might account for variation in violence, results from my survey indicate that respondents across all four counties hear political candidates make similar types of appeals. Broadly speaking then, these regions share important similarities, yet there are both subtle and striking differences as well. Most importantly, perhaps, is the varied history of past election violence between the two regions. As I've explained, the Rift Valley region has witnessed far more election-related violence compared to the Coast. One possible implication, then, is that because the Rift Valley has experienced more violence in the past, it is also more vulnerable to election violence. On this point, existing research provides evidence of this effect, suggesting that exposure to political violence can

---

[4] See Chapter 8 for further details and discussion on this measure.

increase ethnic antipathies (Hadzic et al. 2017; Lupu & Peisakhin 2017), reduce political trust (e.g. de Juan & Pierskalla 2016; Linke 2013), and undermine preferences for peace (e.g. Grossman et al. 2015).

Indeed, it's possible that election violence is more feasible across parts of the Rift Valley due to its history of violence. While I cannot rule out this argument, three points are worth noting. First, while several studies provide evidence for the idea that "violence begets violence," numerous other studies point to the opposite effect: that exposure to violence generates prosocial outcomes. People who have experienced political violence may display greater levels of social capital and altruism (Hartman & Morse 2018; Bauer et al. 2014; Voors et al. 2012), are more likely to participate in politics (e.g. Bateson 2012; Blattman 2009), and have stronger preferences for peace (e.g. Tellez 2019; Horowitz and Klaus 2018). These studies challenge the conventional wisdom that spaces of violence are necessarily more prone to future violence.

Second, and importantly, while violence in the Rift Valley has been broader in scale and scope compared to the Coast, parts of the Coast region have experienced notable instances of election violence. The most significant election violence occurred in Likoni Ward (Mombasa County) during the 1997 preelection period. KANU elites, fearing the loss of parliamentary seats, organized vigilante groups to attack so-called migrants (i.e. Kikuyu, Meru), resulting in the deaths of over 100 people, and the displacement of approximately 100,000 people (Boone 2011).[5] Specifically, prominent KANU leaders recruited, organized, and trained a vigilante group known as Kaya Bombo – comprised primarily of youth from Kwale District – to evict residents from "upcountry" (Anderson 2002). Violence escalated in August 1997 when Kaya Bombo raided a police station in Likoni, stealing weapons and killing police officers. Despite KANU involvement in organizing the raid, the government responded with extreme repression across Likoni and many towns in nearby Kwale – killing or imprisoning anyone suspected of being part of Kaya Bombo, destroying homes, and raping women (see Goldsmith 2011; HRW 2002b). The violence in Likoni is not the only prior episode of election-related violence, but is certainly the

---

[5] KANU lost parliamentary seats in the region in 1992, and hence were likely concerned about losing seats again in the 1997 electionerso.

most significant. Hence, while violence was relatively isolated to Likoni and the bordering villages in Kwale County, the effects of the violence endure. Notably, there remains significant distrust in the government and police, and a fear that anti-outsider violence during elections is always possible.

Third, while it may be true that repeated episodes of election violence make a region more vulnerable to violence, it's important to identify why the Rift Valley was more vulnerable to election violence in the first place – beginning with multiparty elections in 1992. I would argue that election violence in 1991–1992 was more likely in the Rift Valley for the same reasons that make it more vulnerable to violence today. Specifically, in 1992, just as in 2007, we can observe moderate land inequality, contentious land narratives that delineate between "insiders" and "outsiders," political incentives to use violence to ensure victory in a politically divided, but vote-dense region, and a tradition of political leaders acting as strong land patrons. In sum, I make the case that while histories of violence differ between the two regions, there are also important similarities. These similarities – intergroup land inequality, contentious land narratives, and political appeals around land – make the relative absence of election violence in Kwale and Kilifi puzzling.

Argument

One of the main arguments in this book is that in certain contexts, political leaders can use contentious land narratives to mobilize violent forms of political action. These land narratives provide a particularly useful organizing mechanism when supporters believe that their land rights hinge on the outcome of elections. In such scenarios, land narratives work when they help establish two main logics of violence. The first is based on the logic of preemption and defense – "evict them before they can evict us" – and emphasizes impending threats to land rights from political or ethnic rivals. This narrative or campaign appeal acquires particular resonance when it's based on a group's memories of past eviction and the rumors that circulate during elections. The second is based on the logic of opportunity: the belief that elections present a narrow window to strengthen the land rights of group members. Violence becomes a strategy for physically seizing land during the electoral process or ensuring the victory of one's leader at all costs

(Höglund 2009). In each scenario, land narratives provide a way of coordinating followers' beliefs about how electoral outcomes will alter land rights.

Yet even when land narratives are salient and divisive, they do not necessarily provide the sufficient conditions for electoral violence. While land narratives in Kwale and Kilifi are often contentious, many leaders are limited in their ability to use these narratives as a tool to organize violence, and specifically, to signal the risks or opportunities linked to electoral outcomes.

Two factors help explain the weaker link between land and elections along the Coast. The first is the strength of the local political patron (e.g. the Member of Parliament). Elections only present opportunities to strengthen land rights when political patrons have the capacity to allocate land or protect the land security of supporters. The second factor is the political power of "outsiders" relative to the "host" community. While this delineation is rarely drawn in such stark terms, elections are more likely to invoke a sense of threat when outsiders can compete politically with insiders.

Figure 7.1 illustrates how patronage strength and group size interact to shape perceptions of threat and opportunity. The interaction of perception and opportunity, in turn, help explain varying motives for participation in election violence. Ordinary actors only have a motive to participate in violence when they believe that elections present both a threat to their land security and an opportunity to secure land.

This scenario captures much of the Rift Valley in 2007.[6] By contrast, the lower right quadrant captures the dynamics of the Coast region in 2007: most citizens did not associate elections with threats to their land or with opportunities to strengthen rights. Hence, there were few motives for participating in violence. Alternatively, when citizens view elections as opportunities to gain but do not perceive a salient threat, the motivation to engage in violence is weak (upper right quadrant). That is, the opportunity to gain, absent of any perception of threat, is rarely a strong enough incentive for individuals to run the high risk of participating in violence. Violence is possible, but the barriers to collective action are much higher.

---

[6] This does not imply that every resident has a motive to fight.

	STRONG LAND PATRON	WEAK LAND PATRON
MIGRANTS: LARGE MINORITY/ SMALL MAJORITY	Threat & Opportunity: *Strong motive for violence* (Rift Valley: 2007–'08)	Threat; No Opportunity *Weak motive for violence*
MIGRANTS: SMALL MINORITY	Opportunity; No Threat: *No motive for violence*	No Threat; No Opportunity *No motive for violence* (Coast Region: 2007–'08)

Figure 7.1 Land patronage, group size, and potential for violence.

Strength of the Political Patron

A growing literature examines the way that patronage politics shapes the possibilities for electoral violence (Soderberg Kovacs & Bjarnesen 2018), particularly in countries with majoritarian electoral institutions (Fjelde & Höglund 2016a). One argument is that in contexts of competitive elections where patronage politics is more entrenched, the likelihood of electoral violence is greater (Staniland 2014). Taylor et al. (2017) argue that political elites and supporters are more willing to rely on violence where there is a reliable incumbent whose "established, personalistic patronage is already in place" (2017: 401). Applying this argument to Kenya's 2007–2008 postelection violence, the authors suggest that because Mwai Kibaki had developed a strong patronage relationship with his clients, he was confident enough in the loyalty of his supporters and security apparatus to use violence. Likewise, his supporters were more willing to accept the costs associated with election violence.

Patronage politics refers to relationships of exchange where the patron uses state or private resources to build a network of loyal political followers, providing protection, services, jobs, or other goods in exchange for political support (Van de Walle 2007: 51). In countries such as Kenya, where state actors leverage considerable control over the allocation of land, land can provide a powerful source of patronage, particularly in the face of declining state revenues (Boone 2014; Kanyinga 2000). Leaders reward loyal followers with land or land rights, and revoke and reallocate land rights to coerce or punish political opponents (Boone 2011). Where patronage politics is the defining feature of distributive politics, clients are more likely to believe that their ability to access land rights, employment, and security requires that their patron is in power, thus heightening the perceived stakes of elections.

Patronage politics also provides a mechanism of authority and control. Where patronage networks are strong, leaders are better able to organize and recruit potential fighters. The ability to control clients can work through trust and reciprocity (Kitschelt & Wilkinson 2007) or through coercion and punishment (Reno 2007). The capacity for political leaders to mobilize followers during elections relies in part on their ability to leverage patronage networks. The more resources at their disposal – and the more entrenched these networks – the more power leaders have to organize followers.

Citizens are more likely to participate in violence when they believe that the victory of their candidate will strengthen their land security or land holdings. Yet for individuals to risk the high costs of participation in violence, they must also believe that their leader has the capacity and political will to follow through on land-related promises.

Rift Valley: Strong Land Patronage

Leaders can signal their commitment to implement land promises through tradition and precedent. In the Rift Valley, the political patron is well institutionalized; a figure who has the political and financial power to "feed" and protect his community. This leadership image perpetuates the expectation that incoming politicians will continue to fulfill patron–client obligations. While leaders may fall short of their promises, the tradition of patronage bolsters the credibility of campaign appeals. Patronage in this sense is not only about votes in exchange for money or gifts, but about the patron's ability to distribute land rights to loyal followers and protect his community from threats such as eviction and attacks on land or livestock.

Since the reintroduction of multiparty politics in 1992, there are several examples of powerful and high-profile political leaders from the Rift Valley who issue divisive and inflammatory appeals. These appeals resonate with political supporters in part because the leaders who issued such statements tend to be strong political patrons. These leaders have often been high-ranking and inner-circle members of the governing party, with an established recording of lobbying for the land rights of their community.

The most notorious of these leaders includes William Ole Ntimama, a vocal advocate for Maasai land rights and one of Kenya's longest serving politicians. His political career began with his position as Division Officer (DO) with the colonial administration. He went on to become a powerful member of the KANU regime and served as MP for Narok North, in the Southern Rift Valley, for fifteen years. He also owned several parcels of land in Narok district, which measured about 600 acres (Kemei 2016). He is most famous for his anti-outsider remarks in the 1990s, where he warned Kikuyu and other "immigrant" communities to "lie low like antelopes or face the consequences."[7] He clarified later that he meant Kikuyu should "lie low to avoid being preyed by the leopard."[8] In other words, Kikuyus should vote for KANU or avoid the polls, lest they risk punishment from hosts (i.e. Maasai). At a rally in 1992, Ntimama urged people who had settled in the constituency not to provoke the Maasai "or else they would have themselves to blame for whatever happens."[9] In a 1993 speech to parliament, he remarked: "Mr. Deputy Speaker ... I am saying this one very clearly: if people want us to live together, they must not think that we are 'second-class' in this country ... The British suppressed us, and we cannot have the Kikuyu suppressing us again!"[10] These

---

[7] *Weekly Review* 1 March 1999. Ntimama accused Kikuyus of being land grabbers and agitators. He later clarified in the Akiwumi Report (Republic of Kenya 1999) that he meant that Kikuyu should "lie low to avoid being preyed by the leopard." In other words, Kikuyus should vote for KANU or risk retribution.

[8] This clarification is recorded in the Akiwumi Report (Republic of Kenya 1999).

[9] Comments made by Ntimama in the *Sunday Standard*, November 15, 1992 (Republic of Kenya 1999: 167).

[10] MP William Ole Ntimama, speech to Parliament, October 19, 1993. Proceeds accessible through the Kenya National Assembly Official Record (Hansard), pp. 1957–1958.

comments are notable in part, because they were followed by violence against Kikuyus across Narok district and the larger Southern Rift Valley (see Boone 2011).

I highlight Ntimama's remarks because they illustrate the way that a powerful political patron with strong connections to national government can draw on existing land narratives to organize and encourage violence (Matter 2010). While politicians in many regions rely on nativist and anti-outsider political appeals, Ntimama represents a particular land patron prototype in my theory of election violence. His statements are powerful in large part because he has positioned himself as a powerful and credible land patron: supporters trust that he has the political power and will to follow through on land-based appeals. As one resident remarked in an interview with a Kenyan newspaper, "Ntimama meant every word. When he said something, the Maa took it like a law and went ahead to accomplish what he said."[11] And while Ntimama is perhaps the clearest example, there are numerous other examples of political elites whose proximity to national power has enabled them to accumulate land and status. In turn, they have had greater power to exploit land narratives in order to mobilize violence.[12]

Coast Region: Weak Land Patronage

In contrast to the types of patrons we find in the Rift Valley, I suggest that political patrons in much of the Coast region – including chiefs, district officers, and parliamentarians – are historically much weaker. With a few notable exceptions, most leaders from the Coast have not had the same ability to use land as a source of political patronage because they lack the land wealth of many Rift Valley politicians. Equally, many lack the close connections to executive power that is often necessary for acquiring land and controlling land rights. Without political status or wealth in land, coastal politicians have tended to act

---

[11] *Kenya News Agency*, "The Life and Times of the Late William Ole Ntimama." September 5, 2016.

[12] Other examples of strong land patrons who have organized violence include Moses Cheboi (current MP of Bahati North), David Kiptanui Koros (incumbent MP for Eldoret South in 2007), and William Ruto (Current Deputy President of Kenya and former MP of Eldoret North), and Raila Odinga (former Prime Minister of Kenya, leading opposition presidential candidate in 2007, 2013, and 2017, and MP of Langata, 1992–2013).

as brokers to both national-level political elites and regional business elites. Many locals have come to view their leaders as brokers to outsiders rather than their own patrons. A resident from Kilifi provides an example of how this broker-style leadership limits possibilities for reform:

> When we elect our leaders, rich people target them. They don't want leaders who represent the issues of the common man. If a politician or MP is deemed to do so, then the rich people call him and tell him to stop discussing the issues of the poor because the poor will realize they are being denied their rights and start asking questions. They bribe these politicians too.[13]

A long tradition of weak or constrained leaders means that many residents do not believe that their leaders have the capacity or autonomy to follow through on campaign commitments to protect land rights. By extension, they have few incentives to run the high costs of participation in violence. Several factors explain these weak patron–client ties. First, while Mijikenda are the majority across many Coast counties they constitute only 5 percent of the national population (2009 Kenya census in Kenya National Bureau of Statistics 2010).[14] Hence, Mijikenda have not played a strategic or consistent role in any national-level party alliances. National politicians have therefore had few incentives to empower Mijikenda politicians. More so, political leaders have had few incentives to distribute state- or privately owned coastal land to develop a grassroots patronage base. Instead, these politicians have used coastal land to enrich themselves and reward close allies, failing to build the political coalitions that they have developed in more politically strategic regions (Kanyinga 2000).

Second, many Mijikenda leaders have far smaller landholdings compared to political leaders from "upcountry." Individuals with significant landholdings at the Coast region are rarely local elected officials, but instead, members of an entrenched and "nonindigenous" landed elite.[15] This wealthy minority group controls much of the local economy, including import–export businesses, land and real

---

[13] Interview-Kijipwa-Kilifi-Rift Valley, November 20, 2012.

[14] The logic of Kenyan party politics is that larger ethnic voting blocs led by Kikuyu (GEMA), Kalenjin (KAMATUSA), and Luo determine presidential outcomes

[15] Throughout most of the twentieth century, the British followed by Germans and Italians comprised the most significant presence of foreign landowners and investors. Since the early 2000s, nationals from China, India, and the Arab Peninsula are the most active players in Kenya's land market on the coast.

estate-development (centered around the tourism industry), large-scale commercial farming (sugar, sisal, cashews, sugar), and mining (titanium, oil, salt). In the last several decades, the tourist industry has played a particularly important role in reshaping the strategic importance of the Coast region. Kanyinga (1998) writes that when the Kilifi coastline was identified as having "high potential for tourism," national elites were able to act through local elites to acquire and exploit coastal lands (Kanyinga 1998: 88). The demand for beachfront land among KANU elite was so great that the "local elites tended to be overshadowed by the national elites" (Kanyinga 1998; 87). As a result, many coast politicians and local leaders lack the power to act as landlords who can protect, allocate, and remove land rights. The powerful landlords are instead prominent landed elite and business elite who tend to stay away from formal politics. Coast politicians have become brokers to a small and powerful class of business elites and upcountry politicians, diminishing their capacity to act as reliable patrons to their land-poor electorate.

A long tradition of weak or constrained leaders means that many residents do not trust that their leaders have the capacity or autonomy to follow through on campaign commitments to protect their land rights. A group of youth in Kwale remark, "The government has always marginalized the coast people. What the government does upcountry is not what it does here. Our counterparts living upcountry all have title deeds, even the poorest."[16] The comments illustrate the perception that Rift Valley politicians provide land rights while coastal leaders have failed to protect their constituents.

Broker-style leadership across the Coast region means that many residents do not think their leaders have the power and agency to promote or protect local land claims. As one respondent explains, "MPs have no power to solve this [land] issue, otherwise they would have done so."[17] A group of Kilifi elders remark, "Even if I elect a good MP they will be influenced at the highest level with money, so they won't take care of my interests."[18] Citizens emphasize that their leaders have far less autonomy or power than their upcountry counterparts. Politicians prove unable or unwilling to alter the status quo distribution

[16] Focus group with youths-Msambweni-Kwale County, November 18, 2012.
[17] Interview-Kijipwa SS-Kilifi County, November 21, 2012 (6).
[18] Focus group with elders-Kijipwa SS-Kilifi County, November 28, 2012.

of land rights. In an interview with a farmer in Kilifi, he explains why coastal leaders, much like the people, find themselves marginalized in national-level politics:

If we look at these people who have been grabbing this land, they don't come from the coast ... Even our people down here, the Giriama, have no say. Once they leave they go to the government. They have got no say! They can do nothing. The party leaders are all from that place [upcountry Kenya]. So they [coast MPs] just sneak into these parties. So if you just sneak in, or they let you in, you have no say. You can't do anything.[19]

The respondents' comments illustrate the belief that local politicians lack the power to protect or strengthen the rights of local people because they have no real power themselves. Participants in a youth focus group describe the constraints on their leaders in even starker terms: "As per history, all the good leaders who fought for the local people have been killed. If you don't toe the status quo, they kill you. So some of these leaders don't act about some issues because they are scared."[20]

While local MPs may lack the political power to advocate on behalf of locals, most local residents believe that these same politicians knowingly and willingly cooperate with higher-ranking politicians or investors to undermine the land rights of coastal residents. One particular accusation is that MPs and local councilors are complicit in land grabs that have denied Mijikenda their ancestral land. A resident in Kwale describes the complicity of local politicians:

The politicians are the corrupt ones. They sold the land off. For example, the Chale Islands were sold off to foreigners and the locals were not given anything. People like Mwamzandi, Boy Juma Boy, and Shariff Nassir helped people grab our land.[21]

A group of youth from Kwale provides a similar view of their MPs:

---

[19] Interview-Kijipwa SS-Kilifi County, November 21, 2012 (5).

[20] Focus group with youths-Kijipwa SS-Kilifi County, November 23, 2012. The most notorious death was former MP Ronald Ngala, who championed coastal land rights and advocated for regionalism

[21] Interview-Kinondo Chale SS-Kwale County, November 14, 2012 (A3). Mwamzandi, elected to the first parliament of Kenya until 1992 (KANU, Msambweni, Kwale), Boy Juma Boy, and Shariff Nassir are all MPs from Kwale District.

The fat cats have the financial muscle to do anything. If it's title deeds, they have the money to fly to Nairobi so that their titles are processed faster. A good example is our own MP who helped rich people acquire our Chale Forest and built a five-star resort without the knowledge of the community. So for whom are these political leaders fighting?[22]

Community elders in Kwale claim that political leaders "have failed us" because they "have forced these foreigners on us. The Kikuyu and Kamba own the biggest land around here."[23] A fisherman in Chale (Kwale) claims, "Political leaders don't help at all. They even bring people from upcountry to buy land at horrible prices."[24] The comment illustrates a common view that politicians are mere brokers who cater to Nairobi's elite and facilitate the gains of "outsiders."

The inability or unwillingness of coastal leaders to advocate for followers has affirmed the view among many local residents that electoral outcomes have little bearing on their land security or their everyday livelihood. The electoral process has become a mechanism for aspirants to attain political office. Yet in Kwale and Kilifi, where the voter base is relatively homogeneous and where leaders and political parties change frequently, the stakes of each election are low. Despite being able to elect co-ethnic representatives, citizens feel insulated from any changes that elections might otherwise bring. Mijikenda politicians are largely constrained actors who act as brokers to national elites and the landowning class rather than strong patrons who can distribute or protect the land of supporters. The result is that most politicians do not have the political legitimacy or authority to organize violence.

Patronage Strength and Strategies of Claim Making

I argue further that the ability of political leaders to act as strong land patrons affects the claim-making strategies that constituents pursue. Specifically, where citizens perceive their leaders to be strong land patrons, they are more likely to rely on formal land claims. Yet where citizens view their leaders as weak or constrained, they may be more likely to rely on ancestral claims to land rather than advocate for formal tenure rights.

[22] Focus group with youths-Msambweni-Kwale County, November 18, 2012.
[23] Focus group with elders-Msambweni-Kwale County, November 18, 2012.
[24] Interview-Kinondo Chale SS-Kwale County, November 17, 2012.

This link between the strength of the land patron and the type of land claim that citizens pursue is based on the observation that citizens articulate land claims based partly on a sense of moral or legitimate right. Equally however, residents or group members must believe that they have the resources and capacity to counter a competing claimant (e.g. state, rival group, or private developer) through legal, political, or coercive means. Yet in the absence of a powerful political patron, individuals or groups may doubt the willingness of their leaders to capably advocate for their formal tenure rights. Group members may thus rely on ancestral claims because such claims provide a more viable strategy for asserting rights, and equally, a means of protesting the power of title-based claims.

As evidence for this relationship between patronage strength and type of land claim, I draw on results from a survey question where we ask respondents about which land claim they see as more legitimate: title-based claims or ancestral claims.[25] As Table 7.3 indicates, there is clear difference between residents from counties in the Rift Valley compared to those in the sampled coast counties. Specifically, a large majority of residents from Nakuru and Uasin Gishu believe that having a title deed is the more legitimate method of claiming land. In contrast, most respondents from Kilifi and Kwale believe that having an ancestral claim is more legitimate. The difference in claim-making strategies is visible when comparing Uasin Gishu with Kilifi County, where 92 percent of respondents in Uasin Gishu see the title deeds as the more legitimate claim, compared to only 20 percent in Kilifi.

Many Kwale and Kilifi residents view the title deed as a tool used by outsiders or the government to evict them. Despite the power of a title deed to secure land rights, the process of acquiring a title feels beyond the reach of many people. This feeling is largely a function of the ambiguity and dysfunction of formal land institutions that favor wealthy and well-connected individuals who can navigate complex bureaucracy or have the power to subvert the formal process. While residents from Uasin Gishu

---

[25] A survey question asks respondents to imagine a situation where two groups argue over the same piece of land. The first group claims that they are the true owners because they have the ancestral rights to the land. The second claims they are the legitimate owners because they have purchased the land and hold a title deed. Enumerators ask respondents to select the stronger claim.

Table. 7.3 *Preferred strategy of claiming land rights*

	Nakuru	Uasin Gishu	Kilifi	Kwale
Title deed	83%	92%	20%	38%
Ancestral claims	17%	8%	80%	62%
Observations 710				

and Nakuru also struggle to obtain title deeds – and may likewise feel daunted by the process of obtaining a title deed – I suggest that the power of Rift Valley patrons helps account for these regional differences. Specifically, while Rift Valley patrons have facilitated the process of acquiring title deeds, very few coastal leaders have been in such a position. Coast residents thus tend to place greater weight on ancestral claims. As one resident of Kilifi remarks, "Our community does not really care about the title deed. They fear the process, the time, and the finances involved … we know the importance of the title but it's complicated to follow it up."[26]

Ancestral land claims are compelling in part because they have greater legitimacy and moral resonance among many people. One interviewee explains how "selling land is like selling your own mother."[27] Another respondent provides a similar view: "The title deed in the African context is not valid. We used to plant trees to mark which land belongs to us. These title deeds were brought in to take away land from the local people."[28] According to these remarks, formal land sales fall beyond the established norms of Mijikenda culture. Residents understand the pragmatic potential of the title deed but make ancestral claims as a way of protesting the power of title-based claims. Knowing the power of title deeds, yet viewing them as illegitimate or inaccessible, has created what Sharon Hutchinson describes as a "simultaneous dependence on and estrangement from the powers of the government" (in Willis & Gona 2012: 51). The comments of one interviewee hint at this dilemma, whereby local residents understand the power of the titleholder, "according to the law":

[26] Interview-Kijipwa SS-Kilifi County, November 21, 2012 (7).
[27] Interview-Makongeni-Kwale County, November 13, 2012 (2).
[28] Interview-Kijipwa SS-Kilifi County, November 22, 2012 (8).

We cannot confirm who has the right: the locals or people from upcountry. A title deed confirms you as the real owner by law. That's the most important. The people who have the right to ownership are the titleholders, according to the law. Yet the local people who have stayed here for a long time deserve land too.[29]

The comment hints at how coastal residents struggle to develop a single and coherent discourse for asserting rights to land. On the one hand, residents assert their rights through a language of ancestral belonging and a rejection of land commodification. At the same time, they seek the private benefits and security of participating in the formal land economy by acquiring an individual title deed. An interviewee from Kilifi reflects on the challenges of adjudicating between competing claims:

A title deed is very important because when these rich people come asking for title deeds [we don't have one]. Therefore it means the title deed shows that you are the true owner of this land. The people who have stayed there for the longest need to be allocated land first, forget about those people who come with title deeds.[30]

Ancestral claim making becomes not only a form of protest, but a livelihood strategy that emerges from a longer tradition of demarcating and asserting a household's plot and acknowledging the lineage rights of the family.

By contrast, across much of the Rift Valley, ancestral claims to land have become a political rather than livelihood strategy. Kalenjin youth in Nakuru explain, "If you advocate for your ancestral land claims by saying that the land belonged to your forefathers, nothing will happen. You will be ignored. It's not as strong as having a title deed."[31] The ancestral claim is instead a political tool that gives one group the right to reclaim land from another "invading" group. This narrative acquires political power because it is linked to a group's belief in their right to occupy or reclaim territorial space.

Yet in much of Kwale and Kilifi, the ancestral narrative is not a call to exclude or deny the rights of non-natives, nor is it a zero-sum narrative where the balance between land rights and political power are one and

[29] Interview-Kijipwa SS-Kilifi County, November 21, 2012(6). By "local," the respondent refers to people "from the Coast" (i.e. Mijikenda and Swahili).
[30] Interview-Kijipwa SS-Kilifi County, November 23, 2012 (16).
[31] Focus group with youths-Mauche SS-Nakuru County, July 5, 2012.

the same. What this means is that across much of the coast region, elite appeals to land made during the electoral campaign rarely provide a rationale to attack another group. Instead, "ancestral land" is the only claim-making strategy that squatters have at their disposal. This varies from the Rift Valley where residents can demand title deeds from their political representatives as their primary form of land tenure (with varying degrees of success), while at the same time mobilizing politically around a discourse of ancestral rights to territory.

In sum, while residents across parts of the Rift Valley expect political leaders to provision or protect title-based land claims, coast residents are far more skeptical of their leaders' ability to provision tenure rights. One implication is that many Mijikenda do not see elections as moments of opportunity to reclaim or improve individual or group-level land rights.

Group Size

Several scholars suggest that electoral violence is more likely when the anticipated margin of victory between leading candidates is narrow (Wilkinson 2004) and when voting occurs primarily along ethnic lines (Collier & Vicente 2012). These arguments assume that ethnic identity provides a mechanism of electoral mobilization, shaping voters' expectations of resource allocation, and strengthening the salience of identity-based cleavages during elections (Eifert et al. 2010). Building on these observations, I suggest that when outsiders and insiders make up similarly sized groups at the subnational level (i.e. constituency), they serve as viable bases for political mobilization and competition (Posner 2005). Yet when either the migrant or host group are a small proportion of the population within the subnational arena of electoral competition, the insider–outsider distinction rarely provides a useful cleavage line around which to mobilize voters (Klaus & Mitchell 2015). This means that where political competition closely aligns with a salient insider–outsider cleavage, elections become a zero-sum game where outsiders compete with insiders over political office and resources. In this scenario, each side has the incentive and power to use coercive strategies (e.g. forced evictions) to alter electoral outcomes in the pre- and postelectoral periods. Civilians on each side are thus likely to associate elections with an increased threat of eviction or attack.

This dynamic has played out in some constituencies of the Rift where "natives" are a smaller but still competitive minority group relative to migrants. So-called natives have used violence to "remove" outsiders as a way to alter the balance of political power while seeking opportunities to acquire the land of those killed or displaced. The ethnically competitive nature of elections in the Rift Valley since 1992 has enabled political leaders and party activists to frame elections as windows of opportunity to claim or reclaim land, but equally, as moments of threat to land security and the balance of power.

In Kwale and Kilifi, several factors have constrained this particular logic of electoral violence. First, Mijikenda constitute the large majority across most constituencies in Kwale and Kilifi and hence, the ethnic balance of power favors Mijikenda locally.[32] While non-Mijikenda aspirants are on the ballot, electoral competition tends not to be ethnically competitive: they are not races where party affiliation divides the population ethnically. This is not to say that candidates have not used ethnic identity to build political support. In the 1990s, KANU politicians used outsiders as a scapegoat for rising landlessness and insecurity (and continue to do so). Indeed, many Mijikenda voters supported KANU candidates because – among other reasons – these candidates presented themselves as "anti-outsiders" who could defend locals from the land acquisitions of Kikuyus and other groups from upcountry (Kanyinga 2000). Yet while local politicians have exploited Mijikenda anxieties around the in-migration of Kikuyus, this narrative has served primarily as a tool of co-ethnic outbidding. Mijikenda politicians use the issue to prove who has the political muscle to defend locals from outsiders. In most cases, however, rival candidates are also Mijikenda or Swahili. Further, candidates tend to gravitate toward parties based on perceptions of opportunity rather than perceived ethnic affiliation. Candidates calculate the resources that will be made available through the party network and the possibilities for political and social advancement, regardless of the electoral outcome.

What all of this means is that in most constituencies, Mijikenda residents are able to elect their co-ethnics into office. Mijikenda residents are thus confident that they have the demographic advantage to

---

[32] Mijikenda make up 86 percent of the population in Kilifi County and 83 percent in Kwale County (2009 Kenya census in Kenya National Bureau of Statistics 2010).

keep outsiders from gaining local political power. Hence, there are few incentives to use violence as means of removing outsiders, as they do not present a significant political threat.

Many coastal residents are, however, preoccupied with fears of their eviction. This fear is a fact of daily life rather than a unique feature of the campaign period. A respondent in Kilifi emphasizes this sense of *daily* land insecurity: "I have never been allocated land and I don't know if I will ever get land. I don't have any paperwork to show that I own this land. I know I can be evicted any time."[33] Another respondent in Kilifi explains, "I cannot say that the land issue is caused by a particular tribe. It is the rich people who are taking advantage of us. The government was involved in my eviction."[34] These comments illustrate how many coast residents understand the source of threat: not from a neighboring ethnic community or rival political party, but from companies, the state, and powerful individuals who seek to clear the land for private development.[35]

Beyond Ethnic Demography: Ambiguous Constructions of Rivalry and Threat

Ethnic demography only partially explains how and why contentious land narratives vary so markedly in their power to incite violence. Many theories of ethnic conflict overlook how the boundaries, meanings, and political salience of group identity change over time (e.g. Cederman et al. 2013; Horowitz 1985). In much of the Rift Valley, land narratives have worked to sustain and deepen the meanings and salience attached to certain ethnic identities (Lynch 2011). Yet along much of the coast, land narratives are constantly reshaping the meaning and significance of group identity. At first glance, the nativist tone of Mijikenda land narratives parallel Kalenjin narratives in the Rift Valley. I recorded many stories about how outsiders have migrated from upcountry regions to take over the lands of local people. Yet the insider–outsider distinction does not provoke the same political narrative in Kwale and Kilifi as it does in much of the Rift Valley.

---

[33] Interview-Kijipwa SS-Kilifi County, November 22, 2012.
[34] Interview-Kijipwa SS-Kilifi County, November 20, 2012 (2).
[35] The industries with reputations for eviction orders on the Coast include sugar, sisal, and cashew plantations and cement and salt plants.

One reason for this regional difference, I suggest, it that the category of the outsider is neither as well defined nor as visible as, for example, the narrative about Kikuyu outsiders in the Rift Valley. The term "outsider" can refer to private developers, government bureaucrats in the land ministry or provincial administration, European investors, upcountry Kenyans, Arab families who have lived on the coast since the nineteenth century, or even Mijikenda who must rent land or property from other locals. The ubiquity of the term "outsider" along the coast makes it difficult for politicians to appropriate. It is too broad to effectively divide followers and opponents.

In many interviews with coast residents, respondents expressed a willingness or desire to fight for land rights or to seek revenge for land that they had lost. But unlike in the Rift Valley, respondents rarely specify the ethnic identity of their target. When I asked an interviewee to specify whom they would fight, respondents often conflated an ethnic outsider with a bureaucratic official or the state. The perception of crime and injustice, absent an identifiable target group, limits the possibilities for violence. The following excerpt from an interview with a Kilifi respondent helps demonstrate how residents understand culpability and envision the target.[36] The respondent states:

We are getting ready.

Q: What do you mean?

Whether they like it or not, I will fight first before they get my piece of land. I won't let [the land] go like that. No, because I don't come from America or India. I was born here. I am a Kenyan. And I'm above fifty, how come I can't have a piece of land? Why? What happened? Why does someone have to come and say that this is his piece of land?

Q: You say that you would fight for your land. So whom would you fight?

[I would fight] the people coming from Nairobi with their title deeds, those who claim that these pieces of land are theirs.

The respondent makes an implicit claim to the land based on his citizenship, on "being born here," on not being a foreigner. Yet when he envisions the perpetrator of this land injustice, it is not the American or the Indian or even the Kikuyu. Instead, he remarks that the target of

---

[36] Interview-Kijipwa SS-Kilifi County, November 21, 2012 (5).

his violent acts would be "the people coming from Nairobi." His comments hint at how coast residents construct the concept of outsider: not along lines of ethnic identity or belonging, but by the method through which a person claims land.

Land narratives are, in part, stories that ascribe blame. Yet the subjects of this blame are vague at best. For one elderly interviewee, land insecurity is the fault of Arab families, who "really sold us out." Many other respondents blame state officials or political elites. One interviewee claims, "Our land was taken away by the big fish in government. Most of it was allocated to government officials."[37] For many respondents, the term "outsider" describes a lack of authenticity or legitimacy in how one acquires land. These narratives frame outsiders as wealthy, greedy, and powerful individuals who leverage their connections (to the state apparatus) to disinherit local communities. A respondent in Kilifi demonstrates how the perceived method of land acquisition – "buying land in the right way" – shapes attitudes toward "outsiders:"[38]

I don't consider anyone an outsider, so long as you go [about acquiring land] in the right way. I will not complain because he comes from Nakuru, as long as he does not displace anyone I don't mind ... Down here [on the coast] we have accepted everyone. We want peace. We want everyone to feel at home. But do not grab land just because you have money.

The response reveals a degree of tolerance toward outsiders with the caveat that the outsider should "follow the rules and not displace local residents." As another respondent from Kilifi explains, "an outsider is somebody who has land in their motherland but comes down here to grab land. People from other countries buy land or arrange partnerships, but upcountry people use corrupt deals to access land."[39] An elderly resident living in Likoni provides a similar view: "There are two groups of people living here: Those who were born here, and those who bought land from the local people."[40]

Other residents use the term "outsider" to describe their own feelings of insecurity and rootlessness: a person who does not have the social or political power to attain the status of belonging. A respondent from

---

[37] Interview-Kijipwa SS-Kilifi County, November 21, 2012 (4).
[38] Interview-Kijipwa SS-Kilifi County, November 21, 2012 (5).
[39] Interview-Kijipwa SS-Kilifi County, November 22, 2012 (8).
[40] Interview-Likoni-Mombasa County, December 2, 2012 (Elders focus group).

Kwale suggests, "An outsider is someone who doesn't own land. Maybe they stay in rental houses ... when I get land and a title deed I will feel less of an outsider."[41] In Kilifi, a respondent describes a similar feeling: "My land rights are not protected because I don't have a title. I am like a stranger here, as much as I am a local person."[42] These responses demonstrate that the meaning of the term outsider – while ubiquitous in everyday discourse – does not have a single and commonly agreed-upon meaning, nor does it describe a particular group identity.

Despite anxieties around "outsiders," land narratives in much of the coast region reflect a greater level of tolerance toward outsiders compared to the narratives that I document in parts of the Rift Valley. Different histories of political patronage and migration help account for this variation. In the more arable regions of the Rift Valley, elites created patronage networks along ethnic lines. In these spaces, residents learned to fear a political leader from another ethnic community because it signaled their exclusion from the "national cake." Yet in the sparsely populated coast region, KANU elites felt no great rush to build networks of political supporters.[43] Without strong co-ethnic patrons who could offer land or employment, residents have had to negotiate access to land or employment through relationships with strangers – including Europeans, Arabs, Indians, or upcountry Kenyans rather than rely on party or ethnic networks (Cooper 1980; Kanyinga 2000). Relations of interdependence have developed between nonlocals, who required labor on their plantations, and Mijikenda, who require access to land to sustain their livelihoods (Cooper 1980). Outsiders, notably Arab landlords, have become central to the local political economy, despite the widespread resentment of their vast landholdings. The outsider in this sense has become an imperative for survival more than a political and economic threat.

In sum, Mijikenda land narratives have not provided coastal leaders with the same mechanism for organizing violence as land narratives have in parts of the Rift Valley. The reason for this, I argue, is because there is not a well-defined outsider or target group that elites and

---

[41] Interview-Kinondo Chale SS, Kwale County, November 14, 2012 (2).
[42] Interview-Kijipwa SS-Kilifi County, November 22, 2012 (10).
[43] In addition, because Mijikenda constitute a very small proportion of the national population, and hence, the national electorate, KANU leaders have had few incentives to build and mobilize support in primarily Mijikenda districts.

followers can clearly link to electoral outcomes. Beyond towns and cities, many upcountry residents are a small and largely invisible minority who occupy a well-protected stratum of society. In addition, while many residents have strong feelings against outsiders, there is also a tradition of working with and for outsiders that does not exist in other parts of Kenya.

Violence in Tana River and Lamu Counties

The theory I've outlined in this chapter has aimed to explain why election violence is more likely in parts of the Rift Valley compared to the Coast. In my analysis thus far, I've characterized the Coast region as relatively peaceful and stable. In this characterization, however, I refer only to the relative absence of violence linked explicitly to elections, particularly the 2007 general election.

Yet in the last decade alone, parts of the Coast have witnessed significant episodes of political violence. Two events warrant specific mention. The first involved a series of tit-for-tat clashes between Pokomo farmers and Orma pastoralists in Tana River Country between August 2012 and January 2013. The conflict was partly about competing claims over land and water-use rights between the Pokomo and Orma. Yet there is compelling evidence that local political elites instigated the violence, which resulted in the deaths of 185 people and the displacement of an estimated 12,000 people (Malik 2018; HRW 2013). According to many accounts, elites orchestrated the violence as a way to suppress the Pokomo vote in advance of the March 2013 election, enabling the Orma community to gain control at the level of the newly created county (Malik 2018).

The second notable event was a series of attacks in June 2014 carried out by Al-Shabaab, a Somali-based terrorist group (HRW 2015). The attacks, which killed eighty-seven people, occurred in Mpeketoni, a small town located in Lamu County. Two motives likely guided these attacks. First, and as Al-Shabaab claims, the attacks were a way of punishing Kenya for its intervention in Somalia and its persecution and killing of Muslims, including a prominent Muslim cleric (HRW 2015).[44] The location of the attack is also significant because the town

---

[44] In a campaign known as Operation Linda Nchi, Kenya Defense Forces (KDF) invaded southern Somalia in October 2011 in response to cross-border attacks

is part of a controversial settlement scheme that Jomo Kenyatta created for Kikuyus. Since its creation in 1973, resentment has grown among local residents, who see Kikuyu settlers as invaders who have taken their ancestral land. An additional explanation then, is that the Mpeketoni attacks were a way for Al-Shabaab to win over a sympathetic audience, one made up of aggrieved locals who resented the power and land that Kikuyu residents held locally (Butime 2014).

The Tana River clashes and the Mpeketoni attacks are in many ways emblematic of the conflict dynamic that I've presented in this book. Like other cases I've described, there are competing claims over rights to land. In Tana River, these competing claims play out between farmers (Pokomo) and pastoralists (Orma) over farming and grazing rights. In Mpeketoni, there are competing claims between Kikuyu "settlers" who have formal land rights and "natives" who feel displaced from their ancestral land. In both cases, there is evidence that political and militia leaders tapped into existing narratives to organize violence, strengthening the insider–outsider divide and framing violence as a strategy to maintain or reclaim control over land and territory.

Yet despite the important similarities that these cases share with the cases I've presented, I preclude them because they fall outside the scope of my analysis, which I have limited to election-related events occurring during or prior to the 2007–2008 electoral period. Further, these events escalated in distinct political contexts. The Mpeketoni attacks in particular were not linked explicitly to national elections, occurring more than a year after the March 2013 elections and several years before the August 2017 elections.

There is, however, a strong argument for categorizing events in Tana River as preelectoral violence, given that events occurred three to six months in advance of the 2013 elections. Nonetheless, I preclude Tana River because the institutional context differs from the coastal counties of Kwale and Kilifi on a few important dimensions. First, while Kwale and Kilifi are relatively ethnically homogenous, with a large majority and small minority, group dynamics in Tana River are distinct, with the Pokomo and Orma each constituting large minorities.[45] With each

by Al-Shabaab. The operation ended officially in March 2012, but the KDF remain in Somalia as part of the African Union Mission in Somalia (AMISOM).
[45] As of 2010, the Pokomo were the largest ethnic community in Tana River, comprising 28 percent of the county population, followed by the Orma (Burbidge 2015).

group competing over land and political power, the most salient clea-vage line is ethnic rather than class. Second, in contrast to Kwale and Kilifi, there is not a well-established landed elite. The absence of a landed elite is due in large part to the county's geography. The majority of the county is rangeland, with only 7 percent of the land categorized as arable.[46] The lack of land arability likely dissuaded British settlers and domestic elites alike. And unlike Kwale and Kilifi, its inland location placed it beyond the reach of the Zanzibari Sultanate in the nineteenth century.

Hence, I'd characterize the county as having a salient ethnic cleavage, as I observe in much of the Rift Valley. Yet unlike much of the Rift Valley, local political leaders have historically acted as weak land patrons – not because they are constrained by more powerful land-lords, as is the case in Kwale and Kilifi – but because the entire region has been marginalized. The theory that I present in this chapter would predict that where there is a large minority and small majority along-side weak patrons, there is little likelihood for violence. That is, while there's a salient threat, there is not a leader with the capacity and legitimacy to organize violence. Indeed, this may have explained the previously low levels of election violence in Tana River. This dynamic changed, however, after the implementation of the 2010 constitution, which devolved power to the county-level. Devolution altered the perceived stakes of the election, elevating the importance of county-level contests. With the decentralization of power, formerly marginal leaders now had significant control over the distribution of resources and the implementation of land law (Boone et al. 2019). Hence, in Tana River and elsewhere, the new constitution created more opportunities for formerly weak or constrained "land patrons" to become relatively strong.

In sum then, violence was possible in Tana River and Lamu because the institutional context was different from Kwale and Kilifi. In Tana River, tensions between two similarly sized groups fighting over access to land and power shaped a salient ethnic cleavage. Most importantly, however, the 2010 constitution created new political rules, creating mechanisms for formerly weak leaders to acquire significant control

---

[46] Title deeds have been issued to only about 4 percent of all land holdings. All other land falls under communal land tenure. See Republic of Kenya/World Bank 2015, "Climate Risk Profile: Tana River County."

and political power (Malik 2018). More so, devolution has shifted the perceived stakes of the election from the national to the county-level. Hence, with more at stake, local politicians have greater incentives to use violence, and likewise, more power to mobilize violent political action.

Conclusion

Within certain contexts, contentious land narratives can provide political elites with an effective tool to mobilize election violence. The Coast region, and Kilifi and Kwale counties in particular, provides an important site to explain why and how the relationship between land narratives and violence breaks down. By selecting two regions where land is of central importance to residents, I aimed to explain why land narratives can provide elites with an effective tool to organize violence in parts of the Rift Valley but not the Coast.

This question frames the mobilization of violence along two axes. The first is patronage capacity: does the candidate have the power and legitimacy to exploit narratives around land? The second concerns the narrative itself: how do ideas about land rights shape beliefs about threats of losing land or opportunities gain land rights during an election period?

I have specified several factors that make electoral violence more likely. These include strong patron–client relations, the power of group land claims to counter contesting claims, the proportion of outsiders relative to insiders, and the social and political power of the "outsider" relative to other groups. When citizens believe that elections create either a threat of land appropriation or an opportunity to strengthen land rights, there may be stronger motives to engage in violence.[47] Yet when citizens do not view elections as a significant threat to their land security or as an opportunity to strengthen their land rights, there are far fewer incentives to fight. The strength of the political patron and the number of outsiders relative to insiders help explain whether citizens associate threat and opportunity with the electoral process.

The story of the Coast is one where citizens do not feel part of the formal political system (see Willis & Chome 2014). Citizens have few

---

[47] The caveat being that these are necessary but not sufficient conditions to explain electoral violence.

incentives to participate in the political process because many feel insulated from both the positive and negative effects of political participation. Yet this feeling of marginalization does not preclude all forms of political violence. On the contrary, while election violence is not common, there is a growing window for new forms of violence, particularly as citizens come to believe that their politicians and the government do not represent them. These sentiments have helped generate a secessionist movement under the slogan of *Pwani si Kenya* – the Coast is not Kenya.[48]

There is also a rise in new forms of violence along the Coast: attacks on churches, grenade attacks on buses and hotels, targeted attacks on religious leaders, and attacks on sites that symbolize the success of migrants at the expense of locals. This escalation of violence points to new and growing forms of authority in the region with links to extremist religious organizations, secessionist groups, and Al-Shabaab in particular. Future research might consider how the recent devolution of power away from the central state is reshaping patronage networks and, by extension, altering how citizens choose to engage or subvert the formal political process.

---

[48] See Willis and Gona (2012); Botha (2014).

PART III

Consequences of Electoral Violence

8 | Individual-level Causes and Effects of Election Violence

In the preceding chapters, I have focused on the process of electoral violence, examining the institutional origins that shape land inequality, the emergence of contentious narratives between groups, and how land narratives facilitate the joint production of election violence. The analysis thus far has taken a primarily inductive approach, using qualitative case studies to develop a theory about the process of violence. This chapter is distinct in a few important ways. First, the chapter takes a primarily deductive approach, using my survey data to test existing theories about the causes and consequences of electoral violence. Second, and relatedly, I shift the unit of analysis. Whereas previous chapters focused on the region or the group, the focus here is on the individual. Third, and importantly, whereas previous chapters focused on the causes and dynamics of election violence, my main research question here focuses on the individual-level effects of exposure to election violence.

I organize this chapter into two parts, guided by distinct research questions. In Part I, my question remains focused on the causes of election violence. Specifically, I test whether exposure to divisive land appeals affects an individual's likelihood of experiencing violence. Drawing on the theory that I outline in previous chapters, I argue that where elites use contentious land narratives in their campaign appeals, electoral violence is more likely. In particular, the use of divisive campaign appeals heightens the stakes of an election by framing the electoral period as a window to gain or lose land. The use of such appeals can also establish a logic for ordinary Kenyans to participate in violence by framing violence as a means to defend or reclaim land and power.

The second part of the chapter focuses on the effects of violence, asking how the experience of election violence shapes openness toward ethnic outgroups, trust in political leadership, and social engagement across ethnic lines. Broadly, I argue that the experience of election violence has an enduring effect on how an individual perceives and engages with her political and social world. These effects have important implications for postconflict reconstruction and democratic consolidation. Analyzing the effects of election violence on people's attitudes, beliefs, and political behaviors also helps in understanding the process of violence. Doing so helps unpack the potential endogeneity of violence, enabling us to better specify the mechanisms through which election violence increases or diminishes the prospects for democratic consolidation and durable peace, and specifically, the mechanisms through which exposure to violence affects the likelihood for future violence. Further, I suggest that the often cyclical nature of election violence, its highly localized escalation, and its close association with the failure of democracy can have important implications for how affected individuals interact with other members in society and engage in or opt out of the democratic project.

To evaluate these two research questions, I rely primarily on survey data that I collected in January of 2013 – five years after Kenya's 2007–2008 postelection violence. The survey includes geocoded-data, revealing spatial patterns in the intensity of electoral violence at the polling-station level. As I explain at the outset of the book, the survey sampled individuals in four counties: two that experienced significant election violence in 2007–2008 (Nakuru and Uasin Gishu), and two where reported levels of violence were very low (Kilifi and Kwale). While this data source has its own limitations, I overcome several of the biases inherent in relying on government reports, such as the CIPEV Report, or datasets based on media reports.

In examining the predictors of electoral violence, I find that individuals who are exposed to divisive land appeals are indeed, more likely to experience election violence. Importantly, and as I've explained in earlier chapters, exposure to such appeals is only one of several factors that can increase the likelihood for violence. In evaluating the effects of electoral violence, I find that people who directly or indirectly experienced the postelection violence are less open to ethnic outsiders settling in their community and less trusting of political authority. Yet despite diminished trust, they are also more likely to participate in interethnic forms of community engagement.

I Predictors of Individual-level Violence

In this first section, I draw on my survey data to evaluate the theory of election violence that I've outlined in preceding chapters, narrowing in on the second stage in the process of election violence, which focuses on how elites exploit existing land narratives to organize violence. To do so, I analyze whether exposure to divisive land appeals affects one's likelihood of experiencing violence. However, because these inflammatory remarks are so often made "off the record," for example, in secret meetings or through veiled statements made in a group's mother tongue, it is difficult to observe these appeals directly.[1] As a proxy for these strategies, I ask respondents how often – if at all – they hear leaders make such statements. While this approach does not measure how an individual interprets these campaign appeals, it does indicate whether divisive and land-based appeals are commonplace. My expectation is that people's vulnerability to election violence – whether as participants, victims, or bystanders – should be higher where the use of divisive appeals is common. This expectation draws on the theory I've presented over the preceding chapters. That is, where there are salient and contentious land narratives, political leaders will be better able to use such narratives as a tool to mobilize and organize violence. I specify this expectation as follows:

Hypothesis 1: Election violence is more likely where politicians use contentious land narratives as campaign appeals.

Measurement: Part I

The dependent variable at this first stage of analysis is an individual's exposure to violence, and specifically, indirect exposure to election violence. This measure is distinct from a variable that I introduce in the next section ("direct exposure") which measures whether an individual experienced direct physical violence – against herself, members of her family, or personal property.[2] As a way of measuring whether an individual experienced violence *indirectly*, I measure a resident's perception of the violence as it escalated in her own community. Specifically, I rely on a survey question that asks: "When you remember

---

[1] Interview respondents and human rights reports provide evidence that politicians engaged in "hate speech" or divisive political appeals. See for example, KNCHR's (2008) report "Back from the Precipice." By mother tongue, I refer to the practice of speaking in, for example, Kalenjin or Kikuyu. This practice is effective because it signals who is included in the "in-group," while excluding broader audience who may not know the language.

[2] I also refer to these two variables as "indirect violence" and "direct violence."

the time following the elections, how would you describe events within this community?"[3] Using this question provides a measure of how an individual, regardless of whether they were personally attacked, interpreted the level of violence in their community. Importantly, an individual need not witness violence firsthand to experience posttraumatic effects. Hearing about the losses that other community members have endured or knowing that violence has occurred within one's community can have enduring psychological and political consequences (Canetti-Nisim et al. 2009). I also analyze how exposure to appeals affects the likelihood of experiencing direct violence. I show these results in the appendix.[4] These measures of direct and indirect exposure to violence are distinct from many other studies on the causes and consequences of political violence, most of which use event data (e.g. de Juan & Pierskalla 2016; Voors et al. 2012).[5] Despite certain advantages in using event datasets, doing so can also conceal the significant local variation in violence.[6] More so, many existing measures do not distinguish between the experience of direct and indirect exposure to violence.

Independent Variables: Exposure to Land-based Political Appeals

My main explanatory variable measures exposure to divisive land appeals that leaders or party activists use during an election campaign. I test for the effects of four political appeals – all of which are similar, but vary in the degree to which they condone the use of violence. Table 8.1 shows the frequency of such appeals by region and ethnic identification.

The first and most inflammatory appeal asks whether a respondent has heard politicians or party activists make the following type of statement: "If you kick out the other tribe, you will get their land." I refer to this as

---

[3] Respondents could answer in one of four ways: 1) peaceful or mostly calm: no problem; 2) tension; no fighting; 3) some fighting; only in certain areas; and 4) a lot of fighting; people were very scared.
[4] In appendix, see Table C.2.
[5] There are however, several studies that do use individual-level survey data (e.g. Bauer et al. 2014; Linke, 2013; Dercon & Gutierrez-Romero 2012).
[6] By relying on first-hand accounts of violence, the survey data presented avoids the potential counting biases that characterize many event-datasets, particularly those compiled by governments.

Table 8.1 *Frequency of land-related political appeals, by region and ethnic identity*

	Rift Valley		Coast
	(Kalenjin)	(Kikuyu)	
Appeal 1: "Violence"	43%	58%	44%
If you kick out the other tribe, you will get their land.			
Appeal 2: "Title Promise"	48%	59%	72%
I will help you get title deeds or resettle when I win.			
Appeal 3: "Free Land"	39%	47%	52%
Other groups have land b/c they received it for free, while you did not receive anything. This is not fair to you.			
Appeal 4: "Defend Land"	46%	52%	68%
This is your ancestral land. If I win, I will help you defend this land.			
Observations	213	157	378

the "violence appeal." I formulated this question based on qualitative interviews where respondents described candidates encouraging violence against opponents in exchange for land. For example, an interviewee in Oljorai settlement scheme explains, "Politicians are the main perpetrators of conflicts we experience. They tell their community members to kick off a certain tribe so that they take over the land."[7] As I have mentioned, political leaders issue divisive messages through speeches, most of which they conduct in the local language of co-ethnics. Candidates also hold low-profile or secret meetings with prominent community members, youth groups, or gangs. Candidates and party activists also distribute pamphlets "to spread messages of hate,"[8] and coordinate with local radio stations to issue divisive statements, often using coded language. The most infamous case of a local radio station spreading "hate speech" is the case of Joshua Arap Sang, who headed a local Kalenjin radio station known as KASS FM. The International

---

[7] Interview-Oljorai-Nakuru County, September 12, 2012 (4).
[8] Interview-Mauche SS-Nakuru County, October 4, 2012 (3).

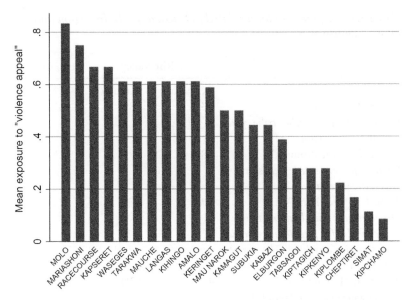

Figure 8.1 Exposure to divisive political appeals: electoral wards in Nakuru and Uasin Gishu counties.

Criminal Court accused Sang of using the radio station to allow William Ruto – the former MP for Eldoret North and current deputy president – to propagate hate messages directed against PNU supporters.[9]

Exposure to this type of appeal is surprisingly common, with 46 percent of respondents indicating that they heard candidates make remarks similar to the one above. Yet as Figure 8.1 indicates, disaggregating responses reveals significant local-level variation in exposure to this appeal, and specifically, variation across sampled electoral wards in Nakuru and Uasin Gishu counties. The expectation then, is not that exposure to divisive appeals causes election violence, but that local spaces where such appeals are common may indicate a contentious political space where elites may more easily organize violence.

The second appeal tests the effects of hearing politicians or party activists promising that "I will help you get a title deed or will help you resettle when I win." This type of statement is more benign. It promises

---

[9] For more details, see the ABA-ICC Project: www.aba-icc.org/accused/joshua-arap-sang/

land in exchange for votes, but makes no explicit reference to the use of violence. This is perhaps why it appears to be a more common appeal, with nearly 62 percent of sampled respondents indicating that they have heard a statement along these lines. Yet while this statement is not explicitly divisive or violent, I include this measure because any appeal that links access to land with an electoral outcome is likely to heighten the perceived stakes of an election. Hence, it may also help explain where elites can more easily organize violence. This particular appeal also appears more common in Coast counties. In many ways, this is not surprising: because fewer citizens have title deeds in the Coast compared to the Rift Valley, the appeal may resonate more with Coast voters. Yet very few residents from the Coast experienced violence. This indicates that while promises of land can shape an environment more conducive to violence, it is one among other factors that need to be present.

The third variable measures whether respondents have heard politicians or party activists make statements along the following lines: "Other groups have land because they received it for free, while you did not receive anything. This is not fair to you." I refer to this as "Free Land" appeal. Across sampled respondents, 47 percent have heard candidates use this type of statement. This appeal taps into narratives of injustice; heightening feelings of marginalization and resentment toward outgroups (i.e. political opponents) who have received land "for free."

The fourth appeal taps into narratives of land injustice and insecurity, reminding voters that they have a right to their ancestral land, while also invoking potential threats to land, reminding voters that their ancestral land rights are not secure without the protection of a political leader who can protect the rights of supporters. This appeal is also similar to the "title promise" appeal in that it is more common in sampled spaces of the Coast. I'd attribute the ubiquity of this particular appeal to the fact that far more residents in the Coast rely on ancestral claims compared to residents from the Rift Valley.

Measuring Alternative Explanations

I also engage with a set of alternative accounts that may help explain variation in exposure to election violence. I do so by analyzing hypotheses that emphasize the predictive power of political competition and local ethnic heterogeneity. The first theory suggests that electoral violence is more likely in electoral spaces such as constituencies or districts where political competition is most intense. Elites should have greater incentives to use violence to alter electoral outcomes where the predicted vote margins are narrow (e.g. Hafner-Burton & Hyde 2013; Wilkinson 2004). Wilkinson's study of ethnic riots in India, for example, focuses on how the degree of electoral competition at the local level predicts whether the regional-level government chooses to use security forces to prevent or foment ethnic riots. Broadly, these studies find that the use of violence can suppress the turnout of nonsupporters through coercion or intimidation, changing voter preferences, or by displacing opposition voters to alter the political terrain (Kasara 2016; Boone 2011; Klopp 2001). In the results that I present, I use the presidential vote margin for the 2007 election at the constituency level as a measure of political competition.

A second set of theories suggest that political violence is more likely in ethnically heterogeneous or polarized spaces (e.g. Horowitz 1985). Kaufmann (1998), for example, argues that the spatial separation of ethnic groups is often necessary in ethnically diverse and postconflict contexts. Kasara (2013) applies theories of ethnic segregation and interethnic mistrust to the Kenya context, and finds that in contrast to Kaufmann's claim, ethnic segregation decreases tolerance. Further, she suggests that local elites are better able to mobilize violence in spaces of ethnic segregation (Kasara 2016).[10]

To account for the potential effects of ethnic fractionalization, I include a measure of the ethnic fractionalization index (ELF) at the location level, which is Kenya's smallest administrative unit.[11] To construct this measure, I rely on data from the 1989 Kenya census – the last census to record information about an individual's ethnic identity.[12] This measure is thus potentially problematic given that

---

[10]   Much of this literature draws on debates within social psychology and sociology about the origins of prejudice and ethnic tolerance, particularly within the US context.

[11]   The ELF measures the probability that two randomly chosen individuals will not belong to the same group.

[12]   See Table A.1 in the appendix for location-level details on the ELF. Mai Hassan generously provided the data to construct this measure.

ethnic demography, especially at the local level, is constantly changing. Notably, electoral violence in the 1990s altered local ethnic demography such that some areas became more ethnically homogenous as targeted groups fled or migrated out of ethnically diverse and politically contested spaces (Boone 2011). At the same time, the Moi government also created new settlement schemes, turning previously homogenous locations into more diverse areas. I report the results of these two variables in the section below.

In addition to the key independent variables and alternative explanations that I aim to measure, each of the model specifications that I report below also include a number of socioeconomic and demographic variables that serve as controls. The first is a binary variable for region, which controls for whether a respondent lives in the Coast (Kwale or Kilifi) or the Rift Valley (Uasin Gishu or Nakuru). The second is a categorical variable for ethnic identification. This variable is based on a question that asks respondents to specify their home language. I've collapsed the fourteen possible respondents into four categories: 1) Kikuyu, 2) Kalenjin, 3) Mijikenda, and 4) all other groups. The appendix provides a detailed breakdown of these responses. I also proxy for local state capacity, which I measure by the distance a respondent must walk to reach the nearest police station. The theory here is that police presence serves as an extension of the state, surveilling and protecting the population. Areas that the police cannot easily reach can indicate spaces of state weakness (e.g. Herbst 2000). Other control variables include a respondent's age, which I treat as a categorical variable consisting of six age group categories (Age), a respondent's gender identification (Male), the education level of the household (School), a household's proximity to an urban area or paved road (Distance),[13] the respondent's reported daily household income (Wealth), the population of the respondent's constituency in 2009, and the population density of the constituency in 2009. Table 8.2 shows the summary statistics for variables included in model estimations for both Part I and II of the chapter's analysis.

---

[13] Where 1= urban area, 2=trading center, 3= roadside, 4= remote (within 2 km of paved road), 5= remote (more than 2 km from paved road).

Table 8.2 *Summary statistics: part I and II*

Variable	Obs	Mean	Std. dev	Min	Max
Direct violence	750	0.15	0.35	0	1
Indirect violence	746	0.27	0.45	0	1
Appeal 1: Violence	747	0.46	0.50	0	1
Appeal 2: Title promise	748	0.62	0.48	0	1
Appeal 3: Free land	750	0.47	0.59	0	1
Appeal 4: Defend land	748	0.58	0.49	0	1
Anti-settlement	729	0.64	0.48	0	1
Pres. Vote margin ('07)	750	41.2	21.8	5.1	91.6
PM Vote margin ('02)	750	16.9	14.5	0.88	50.2
Ward rep: vote margin ('07)	363	0.29	0.19	0.04	0.72
ELF: location level ('89)					
Fear of ethnic border	738	0.34	0.47	0	1
Interethnic engagement	647	0.56	0.5	0	1
Trusts leader	744	0.76	0.42	0	1
Has a title deed	750	0.45	0.5	0	1
Ethnicity	741	2.5	0.93	1	4
Kalenjin: dummy	741	0.32	0.47	0	1
Region	750	1.5	0.5	1	2
Age category	748	2.9	1	1	5
Degree urban (distance from road)	750	3.2	1	1	4
Gender (male)	747	0.51	0.5	0	1
Level of education	739	3.6	1.4	1	6
Wealth (reported monthly earning)	733	1.8	0.72	1	4
Constituency population (2009)	750	11.9	0.22	11.45	12.24
Pop. density of constituency (2009)	750	5.4	0.81	3.2	6.3

Notes: Direct and indirect violence refer to one's degree of exposure to election violence. Ethnicity is a categorical variable that indicates the ethnic identity which the respondent identifies (where 1=Kikuyu, 2=Kalenjin, 3= Mijikenda, and 4= other group). "Region" is a binary variable for the respondent's region, where 1=Rift Valley and 2=Coast.

Analysis: Part I

Recall that this stage of analysis examines the predictors of election violence (indirect violence). My main hypothesis is that exposure to divisive land appeals should increase one's probability of experiencing election violence. I examine this hypothesis and other alternative explanations through a series of hierarchal linear models with random effects.[14] For variables of interest, I report the predicted probabilities or average marginal effects. In addition to key explanatory variables, I also include a set of controls which I've explained in the preceding section. I retain all controls in each model unless otherwise specified.

Table 8.3 reports results from six different models that estimate how each of the key independent variables that I've described above predicts the likelihood of experiencing election violence.[15] Table C.2 in the appendix presents a series of models that estimates the likelihood of an individual experiencing *direct* election violence. I estimate the effects across my full sample of respondents in the Coast and Rift Valley.

I begin by analyzing the effects of hearing the first appeal, which makes the most explicit reference to violence. As results from Model 1 indicate, exposure to the first appeal has positive and statistically significant effects. Not surprisingly, the size of these effects is most profound for sampled respondents from the Rift Valley. An individual from the Rift Valley has a 29 percent probability of experiencing violence if she has not been exposed to Appeal 1, compared to a 48 percent probability if she has been exposed to the appeal. For sampled respondents from the Coast, an individual's probability of experiencing violence increases from 2 percent if they haven't heard Appeal 1 to 5 percent if they have.

The next model (Model 2) estimates the effects of hearing Appeal 2 (Title Promise). The results indicate very similar effects: a respondent from the Rift Valley has a 28 percent probability of experiencing

---

[14] Using logistic random effects is a common approach when the outcome is binary and data is nested into two or more groups. In the model specifications here, the groups include region, constituency, and individual. In most specifications, I set the panel-level observations to the level of the constituency (n=14). However, in models where I only include respondents from the Rift Valley, there are only seven panel-level observations.

[15] By "experience" of violence, I refer to a survey question that asks respondents to rate the level of election violence in their community.

violence if they've never heard the appeal and 46 percent if they have. For respondents from the Coast, hearing this appeal raises an individual's probability of experiencing violence from two to five percent.

Model 3 estimates the effects of hearing Appeal 3 (Free Land). Again, results indicate very similar effects. For Rift Valley respondents, one's probability moves from 29 percent if they've never heard such appeals to 48 percent if they have. Meanwhile, a respondent from the Coast has a 2 percent probability of violence if they've never heard such an appeal, and a 5 percent probability if they have. These results are replicated in Model 4, which estimates the effects of hearing Appeal 4, which references politicians defending one's ancestral land (Defend).[16]

In Models 5 and 6, I test the effects of political competition and ethnic fractionalization. Specifically, Model 5 retains the measure of Appeal 1 (Violence) but also includes a measure of the 2007 presidential vote margin at the constituency level. As the results in Model 5 in Table 8.3 indicate, the presidential vote margin (e.g. between Kibaki and Odinga) does appear to have statistically significant effects on one's likelihood of experiencing violence. Figure 8.2 illustrates this downward and linear relationship. Specifically, it shows that as the vote margin expands from the narrow margin of 5 percent to over 90 percent, the likelihood that an individual experiences election violence decreases significantly. The figure also shows how exposure to the first appeal interacts with the presidential vote margin. While the probability of violence diminishes for respondents as vote margin increases, the probability at each vote margin is lower for those who have never heard candidates issue statements similar to Appeal 1, with effects narrowing as vote margin increases.

There are, however, limitations in my measure of political competition. First, because my sample includes only fourteen of Kenya's 210 constituencies in 2007, I am limited in the claims that I can make about the effects of political competition at this level. Further, because I am only analyzing the vote margins of fourteen constituencies, the results may be skewed by the very narrow vote margins of two constituencies (Molo and Njoro), where there was significant violence. Second,

---

[16] There is a slight difference in the predicted probabilities between Model 3 and Model 4. Specifically, a Rift Valley respondent who has heard Appeal 4 has a 45 rather than a 48 percent (Model 3) predicted probability of experiencing violence.

Table 8.3 *Predictors of indirect exposure to election violence*

Variables	Model 1	Model 2	Model 3	Model 4	Model 5	Model 6 (Rift Valley)
Appeal 1: Violence	1.101***				1.043***	1.111***
	(0.265)				(0.264)	(0.288)
Appeal 2: Title promise		1.098***				
		(0.260)				
Appeal 3: Free land			1.113***			
			(0.259)			
Appeal 4: Defend land				1.008***		
				(0.257)		
Pres Vote Margin ('07)					-0.0426***	-0.0335***
					(0.00747)	(0.0101)
ELF: Location ('89)						-2.975***
						(0.901)
Mijikenda	-1.867**	-1.970**	-2.042**	-2.099**	-1.824**	
	(0.827)	(0.830)	(0.835)	(0.835)	(0.809)	
Coast Region	-3.469***	-3.533***	-3.519***	-3.466***	-3.009***	
	(0.880)	(0.883)	(0.864)	(0.885)	(0.587)	
CONTROLS	Y	Y	Y	Y	Y	Y
Distance: 2 km from road	-1.432***	-1.361***	-1.431***	-1.376***	-1.332***	-0.896
	(0.470)	(0.470)	(0.469)	(0.468)	(0.454)	(0.552)
Constituency Pop. (log)	-0.296	-0.386	-0.221	-0.583	-1.529*	1.686
	(1.551)	(1.518)	(1.477)	(1.549)	(0.894)	(1.452)
Constant	-0.492	0.332	-0.994	2.503	13.89	-14.52
	(17.31)	(17.00)	(16.52)	(17.34)	(9.146)	(13.48)
Observations	714	715	715	715	714	360
Number of constituencies	14	14	14	14	14	7

Note: All columns display results of a logit regression using random effects. Standard errors are clustered at the constituency level and displayed in parentheses. The dependent variable measures indirect exposure to election violence, where a value of 1=indirect exposure. *Pres Vote Margin ('07)* refers to the margin between the two top presidential candidates at the constituency level. *Mijikenda* is a categorical variable measuring a respondent's ethnic identification. *ELF: Location ('89)* measures the ethnolinguistic fractionalization index at the location level based on the 1989 census, where a value of 1= most homogenous. The variable *Distance* is a categorical variable measuring a respondent's distance from the main road. Model 6 is based only on the Rift Valley sample. Controls are included in the model but not reported. *** $p<0.01$, ** $p<0.05$, * $p<0.1$

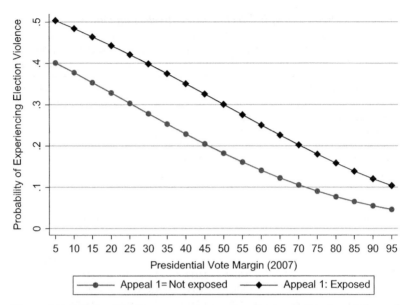

Figure 8.2 Relationship between vote margin, divisive political appeals, and electoral violence.

analyzing vote margins at the level of the constituency does not capture the more local-level competition that may shape spaces of violence. In many cases, the tension or relative stability that people experience is shaped by the degree to which residents share similar political preferences at the very local level rather than the larger electoral constituency.

As a way of analyzing whether political competition at a more local level might affect the likelihood of violence, I also estimate the effects of the vote margin between candidates for ward councilor (for the Rift Valley sample only).[17] I report these results in Table C.1 in the appendix. As the table indicates, vote margin at the ward level has no statistically significant effect on one's likelihood of experiencing violence.[18] The lack of explanatory power may be because the first and second candidates for ward councilor were typically from the same ethnic community. Hence, while co-ethnic outbidding increased the

---

[17] Ward councilors represent the electoral ward. Wards are subunits of electoral constituencies, which contain about three to seven wards.
[18] The model only includes sampled respondents from the Rift Valley.

level of tension and contentious politics, competition at the ward level rarely instigated outright violence.

An additional measure, which I show in Model 2 of Table C.1 in the appendix, shows the effects of the parliamentary vote margin in the 2002 general election, again at the constituency level. The intuition here is that candidates may use violence where vote margins are narrow, but will rely on voting data from the previous election to make inferences about the vote margin. Hence, we should expect that where vote margins were narrow in the preceding election, residents living in that constituency should have a higher probability of experiencing electoral violence. Results indicate, however, that the 2002 parliamentary vote margin is not a statistically significant predictor of election violence.

Model 6 in Table 8.3 includes a variable that measures the ELF index at the location level. As results in column 6 indicate, the ELF is negative and statistically significant: as spaces become more homogenous (approaching 1), the probability that a given individual experiences violence diminishes significantly. Equally however, as Figure 8.3 reveals, an individual's exposure to Appeal 1 ("kick out outsiders"),

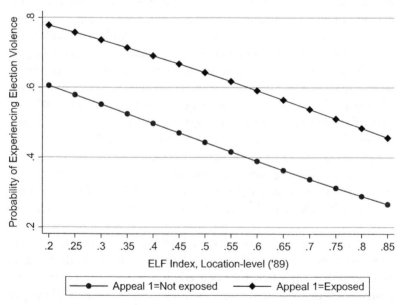

Figure 8.3 Relationship between ethnic fractionalization index (ELF), divisive political appeals, and election violence.

also remains a significant predictor. Specifically, in the most homogenous locations, a respondent exposed to this more violent appeal has a 46 percent probability of experiencing election violence. Yet if this same individual has never heard such appeals, her likelihood of experiencing violence drops to 27 percent. For people living in more ethnically heterogeneous spaces (i.e. higher degree of ethnic fractionalization), they have a much higher likelihood of experiencing violence. Yet still, exposure to divisive appeals matter, with individuals who have heard violent appeals having a 78 percent probability of experiencing violence, while those who have not heard such appeals having a 61 percent probability.

Stepping back from these findings, one could argue that ethnic identity, and specifically, ethnic fractionalization of local spaces, affects where violence escalates. And indeed, the ethnic composition of local and regional space may be an important factor in predicting spaces electoral violence. Yet there are two notable inferential challenges. The first, as I've mentioned, is that the measure of ethnic fractionalization that I use here is based on data that is over thirty years old. During this time, the demography of many local spaces has changed considerably, through forced displacement during elections, in-migration, and the creation of new settlement schemes. Second, even if more recent data on ethnic composition were available, it is difficult to establish the causal role of ethnicity. Drawing on constructivist insights, I suggest that thinking about ethnic identity as having causal power is problematic. The key question is not whether ethnic composition or ethnic identity predicts violence in a given period, but instead, why? Why do particular identities or ethnic arrangements matter in one location and not another, or in one electoral cycle but not another?

I argue that the salience of ethnic identification and the explanatory power of ethnic composition are endogenous to a set of institutional arrangements and political processes (e.g. Lynch 2011; Chandra 2005; Kalyvas 2003). Specifically, we can think of ethnic identity in much the same way as I theorize land narratives, that the meaning and power such identities acquire emerge largely from the histories of land control and distribution of land rights. In the Kenyan context, the distribution of land rights has often followed ethnic lines. In the colonial and postcolonial period, the Kenyan state organized settlement along primarily ethnic lines – first with the native reserves, and later, with government engineered settlement schemes, LBCs, and trust lands. In addition, with the advent of multiparty politics, ethnic identity became an even more powerful predictor of one's land security, as many citizens came to believe that having a co-ethnic patron in power would ensure land and livelihood security. This has been particularly so for communities who have lacked formal land security. In the absence of formal tenure rights, electing a co-ethnic leader has provided an alternative mechanism for securing *de facto* tenure rights. Hence, while variables measuring the ethnic composition of a constituency appear statistically significant in certain model specifications, I argue that greater analytic weight should be placed on the institutional and political factors that may alter the salience of ethnic or political identity at a given moment.

II The Effects of Violence

In this section, I turn to the chapter's second and primary research question, which asks how the experience of election violence shapes a person's social and political trust and modes of social engagement. A growing body of research examines the effects of war and violence. Employing a diverse range of empirical strategies, scholars examine the immediate and multigenerational effects of exposure to violence on political participation and voting behavior (Blattman 2009; Bateson 2012), political trust (de Juan & Pierskalla 2016), preferences for peace (Grossman et al. 2015), inter- and intragroup trust and altruism (Hartman & Morse 2018), and ethnic identification and antipathy toward outgroups (Lupu & Peisakhin 2017).

Many of these studies find that exposure to political violence hardens and polarizes ethnic and political identities (Cassar et al. 2014), erodes intergroup trust and community cohesion (Hadzic et al. 2017; Becchetti et al. 2014), pushes people to hold more extreme political preferences (Getmansky & Zeitzoff 2014) or leads to higher levels of violent crime (Deglow 2018). Yet many other scholars point to the opposite effect: that people who have experienced violence are more empathetic toward ethnic outgroups (Hartman & Morse 2018), more likely to vote (e.g. Blattman 2009), and more likely to behave altruistically toward neighbors and participate in the civic life of their communities (Bauer et al. 2016; Voors et al. 2012). These cumulative findings indicate that one's experience with extreme political violence may not have a single and predictable set of effects.

I engage with this growing literature, focusing on exposure to Kenya's 2007–2008 postelection violence. As I've mentioned in previous chapters, the postelection violence – and the logic of targeting – occurred along ethnic and political lines. The dynamics of violence were often intimate as well: perpetrators attended church, traded, and resided alongside the people whose homes and properties they would destroy or even kill. Speaking less than five years after the violence, a survivor remarked: "The society seems healed. But for sure, there is a gap in between. Because it's hard to trust in a person who butchered your brother."[19] How does this experience with extreme violence, whether as victim, perpetrator, or bystander, affect the way that individuals perceive and engage with their political world?

My main argument is that exposure to violence makes people more fearful and less trusting of ethnic outgroups; pushing people to self-segregate along ethnic lines. Victims of violence are less likely to trust in the ability of their leaders to defend their land and livelihood. The logic here is that victims of ethnically targeted violence will be more likely to see ethnic others as credible threats, and hence will seek to exclude or avoid these groups. Relatedly, having endured physical violence and loss of property, they are also more likely to view their political leaders as unable or unwilling to protect their land rights and physical security. Yet distrust and fear does not imply insularity. While victims of violence may prefer ethnically homogenous spaces, they may also be more invested in preventing future violence than people who have not experienced the trauma and personal loss that election violence brings. Further, as trust in leadership erodes, survivors may be more willing to participate in interethnic forums as a way to advocate for the rights and security of their own households or communities. I expect, therefore, that where trust in other ethnic groups and political leaders erodes, victims of violence should be more likely to engage in interethnic civic associations – not because they are more trusting, but because individuals believe that preventing future violence requires their own participation and engagement.

[19] Interview-Likia LBC-Nakuru County, September 13, 2012 (5).

Fear of Ethnic Others

How does exposure to election violence shape one's perceptions of ethnic outgroups? Existing research provides a number of potential scenarios. Drawing largely on political psychology, Hirsch-Hoeffler et al. (2016) suggest that prolonged exposure to political violence heightens feelings of vulnerability and perceived threat. As a result, affected individuals may be more likely to rely on defensive mechanisms to buffer themselves from perceived threat – typically from another ethnic or political group. Similarly, Becchetti et al (2014) find that victims of Kenya's 2007–2008 election violence were less trusting of non-co-ethnics compared to residents who were not victimized. Hadzic et al. (2017) also find that exposure to political violence increases the salience of ethnic identity, suggesting that where violence takes on ethnic dimensions, individuals take sides and "retreat into ethnic communities." Even after the conflict ends, these coping mechanisms endure, with people linking their own fortunes to the fortunes of the broader ethnic community (Hadzic et al. 2017: 2).

Taken together, these studies suggest that when a violent conflict has a clear ethnic or regional cleavage, exposure to violence may strengthen the salience of ethnic identification, diminish trust of ethnic others, and heighten the perception of threat posed by ethnic outgroups. In the context of election violence, where the main cleavage is often defined along ethnic, regional, and political lines, victims may be less trusting of outsiders and more defensive of group borders and the rights of "insiders." These effects may be particularly visible where contests over land and territory have shaped the dynamics of violence. People may seek to exclude outsiders, not only because they are fearful or distrusting, but because creating ethnically exclusive spaces provides a way of asserting claims to land and territory. Further, where violence takes the form of forced eviction and the destruction of property, survivors may seek to exclude former rivals as a form of retribution, a way of declaring that "you have denied us our land, now we shall do the same to you." Considering the ways that exposure to violence can make people more defensive and fearful of other communities, I make two related predictions about efforts to self-segregate. The first of these is an expectation about how people exposed to violence will become more defensive of their perceived community borders – be it an urban neighborhood, village, or agricultural community. The second is a closely related prediction about how the experience of violence makes people more fearful of living in close proximity to another ethnic community. I specify the following hypotheses:

Hypothesis 2: Individuals who have experienced election violence will be less open to the settlement of ethnic outsiders within their community compared to people who have not experienced election violence.

Hypothesis 3: Individuals who have experienced election violence will be more fearful of ethnic border zones compared to individuals who have not experienced election violence.

Political Trust

Exposure to political violence may also affect an individual's level of political trust. Political trust is a cornerstone of state legitimacy and viability. Many factors help explain levels of political trust, including perceptions of institutional capacity (Hutchison & Johnson 2011), the protection of civil and political liberties (Dahl 1973), or the maintenance of political stability (Branch & Cheeseman 2008). Among the most important factors in shaping political trust, however, is one's experience with both political and everyday violence. As de Juan and Pierskalla (2016) write, "Violent conflict is a blatant sign of the government's inability to uphold its monopoly over the use of violence and to protect citizens from physical harm" (2016: 69). Yet few studies focus explicitly on the link between exposure to violence and trust in political leaders or state institutions. Among these studies, conflicting findings emerge. The dominant finding is that exposure to violence erodes political trust (de Juan & Pierskalla 2016). Other studies, however, find that citizens who experienced violence were more likely to trust local government officials (Sacks & Larizza 2012). These varied effects may have more to do with the context in which people experience violence, and specifically, their relationship to different conflict actors (Deglow 2018). Where state security intervenes to protect civilians, people may see the state as credible and trustworthy, despite the broader context of violence or war. Yet where citizens are victimized directly by state forces or see the state condoning the violent behavior of an armed group, political trust should erode.

In the context of election violence, I expect that exposure to violence will diminish one's trust in political leaders. Specifically, I predict that citizens who have experienced violence will be less likely to trust in their leaders' willingness or capacity to protect their land, property, and livelihood. More so, in settings where questions of land rights are a key campaign issue and source of voter anxiety, one way that citizens evaluate the trustworthiness of political leadership is through their ability to defend the land rights of followers. I thus predict the following:

Hypothesis 4: Individuals who have experienced election violence should be less likely to trust their political leaders compared to individuals who have not experienced election violence.

Interethnic Civic Engagement

If individuals who are exposed to violence become less open toward ethnic others, and less trusting in their political leaders, their forms of social and political engagement might also change. I examine how exposure to violence affects a person's willingness to participate in interethnic forms of community engagement. Interethnic engagement could include attending an alternative dispute resolution forum, a meeting about violence prevention, or proposals to build a new school or road.

One possibility is that exposure to violence creates new cleavages within a community and may thus erode a community's "social glue" (Cassar et al. 2014; Weidmann & Zürcher 2013). Exposure to violence might also strengthen social bonds within a community, with affected individuals becoming more altruistic toward neighbors (Bauer et al. 2016; Biong Deng 2010), or more inclined to participate in political discussions (de Luca & Verpoorten 2015; Bellows & Miguel 2009; Blattman 2009). Yet while exposure to violence may improve levels of social capital within the group, it tends to undermine prosocial norms and civic engagement between ethnic groups (Mironova & Whitt 2018). Scholars studying intergroup conflict have termed this phenomenon "parochial altruism": the idea that conflict reinforces cooperation within the in-group while fueling antipathy toward the out-group (e.g. Bauer et al. 2014; Choi & Bowles 2007). Taken together, these studies suggest that exposure to violence strengthens forms of social capital within a group, but undermines social capital and forms of engagement between identity-based groups.

I suggest that exposure to election violence may actually encourage survivors to engage with ethnic others. This may occur because election violence, while devastating, is often less thoroughly destructive than civil war. Physical violence tends to be more isolated, kills fewer people than civil war, does not always involve the explicit involvement of the state, and is shorter in duration. One implication therefore, is that even while election violence may increase fear and distrust of the out-group, the local institutions that facilitate group interaction may remain functional or intact.[20] In other words, in contrast to many postwar settings, the local institutions in countries affected by election violence – rather than war – may remain sufficiently strong so as to enable cooperation, even absent interethnic trust.

Relatedly, even where people do not trust one another or their political leaders, those affected by election violence may have strong incentives to communicate and cooperate across ethnic lines in order to preserve or rebuild social order. That is, as trust in other groups or political leaders erodes, individuals may be more inclined to advocate for themselves or their communities. Attending intergroup meetings may be one way for citizens to advocate for their own land rights and access to livelihood resources, while also providing them with a space to voice their concerns, fears, and preferences.

In addition, because electoral violence is often cyclical, victims of election violence may be particularly committed to preventing violence in a future election. While some studies find that people exposed to violence may be less committed to peace (Hirsch-Hoeffler et al. 2016; Grossman et al. 2015), other studies find that people exposed to political violence are more fearful of future violence and hence, more committed to ensuring or restoring peace (e.g. Horowitz & Klaus 2018).

Finally, individuals affected by violence may have more opportunity to attend interethnic meetings than individuals living in more stable regions. One reason is because peace-building initiatives, led by non-governmental organizations or the government, are more likely to

---

[20] Local institutions that facilitate intergroup cooperation may include local government offices, institutions of worship, as well as agricultural cooperatives and labor groups.

target their efforts in areas affected by violence. Hence, individuals who have experienced violence will be more likely to participate in inter-ethnic forms of civic engagement, either because citizens have greater access to interethnic venues or because they have greater incentives to participate. I specify this hypothesis as follows:

Hypothesis 5: Individuals who have experienced election violence should be more likely to participate in interethnic forms of civic engagement than those who have not experienced election violence.

Measurement: Part II

In this section I explain how I measure each of the concepts I've outlined above. I draw on my survey data to examine the effects of violence on key outcomes. The first dependent variable measures an individual's openness to ethnic outsiders settling in one's own community (Anti-Settlement*)*, which I base on a survey question that asks whether a respondent is "comfortable with any Kenyan coming to live in this community, even if s/he has a title deed and [you] do not have [your] own title deed." Table 8.4 shows variation in responses to this question by county. The variation between counties in the Rift Valley and the Coast is striking. In Uasin Gishu, where the majority of respondents are Kalenjin, 90 percent say that they do not feel comfortable with "any Kenyan" coming to live in their community. By contrast, only 30 percent of respondents in Kilifi are opposed to "any Kenyan" moving into their community. I suggest this discrepancy is due in part, to the varied histories of election violence. While many Uasin Gishu residents have experienced election violence, very few have in Kilifi.

The wording of the question emerges from debates about whether ethnic outsiders should be able to settle beyond their "ethnic

Table. 8.4 *Respondents who are not comfortable with "any Kenyan coming to live in this community."*

Counties	Nakuru	Uasin Gishu	Kilifi	Kwale
Against settlement	82% (204)	90% (160)	30% (214)	57% (151)

Results not weighted. Pearson Chi-2, p<0.001. Observations in parentheses.

Table 8.5 *Respondents who trust political leader, by county*

Counties	Nakuru	Uasin Gishu	Kilifi	Kwale
Trusts political leader	86% (207)	94% (161)	61% (214)	73% (162)

Results not weighted. Pearson Chi-2, p<0.001. Observations in parentheses.

homelands." While the constitution states that citizens have the legal right to settle anywhere, many interpret this liberal vision of land and citizenship rights as a threat to their livelihood, land security, and political power. From this perspective, ethnic outsiders, particularly when equipped with title deeds, signal the marginalization and disenfranchisement of "first-comers." As Table 8.2 indicates, 64 percent of all sampled respondents agree with the statement. That is, they are not open to outsiders settling in their community. This measure enables me to evaluate Hypothesis 2: that those exposed to election violence should be less open and receptive to the settlement of ethnic outsiders within their own community.

A related dependent variable measures an individual's fear of residing near the boundary lines of two ethnic communities (Hypothesis 3). The measure is based on a survey question that asks respondents to assess the risk that a household faces if they "live near a border of another ethnic community." Across the sample, 34 percent of respondents believe that living near the border with another group poses significant risk, particularly during elections. Yet among respondents who experienced direct violence, this perception of risk is notably higher, with 63 percent indicating that they fear border zones.

The third outcome of interest provides a measure of the fourth hypothesis – that individuals who have experienced election violence will be less likely to trust their leaders compared to those who have not experienced violence. I rely on a survey question that presents the respondent with a set of leader types and then asks, "Tell me who you would trust the most to defend your land rights or physical security.[21]" I code as one those respondents who indicate that they have no trust in any leader. Table 8.5 shows trust in political leadership

[21] Respondents can select from the following list: MP, Government of Kenya, political aspirant, local ward councilor, village elder, or chief.

across the four sampled counties. Across counties, trust appears higher in counties of the Rift Valley – where far more of the population has experienced election violence. This pattern may partly reflect the theory of land patronage that I present in previous chapters. That is, because political leaders in the Rift Valley have historically acted as capable "land patrons" compared to leaders in the Coast, respondents in Uasin Gishu and Nakuru have greater trust in the ability of their leaders to protect their land. Yet as I show in the analysis below, individuals who have experienced violence – most of whom live in Uasin Gishu and Nakuru – are far less likely to trust in their political leaders.

The fourth dependent variable provides a measure of my fifth hypothesis – that exposure to violence should increase the frequency of community engagement across ethnic lines (i.e. interethnic engagement). I rely on a survey question that asks respondents how often they "attend a community meeting with members of another ethnic group."[22] As Figure 8.5 indicates, 56 percent of all sampled respondents frequently attend meetings with members of other ethnic communities. Yet among respondents who directly experienced election violence, this number is 77 percent.

The main independent variable in each of these models is a person's exposure to election violence. I use the same measure of election violence as I do in the first part of this chapter (indirect exposure to violence). The analysis I present here also includes a test of direct exposure to violence, which I measure with a survey question that asks a respondent about their personal loss during the postelection violence. I code a respondent as a victim (i.e. directly exposed) if they experienced any of the following: their animals were stolen, their house was burned or crops destroyed, a family member was injured, family member(s) was killed, or the respondent was injured. Notably, while many election violence scholars use measures of violence that are limited to injuries or deaths, I expand the measure of physical harm to encompass violence to personal property (i.e. land and dwellings) as well as livestock and crops.[23] I do so because the destruction of these goods, while not equivalent to human life, is

---

[22] In the survey respondents could indicate "often/all the time," "sometimes," "occasionally" and "never." I recode as a binary variable where "often" and "sometime" =1 and "occasionally" and "never" = 0.

[23] This measure is similar to Voors et al. (2012) who create a "household-level victimization index" which includes the experience of death, theft, ambush, forced labor, and torture.

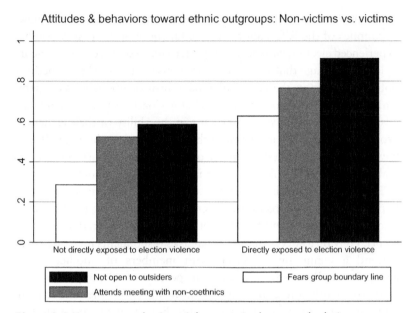

Figure 8.4 Exposure to election violence, attitudes toward ethnic outgroups, and political trust.

nonetheless devastating and violent. This approach is similar to work by Linke (2013) and Becchetti et al. (2014), each of whom use a similar measure of victimization including home destruction and eviction. Finally, I retain the same control variables that I include in the first set of estimations (Part 1), but add a measure for whether or not an individual's household has a title deed to their land or property (Title Deed), and a measure for whether a respondent identifies as Kalenjin or not (Kalenjin).[24]

Figure 8.4 shows differences in the three key outcomes of interest sorted by whether an individual experienced direct electoral violence. Victims of violence appear less open to outsiders and more likely to fear ethnic borders compared to individuals who have not experienced direct violence. It also demonstrates that a larger proportion of election violence victims attend meetings with non-co-ethnics compared to non-victims.

[24] I use this variable only for models that are restricted to my Rift Valley sample. Among respondents who do not identify as Kalenjin ("non-Kalenjin"), 77 percent identify as Kikuyu.

Analysis: Part II

I estimate the effects of exposure to violence along several outcomes of interest: openness to ethnic outsiders, fear of interethnic boundary zones, trust in political leadership, and interethnic community engagement. I estimate these effects with a series of hierarchical linear models with random effects and predicted probabilities.[25]

Effects of Exposure to Violence on Openness to Ethnic Outgroups (Hypothesis 2)

I begin by analyzing whether the experience of violence affects an individual's openness to ethnic outgroups settling within one's community (Hypothesis 2). I present these results in Models 1–4 of Table 8.6. Results from Model 1 show support for this hypothesis: individuals who experienced direct victimization have a significantly higher likelihood of opposing settlement compared to individuals who were not directly victimized. Among respondents from the Rift Valley, an individual who experienced direct violence has an 88 percent probability of opposing settlement by outsiders compared to individuals who did not experience direct victimization (75 percent probability). Model 2 estimates the effects of indirect exposure. While effects are not as strong, they remain statistically significant. Across all sampled respondents, a person's probability of opposing settlement by outsiders decreases by 8 percent if they experienced indirect violence (from 71 percent to 63 percent). In Models 3 and 4, I narrow the sample to residents of the Rift Valley. Doing so shows similar effects: residents who experienced direct or indirect violence are less open to the settlement of ethnic outsiders, though the effects of indirect victimization are not as strong.[26]

[25] Using logistic random effects is a common approach when the outcome is binary and data is nested into two or more groups. In the model specifications here, the groups include region, constituency, and individual. In most specifications, I set the panel-level observations to the level of the constituency (n=14). However, in models where I only include respondents from the Rift Valley, there are only seven panel-level observations.

[26] A Kikuyu respondent who experienced direct exposure to the PEV has a 95% probability of agreement with the anti-outsider statement compared to 89% if they are not direct victims. A Kalenjin resident by contrast, has an 80% probability of agreeing with the statement if s/he is not a direct victim, and a 90% probability is s/he was a victim.

Table 8.6 *Effects of violence exposure on openness to ethnic outsiders*

Variables	Model 1	Model 2	Model 3 (Rift Valley)	Model 4 (Rift Valley)
Direct violence	0.938**		0.785*	
	(0.406)		(0.460)	
Indirect violence		0.505*		0.895**
		(0.306)		(0.366)
Has a title deed	0.132	0.137	0.483	0.549
	(0.219)	(0.219)	(0.370)	(0.376)
Ethnicity: Kalenjin	−0.366	−0.523		
	(0.417)	(0.412)		
Ethnicity: Mijikenda	−1.495***	−1.579***		
	(0.517)	(0.513)		
Ethnicity: Other group	−0.790	−0.858*		
	(0.499)	(0.493)		
Kalenjin dummy			−0.781*	−0.920**
			(0.406)	(0.403)
Region: Coast	−1.114**	−1.106**		
	(0.477)	(0.491)		
Controls	Y	Y	Y	Y
Constituency Pop (2009)	−0.544	−0.484	−1.339	−1.836*
	(0.721)	(0.738)	(0.884)	(0.951)
Pop. Density (2009)	−0.254	−0.249	1.595**	2.015***
	(0.180)	(0.184)	(0.652)	(0.697)
Constant	9.828	9.098	8.421	11.53
	(8.459)	(8.650)	(8.495)	(8.853)
Observations	703	701	355	355
Number of constituencies	14	14	7	7

Note: All columns display results of a logit regression using random effects. Standard errors are clustered at the constituency level and displayed in the parentheses. The dependent variable is a binary measure of a respondent's openness to outsiders settling in their community, where value of 1= not open. All other variables are explained in the text. Controls included in all models but not reported. "Other group" refers to respondents who do not identify as one of the three main groups represented in sample (not Kikuyu, Kalenjin or Mijikenda). *** $p<0.01$, ** $p<0.05$, * $p<0.1$

Qualitative interviews suggest this effect as well. In interviews that I conducted in 2012, many respondents affected by the 2007–2008 postelection violence expressed strong aversions to the settlement of ethnic outgroups within or near their own communities. For example, a Kikuyu respondent living in Likia explains, "We have been fighting for the land in the East Mau [forest]. We don't want Kalenjin to settle there. If they settle, they will surround us and it would be problematic."[27] Many other residents expressed their opposition to Kalenjin settlement, emphasizing that residents lived peacefully "until [Kalenjin] were brought here by the government.[28]"

The anti-outsider narratives that these Kikuyu farmers express are particularly salient and explicit. These attitudes, however, are not a given. Nor are they commonplace. Kikuyu residents and neighboring Kalenjin are particularly against the settlement of the other group because there is a history of violent confrontation between the two – in 1992, 1997, and again in 2007. Both communities see the other as a threat. A Kalenjin living in the neighboring farm of Mauche expresses a similarly exclusive view, claiming that "If it were possible, I would recommend [Kikuyu] exclusion from the rest of the society. They should be provided with passports to enable them to move into other regions until such a time that they will learn to live peacefully."[29] The survey results and qualitative interviews provide strong evidence that people who have experienced election violence will be less receptive to ethnic outsiders settling in or near their own community.

Finally, it is useful to note that respondents from the Coast region sample were far more likely to be open to outsiders. Similarly, respondents who identify as Mijikenda – the main ethnic group along the Coast – are also more likely to remain open to outsiders. This is not surprising, given that less than 5 percent of respondents from the Kwale and Kilifi were exposed to the postelection violence in 2007–2008.

Fear of Intergroup Boundaries (Hypothesis 3)

As an additional way to measure distrust and fear of ethnic others, I estimate the effects of exposure to violence on an individual's

---

[27] Interview-Likia LBC-Nakuru County, June 27, 2012 (1).
[28] Interview-Likia LBC-Nakuru County, June 28, 2012 (5).
[29] Interview-Mauche SS-Nakuru County, July 21, 2012 (15).

likelihood of viewing boundaries between ethnic groups as high-risk spaces. I present results of these estimations in Table 8.7. In line with my expectations, results indicate that direct victimization increases an individual's fear of ethnic borderlands. Respondents who were directly victimized have a 46 percent probability of fearing border zones. Yet among respondents who did not experience direct violence, this probability drops by 16 percent. Further, while holding a title deed has little effect on one's openness to ethnic outsiders, it does appear to mitigate one's fear of ethnic borderlands. One explanation is that a person's fear of living near a border zone is based partly on a fear of being forcibly evicted or losing one's land or property to the neighboring group. Yet in holding a title deed, an individual may feel more insulated from these threats. These results also indicate the potential implications of formal land tenure to mitigate fear and distrust of ethnic outgroups.

In qualitative interviews too, respondents would remark on risk involved in living near a border zone with another community member. For example, a Kikuyu resident living in Nakuru County comments on the bravery of his family, "because no one else lives on the border but us." He continues, "Almost one kilometer along the Mauche border on the Likia side there are no people. They all fled the wrath of the Kalenjin. They are scared of living in that area with the clashes."[30]

Trust in Leaders (Hypothesis 4)

Table 8.8 shows results from four models that estimate the effects of exposure to election violence on an individual's likelihood of trusting a political leader (Hypothesis 4). As descriptive statistics in Table 8.2 reveal, the large majority of respondents trust at least one authority figure, be it a chief, village elder, or member of parliament. Yet 22 percent indicate that they do not trust any political leader – formal or informal. So how does exposure to violence affect this trust deficit? All four models indicate that both direct and indirect exposure to election violence have a negative and statistically significant effect on one's probability of trusting a political leader. Predicted probabilities from Model 1 indicate that an individual who did not experience election violence has an 80 percent probability of trusting some political

---

[30] Interview-Likia LBC-Nakuru County, June 28, 2012.

Table 8.7 *Effects of violence on fear of intergroup boundary*

Variables	Model 1	Model 2	Model 3 (Rift Valley)	Model 4 (Rift Valley)
Direct violence	0.848***		0.711**	
	(0.282)		(0.278)	
Indirect violence		0.486**		0.430*
		(0.248)		(0.255)
Has a title deed	−0.676***	−0.624***	−0.246	−0.221
	(0.223)	(0.220)	(0.261)	(0.260)
Ethnicity: Kalenjin	−0.505	−0.746**		
	(0.321)	(0.309)		
Ethnicity: Mijikenda	−0.347	−0.539		
	(0.476)	(0.469)		
Ethnicity: Other group	0.163	0.00108		
	(0.414)	(0.407)		
Kalenjin dummy			−0.405	−0.523**
			(0.270)	(0.265)
Region: Coast	−1.304**	−1.227**		
	(0.574)	(0.563)		
Controls	Y	Y	Y	Y
Constituency Pop. (2009)	−1.523	−1.432	1.159*	1.077*
	(0.952)	(0.893)	(0.623)	(0.640)
Pop. Density (2009)	0.0713	0.0845	−1.556***	−1.397***
	(0.278)	(0.263)	(0.465)	(0.472)
Constant	19.31*	18.16*	−4.521	−4.595
	(11.15)	(10.46)	(6.177)	(6.234)
Observations	709	707	361	361
Number of constituencies	14	14	7	7

Note: All columns display results of a logit regression using random effects. Standard errors are clustered at the constituency level and displayed in the parentheses. The dependent variable is a binary measure of a respondent's fear of ethnic borderlands, where 1= fearful. All other variables are explained in the text. Controls included in all models but not reported. "Other group" refers to respondents who do not identify as one of the three main groups represented in sample (not Kikuyu, Kalenjin or Mijikenda). *** $p<0.01$, ** $p<0.05$, * $p<0.1$

Table 8.8 *Effects of violence exposure on trust in political leaders*

Variables	Model 1	Model 2	Model 3 (Rift Valley)	Model 4 (Rift Valley)
Direct violence	−0.854**		−0.959**	
	(0.385)		(0.461)	
Indirect violence		−1.119***		−1.341***
		(0.379)		(0.515)
Has a title deed	1.034***	0.993***	1.440***	1.354***
	(0.262)	(0.263)	(0.517)	(0.509)
Ethnicity: Kalenjin	−0.720	−0.534		
	(0.488)	(0.477)		
Ethnicity: Mijikenda	−0.654	−0.553		
	(0.551)	(0.543)		
Ethnicity: Other group	−1.107**	−0.998*		
	(0.520)	(0.516)		
Kalenjin dummy			0.672	1.045*
			(0.554)	(0.559)
Region: Coast	−1.859***	−2.237***		
	(0.658)	(0.683)		
Controls	Y	Y	Y	Y
Constituency Pop. (2009)	−0.169	−0.202	−2.904	−2.341
	(1.217)	(1.200)	(2.357)	(2.541)
Pop. Density (2009)	−0.420	−0.425	3.083*	2.614
	(0.315)	(0.310)	(1.705)	(1.825)
Constant	7.151	7.945	18.78	15.47
	(14.26)	(14.06)	(22.88)	(24.66)
Observations	713	711	346	346
Number of constituencies	14	14	7	7

Note: All columns display results of a logit regression using random effects. Standard errors are clustered at the constituency level and displayed in the parentheses. The dependent variable is a binary measure of a respondent's trust in political leaders where value of 1= trusting. All other variables explained in the text. Controls included in all models but not reported. "Other group" refers to respondents who do not identify as one of the three main groups represented in sample (not Kikuyu, Kalenjin or Mijikenda). *** $p<0.01$, ** $p<0.05$, * $p<0.1$

authority figure, yet an individual who has experienced violence has only a 68 percent likelihood.

Qualitative evidence based on interviews with survivors of election violence helps illustrate this effect. For example, when I ask a respondent in Likia who he would trust to protect his land, he remarks, "If I have trouble with my land, there is no one whom I trust to protect me. I will fight for what is mine directly."[31] Another respondent points to the impossibility of trusting a set of leaders who failed to protect his land and livelihood: "The government says that they protect us. Meanwhile, our houses are being torched."[32] These effects are perhaps, not surprising. Among the most important role of a liberal democratic state is to protect the life and property of its citizens. When the state fails to uphold this contract, affected citizens will question the capacity and legitimacy of the state, and by extension, local and national political leaders.

Interethnic Community Engagement (Hypothesis 5)

Table 8.9 presents four models that estimate the effects of exposure to electoral violence on one's participation in interethnic community engagement. As I explain in the section above, the dependent variable measures how frequently an individual attends a meeting with members of other ethnic communities. I hypothesized that exposure to violence would increase one's likelihood of engaging in interethnic spaces, including meetings. The results presented in Table 8.8 provide evidence for this hypothesis. People who experienced violence are more likely to attend intergroup meetings compared to people who did not experience the 2007–2008 postelection violence. However, this result only holds for people who have experienced direct physical violence. Exposure to indirect violence appears to have no statistically significant effect on one's likelihood of attending interethnic meetings (Model 3). Model 1, however, indicates that an individual who experienced direct violence has a 70 percent probability of attending intergroup meetings. This probability drops to 53 percent for individuals who were not direct victims. One explanation is that individuals who experienced significant trauma and loss during the postelection violence may be more invested in local-level peace-building and conflict mitigation processes. Many of these peace-

---

[31] Interview-Likia LBC-Nakuru County, June 27, 2012.
[32] Interview-Likia LBC-Nakuru County, June 28, 2012.

Table 8.9 *Effects of violence exposure on interethnic engagement*

Variables	Model 1	Model 2	Model 3 (Rift Valley)	Model 4 (Rift Valley)
Direct violence	0.899***		1.030***	
	(0.304)		(0.328)	
Indirect violence		0.434*		0.519*
		(0.247)		(0.273)
Has a title deed	0.148	0.173	0.398	0.438
	(0.206)	(0.207)	(0.288)	(0.285)
Ethnicity: Kalenjin	−0.156	−0.308		
	(0.308)	(0.297)		
Ethnicity: Mijikenda	0.0247	−0.120		
	(0.475)	(0.468)		
Ethnicity: Other group	1.618***	1.485***		
	(0.486)	(0.477)		
Kalenjin dummy			−0.105	−0.279
			(0.322)	(0.312)
Region: Coast	−0.245	−0.198		
	(0.433)	(0.445)		
Controls	Y	Y	Y	Y
Constituency Pop. (2009)	0.231	0.288	−0.134	−0.201
	(0.510)	(0.518)	(0.674)	(0.694)
Pop. Density (2009)	−0.110	−0.100	0.512	0.693
	(0.142)	(0.144)	(0.484)	(0.492)
Constant	−1.789	−2.431	−0.877	−1.241
	(5.937)	(6.020)	(6.602)	(6.702)
Observations	625	623	320	320
Number of constituencies	14	14	7	7

Note: All columns display results of a logit regression using random effects. Standard errors are clustered at the constituency level and displayed in the parentheses. The dependent variable is a binary measure of the frequency with which a respondent attends interethnic community meetings, where 1=often/sometimes and 0=never/rarely. All other variables are explained in the text. Controls included in all models but not reported. "Other group" refers to respondents who do not identify as one of the three main groups represented in sample (not Kikuyu, Kalenjin or Mijikenda). *** $p<0.01$, ** $p<0.05$, * $p<0.1$

building activities involve meetings with different ethnic communities, including village elders, local politicians, and religious leaders. All three models also indicate that a person's proximity to a paved road or town center also effects their participation. Among people directly victimized by the postelection violence, an individual has an 82 percent probability of attending intergroup meetings if they live near a town center or trading area. Yet for victims who live more than 2 km from a paved road, the probability of attending such a meeting drops to 66 percent. This is likely because people who live far from a main road or trading center are less likely to walk the long distance required to attend community meetings – many of which take place in churches, schools, or assembly spaces that are located near a paved road or town center. In other words, living closer to a town center makes it more likely that an individual will interact with someone from another ethnic community and equally, makes attending such forums more convenient.

Conclusion

This chapter analyzes two research questions: what explains exposure to violence, and what are the effects of such exposure? In analyzing the first question, I aim to analyze whether and how divisive land appeals affect the escalation of violence. Doing so provides an additional way of examining the link between land narratives and the organization or mobilization of violence. While I cannot test how exposure to such appeals shaped decisions to participate in violence, I use exposure to divisive appeals as an indirect measure of a candidate's electoral strategy. Where elites rely on divisive appeals around land, salient and contentious land narratives most likely exist, narratives that a political candidate can exploit and deepen through the use of particular appeals. The results that I've presented in this chapter do indeed indicate that exposure to divisive political appeals increases the likelihood of violence. The likely mechanism, however, is not individual exposure per se. Rather, I suggest that hearing such appeals indicates a political space where using them is advantageous and effective. It is these underlying conditions – fear of losing land or hopes gaining land – that make violence more likely.

The second question considers the effects of violence. In doing so, I engage with a growing literature in conflict studies and cognitive psychology focusing on how exposure to political violence affects social and political trust and interethnic cooperation. Broadly, I find that those who have experienced direct violence are less open to outsiders, more fearful of ethnic borderlands, and less trusting of political leaders. These findings align with other studies demonstrating that victims of violence are less trusting and altruistic toward ethnic outgroups, and less trusting of state institutions. Yet in contrast to other studies, I find that those who have experienced violence are also more likely to participate in interethnic forms of civic engagement.

This chapter also aims to contribute to existing research on election violence. In particular, while there is a vibrant and growing literature on the causes and dynamics of election violence both crossnationally and subnationally, far fewer scholars focus explicitly on the effects of election violence, particularly at the individual level. Instead, most analyses observe broad institutional and behavioral changes, such as a decline in voter registration or turnout (Bekoe & Burchard 2017; Höglund 2009), the erosion of state legitimacy and trust in state institutions, further politicization of the state bureaucracy (Hassan & O'Mealia 2018), changes in the ethnic composition of political units (Kasara 2016), or the increased likelihood for conflict recurrence (Burchard 2015). This last point has received particular attention among studies that focus on the costs of holding elections in weak or postconflict settings (e.g. Flores & Nooruddin 2016; Brancati & Snyder 2013).

Yet very few of these studies specify the micro-mechanisms through which election violence reinforces certain political orders while destabilizing others. By examining how the experience of election violence affects people's attitudes and behaviors, this chapter identifies potential pathways through which changes at the individual level might have broader implications for peace-building, national unity, and future violence. Specifically, my first finding indicates that exposure to election violence may make future violence more likely because citizens become more hostile and less willing to include people from other ethnic communities. As Kasara (2016) observes, the self-segregation that these fears and antipathies produce facilitates the spread of rumors and hate speech that often precede violence.

My second main finding suggests that exposure to election violence makes people less likely to trust their leaders. On the one hand, a decline in trust can undermine spaces of state legitimacy, which can erode the state's monopoly on the use of violence. In addition, if people who have experienced violence are less likely to trust political leaders to protect their land or livelihood – as the findings here suggest – they may turn to more informal sources of authority and power. While some of these alternative institutions may align with the democratic process, others work actively against it. For instance, people may be more inclined to support or join vigilante groups, local gangs, or armed, extralegal organizations. Alternatively, a reduction in political trust can have positive implications as well. It may make citizens more vigilant, and less receptive to the fearmongering of their leaders, and more willing to sanction leaders who use or encourage violence.

My third and more encouraging finding is that while the experience of violence may make people both less trusting of ethnic others and their own leaders, people continue to engage with one another across ethnic lines. One explanation is that the experience of violence makes people feel that they have more at stake in the reconciliation process, and thus these individuals may be more willing to attend community meetings with other ethnic groups. And because citizens often view electoral violence as cyclical – and hence likely to reoccur – they may have particularly strong incentives to enter into dialogue with other ethnic or political groups, including former rivals. More so, as trust in political leadership erodes, affected individuals may see themselves as their own best ambassadors.

Stepping back, these findings challenge the conventional wisdom that "violence begets violence." Instead, the chapter demonstrates that the effects of violence do not fall neatly into pro- or antisocial outcomes. Rather, the responses and coping strategies of individuals can appear contradictory: a deepening of social and political distrust and simultaneously, a greater willingness to reach across ethnic boundary lines to rebuild local social orders. Finally, analyzing the effects of violence provides a more complete view of the process of violence, providing insights into the pathways through which the experience of violence increases and mitigates the likelihood of conflict recurrence.

9 | Conclusion

This book opens with the contrasting stories of Mauche and Ogilgei – two seemingly similar communities with very different experiences of electoral violence: one where significant violence escalated in 2007–2008, and another where there has never been election violence. This very local-level variation in the occurrence of electoral violence motivates one of the main questions in this book: why does violence escalate in one local context, but not another? To answer this question of spatial variation, I ask an additional set of questions about the organization and dynamics of violence. Specifically, I've argued that the occurrence of violence is a joint production between the electoral incentives of political elites and motives of ordinary citizens. This view of violence shifts the focus from one that is a primarily elite-driven process to one in which elites must organize, collaborate with, or coerce local supporters.

One of the main arguments that I've presented in this book is that in contexts where institutions in land are weak, and where land is a key source of livelihood and identification, land narratives can serve as a key device around which elites and citizens coordinate the use of violence. These land narratives work by providing a tool or "script" that elites and citizens use to polarize groups, underscore the urgency and legitimacy of land claims, and specify a program of action that offers symbolic and material benefits at the individual and group level. Taken together, these narratives have the power to mobilize violent forms of collective action when they succeed in convincing people that elections present a threat to their land rights or a window of opportunity to acquire land.

Yet as I emphasize throughout the book, a key challenge is to explain when and how contentious land narratives become viable frames for elites and citizens to jointly produce electoral violence.

I present a theory of electoral violence that proceeds in two main stages. In the first, I focus on explaining variation in contentious land narratives, asking why contentious land narratives become salient features of local politics in some spaces, yet less so in others. Broadly, I show that contentious land narratives are more likely to form where there is inequality in land rights between two distinct groups, defined along ethnic or class lines. I make a further distinction between significant land inequality and moderate land equality. Where there is significant land inequality, the most salient cleavage line tends to be class – not because ethnic identities do not matter, but because the category of landlord and tenant is more profound and salient in everyday life. By contrast, where there is moderate land inequality, ethnic rather than class identity becomes the more powerful line of distinction, and hence the more salient cleavage line.

In the second stage, I focus on explaining variation in the escalation of electoral violence. Using both qualitative interviews and micro-quantitative data based on my survey results, I've shown that local-level electoral violence is most likely to escalate where there is: 1) moderate inequality in land rights between two ethnically distinct groups who share the same political space; 2) salient and contentious land narratives between these two groups; and 3) a "strong land patron" who can deploy these land narratives to convince or compel ordinary citizens to participate in violence.

I place particular emphasis on the condition of moderate land inequality. While contentious land narratives also emerge in contexts of significant inequality, I've argued that moderate land inequality tends to be endogenous to a local political order defined by patronage politics, one where citizens acquire land and tenure security in part, through political leaders who act as "land patrons." In these environments where the political leader acts as a strong land patron, the leader can signal his or her willingness and ability to protect and redistribute land rights, and in particular, the ability to reward violence with land and other goods.

In this sense, we can think of moderate land inequality as being both a feature of patronage politics, but equally, as generating a set of land narratives that are particularly conducive to violent forms of political mobilization; narratives that are ethnically exclusive, establish a program of action for securing or reclaiming land, and specify a clear target group. Further, where there is moderate land inequality, there should also be lower barriers to violent collective action. This is partly because the aggrieved group is likely to identify along ethnic rather than class lines (Bates 1983).

Generalizability

Broadly, I suggest that struggles over land can provide a critical lens to understand the dynamics of electoral violence, and more broadly, struggles over democratic consolidation. The central argument that I have developed can travel to other multiethnic, democratizing, and postconflict societies where property rights are not well institutionalized and can therefore be easily politicized or expropriated. This theory is more likely to travel to contexts where a majority of citizens continue to rely on land for livelihood purposes.

In addition, this book focuses on how political leaders use the issue of land to persuade and mobilize ordinary citizens to fight on their behalf. Hence, because this is a question about why *ordinary* people participate in violence, the theory has less applicability to contexts where state security forces are the primary perpetrators of violence.[1] For example, I would not expect this argument to have much applicability to Iran's 2009 postelection violence, where the government ordered the police and a paramilitary group (the Basij) to suppress people protesting the election results (HRW 2013a). In the African context, the Ethiopian government has used its state security forces to brutally suppress and kill protestors. In the 2005 Ethiopian elections for example, the police were accused of massacring 193 protestors. Yet because these protestors were not also using violence, this case falls beyond the scope of my theory. While security forces have contributed to election violence in Kenya, the 2007–2008 postelection violence is a case where "ordinary citizens" also participated in significant numbers. Further, because I explain the process of mobilization, I do not generalize to contexts where individuals have no agency over their participation, where state or

---

[1] By "ordinary citizens," I refer to cases where individuals who are not elected officials or members of a state security force are recruited into vigilante or paramilitary groups such as the Kalenjin Warriors or *Mungiki* in Kenya, the *Interahamwe* militia in Rwanda, or the *Imbonerakure* in Burundi.

nonstate armed groups force or coerce individuals to fight and kill (Humphreys & Weinstein 2006).[2]

With these scope conditions in mind, I exclude at one end countries with well-consolidated democracies that have strong and inclusive property rights institutions. At the other extreme, I exclude countries that remain under authoritarian regimes where opposition parties do not compete in elections (e.g. *de jure* single party regimes such as Azerbaijan) or countries where violence is carried out almost exclusively by state security forces (e.g. Iran).

As a way of demonstrating how the argument generalizes to other countries, I select a set of country case studies where my theory of electoral violence might extend. Specifically, I suggest that election violence is possible where each of the three conditions that I've outlined in this book are present. These include: 1) *moderate* land inequality between two ethnically distinct groups, 2) contentious land narratives between these groups, and 3) the successful deployment of these narratives to organize election violence[3]. I begin by summarizing three countries where I identify all three conditions. In the second set of cases, I present countries that are possible cases for election violence, yet not all three conditions for election violence are present. I summarize these cases in Table 9.1.

Burundi

I begin by evaluating the context of pre-2015 Burundi. Here we find that the three broad conditions for electoral violence are present. Land had become one of Burundi's most pressing political and socioeconomic challenges. Like Kenya, the vast majority of the population relies on land as its primary income source (90 percent).[4] Yet unlike Kenya, contentious land politics is largely a product of decades of violence and civil war that created mass displacement. The first wave of

---

[2] Both state and nonstate groups have used forced recruitment of fighters. This has been documented in countries such as Sierra Leone, with the Revolutionary United Front, the Liberian National Police led by Charles Taylor, the Lord's Resistance Army in Northern Uganda, and the Revolutionary Armed Forces (FARC) in Colombia.

[3] Specifically, elites have greater ability to mobilize election violence where they act as strong land patrons.

[4] USAID Country Profile: Property Rights and Resource Governance: Burundi. https://www.land-links.org/country-profile/burundi/

Table 9.1 *Comparative case analysis*

Country	Moderate land inequality	Contentious land narratives	Mobilization of narratives	Election violence
Burundi	Yes	Yes	Yes	Yes
Côte d'Ivoire	Yes	Yes	Yes	Yes
Bangladesh	Yes	Yes	Yes	Yes
Tanzania	No	No	Yes	No
Ghana	Yes	No	No	No
Exceptions to theory				
Colombia	No*	No	No	Yes

* Land inequality is best characterized as significant rather than moderate.

displacement came in the wake of the 1972 mass killings that resulted in the deaths of between 150 and 300,000 people (mostly Hutu). These ethnically and selectively targeted killings aimed to suppress Hutu insurgents seeking to overthrow the Tutsi-led regime (Lemarchand 2008).[5] Approximately 300,000 people fled the country following these massacres (Nkurunziza 2018). The second wave of displacement came after the 1993 coup d'état that resulted in the assassination of Melchior Ndadye, the country's democratically elected president and first Hutu president. The coup and the reprisal attacks between Hutu and Tutsi communities that followed pulled the country into a twelve-year civil war (1993–2005). Within the first year following the coup, approximately 50,000 people died (Reyntjens 2005). The war displaced approximately 400,000 people outside Burundian borders and created 880,000 IDPs.[6]

Forty years of war and political instability have pushed a significant portion of the population into refugee camps in Tanzania, the DRC, and Uganda, as well as in internal displacement camps. It is only in the last few years that displaced Burundians are beginning to return home.[7]

---

[5] Educated Hutus were selectively targeted as a way of "incapacitating" future Hutu leadership (Minorities at Risk 2009).

[6] UNHCR-WFP 2007.

[7] I refer to the relative stability that existed prior to the May 2015 coup attempt and the political violence that escalated in the months and years since.

Yet as thousands of families return home, some after an absence of forty years, many find their land occupied by new owners.[8]

Decades of violence have produced two groups of competing claimants: *returnees* who see themselves as the rightful owners of their family land and *current owners* who claim that they have purchased the land legally from neighbors, private sellers, or the state (Schwartz 2019). Many returnees view the new owners of their plots as perpetrators in the violence (Binder & Murithi 2013). In this regard, competing claims over land also overlap with narratives of justice and reconciliation.

The government created the National Land Commission (CNTB) to mediate and adjudicate competing claims.[9] In its first iteration, the commission suggested that the returnees and current residents split the plots of land under dispute. More recently, the CNTB shifted its favor to repatriated citizens over current landowners, declaring that all repatriated citizens would have full claim to contested plots.[10] Perceived state bias toward returnees at the expense of current owners has generated a narrative that the government is using land policy as a mode of "revenge-seeking."[11] These land narratives articulate competing claims over land but equally, fears of losing land to the rival group (returnees).

These narrative themes provide an extremely useful and dangerous device for political entrepreneurs to mobilize segments of the population. Land narratives in Burundi are powerful, in part because they invoke fears of losing land and underscore the right to reclaim lost or "stolen" land. Politicians on both sides use the land issue to make appeals like, "I promise to return to you what is rightfully yours" (Keenan 2015). These promises are credible among large segments of the population – especially supporters of the current president, Pierre Nkurunziza – because the Hutu-led government retains significant control over the country's land institutions. The power that the ruling

---

[8] Following the 1972 violence, the Burundian government redistributed vacated lands to new owners through agricultural settlement schemes (*paysannats*).

[9] The CNTB was formed as part of the Arusha Accords in 2000. These accords formalized a peace agreement (ethnic power sharing agreements) and put in place several measures to bring about more ethnically inclusive and democratic governance.

[10] "Fields of Bitterness II", Africa Report No. 214 17 Feb 2014 (ICG 2015).

[11] Ibid.

party has over the adjudication of land rights raises the stakes of upcoming 2020 elections.

Côte d'Ivoire

Political dynamics in Côte d'Ivoire provide an additional example of how inequality in land rights and contentious land narratives can shape the prospects and occurrence of election violence. One particularly salient division in Côte d'Ivoire exists between people who see themselves as native Ivorians (*autochthones*) and people seen as migrants or foreigners.[12] At different points in time, land rights have skewed either in favor of autochthones or "foreigners." This inequality, in the context of larger civil war dynamics, has contributed to a set of contentious land narratives between these two groups. During the 2010 electoral crisis, these narratives provided an effective tool for elites seeking to gain political support and organize violence.

The origins of Côte d'Ivoire's current land conflict date back to the early postcolonial period when President Félix Houphouët-Boigny encouraged the in-migration of foreign labor to stimulate the growth of cocoa and coffee sectors in the south. To incentivize migrants, Houphouët-Boigny declared in 1963 that the "land belongs to those who make it productive." The language of this policy implied, however, that as migrants entered the region in mass, there was not a clear policy for adjudicating land rights between migrants and autochthons. In the absence of unambiguous *de jure* land rules, the longer-standing informal system known as the *tutorat* shaped rights between new migrants and Ivoirians. Under this patron–client system, migrants gained access to land in exchange for the labor or annual payments they offered to autochthons who retained moral authority over the land (Klaus & Mitchell 2015).

The political climate shifted from pro-migrant under Houphouët-Boigny to ultranationalist in the 1990s. This culminated in the 1998 Land Law declaring that only Ivoirian citizens could own land. This decisive nativist shift in land policy prompted both groups to question the strength and legitimacy of their land claims relative to the other group. Legally, native Ivoirians (autochthons) had stronger land

---

[12] Migrant refers to internal migrants (e.g. from the Baoulé region) and from neighboring countries (Mali, Bukina Faso, and Guinea).

tenure security. As citizens, they were entitled to make individual claims to the land. Yet many Ivoirians believed so-called "migrants" had benefited disproportionally from the productive use of the land. As migrants reaped the benefits from the soil, autochthons feared that they would lose their user rights as "sons-of-the soil." Meanwhile, migrants feared evictions from the lands they had farmed for generations.

In the context of the contentious election of 2010 and the larger civil war, these narratives provided a mechanism for political elites to organize violent collective action among ordinary citizens in the pre- and postelectoral period. Elites drew on existing narratives to convince supporters that violence was necessary for defending and strengthening land rights. This strategy is evident in the cocoa regions, where pro-Gbagbo media outlets bombarded radio listeners and television viewers with hate messages that encouraged violence against migrants (Klaus & Mitchell 2015: 631). At the time, many autochthons threatened to expropriate migrants' lands if Gbagbo were to lose the elections (Airault 2010). In the early days of the postelectoral crisis, pro-Gbagbo supporters distributed anti-migrant propaganda leaflets, which read: "the hour has come for ultimate vengeance" (Klaus & Mitchell 2015: 632). The handouts urged autochthons to kill and chase away migrants.

In this context, land narratives rooted in fears of losing land provided a rhetorical device for politicians to mobilize violence. These dynamics exist in various forms throughout the African continent, particularly in countries where the state or political elites retain formal or informal control over the distribution of land rights. In these cases, elections become high stakes events for ordinary citizens because they believe that their access and rights to land hinge on the victory of a particular party (Boone 2009).

Bangladesh

I also consider how my theory applies to democratizing contexts outside of Africa. One such example is the violence that escalated in certain regions of Bangladesh during the 2014 parliamentary elections. At the national level, the opposition Bangladesh Nationalist Party (BNP) violently protested the elections when the ruling party, Awami League (AL) refused to allow a "neutral caretaker government" to monitor the election. Awami League supporters became targets of attacks across the country. I focus on how local tensions around land access and tenure security shaped the dynamics of conflict locally, focusing specifically on land tensions in the southwest, where minority Hindu communities faced violent evictions and seizures of their land by supporters of the opposition party (BNL) and the alliance party, Jamaat-e-Islami.

Much of the violence occurred in the southwestern districts (Satkhira district) along the border with India. The region is characterized by extreme land scarcity due to both population pressures and environmental fragility of the region, a very weak and highly politicized property rights system, and intercommunal tensions between Bengali Hindus who constitute a large minority and Muslims who are the small majority (Allchin 2014). Members of both communities believe that their land rights hinge on the election of their party (AL for Hindus and BNL and the smaller Jamaat-e-Islami for Muslims). The two main political parties tap into narratives of land insecurity and political representation to divide communities during elections. Politicians tell supporters, "if you burn their house, you will get their land," referring to opposition supporters (ibid.). The seizure of land and land documents provides politicians with an easy source of patronage to reward loyal followers. Equally, displacing or burning the lands of minority Hindus (i.e. AL supporters) enables the BNL and Jamaat-e-Islami to assert their political dominance in the region. Further, the destruction of land and the abrogation of land rights enable parties to punish political rivals. Human Rights Watch, for example, has documented how the security forces of the AL destroyed the homes of BNL activists and then "took all the land registration documents into the courtyard and set them on fire" (HRW 2014a). Equally, by convincing supporters to destroy the homes, properties, and land documents of rival groups, opposition leaders from the BNL and Jamaat-e-Islami were able to undermine support for the governing party while redistributing land to supporters.

Tanzania

Tanzania provides a puzzling foil to Kenya's political trajectory. Kenya and Tanzania share many important similarities: common geography, national language (Swahili), and a shared history of European colonial rule.[13] Despite these similarities, Tanzania has never experienced significant electoral violence on the country's mainland, with the important exception of the 2000 elections on the island of Zanzibar.[14]

One factor that has likely mitigated possibilities for election violence is that land inequality, while present, tends not to fall on ethnic lines. That is, one's ethnic identity has not been a significant factor in whether and where a household obtains land. As a result, land narratives are not nearly as divisive as I observe in Kenya, despite internal migration and land shortages. This is not to say that there are not conflicts over land, but in most cases conflicts emerge between large companies (foreign owned) and indigenous groups (e.g. Maasai) or between farmers and pastoralists (Benjaminsen et al. 2009).

Drawing on the observations of Boone and Nyeme (2015), I outline three factors that help explain the absence of both group-based land inequality and contentious land narratives. First, at independence, the newly independent government significantly revised preexisting colonial institutions, undermining the power of customary authorities to allocate or manage land on behalf of the central state (Boone & Nyeme 2015; Miguel 2004). In doing so, the state cut one of the main links that facilitated the institutionalization of ethnicity under colonial rule. Boone and Nyeme (2015) note that even before independence, Tanzania's property rights institutions were unique in the region. A 1923 land law "recognized customary rights ... and invested these in the *land user,* not the ethnic group." These users were granted with titles. This policy stands in stark contrast to many colonial policies in Kenya and elsewhere, which transformed customary lands into "native reserves" or ethnically defined units where land titles were held by the colonial state (i.e. the British Crown).

A second important factor was the forced state-led villagization process that formed part of Julius Nyerere's Ujamaa policy. Under this socialist vision of rural re-engineering, about 50 percent of the

---

[13] Edward Miguel (2004) suggests that Kenya and Tanzania make for natural paired comparison. Importantly, they have quite different colonial experiences, with Kenya being administered by the British Crown and having a population of white settlers, while Tanzania fell under German rule (until World War I).

[14] In January 2001, state security forces violently suppressed protestors in Zanzibar who were protesting the alleged irregularities of the October 2000 election. Security forces opened fired, killing 35–40 Zanzibar residents. They also went door-to-door, "arresting, beating, and sexually abusing island residents" (HRW 2002a).

population was uprooted from rural and urban homes and resettled in Ujamaa villages (Boone & Nyeme 2015: 13). The policy altered how people and communities could make land claims. By moving families and communities away from what they viewed as their ancestral or community land, villagization undermined land claims based on ethnic identity or first-comer rights. Equally, villagization produced the opposite effect from settlement schemes in Kenya: it made villages more ethnically and culturally heterogeneous by opening them up to Tanzanians from different regions of the county, in effect "[chipping] away at the principle of ethnic homelands by altering facts on the ground" (Boone & Nyeme 2015: 13). Further, the relatively equal distribution of land plots across families, regardless of ethnic identification, meant that contentious land narratives were less likely to form along ethnic lines.

In sum, Tanzania is not a likely case for land-related electoral violence because ethnic identity does not provide a mechanism for claiming or acquiring land. Land politics emerged from a set of nation-building policies that aimed to restructure land rights along political and administrative lines rather than ethnicized territorial space.

Ghana

Ghana provides a further test of the theory. I suggest that while there is moderate land inequality between groups in certain spaces, land narratives are rarely contentious, with a few important exceptions.[15] Hence, while politicians may appeal to the tenure rights of a particular group, such appeals tend to be isolated to a few ethnically diverse urban constituencies (see Klaus & Paller 2017). I highlight a few reasons why inequality in land tends not to produce the type of contentious land narrative that can shape violent political mobilization.

First, while there is land inequality between insiders and outsiders, this insider–outsider cleavage is distinct from Kenya or Côte d'Ivoire. In Ghana, ethnic insiders typically benefit from customary land tenure rights, while ethnic outsiders (strangers) must bargain for subordinate and hence more tenuous land rights (Boone 2014). Ghana's customary land regime means that traditional authorities, rather than the state,

---

[15] See Lund (2003), "Bawku is still volatile."

control, manage, and sell the land in trust of the communities (Boone 2014).[16] Tenure rights are distributed along ethnic lines with preference given to members of the group (i.e. members under a particular "stool"). Chiefs can sell land to outsiders, such as ethnic outsiders, investors, or politicians, but a good chief is expected to prioritize and protect the land and development needs of his or her people.

Second, my theory predicts that contentious land narratives are most likely to form at the local level when "ethnic insiders" feel that outsiders threaten their land claims. Yet in Ghana, the insider–outsider cleavage is rarely cast in such stark terms. Historically, the demand for labor and the availability of land created incentives for chiefs to absorb strangers into communities. The institutionalization of a two-party system in the 1960s, alongside the rising demand for land, politicized access to land. Despite these changes, land narratives in Ghana are still less contentious than they are in Kenya and Côte d'Ivoire. In part, this is because the customary land rights system has favored indigenous rights over the rights of migrants or strangers. Migrants tend not to assert claims to land, as they often have their own "ethnic homelands" elsewhere. As a result, indigenous residents are less likely to feel threatened because they maintain relatively strong land rights in their ethnic homeland.[17]

There are scenarios however, where changing inequalities in land rights have exacerbated contentious narratives around land and territory. These narratives form where migrants become a large minority or small majority in a region or district, becoming large enough to alter the local balance of power, and by extension, large enough to alter the distribution of material goods and developmental resources. This is the case in rapidly growing cities like Accra, where migrants have supplanted the indigenous Ga as the majority (Nathan 2019; Paller 2019).

I also predict that electoral violence is more likely when political leaders have the incentive and ability to exploit existing land narratives during electoral campaigns. While Ghana has not experienced significant election violence, there are scenarios when political elites have incentives to resort to low-level forms of violence, particularly when

[16] Lands under traditional authority (referred to as "stool" or "skin" lands) cover about 75 percent of the country territory (Onoma 2009).

[17] Geschiere and Gugler (1998) term the idea of local citizenship, "primary patriotism." The term also describes why migrants maintain strong relationships with their own families back home (see also Lentz 2013).

the margin of victory is narrow and, more importantly perhaps, when the politician's party has an "indigene advantage" at the local level (Klaus & Paller 2017).[18] These low-level forms of violence escalated in the run-up to the 2012 presidential election and included intimidation, the use of "thugs" (i.e. macho-men), physical assaults against targeted individuals, death threats, and damage to property belonging to rival party members (Bob-Milliar 2014).[19]

In sum, while low-level election violence has escalated in a few local cases, Ghana is not a likely case for large-scale electoral violence. One of the key mechanisms of restraint is the role that customary land tenure institutions play in diffusing the stakes of electoral outcomes (Boone 2014). Specifically, because state actors do not have direct control over the distribution of land rights, traditional authorities are able to mediate identity-based tensions around access to land and other resources. Further, because traditional authorities have considerable autonomy over land, they can insulate their members from the negative effects of an electoral loss. Even if a community supports the losing political party, a strong chief will ensure that ethnic insiders can access and secure land, regardless of election outcomes. Hence, national elections are rarely cast in such zero-sum terms as they are in countries such as Kenya and Burundi where the central state leverages significant control over the rights to land.

Colombia

I consider the case of Colombia, a country marked by decades of civil war violence and extremely high rates of land inequality alongside a relatively stable democracy. Colombia's civil war began in the 1960s with the formation of the *campesino*-based movement known as the Revolutionary Armed Forces of Colombia (FARC). The movement aimed to evade and eventually resist the state (Arjona 2014). Struggles to access and secure land have played an important role in

---

[18] This finding draws largely on a paired-case comparison of two electoral
      constituencies in Accra (Ayawaso Central and Odododiodioo), where
      I conducted in-depth interviews and focus groups with party organizers,
      candidates, and supporters (January–April 2012).
[19] In the Accra, the "indigenous" are the Ga. During the voter registration process,
      for example, there have been attempts to prevent Akan market and tradespeople
      from registering to vote in "Ga Lands."

the ongoing conflict between the FARC rebels, the government, and paramilitary groups. These struggles have also taken on new dynamics in the post-civil war period, particularly between right-wing paramilitary groups and campesinos.

The Colombia case is distinct from the scenarios I outline in a few important ways. First, competing land claims tend to play out between smallholder farmers and paramilitary groups, rather than between ethnic "insiders" and "outsiders." In the postconflict period, campesinos have struggled to reclaim the land they lost during the war (Arjona 2014; Romero 2000).[20]

Second, while there is election violence, the violence is based primarily on perceived political loyalties rather than ethnic identification (Steele 2018). Political parties and armed groups have targeted ordinary citizens, often with the aim of forcing them off their land, but many of the recorded incidents of election violence are against local politicians.[21]

Third, while landlord–tenant dynamics mitigate the potential for election violence in Kenya, the case of Colombia points to the opposite effect: the likelihood for electoral violence tends to correspond with spaces where land holding inequality is highest. Nieto-Matiz (2019) suggests that this relationship exists because in such spaces, elites and armed actors alike have greater incentive and capacity to organize violence.

An additional factor that distinguishes Colombia is the presence and power of multiple and competing armed groups, including rebel groups such as FARC, paramilitaries, and drug cartels. The power of these groups is an enduring legacy of the country's decades-long civil war. Where land concentration is high, armed groups are likely to be more active, in large part because these groups seek to gain control over valuable territory (Nieto-Matiz 2019). Violence is possible then, either when armed actors use violence to alter elections or when landed elite, seeking to preserve the status quo, collude with armed actors to ensure a particular electoral outcome (Nieto-Matiz 2019; Albertus 2017).

In sum, land shapes the dynamics of violence in Colombia, but the mechanisms are distinct. First, political party actors are not directly

---

[20] *The Economist* (September 16, 2010), "This Land Is Our Land."

[21] The Independent Electoral Observer Mission (MOE) has recorded numerous murders and kidnappings, mostly against local political candidates (MOE 2011).

responsible for organizing election-related attacks. Instead, non-state armed groups carry out the majority of assassinations or other violent attacks.[22] Behind these groups are a class of powerful landowners who seek to protect their landed property. In addition, the targets of election-time violence are not typically civilians defined by their ethnic identification. Instead, they tend to be local political candidates and state officials such as mayors, legislators, city council members, or governors and candidates who threaten the landholdings of powerful elites.[23]

In this context, violence has become an effective strategy for private and political actors to influence the electoral process. By employing targeted assassinations or threats, armed groups and wealthy landowners can ensure that local politicians do not interfere with their control over land and territory.[24] In many ways, electoral violence reproduces civil war dynamics whereby the use of violence provides a way of (re)asserting control over territory.

Implications

This book has four broad implications for the study of mobilization and electoral violence. First, the book demonstrates the importance of incorporating micro- and meso-level analyses into studies of electoral violence. By shifting from the macro- to the micro-level, scholars are able to develop more precise explanations about why electoral violence might emerge in one subnational region – city, neighborhood, or village – and not another. Being able to explain or predict why one community or region is more vulnerable to violence than others enables governments and aid agencies to make more targeted and locally appropriate interventions aimed at building resilience, mitigating conflict, or implementing postconflict peacebuilding programs.

Second, the theory and empirics I present point to the value in analyzing electoral violence as a process of mobilization rather than

---

[22] These armed groups include FARC, and the National Liberation Army (ELN) and paramilitary groups such as Rastrojos and Aguilas Negras (Ramsey 2011).

[23] In 2011, the MOE recorded 253 acts of election-related violence across 233 municipalities. Of these, 157 targeted political candidates.

[24] The resources at stake vary by region. In some areas paramilitary groups seek to maintain control over the cocoa trade, while in other areas it is oil (Casanare) or coal (Guajira).

an event based largely on the strategic calculations of elites. This process of mobilization requires coordination between elites and ordinary citizens. While scholars such as Kalyvas (2006, 2003) have made this claim with respect to the organization of civil war violence, most studies of electoral violence focus more narrowly on the electoral interests of political candidates and parties. Further, analyzing violence as a process also means that we think about the effects of violence, and the ways that experiencing or participating in violence shape the prospects for and dynamics of future violence.

Third, I suggest that narratives themselves – as frames, scripts, and collective stories – are a key yet overlooked causal mechanism linking institutional effects with the organization of violence. Scholars can analyze narratives as coordinating devices, methods of mobilization, and part of a process or mode of meaning-making. In particular, by studying the content and salience of particular narratives, conflict scholars gain insight into why certain actions become thinkable, possible, and even necessary (Autesserre 2017; Schatzberg 2001).

Lastly, this book reveals the ways that a focus on land – as a livelihood resource, source of identification, and form of territory – can provide a lens for explaining the process and dynamics of political violence. For much of the world's population, land sustains livelihoods, shapes identities, and provides a source of investment and security. Yet the centrality of land in political and everyday life also means that it can become a source of contentious politics and violence. This study provides a theory that links group struggles over land with different forms of conflict or violence: between squatters and large corporations, different ethnic communities, or rebels and the state. Land is a particularly powerful explanatory lens because it combines institutional, ideational, and material factors. By examining the meanings that people attach to land, property, and territory, scholars can gain a better understanding of why and when people are willing and able to mobilize or fight around issues of land security, territory, and identity.

Appendix A

Interview Protocol and List of Interviews

Methodological Note on Qualitative Interviews

During the comparative case study portion of this project, I interviewed 230 Kenyan residents living on settlement schemes and LBCs and conducted nineteen focus groups with youth and elders of these farms and communities. The majority of interviews were conducted in Swahili (Kenya's national language). All interviews were recorded using an audio recorder. Research assistants translated and transcribed these interviews. A research assistant who was fluent in Swahili or the relevant language, such as Kikuyu or Kalenjin, was always present during the interview and often assisted in conducting the interview. The average length of an individual interview was 45 minutes (ranging from 25 minutes to 90 minutes). I interviewed individuals in the privacy of their residence. Village escorts were never present during the actual interview. To protect the privacy of the respondent, escorts stood beyond earshot (outside the home or at the edge of the property) during the interview. The selection of respondents was not random. Village elders (or designated community leaders) escorted me though the interview process and hence were able to influence the selection of respondents. This selection was based on the respondent's willingness to speak, whether they were near the home, and their trust in the village elder or village guide (and by extension, trust in my agenda and my research assistant). Respondents were never asked to provide their name, or to identify their role in the electoral violence, although some chose to volunteer this information.

I held focus groups in each community after completing individual interviews. I grouped focus groups by two age-sets: youth and elders. The category of "youth" refers to young members of society who have not acquired a position of leadership in the family or community (in general, 18–35). Elders, meanwhile, refer to community leaders, usually older men. Focus group discussions followed a very similar questionnaire that I used in the one-on-one interviews. One objective of the focus groups was to use the group structure to facilitate a discussion around each question. The group format helped to highlight the beliefs, opinions, or narration of events that were widely shared, and those that were more idiosyncratic.

In addition to interviews with ordinary citizens, I also conducted interviews with key informants on issues relating to elections, electoral violence, human rights, and land. Informants in this category include Kenyan lawyers that have chaired commissions such as the Commission of Inquiry into the Illegal/Irregular Allocation of Land, the Truth Justice and Reconciliation Commission (TJRC), or the National Cohesion and Integration Commission, Kenyan academics and activists, and politicians and political officials (e.g. officials working for the Ministry of Lands). A list of these informants is available upon request.

Selected Interview Questions

The questions listed below are based on the two rounds of questionnaires that guided the research design that I outline in Chapter 1. Each stage aimed to uncover a different part of the process of violence. The first questionnaire (round 1) focused primarily on the respondent's land tenure and beliefs about land rights. The second questionnaire (round 2) focused on the respondent's interpretations and experiences of the electoral violence, and specifically, the postelection violence of 2007–2008. Because I repeated each questionnaire in multiple communities, I made several small changes to the questionnaire (either to improve the wording of the question or to adjust for the particular location). Hence, the numbering and exact wording of each question is not consistent. Further, because I translated these questions into Swahili and because of the semistructured style of the interview, the questions below served as "guide posts" for each interview, but wording and question order varied slightly.

Part I

Background
• In which community or region were you born?
• Where do you stay (live) now?

- When did you come to this village or community?
- Can you tell us why you first came to this community?
- How would you describe the type of farm or village where you are now staying?

Land Ownership and Access
- In this area (location/scheme/LBC) who owns most of the land?
- In the past, who owned or used this land?
- In your view, is there a certain group that has the right to use or cultivate this land today?
- Are you able to access a piece of land for your own family?
- If yes, what method do you use to access this land?
- If you do not have land access, what factors prevent you from accessing land?
- If you do not have access to a plot of land right now, did you have land in the past? Where did you have this land?
- If you have land, can you explain how and when you or your family first acquired this land? (i.e. who first helped you join the society or the settlement scheme?)
- What is the size and location of your plot now? Has this land been subdivided? How do you use this land?
- Would you say that the method of accessing land is different today than in the past?

Land Narratives
- When you hear people use the words "outsider" or "newcomers," what do these words mean to you?
- In your community, would you say that there is a certain group that arrived here first?
- Does this community have important boundaries?
- People and groups use different arguments to make claims to the land. Some people say they have the ancestral right to land. Others say they have purchased the land, and hence, they are the rightful owners. In your opinion, what does it mean when people say that they have the ancestral right (or historical right) to the land?
- Imagine that there are two groups arguing over the same space of land. The first group says that they are the true owners because they have ancestral rights to the land. The second group says that they are the real owners because they purchased the land and they hold the title deed. In your opinion, which group has the right to claim the

land? If these groups came to you to seek you help, what would you say?

- If a person holds a title deed to the land, does he or she have the right to own that piece of land? Why or why not?
- If you had a title deed to your land, would you feel that your land rights were safe?
- If there were clashes, would you feel safe remaining in your home if you held a title deed? Why or why not?
- If you felt that someone was threatening to take away your land, how would you try to protect your land? Whose help would you seek?
- After independence, do you think that the government tried to allocate the land equally between the different ethnic groups? Why or why not?
- How do you view the settlement schemes that President Kenyatta created? Were they mostly a success or a failure?
- How do you view the settlement schemes that President Moi created? Were they mostly a success or a failure?
- In your opinion, do you think that some settlement schemes and companies have been more successful than others? If so, where are these farms? Why do you think they have been more successful?
- In your view, do you think that politicians should consider history (historical events) when they distribute land or draw boundaries? In other words, do you think that the history of different groups should matter today?

Land Institutions
- Do you think the national government has done a good job managing land in this country? Why or why not?
- Do you think that the district level government (Ministry of Land, district offices, county council, MPs) have tried to allocate land in a way that is fair, legal, and transparent? Why or why not?
- Do you know how to access the Ministry of Lands or other offices related to land documentation and land security?
- Have you witnessed land grabbing, illegal allocation of land, or other forms of corruption among government officials? If so, when?

- If you have witnessed land grabbing, who are the main types of people grabbing land?
- Do you think political leaders can help people gain land? If so, can you describe the ways that politicians have given land to people in the past?
- Have you or your family benefited from land that the government has provided?
- Do you think the government or politicians have the right to take land away from people? Has the government ever taken land away from you or others in this area?
- Do you think that the local and national government has the power to protect the land rights of your community?
- In general, would you say that you trust the government, including the police and military, to protect your safety? Why or why not?

Part II

Remembering the Postelection Violence:
- Can you please share with us your own experiences during the most recent clashes (2007–2008)? Please take some time to provide as much detail as you can recall or feel comfortable providing (Guiding questions: *Were there warning signs? What happened first? What was the order of events? The first day, the second day . . . ? Where did the worst fighting take place?*)
- Some people have said they were able to see warning signs before the clashes. For example, people talk about rumors against "outsiders," secret meetings, cattle theft, and growing tension between communities. Did you see any warning signs before the violence broke out? If so, what were some of these signs?
- During the clashes, people sometimes remember a certain event that started the fighting between the two sides. Can you recall any particular event here?
- After the election results were announced, and the violence started to break out in certain places in the country, how did the youth here respond?
- During the violence, how did the elderly respond? How did they advise the youth? Did the young people listen to the elderly during this time?

- Can you remember if certain sections in ____ experienced worse fighting than other parts? If so, which sections were these?
- If you noticed that certain areas were affected more than others, do you know why?
- Did you notice if certain people were targeted more than others? If yes, what types of people seemed to be targeted?
- During the attacks, can you recall the main methods of violence that each side used? (e.g. burning homes, panga, theft, barricades in the road).
- How many people do you think left this community during or after the violence? How many have returned?
- Why do you think the areas such as X and Y were hotspots during the violence, but other areas with both Kikuyu and Kalenjin (or ODM and PNU) remained calm?
- Overall, would you describe the violence here as "politically organized," "spontaneous," or a combination of both? Can you explain?

Participation in the Election Violence
- In your opinion, what are some of the main reasons that people join in the clashes or become involved in the clashes?
- Do you think some young people believed they would gain something by fighting, such as land or money? Are they made promises by leaders?
- Which types of leaders (or politicians) are known to make promises of land or money to youth? Do you think they are usually from the local level (local councilors, party chairmen) or the "big men" at the top (like MPs)?

Mobilization
- In your time living here, have you ever experienced land disputes or other land problems? Have you ever felt that your own land rights were not secure?
- During campaign season, do you hear politicians using issues of land (such as promises to provide land titles) to win the support of people here? What are some ways that you hear politicians talking about land during campaigns?
- During election season (in the past or now) did you hear politicians sending messaging about removing outsiders? If yes, how do these statements make you feel?

- Do you believe that your land rights will be more secure if a certain political party or politician wins? If so, can you explain why you feel this way? If not, can you say why you think it does not matter?
- Do you think that some politicians send messages that can incite people or communities? If so, can you explain how these messages work?
- In your opinion, why do you think politicians use violence during election time?
- Do you feel safe living in your home now as the next election approaches? If yes, why do you feel safe this time, when violence has happened so many times in the past? If not, what makes you feel insecure or worried?
- In your opinion, what are the major obstacles to peace that still remain in this community?

Table A.1 *List of individual interviews*

Case	Location (constituency, county, region)	Total interviews	Men	Women	Date range
Likia LBC	Njoro, Nakuru, Rift Valley	37	28	13	6/27–07/03/12; 9/13–10/03/12
Mauche SS	Njoro, Nakuru, Rift Valley	42	38	8	7/18–7/21/12 10/4–10/10/12
Giwa resettlement farm	Rongai, Nakuru, Rift Valley	15	11	10	7/25–8/6/12
Belbar SS/ Umoja LBC	Rongai, Nakuru, Rift Valley	8	7	4	8/8–8/14/12
Ogilgei SS	Rongai, Nakuru, Rift Valley	16	15	4	8/15–9/5/12
Oljorai SS	Gilgil, Nakuru, Rift Valley	19	19	6	9/6–11/1/12
Hell's Gate	Naivasha, Nakuru, Rift Valley	14	7	7	10/13–10/20/12
Mwisho wa Lami SS	Njoro, Nakuru, Rift Valley	7	4	2	10/15–10/17/12
Tipis SS/Group ranch	Njoro, Nakuru, Rift Valley	14	13	2	10/18/2012

Table A.1 (*cont.*)

Case	Location (constituency, county, region)	Total interviews	Men	Women	Date range
Kisima IDP camp	Njoro, Nakuru, Rift Valley	4	2	2	10/29/2012
Ramisi I & II SS	Msambweni, Kwale, Coast	9	9	1	11/12–11/13/12
Kinondo SS	Msambweni, Kwale, Coast	15	16	2	11/14–11/17/12
Kijipwa SS	Kilifi South, Kilifi, Coast	23	18	6	11/20–11/25/12
Waitiki settlement	Likoni, Mombasa, Coast	6	4	2	12/02/12
Kembu farms (private)	Njoro, Nakuru, Rift Valley	1	1	0	8/10/2012

Note: The number of men and women interviewed in a given case may exceed total number of interviews where a single interview is conducted with more than one person. Total interviews: 230. SS signifies "settlement scheme" and LBC signifies "land-buying company."

Table A.2 *Focus group discussions*

Participants	Sublocation	Location	Date	Duration
Youth	Mauche settlement scheme	Njoro, Nakuru, RV	07/05/12	1:28:17
Elders	Mauche settlement scheme	Njoro, Nakuru, RV	07/21/12	1:39:25
Youth	Giwa settlement scheme	Rongai, Nakuru, RV	07/26/12	1:54:44
District Commissioners	Bontana Hotel, Nakuru Town	Nakuru, Nakuru, RV	08/13/12	38:15
Elders	Ogilgei LBC	Rongai, Nakuru, RV	08/14/12	1:35:14
Turkana squatters	Oljorai settlement scheme	Gilgil, Nakuru, RV	09/06/12	48:35:00
Youth	Oljorai settlement scheme	Gilgil, Nakuru, RV	09/11/12	1:35:03

Table A.2 (*cont.*)

Participants	Sublocation	Location	Date	Duration
Elders	Mauche settlement scheme	Njoro, Nakuru, RV	10/02/12	1:48:02
Youth group 1	Mauche settlement scheme	Njoro, Nakuru, RV	10/10/12	1:06:41
Youth group 2	Mauche settlement scheme	Njoro, Nakuru, RV	10/10/12	1:40:48
Youth	Likia LBC	Njoro, Nakuru, RV	10/03/12	1:12:18
Combined	Hell's Gate sublocation	Naivasha, Nakuru, RV	10/20/12	1:48:10
Maasai youth	Tipis Scheme/ Group Ranch	Njoro, Nakuru, RV	10/18/12	39:15:00
IDP youth	Kisima IDP Camp	Njoro, Nakuru, RV	10/29/12	45:54:00
Youth	Kinondo settlement scheme	Msambweni, Kwale, Coast	11/18/12	1:58:55
Elders	Kinondo settlement scheme	Msambweni, Kwale, Coast	11/18/12	1:10:54
Youth	Kijipwa settlement scheme	Kilifi South, Kilifi, Coast	11/28/12	1:23:48
Elders	Kijipwa settlement scheme	Kilifi South, Kilifi, Coast	11/28/12	1:15:03
Elders/MRC	Waitiki Settlement	Likoni, Mombasa, Coast	12/02/12	1:22:38
Youth	Kinondo settlement scheme	Msambweni, Kwale, Coast	11/18/12	1:58:55
Elders	Kinondo settlement scheme	Msambweni, Kwale, Coast	11/18/12	1:10:54
Youth	Kijipwa settlement scheme	Kilifi South, Kilifi, Coast	11/28/12	1:23:48
Elders	Kijipwa settlement scheme	Kilifi South, Kilifi, Coast	11/28/12	1:15:03
Elders	Waitiki Settlement	Likoni, Mombasa, Coast	12/02/12	1:22:38

Appendix B

Household-Level Survey

Table B.1 *Key independent and dependent variables*

Variable	Question Wording	Range
Direct violence	Please let me know if any of the following happened to your household: a) Your animals were stolen; b) Your house was burned or crops destroyed; c) You or other family members were injured; d) Several family members were injured; e) Family member(s) killed; f) None of these apply to you.	1–6 (recoded 0–1)
Indirect violence	When you remember the time following the elections, how would you describe events (within this ward)? a) Peaceful: no problems; b) some tension; c) some fighting; d) a lot fighting.	1–4 (recoded, 0–1)
Appeal 1: Violence	Please tell me if you have heard candidates make the following type of statement: *"If you kick out the other tribe, you will get their land"*: a) Yes; b) something like this; c) No.	1–3 (recoded, 0–1)
Appeal 2: Title promise	Have you heard candidates make the following type of statements? *"I will help you get title deeds or I will help to resettle you when I win."* a) Yes; b) Statement like this; c) No.	1–3 (recoded, 0–1)
Appeal 3: Free land	Have you heard candidates make the following type of statements? *"The other groups have land because they received it for free, while you did not receive anything. This is not fair to you."* a) Yes; b) Statement like this; c) No.	1–3 (recoded, 0–1)

Table B.1 (*cont.*)

Variable	Question Wording	Range
Appeal 4: Defend land	Have you heard candidates make the following type of statements? This is your ancestral land. If I win, I will help you defend this land: a) Yes; b) Something like this; c) No.	1–3 (recoded, 0–1)
Narrative 1: Anti-settlement	How much do you agree with the following: *I am comfortable with any Kenyan coming to live in this community, even if he has a title deed and I do not have my own: a) strongly agree; b) agree; c) disagree; d) strongly disagree, e) don't know (recoded where 1=disagree; 0 = agree).*	1–5 (recoded, 0–1)
Narrative 2: Invader	How much do you agree with the following: *Our community is landless today because other tribes have invaded and taken the land that belongs to us: a) strongly agree; b) agree; c) disagree; d) strongly disagree; e) don't know.*	1–5 (recoded, 0–1)
Narrative 3: Anti-outsider	How much do you agree with the following: *Outsiders do not deserve to own land here. The problem is that they only use corrupt means to buy land from indigenous people: a) strongly agree; b) agree; c) disagree; d) strongly disagree; e) don't know.*	1–5 (recoded, 0–1)
Fear of ethnic border	If a household lives near a border of another [ethnic] community, do they face greater risk of attack from another group, especially during elections? a) No (border makes no difference); b) a little; c) somewhat more risk; d) much more risk.	1–4 (recoded, 0–1)
Interethnic engagement	How often do you attend a community meeting with members from another tribe? a) Often; b) sometimes; c) occasionally; d) never.	1–4 (recoded 0–1)

Table B.1 (*cont.*)

Variable	Question Wording	Range
Trusts Leader	I am going to read a list of leaders. Tell me who you would trust the most to defend or promote your land rights or your land security: a) MP; b) GoK; c) political aspirant; d) ward councilor; e) village elders; f) chief; g) No trust.	1–7 (recoded, 0–1)

Table B.2 *Control variables*

Variable	Question wording	Range
Has a title deed	What type of documents, if any, do you have showing that you own your land? a) Title deed (real); b) title deed (fraudulent); c) plot allotment letter; d) shareholder certificate; e) letter; f) no document.	1–6 (recoded, 0–1)
Ethnicity	Which Kenyan language is your home language? All groups listed. Variable recoded into a) Kikuyu; b) Kalenjin; c) Mijikenda; d) other group.	
Age category	What is your age? a) 18–25; b) 26–35; c) 36–49; d) 50–65; e) 66 or over.	
Degree urban	Household is located in: a) urban area; b) trading center; c) roadside; d) within 2 km of paved road; e) more than 2 km from paved road.	1–5
School level	What is the highest level of education that you have completed? a) No formal school; b) some primary; c) some secondary; d) some university; e) university graduate.	1–6
Wealth	About how many shillings does your household earn on a normal day? a) Less than 200; b) 250–500; c) 600–1000; d) 1100–2000; e) over 2,000; f) don't know.	
Police station	How far is the nearest police station to your home? A) Very close (<10 minutes walking); b) close (20 minutes walking); c) somewhat near (30 mins walking); d) far (40 minutes walking); e) no police station.	1–5

Table B.3 *Other important variables (mentioned in various chapters)*

Variable	Question wording	Range
Displaced	Did you move to this area because you were displaced by the 2007–2008 postelection violence?	0–1
Past eviction	Have you or any members of your family ever been evicted by the government?	0–1
Eviction fear	How much do you fear being evicted by the government or another group? a) Not at all; b) a little; c) somewhat; d) a lot.	1–4 (recoded, 0–1)
Land security	Please tell me which statement you agree with most: a) I have land security because I have a title deed; b) I have land security because this is family land; c) I have land security because my tribe is the majority here; d) I have land security because there are no problems here; e) none of above: no land security.	1–5 (recoded, 0–1)
Ancestral land	Two different groups are arguing over the same space of land. The first group says that they are the true owners because they have ancestral rights to the land. The second group says that they are the real owners because they purchased the land and hold the title deed. In your view, which group has the right to the land? a) The group with the title deed; b) the group with ancestral rights; c) can't say.	1–3 (recoded, 0–1)
Pamphlets	In your community, how often do the following activities occur? Candidates distribute pamphlets with strong messages against the opposition groups: a) Often; b) sometimes; c) occasionally; d) never.	1–4
SMS messages	In your community, how often do the following activities occur? Candidates or party officers send out SMS messages giving warnings to the opposition or encouraging or inciting supporters against opposition: a) often; b) sometimes; c) occasionally; d) never.	1–4

Table B.3 (*cont.*)

Variable	Question wording	Range
Motivation	Many people say that politicians are able to convince youth to fight because they provide motivation. In this area, how much do these offers affect young people's involvement in the clashes or violent activities? a) A lot; b) somewhat; c) only a little; d) none.	1–4
Organization of violence	How would you describe the fighting that started after the election results? a) Not planned; b) planned by people at the grassroots; c) planned by people at the top; d) planned by people at the top and bottom; e) can't say/don't know; f) not applicable.	1–6 (recoded 0–1)

Table B.4 *Home language of respondents*

Rift Valley				Coast	
	Nakuru	Uasin Gishu	Kilifi	Kwale	Total
Kalenjin	45.67	72.84	0.0	16.13	32.12
	(95)	(118)	(0)	(25)	(238)
Kikuyu	48.08	16.0	0.93	1.94	16.87
	(100)	(20)	(2)	(3)	(125)
Mijikenda	0.0	0	77.78	66.45	36.57
	(0)	(0.0)	(168)	(103)	(271)
Kiswahili	0.48	0.62	13.43	0.0	4.18
	(1)	(1)	(29)	(0)	(31)
Kamba	0.48	1.23	1.85	12.16	3.51
	(1)	(2)	(4)	(19)	(26)
Luo	0.48	4.94	1.39	1.29	1.89
	(1)	(8)	(3)	(2)	(14)
Luhya	1.44	3.7	1.39	0.0	1.62
	(3)	(6)	(3)	(0)	(12)
Kisii	2.88	3.09	0.0	0.0	1.48
	(6)	(5)	(0)	(0)	(11)
Taita	0.0	0.0	2.78	0.65	0.94
	(0)	(0)	(6)	(1)	(7)

Table B.4 (*cont.*)

Rift Valley	Nakuru	Uasin Gishu	Kilifi	Coast Kwale	Total
Maasai	0.0	0.62	0.46	0.65	0.40
	(0)	(1)	(1)	(1)	(3)
Turkana	0.48	0.0	0.0	0.65	0.27
	(1)	(0)	(0)	(1)	(2)
Somali	0.0	0.62	0.0	0.0	0.27
	(0)	(1)	(0)	(0)	(2)
Total observations	208	162	216	155	741

Table B.5 *Location-level ELF index with predicted probabilities of direct exposure to violence*

County	Ward	ELF - 1989	Margins (PP)
Uasin Gishu			
	Kamagut	0.625	0.23
	Kiplombe	0.848	0.16
	Tabsagoi	0.396	0.31
	Cheptiret	0.789	0.17
	Kipchamo	0.789	0.17
	Kapseret	0.359	0.32
	Kipkenyo	0.213	0.4
	Langas	0.213	0.4
	Racecourse	0.213	0.4
	Simat	0.359	0.32
	Tarakwa	0.424	0.3
Nakuru			
	Amalo	0.409	0.31
	Keringet	0.328	0.34
	Kiptagich	0.723	0.19
	Elburgon	0.712	0.2
	Kihingo	0.838	0.16
	Mariashoni	0.414	0.31
	Mau Narok	0.826	0.16
	Mauche	0.838	0.16
	Molo	0.523	0.26
	Waseges	0.466	0.29

Note: In this coding of the ELF, the closer the unit (ward) is to one, the more homogeneous it is. 1989 ethnicity data provided by Mai Hassan.

Table B.6 *Pairwise correlation matrix: land narratives and violence*

	Anti-outsider	Anti-Settlement
Anti-settlement	0.45* 0.000 (711)	
Indirect violence	0.29* 0.000 (719)	0.31* 0.000 (727)
Direct violence	0.21* 0.000 (721)	0.25 0.000 (729)

Notes: Table shows the pairwise correlation between contentious land narratives (measured by the variables: *anti-outsider* and *anti-settlement* and election violence, direct and indirect). Observations in parentheses. Source: author's survey.

Summary of Sampling Strategy

I conducted the household survey, which I administered to 750 respondents, across four counties of Kenya, from January to February 2013. The selection strategy relied on multistage sampling (cluster sampling) to select respondents. I purposely selected two counties in the Rift Valley (Nakuru and Uasin Gishu) and two counties in the Coast region (Kwale and Kilifi). Within Kilifi and Nakuru, I selected four constituencies and within Uasin Gishu and Kwale, I selected three constituencies, all randomly. Within the constituency, I selected three electoral wards randomly and at each electoral ward, I selected six polling stations to randomize the selection of respondents. Thus, the sampling strategy uses the polling station as a rough approximation of population density and distribution. In most cases, polling stations are prominent community centers such as schools or churches. Using the polling station provided a feasible way to create enumeration areas. At each polling station, enumerators followed a "random walk" method to select three households (one respondent within each household). Enumerators received instructions on how to randomize the selection of household members to avoid selection bias at the household level.

Enumerators indicated and described all nonresponses. In total, the survey sampled 210 respondents in Nakuru, 216 respondents in Kilifi and 162 respondents in Uasin Gishu and Kwale. Each constituency consists of 54 respondents, while each electoral ward contains of eighteen respondents.

The survey instrument consisted of 97 observational questions. These questions were divided into several sections, including basic information recorded by the enumerator (i.e. location, type of shelter, material of roof, respondent's gender), basic background information on respondents (i.e. age, weekly income, other income sources, home area, home language, etc.), questions on land (access, tenure type, perceived security, plot size, arability, view of land institutions, history of eviction, agreement with particular land narratives), questions on political mobilization, experience with and views on election violence, and forms and degree of ethnic interaction (e.g. frequency of sharing a meal or attending a meeting with ethnic outgroup). In addition, the survey also included three experimental questions, two of which were list experiments.

There were two survey teams: one team sampled households in Rift Valley counties, while the other sampled households in the Coast counties. There were eighteen enumerators in total. Enumerators working in the Rift Valley were selected based on their previous experience working for Afrobarometer. The Rift Valley team consisted of Kikuyu, Kalenjin, Kamba and Luo enumerators. At the Coast, I selected and trained respondents who had previous experience working for the Kenya census or other research firms. Coast enumerators identified as Mijikenda, Pokomo, and Kamba.

Appendix C

Additional Regressions

Table C.1 *Alternative measures of political competition*

Variables	Model 1 (Rift Valley)	Model 2	Model 3
Ward rep: vote margin	0.504		
	(0.732)		
PM vote margin ('02)		−0.0223	
		(0.0228)	
PM vote margin ('07)			−0.0196
			(0.0352)
CONTROLS	Y	Y	Y
Const. population ('09)	3.051*	−0.837	0.0719
	(1.668)	(1.560)	(1.964)
Population density ('09)	−2.019*	0.852	1.292
	(1.192)	(0.693)	(0.983)
Region		−3.447***	−3.691***
		(0.888)	(1.076)
Constant	−24.18	6.581	−6.414
	(16.26)	(17.78)	(23.84)
Observations	351	715	715
Number of constituencies	7	14	14

Notes: PM vote margin refers to the vote margin between the top two parliamentary candidates at the constituency level. Standard errors in parentheses.
*** p<0.001, ** p<0.01, * p<0.05

Table C.2 *Predictors of election violence (dependent variable: direct violence)*

Variables	Model 1	Model 2	Model 3	Model 4	Model 5	Model 6 (Rift Valley)
Appeal 1: Violence	1.346*** (0.306)				1.286*** (0.307)	1.573*** (0.340)
Appeal 2: Title promise		1.382*** (0.318)				
Appeal 3: Free land			1.484*** (0.294)			
Appeal 4: Defend land				1.311*** (0.308)		
Pres Vote Margin ('07)					-0.0386*** (0.0125)	-0.0536*** (0.00968)
ELF: Location ('89)						-4.585*** (1.185)
Kalenjin	-1.375*** (0.400)	-1.381*** (0.397)	-1.358*** (0.399)	-1.386*** (0.395)	-1.213*** (0.404)	-1.429*** (0.405)
Mijikenda	-2.536** (1.005)	-2.663*** (1.008)	-2.578** (1.015)	-2.566** (1.001)	-2.391** (1.008)	
Coast region	-2.597*** (0.995)	-2.643*** (0.976)	-2.734*** (0.952)	-2.737*** (0.959)	-1.977** (0.831)	
CONTROLS	Y	Y	Y	Y	Y	Y
Const. Pop. (log)	1.724 (1.588)	1.473 (1.500)	1.568 (1.423)	1.317 (1.472)	0.0767 (1.259)	0.0740 (1.263)
Constant	-21.67 (18.47)	-19.54 (17.43)	-20.22 (16.52)	-17.22 (17.08)	-4.487 (14.24)	-12.43 (11.78)
Observations	705	706	706	706	705	362
Number of CONST2	14	14	14	14	14	7

Note: All columns display results of a logit regression using random effects. Standard errors are clustered at the constituency level and displayed in parentheses. The dependent variable measures direct exposure to election violence, where a value of 1=indirect exposure. *Pres Vote Margin ('07)* refers to the margin between the two top presidential candidates at the constituency level. *Mijikenda* and *Kalenjin* are categorical variables measuring a respondent's ethnic identification. *ELF: Location ('89)* measures the ethnolinguistic fractionalization index at the location level based on the1989 census, where a value of 1= most homogenous. The variable *Distance* is a categorical variable measuring a respondent's distance from the main road. Model 6 is based only on the Rift Valley sample. Controls are included in the model but not reported. *** p<0.001, ** p<0.01, * p<0.05

Appendix D

National-level Data on the 2007–2008 Postelection Violence

Table D.1 *Reported fatalities*

County	CIPEV	ACLED	UCDP	Total	Code
Baringo	23	94	0	117	4
Bomet	9	22	0	31	2
Bungoma	28	40	11	68	3
Busia	9	31	0	41	2
Elgeyo-Marakwet	0	0	0	0	0
Embu	0	0	0	0	0
Garissa	0	0	0	0	0
Homa Bay	8	28	0	36	2
Isiolo	0	0	0	0	0
Kajiado	0	0	0	0	0
Kakamega	43	12	4	55	3
Kericho	74	65	4	139	4
Kiambu	4	24	0	28	2
Kilifi	1	0	0	1	1
Kirinyaga	0	2	0	2	1
Kisii	9	35	0	44	2
Kisumu	81	119	58	154	4
Kitui	0	0	0	0	0
Kwale	0	11	0	11	2
Laikipia	0	42	6	48	2
Lamu	0	0	0	0	0
Machakos	0	0	0	0	0
Makueni	0	0	0	0	0
Mandera	0	0	0	0	0
Marsabit	0	0	0	0	0
Meru	0	2	0	0	0
Migori	26	16	0	42	2
Mombasa	0	37	19	37	2

Table D.1 (*cont.*)

County	CIPEV	ACLED	UCDP	Total	Code
Murang'a	0	1	0	1	1
Nairobi	125	124	55	209	4
Nakuru	263	219	98	431	4
Nandi	7	4	0	11	1
Narok	19	6	5	25	2
Nyamira	0	0	31	31	2
Nyandarua	1	1	1	1	1
Nyeri	0	13	13	13	2
Samburu	0	0	0	0	0
Siaya	10	8	0	18	2
Taita-Taveta	0	1	0	1	1
Tana River	0	0	0	0	0
Tharaka-Nithi	0	0	0	0	0
Trans Nzoia	104	60	13	160	4
Uasin Gishu	230	111	42	306	4
Vihigia	18	4	0	22	2
Wajir	0	0	0	0	0
West Pokot	0	0	0	0	0

Note: There are several counties listed here for which the total row is not the sum of columns 2–4. In these cases, the three data sources count the same fatality or incident of violence. The "total" column therefore reflects separate incidents of violence (i.e. deaths) that are unique across all three datasets. In other words, the totals shown here avoid "double-counting" fatalities across the three data sources.

Table D.2 *Coding scheme for levels of election violence*

Code	Level of violence	Recorded deaths/county
0	No violence	No recorded deaths
1	Low level of violence	1–10
2	Moderate level of violence	11–50
3	High level of violence	51–100
4	Mass violence	Over 100

Notes: The coding scheme here explains the map of election violence that appears in Chapter 1.

Appendix E

Data on Settlement Schemes

Table E.1 *Allocation of settlement schemes: temporal and provincial view*

Province	Number of schemes	Scheme size	Number of settlers (households)	Mean plot size (ha)	Range (min-max)
Kenyatta era settlement schemes (1962–1978)					
Coast	11	53,583	9,341	5.7	0.65–24.0
Rift Valley	100	186,060	26322	7.1	1.0–67.0
Central	67	179,507	22274	8	0.7–44.0
Eastern	19	48,599	5306	9.2	2.3–80.0
Western	19	76,251	7708	9.9	7.0–19.0
Nyanza	20	40295	5851	6.9	0.8–43.0
Moi era settlement schemes (1979–2002)					
Coast	65	214,982	38,721	5.6	0.01–68.2
Rift Valley	57	74448	20508	3.6	0.8–97
Central	23	60,241	14,478	4.2	0.075–12.3
Eastern	17	69,972	27336	2.6	0.4–6.5
Western	3	6452	4393	1.5	0.8–2.3
Nyanza	1	256	167	1.5	1.5–1.5
Kibaki era settlement (2003–2012)					
Coast	36	70,805	42385	1.7	0.006–13.8
Rift Valley	24	89,883	29,432	3.1	0.4–4.0
Central	1	100	486	0.2	0.07–1.2
Eastern	15	71,833	18587	3.9	0.52–21.7
Western	1	2,500	1735	1.4	0.8–2.3
Nyanza	1	2,500	683	3.6	0.93–3.6
Totals	480	1,248.267	275,713		0.006–96.8

Note: The data was made available by Kenya's Ministry of Lands & Settlement (unpublished data, 2013).

References

Acemoglu, Daron, & James A. Robinson. (2006). *Economic Origins of Dictatorship and Democracy*. Cambridge: Cambridge University Press.

Agiboa, Daniel E. (2018). "Patronage Politics and Electoral Violence in Lagos, Nigeria: Understanding the Micro-level Dynamics." In Mimmi Söderberg Kovacs & Jesper Bjarnesen, eds. *Violence in African Elections: Between Democracy and Big Man Politics*. London: Zed Books, 215–232.

Airault, Pascal (2010) Présidentielle: La bataille de l'ouest n'est pas gagnée par Laurent Gbagbo [Presidential: The Battle in the West Is Not Won for Laurent Gbagbo]. October 27. *Jeune Afrique*. www.jeuneafrique.com/Article/ARTJAJA2597p038-039.xml0/.

Albertus, Michael. (2015). *Autocracy and Redistribution: The Politics of Land Reform*. Cambridge: Cambridge University Press.

Albertus, Michael. (2017). "Landowners and Democracy: The Social Origins of Democracy Reconsidered." *World Politics* 69(2): 233–276.

Albertus, Michael, & Oliver Kaplan. (2013). "Land Reform as a Counterinsurgency: Policy Evidence from Colombia." *Journal of Conflict Resolution* 57(2):198–231.

Albertus, Michael, Thomas Brambor, & Ricardo Ceneviva. (2018). "Land Inequality and Rural Unrest: Theory and Evidence from Brazil." *Journal of Conflict Resolution* 62(3): 557–596.

Alesina, Alberto, & Roberto Perotti. (1996). "Income Distribution, Political Instability, and Investment." *European Economic Review* 40(6): 1203–1228.

Alesina, Alberto, Stelios Michalopoulos, & Elias Papaioannou. (2016). "Ethnic Inequality." *Journal of Political Economy* 124(2): 428–488.

Allchin, Joseph. (2014) "The Hindus of Bangladesh Fear for Their Future." *Time*. January 14. http://world.time.com/2014/01/14/the-hindus-of-bangladesh-are-fearing-for-their-future/

Alvin, Rabushka, & Shepsle Kenneth. (1972). *Politics in Plural Societies: A Theory of Democratic Instability*. Columbus, OH: Charles E. Merrill.

Amnesty International and Human Rights Watch. (2017). "Kill Those Criminals: Security Forces Violations in Kenya's August 2017

Elections." Report. www.amnesty.org/en/documents/afr32/7249/2017/en/

Anderson, David. (2002). "Vigilantes, Violence and the Politics of Public Order in Kenya." *African Affairs* 101(405): 531–555.

Anderson, David, & Lochery, Emma. (2008). "Violence and Exodus in Kenya's Rift Valley, 2008: Predictable and Preventable?" *Journal of Eastern African Studies* 2(2): 328–343.

Arjona, Ana. (2014). Wartime Institutions: A Research Agenda. *Journal of Conflict Resolution* 58(8): 1360–1389.

Arjona, Ana. (2016). *Rebelocracy: Social Order in the Colombian Civil War.* Cambridge: Cambridge University Press.

Arriola, Leonardo. (2009). "Patronage and Political Stability in Africa." *Comparative Political Studies* 42(10): 1339–1362.

Ashforth, Adam. (2005). *Witchcraft, Violence, and Democracy in South Africa.* Chicago: University of Chicago Press.

Asunka, Joseph, Sarah Brierley, Miriam Golden, Eric Kramon, & George Ofosu. (2019). "Electoral Fraud or Violence: The Effect of Observers on Party Manipulation Strategies." *British Journal of Political Science* 49(1): 129–151.

Autesserre, Séverine. (2009). "Hobbes and the Congo: Frames, Local Violence, and International Intervention." *International Organization* 63(2): 249–280.

Autesserre, Severine. (2012). "Dangerous Tales: Dominant Narratives on the Congo and Their Unintended Consequences." *African Affairs* 111(443): 202–222.

Autesserre, Severine. (2017) "International Peacebuilding and Local Success: Assumptions and Effectiveness." *International Studies Review* 19(1): 114–132.

Baland, Jean-Marie, & James Robinson. (2012). "The Political Value of Land: Political Reform and Land Prices in Chile." *American Journal of Political Science* 56(3): 601–619.

Balcells, Laia. (2017). *Rivalry and Revenge: The Politics of Violence During War.* Cambridge: Cambridge University Press.

Balcells, Laia, & Patricia Justino. (2014). "Bridging Micro and Macro Approaches on Civil Wars and Political Violence Issues, Challenges, and the Way Forward." *Journal of Conflict Resolution* 58(8): 1343–1359.

Balcells, Laia, Lesley-Ann Daniels, & Abel Escribà-Folc. (2016). "The Determinants of Low-intensity Intergroup Violence: The Case of Northern Ireland." *Journal of Peace Research* 53(1): 33–48.

Baldwin, Kate. (2014). "When Politicians Cede Control of Resources: Land, Chiefs, and Coalition-building in Africa." *Comparative Politics* 46(3): 253–271.

Baldwin, Kate, & John Huber. (2010). "Economic Versus Cultural Differences: Forms of Ethnic Diversity and Public Goods Provision." *American Political Science Review* 104(4): 644–662.

Bangura, Ibrahim, & Mimmi Soderberg Kovacs. (2018). "Competition, Uncertainty and Violence in Sierra Leone's Swing District." In Mimmi Söderberg Kovacs & Jesper Bjarnesen (eds.) *Violence in African Elections*. London: Zed Books, 114–134.

Barume, Albert. (2005) "Indigenous Battling for Land Rights: The Case of the Ogiek in Kenya." In Joshua Castellino & Niamh Walsh (eds.) *International Law and Indigenous People*. Leiden: Nijhoff, 365–391.

Basset, Thomas. (2011). "Winning Coalition, Sore Loser: Cote d'Ivoire's 2010 Presidential Elections." *African Affairs* 110(440): 469–479.

Bates, Robert. (1983). "Modernization, Ethnic Competition, and the Rationality of Politics in Contemporary Africa." In Donald Rothchild & Victor A. Olorunsola (eds.) *State Versus Ethnic Claims: African Policy Dilemmas*. Boulder, CO: Westview Press, 152–171.

Bateson, Regina. (2012). "Crime Victimization and Political Participation." *American Political Science Review* 106(3): 231–247.

Bauer, Michal, Christopher Blattman, Julie Chytilova, Joseph Henrich, Edward Miguel, & Tamar Mitts. (2016). "Can War Foster Cooperation?" *Journal of Economic Perspectives* 30 (Summer): 249–274.

Bauer, Michal, Alessandra Cassar, Julie Chytilova, & Joseph Henrich. (2014). "War's Enduring Effects on the Development of Egalitarian Motivations and In-group Biases." *Psychological Science* 25 (January): 47–57.

Becchetti, Leonardo, Conzo Pierluigi, & Romeo Alessandro. (2014). "Violence, Trust and Trustworthiness: Evidence from a Nairobi Slum." *Oxford Economic Papers* 66(1): 283–305.

Bedford, Robert, & David Snow. (2000). "Framing Processes and Social Movements: An Overview and Assessment." *Annual Review of Sociology* 26: 611–639.

Bekoe, Dorina. (2012). "The Scope, Nature, and Pattern of Electoral Violence in Sub-Saharan Africa." In Dorina A. Bekoe (ed.) *Voting in Fear: Electoral Violence in Sub-Saharan Africa*. Washington, DC: United States Institute of Peace, 1–14.

Bekoe, Dorina A., & Stephanie Burchard. (2017). "The Contradictions of Pre-election Violence: The Effects of Violence on Voter Turnout in Sub-Saharan Africa," *African Studies Review* 60: 73–92.

Bellows, John, & Edward Miguel. (2009). "War and Local Collective Action in Sierra Leone." *Journal of Public Economics* 93(11–12): 1144–1157.

Benjaminsen, Tor A., & Ian Bryceson. (2012). "Conservation, Green/Blue Grabbing and Accumulation by Dispossession in Tanzania." *Journal of Peasant Studies* 39(2): 335–355.

Benjaminsen, Tor A., Faustin P. Maganga, & Jumanne Moshi Abdallah. (2009). "The Kilosa Killings: Political Ecology of a Farmer–Herder Conflict in Tanzania." *Development and Change* 40(3): 423–445.

Berger, Peter L., & Thomas Luckmann. (1967). *The Social Construction of Reality: A Treatise in the Sociology of Knowledge*. New York: Anchor Books.

Berman, Sheri. (2007). "How Democracies Emerge: Lessons from Europe." *Journal of Democracy* 18(1): 28–41.

Berman, Bruce, & John Lonsdale. (1992). *Unhappy Valley: Conflict in Kenya & Africa*. Volume 2. Oxford: James Currey.

Berry, Sara. (1993). *No Condition Is Permanent: The Social Dynamics of Agrarian Change in Sub-Saharan Africa*. Madison, WI: University of Wisconsin Press.

Besley, Timothy. (1995). Property Rights and Investment Incentives: Theory and Evidence from Ghana. *Journal of Political Economy* 103 (5): 903–937.

Bhavnani, Rikhil, & Bethany Lacina. (2015). "The Effect of Weather-Induced Migration on Sons of the Soil Violence in India." *World Politics* 67(4): 760–794.

Binder, Judith, & Tim Murithi. (2013). "Home at Last? Land Conflicts in Burundi and the Right of Victims to Reparations." Institute for Justice and Reconciliation Policy Brief (No. 11). www.africaportal.org/publica tions/home-at-last-land-conflicts-in-burundi-and-the-right-of-victims-to-reparations/

Biong Deng, Luka. (2010). "Social Capital and Civil War: The Dinka Communities in Sudan's Civil War." *African Affairs* 109(435): 231–250.

Birch, Sarah, & David Muchlinski. (2017). "The Dataset of Countries at Risk of Electoral Violence." *Terrorism and Political Violence* 1–20. www .tandfonline.com/doi/full/10.1080/09546553.2017.1364636

Blattman, Christopher. (2009). "From Violence to Voting: War and Political Participation in Uganda." *American Political Science Review* 103(2): 231–247.

Blattman, Christopher & Edward Miguel. (2010). "Civil War." *Journal of Economic Literature* 48(1): 3–57.

Blattman, Christopher, Alexandra Hartman, & Robert Blair. (2014). "How to Promote Order and Property Rights under Weak Rule of Law? an Experiment in Changing Dispute Resolution Behavior through Community Education." *American Political Science Review* 108(1): 100–120.

Bob-Milliar, George. (2014). "Party Youth Activists and Low-Intensity Electoral Violence in Ghana: A Qualitative Study of Party Foot Soldiers' Activism." *African Studies Quarterly* 15(1): 125.

Boix, Carles. (2003). *Democracy and Redistribution.* New York: Cambridge University Press.

Boone, Catherine. (2007). "Property and Constitutional Order: Land Tenure and the Future of the African State." *African Affairs* 106(425): 557–586.

Boone, Catherine. (2009). "Electoral Populism Where Property Rights are Weak: Land Politics in Contemporary Sub-Saharan Africa." *Comparative Politics* 41(2): 181–201. .

Boone, Catherine. (2011). "Politically-Allocated Land Rights and the Geography of Electoral Violence: The case of Kenya in the 1990s." *Comparative Political Studies* 44(1): 1311–1342.

Boone, Catherine. (2014). *Property and Political Order in Africa: Land Rights and the Structure of Politics.* Cambridge: Cambridge University Press

Boone, Catherine, & Norma Krieger. (2012). "Land Patronage and Elections: Winners and Losers in Zimbabwe and Côte D'ivoire." In Dorina A. Bekoe (ed.) *Voting in Fear: Electoral Violence in Sub-Saharan Africa.* Washington, DC: USIP Press, 75–117.

Boone, Catherine, & Lydia Nyeme. (2015). "Land Institutions and Political Ethnicity in Africa: Evidence from Tanzania." *Comparative Politics* 48(1): 67–86.

Boone, Catherine, Alex Dyzenhaus, Ambreena Manji, Catherine Gateri, Seth Ouma, James Owino, Achiba Gargule, & Jacqueline Klopp. (2019). "Land Law Reform in Kenya: Devolution, Veto Players, and the Limits of an Institutional Fix." *African Affairs* 118(471): 215–237.

Botha, Anneli. (2014). "Radicalisation in Kenya: Recruitment to Al-Shabaab and the Mombasa Republican Council." ISS Paper 265, Institute for Security Studies. https://issafrica.org/research/papers/radicalisation-in-kenya-recruitment-to-al-shabaab-and-the-mombasa-republican-council

Brancati, Dawn, & Jack Snyder. (2013). "Time to Kill: The Impact of Election Timing on Post-Conflict Stability" *Journal of Conflict Resolution* 57(5): 822–853.

Branch, Daniel. (2009). *Defeating Mau Mau, Creating Kenya: Counterinsurgency, Civil War, and Decolonization.* Cambridge: Cambridge University Press.

Branch, Daniel, & Nic Cheeseman. (2009). "Democratization, Sequencing, and State Failure: Lessons from Kenya." *African Affairs* 108(430): 1–26

Brennan, James. (2008). "Lowering the Sultan's Flag: Sovereignty and Decolonization in Coastal Kenya." *Comparative Studies in Society and History* 50(4): 831–861.

Brockett, Charles. (1992). "Measuring Political Violence and Land Inequality in Central America." *American Political Science Review* 86(1): 169–76

Brown, Stephen, & Chandra Lekha Sriram. (2012). "The Big Fish Won't Fry Themselves: Criminal Accountability for Post-Election Violence in Kenya." *African Affairs* 111(443): 244–260.

Bruner, Jerome, S. (1986). *Acts of Meaning: Four Lectures on Mind and Culture.* Cambridge, MA: Harvard University Press.

Buhaug, Halvard, Tor Benjaminsen, Espen Sjaastad, & Ole Magnus Theisen. (2015). "Climate Variability, Food Production Shocks, and Violent Conflict in Sub-Saharan Africa." *Environmental Research Letters* 10(12).

Burbidge, Dominic. (2015). "Democracy Versus Diversity: Ethnic Representation in a Devolved Kenya." Working Paper. Princeton, NJ: Princeton University.

Burchard, Stephanie. (2015). *Electoral Violence in Sub-Saharan Africa: Causes and Consequences.* Boulder, CO: Lynne Rienner Publishers.

Butime, Herman. (2014). "Unpacking the Anatomy of the Mpeketoni Attacks in Kenya." *Small Wars Journal.* https://smallwarsjournal.com/jrnl/art/unpacking-the-anatomy-of-the-mpeketoni-attacks-in-kenya

Canetti-Nisim, Daphna, Eran Halperin, Keren Sharvit, & Stevan E. Hobfoll. (2009). "A New Stress-Based Model of Political Extremism: Personal Exposure to Terrorism, Psychological Distress, and Exclusionist Political Attitudes." *Journal of Conflict Resolution* 53(3): 363–389.

Carlson, Elizabeth. (2015). "Ethnic Voting and Accountability in Africa: A Choice Experiment in Uganda." *World Politics* 67(2): 353–385.

Carothers, Thomas. (2007). "The 'Sequencing' Fallacy." *Journal of Democracy,* 18(1): 12–27.

Cassar, Alessandra; Pauline Grosjean, & Sam Whitt. (2014). "Social Preference of Ex-Combatants: Survey and Experimental Evidence from Postwar Tajikistan." In Karl Wärneryd (ed.) *The Economics of Conflict: Theory and Empirical Evidence.* Cambridge, MA: MIT Press, 231–262.

Cederman, Lars-Erik, & Luc Girardin. (2007). "Beyond Fractionalization: Mapping Ethnicity into Nationalist Insurgencies." *American Political Science Review* 101(1): 173–185.

Cederman, Lars-Erik, & Julian Wucherpfennig. (2017). "Inequalities Between Ethnic Groups, Conflict, and Political Organizations." *Ethnopolitics* 16(1): 21–27

Cederman, Lars-Erik, Andreas Wimmer & Brian Min. (2010). "Why Do Ethnic Groups Rebel? New Data and Analysis." *World Politics* 62(1): 87–119.

Cederman, Lars-Erik, Nils B. Weidmann, & Kristian Skrede Gleditsch. (2011). "Horizontal Inequalities and Ethnonationalist Civil War:

a Global Comparison." *American Political Science Review* 105(3): 478–495.

Cederman Lars-Erik, Kristian Gleditsch & Simon Hug. (2013). "Elections and Ethnic Civil War." *Comparative Political Studies* 46(3): 387–417.

Cederman, Lars-Erik, Kristian Gleditsch, & Julian Wucherpfennig. (2017). "Predicting the Decline of Ethnic Civil War: Was Gurr Right and For the Right Reasons?" *Journal of Peace Research* 54(2): 262–274.

Chandra, Kanchan. (2004). *Why Ethnic Parties Succeed: Patronage and Ethnic Head Counts in India*. Cambridge: Cambridge University Press.

Chandra, Kanchan. (2005). "Ethnic Parties and Democratic Stability." *Perspectives on Politics*, 3(2): 235–252.

Chandra, Kanchan (ed.) (2012). *Constructivist Theories of Ethnic Politics*. Oxford: Oxford University Press.

Chandra, Kanchan, & Steven Wilkinson. (2008). "Measuring the Effect of Ethnicity." *Comparative Political Studies* 41(4–5): 515–563.

Chaturvedi, Ashish. (2005). "Rigging Elections with Violence." *Public Choice* 125: 189–202.

Checkel, Jeffrey. (2017). "Socialization and Violence: Introduction and Framework." *Journal of Peace Research* 54(5): 592–605.

Cheeseman, Nic. (2008). "The 2007 Kenyan Election: An Introduction." *Journal of Eastern African Studies* 2(2): 166–184.

Choi, Jung-Kyoo, & Samuel Bowles. (2007). "The Coevolution of Parochial Altruism and War." *Science*, 318: 636–640.

Collier, Paul. (2009). "The Political Economy of State Failure." *Oxford Review of Economic Policy* 25(2): 219–240.

Collier, Paul, & Anke Hoeffler. (2004). "Greed and Grievance in Civil War." *Oxford Economic Papers* 56(4): 563–95.

Collier, Paul, & Pedro C. Vicente. (2012). "Violence, Bribery, and Fraud: The Political Economy of Elections in Sub-Saharan Africa." *Public Choice* 153(1–2): 117–147.

Cooper, Fredrick. (1980). *From Slaves to Squatters: Plantation Labor and Agriculture in Zanzibar and Coastal Kenya: 1980–1925*. New Haven, CT: Yale University Press.

Côté, Isabelle, & Matthew I. Mitchell. (2017) "Deciphering 'Sons of the Soil' Conflicts: A Critical Survey of the Literature." *Ethnopolitics* 16(4) 333–351.

Cramer, Katherine. (2012). "Putting Inequality in Its Place: Rural Consciousness and the Power of Perspective." *American Political Science Review* 106(3): 517–532.

Dahl, Robert A. (1973). *Polyarchy: Participation and Opposition*. New Haven, CT: Yale University Press.

Daxecker, Ursula. (2012.) "The Cost of Exposing Cheating: International Election Monitoring, Electoral Manipulation, and Violence." *Journal of Peace Research* 49(4): 503–516.

Daxecker, Ursula. (2014). "All Quiet on Election Day? International Election Observation and Incentives for Pre-election Violence in African Elections." *Electoral Studies* 34: 232–243.

Daxecker, Ursula. (2019). "Unequal Votes, Unequal Violence: Malapportionment and Election Violence in India." *Journal of Peace Research*. Online First. https://doi.org/10.1177/0022343319884985

Daxecker, Ursula, Elio Amicarelli, & Alexander Jung (2019) "Electoral Contention and Violence (ECAV): A New Dataset." *Journal of Peace Research* 56(5) https://journals.sagepub.com/doi/full/10.1177/0022343318823870

De Figueiredo, Rui J.P Jr. & Barry Weingast. (1999). "The Rationality of Fear." In Barbara F. Walter & Jack Snyder (eds.) *Civil Wars, Insecurity, and Intervention*. New York: Columbia University Press, 261–302

De Juan, Alexander & Jan Pierskalla. (2016). "Civil War Violence and Political Trust: Microlevel Evidence from Nepal." *Conflict Management and Peace Science* 33(1): 67–88.

De Luca, Giacomo, & Marijke Verpoorten. (2015). "Civil War, Social Capital and Resilience in Uganda." *Oxford Economic Papers* 67: 661–686.

De Soto, Hernando. (2000). *The Mystery of Capital. Why Capitalism Triumphs in the West and Fails Everywhere Else*. New York: Perseus.

Deglow, Annekatrin. (2018). "Forces of Destruction and Construction: Local Conflict Dynamics, Institutional Trust and Postwar Crime." Dissertation Manuscript, Department of Peace and Conflict Research. Uppsala: Uppsala University.

Denny, Elaine, & Barbara F. Walter. (2014). "Ethnicity and Civil War." *Journal of Peace Research* 51(2): 199–212.

Dercon, Stefan, & Roxana Gutierrez-Romero. (2012). "Triggers and Characteristics of the 2007 Kenyan Elections." *World Development* 40 (4): 731–744.

Diamond, Larry, Juan J. Linz, & Seymour Martin Lipset. (1995). *Politics in Developing Countries: Comparing Experiences with Democracy*. Boulder, CO: Lynne Rienner.

Dunning, Thad. (2011). "Fighting and Voting: Violent Conflict and Electoral Politics." *Journal of Conflict Resolution* 55(3): 327–339.

Easterly, William, & Ross Levine. (1997). "Africa's Growth Tragedy: Policies and Ethnic Divisions." *The Quarterly Journal of Economics* 112 (4): 1203–1250.

Eifert, Benn, Edward Miguel, & Daniel N. Posner. (2010). "Political Competition and Ethnic Identification in Africa." *American Journal of Political Science* 54(2): 494–510.

Ellman, Matthew, & Leonard Wantchekon. (2000). "Electoral Competition under the Threat of Political Unrest." *The Quarterly Journal of Economics* 115(2): 499–531.

Falleti, Tulia, & Julia Lynch. (2009). "Context and Causal Mechanisms in Political Analysis." *Comparative Political Studies* 42(9): 1143–1166.

Fearon, James, & David Laitin. (2000). "Violence and the Social Construction of Ethnic Identity." *International Organization* 54(4): 845–877.

Fearon, James, & David Laitin. (2003). "Ethnicity, Insurgency, and Civil War." *American Political Science Review* 97(1): 75–90.

Fearon, James, & David Laitin. (2011). "Sons of the Soil, Migrants, and Civil War." *World Development* 39(2): 199–211.

Ferree, Karen. (2011). *Framing the Race in South Africa: The Political Origins of Racial Census Elections.* Cambridge: Cambridge University Press.

Finkel, Evgeny, Scott Gehlbach, & Tricia Olsen. (2015). "Does Reform Prevent Rebellion? Evidence From Russia's Emancipation of the Serfs." *Comparative Political Studies* 48(8): 984–101

Finkel, Steven E., Jeremy Horowitz, & Reynaldo T. Rojo-Mendoza. (2012). "Civic Education and Democratic Backsliding in the Wake of Kenya's Post-2007 Election Violence." *Journal of Politics* 74(1): 52–65.

Fischer, Jeff. 2002. "Electoral Conflict and Violence." IFES White Paper (1). www.ifes.org/sites/default/files/econflictpaper.pdf

Fjelde, Hanne, & Kristine Höglund. (2016a). "Electoral Institutions and Electoral Violence in Sub-Saharan Africa." *British Journal of Political Science* 46.2: 297–320.

Fjelde, Hanne, & Kristine Höglund. (2016b). "Electoral Violence: The Emergence of a Research Field." *APSA Comparative Democratization Newsletter* 14(2).

Flores, Thomas E., & Irfan Nooruddin. (2012). "The Effect of Elections on Postconflict Peace and Reconstruction." *The Journal of Politics* 74 (2): 558–570.

Flores, Thomas E., & Irfan Nooruddin. (2016). *Elections in Hard Times: Building Stronger Democracies in the 21st Century.* Cambridge: Cambridge University Press and Woodrow Wilson Center Press.

Fridy, Kevin S. (2007). "The Elephant, Umbrella, and Quarrelling Cocks: Disaggregating Partisanship in Ghana's Fourth Republic." *African Affairs* 106(423): 281–305.

Frymer, Paul. (2014). "'A Rush and a Push and the Land Is Ours': Territorial Expansion, Land Policy, and US State Formation." *Perspectives on Politics* 12(1): 119.

Fujii, Lee Ann. (2009). *Killing Neighbors: Webs of Violence in Rwanda.* New York: Cornell University Press.

Fujii, Lee Ann. (2010). "Shades of Truth and Lies: Interpreting Testimonies of War and Violence." *Journal of Peace Research* 47(2): 231–241

Gamson, William. (1992). *Talking Politics.* Cambridge: Cambridge University Press.

Gates, Scott. (2002). "Recruitment and Allegiance: The Microfoundations of Rebellion." *Journal of Conflict Resolution* 46(1): 111–130.

Geschiere, Peter. (1997). *The Modernity of Witchcraft: Politics and the Occult in Postcolonial Africa.* Charlottesville: University of Virginia Press.

Geschiere, Peter. (2009). *The Perils of Belonging: Autochthony, Citizenship, and Exclusion in Africa and Europe.* Chicago: University of Chicago Press.

Geschiere, Peter, & Josef Gugler. (1998). "Introduction: The Urban–Rural Connection: Changing Issues of Belonging and Identification." *Africa* 68 (3): 309–319.

Getmansky Anna, & Thomas Zeitzoff. (2014). "Terrorism and Voting: The Effect of Rocket Threat on Israeli Elections." *American Political Science Review* 108(3): 588–604.

Ghai, Yash P., & Patrick McAuslan. (1970). *Public Law and Political Change in Kenya: A Study of the Legal Framework of Government from Colonial Times to the Present.* Oxford: Oxford University Press.

Giuliano, Elise. (2011). *Constructing Grievance: Ethnic Nationalism in Russia's Republics.* Ithaca, NY: Cornell University Press.

Goffman, Erving. (1974). *Frame Analysis. An Essay on the Organization of Experience.* Cambridge, MA: Harvard University Press.

Goldsmith, Paul. (2011). *The Mombasa Republican Council Conflict Assessment: Threats and Opportunities for Engagement.* Nairobi: United State Agency for International Development.

Government of Kenya. (2007). "Kenya: President Kibaki Opens Mombasa Show, Announces the Revival of Ramisi Sugar Factory." August 30. *Reliefweb.* https://reliefweb.int/report/kenya/kenya-president-kibaki-opens-mombasa-show-announces-revival-ramisi-sugar-factory

Government of Kenya. (2009). "Report of the Prime Minister's Task Force on the Conservation of the Mau Forest Complex." www.kws.go.ke/file/1446/download?token=xDBvXH_o

Grossman, Guy, Devorah Manekin, & Dan Miodownik. (2015). "The Political Legacies of Combat: Attitudes Towards War and Peace among Israeli Ex-combatants." *International Organization* 69: 981–1009.

Gurr, Ted. (1970). *Why Men Rebel.* Princeton, NJ: Princeton University Press.

Gurr, Ted. (1993). "Why Minorities Rebel: A Global Analysis of Communal Mobilization and Conflict since 1945." *International Political Science Review* 14(2): 161–201.

Gurr, Ted. (2000). *Peoples Versus States: Minorities at Risk in the New Century*. Washington, DC: US Institute of Peace Press.

Gutiérrez-Romero, Roxana. (2014). "An Inquiry into the Use of Illegal Electoral Practices and Effects of Political Violence and Vote-Buying." *Journal of Conflict Resolution* 58(8): 1500–1527.

Gutierrez Sanin, Francisco, & Elisabeth Wood. (2014). "Ideology in Civil War: Instrumental Adoption and Beyond." *Journal of Peace Research* 51 (2) 213–226.

Hadzic, Dino; David Carlson, & Margit Tavits. (2017). "How Exposure to Violence Affects Ethnic Voting." *British Journal of Political Science* 1–18.

Hafner-Burton, Emilie M., Susan Hyde, & Ryan S. Jablonski. (2016). "Surviving Elections: Election Violence, Incumbent Victory and Post-Election Repercussions." *British Journal of Political Science* 48(2): 459–458.

Hafner-Burton, Emilie, Susan Hyde, & Ryan Jablonski. (2014). "When Do Governments Resort to Election Violence?" *British Journal of Political Science* 44(1): 149–179.

Harbeson, John. (1973). *Nation-Building in Kenya: The Role of Land Reform*. Evanston, IL: Northwestern University Press.

Harish, S. P., & Andrew T. Little. (2017). "The Political Violence Cycle." *American Political Science Review* 111(2): 237–255.

Harris, J. Andrew. (2012). "'Stain Removal': Measuring the Effect of Violence on Local Ethnic Demography in Kenya." Working Paper. Cambridge, MA: Harvard University.

Hartman, C. Alexandra, & Benjamin S. Morse. (2018). "Violence, Empathy and Altruism: Evidence from the Ivorian Refugee Crisis in Liberia." *British Journal of Political Science*, 1–25.

Hassan, Mai. (2017). "The Strategic Shuffle: Ethnic Geography, the Internal Security Apparatus, and Elections in Kenya." *American Journal of Political Science* 61(2): 382–395.

Hassan, Mai. (2020). *Regime Threats and State Solutions: Bureaucratic Loyalty and Embeddedness in Kenya*. Cambridge: Cambridge University Press.

Hassan, Mai, & Kathleen Klaus. (2019). "Beyond State Capacity: The Electoral Logics of Land Formalization in Kenya." Working Paper presented at the American Political Science Association, Washington DC (August 2018).

Hassan, Mai, & Thomas O'Mealia. (2018). "Uneven Accountability in the Wake of Political Violence: Evidence from Kenya's Ashes and Archives." *Journal of Peace Research* 55(2): 161–174.

Haugerud, Angelique. (1989). "Land Tenure and Agrarian Change in Kenya." *Africa* 59(1): 61–90.

Haugerud, Angelique. (1995). *The Culture of Politics in Modern Kenya.* Cambridge: Cambridge University Press.

Hegre, Håvard, Tanja Ellingsen, Scott Gates, & Nils P. Gleditsch. (2001). "Toward a Democratic Civil Peace? Democracy, Political Change and Civil War 1816–1992." *American Political Science Review* 95(1): 33–48.

Herbst, Jeffrey. (2000). *States and Power in Africa.* Princeton, NJ: Princeton University.

Herrera, Yoshiko. (2005) *Imagined Economies: The Sources of Russian Regionalism.* Cambridge: Cambridge University Press.

Herrera, Yoshiko & Devesh Kapur. (2007). "Improving Data Quality: Actors, Incentives, and Capabilities." *Political Analysis* 15(4): 365–386.

Higashijima, Masaaki, & Christian Houle. (2017). "Ethnic Inequality and the Strength of Ethnic Identities in Sub-Saharan Africa." *Political Behavior* 40: 1–24.

Hill, Michael. (1960) The White Settler's Role in Kenya." July. *Foreign Affairs.* www.foreignaffairs.com/articles/kenya/1960-07-01/white-settlers-role-kenya

Hillesund, Solveig. (2015). "A Dangerous Discrepancy: Testing the Micro-Dynamics of Horizontal Inequality on Palestinian Support for Armed Resistance." *Journal of Peace Research* 52(1): 76–90.

Hirsch-Hoefler, Daphna Canetti, Carmit Rapaport & Stevan E. Hobfoll. (2016). "Conflict Will Harden Your Heart: Exposure to Violence, Psychological Distress, and Peace Barriers in Israel and Palestine." *British Journal of Political Science* 46: 845–859.

Höglund, Kristine. (2009). "Electoral Violence in Conflict-Ridden Societies: Concepts, Causes and Consequences." *Terrorism and Political Violence* 21(3): 412–427.

Hornsby, Charles. (2013). *Kenya: A History since Independence.* London: IB Tauris.

Horowitz, Donald. (1985). *Ethnic Groups in Conflict.* Berkeley: University of California Press.

Horowitz, Jeremy, & Kathleen Klaus (2018). "Can Politicians Exploit Ethnic Grievances? An Experimental Study of Land Appeals in Kenya." *Political Behavior* 1–24.

Houle, Christian. (2009). "Inequality and Democracy: Why Inequality Harms Consolidation but Does Not Affect Democratization." *World Politics* 61(4): 589–622.

HRW (Human Rights Watch). (1993). "Divide and Rule: State-Sponsored Ethnic Violence in Kenya." Report. www.hrw.org/report/1993/11/01/divide-and-rule-state-sponsored-ethnic-violence-kenya

HRW (Human Rights Watch). (2002a). "The Bullets Were Raining': The January 2001 Attack on Peaceful Demonstrators in Zanzibar." Report. www.hrw.org/reports/2002/tanzania/

HRW (Human Rights Watch). (2002b). "Playing with Fire: Weapons Proliferation, Political Violence and Human Rights in Kenya." Report. www.hrw.org/reports/2002/kenya/Kenya0502.pdf

HRW (Human Rights Watch). (2008). "Ballots to Bullets: Organized Political Violence and Kenya's Crisis of Governance." Report. www.hrw.org/report/2008/03/16/ballots-bullets/organized-political-violence-and-kenyas-crisis-governance

HRW (Human Rights Watch). (2013a). "High Stakes: Political Violence and the 2013 Elections in Kenya." Report. www.hrw.org/report/2013/02/07/high-stakes/political-violence-and-2013-elections-kenya

HRW (Human Rights Watch). (2013b). "Iran: Threats to Free, Fair Elections., May 24." www.hrw.org/news/2013/05/24/iran-threats-free-fair-elections

HRW (Human Rights Watch). (2014a). "Bangladesh: Elections Scarred by Violence." April 29. Report. www.hrw.org/news/2014/04/29/bangladesh-elections-scarred-violence

HRW (Human Rights Watch) (2014b). "Democracy in the Crossfire: Opposition Violence and Government Abuses in the 2014 Pre- and Post-Election Period in Bangladesh." April 29. Report. www.hrw.org/report/2014/04/29/democracy-crossfire/opposition-violence-and-government-abuses-2014-pre-and-post

HRW (Human Rights Watch). (2015). "Insult to Injury: The 2014 Lamu and Tana River Attacks and Kenya's Abusive Response." June 15. Report. www.hrw.org/report/2015/06/15/insult-injury/2014-lamu-and-tana-river-attacks-and-kenyas-abusive-response

Hughes, Lotte. (2005). "Malice in Maasailand: The Historical Roots of Current Political Struggles." *African Affairs* 104(415): 207–224.

Humphreys, Macartan, and Jeremy Weinstein. 2006. "Handling and Manhandling Civilians in Civil War." *American Political Science Review* 100(03): 429–447.

Huntington, Samuel. (1991). *The Third Wave: Democratization in the Late Twentieth Century.* Norman: University of Oklahoma Press.

Hutchison, Marc L., & Kristin Johnson. (2011). "Capacity to Trust? Institutional Capacity, Conflict, and Political Trust in Africa, 2000–2005." *Journal of Peace Research* 48(6): 737–752.

Hyde, Susan, & Nikolay Marinov. (2012). "Which Elections Can Be Lost?" *Political Analysis* 20(2): 191–201.

ICG (International Crisis Group). (2015). "Fields of Bitterness: Restitution and Reconciliation in Burundi." Report No. 214.

www.crisisgroup.org/africa/central-africa/burundi/fields-bitterness-ii-resti
tution-and-reconciliation-burundi

Jayadev, Arjun, & Sanjay G. Reddy. (2011). "Inequalities Between Groups: Theory and Empirics." *World Development* 39(2): 159–173.

Jenkins, Sarah. (2012). "Ethnicity, Violence, and the Immigrant-Guest Metaphor in Kenya." *African Affairs* 111(445): 576–596.

Jerven, Morten. (2015). *Africa: Why Economists Get It Wrong*. London: Zed Books.

Jervis, Robert (1978). "Cooperation Under the Security Dilemma." *World Politics* 30(2): 167–214.

Joireman, Sandra F. (2011). *Where There Is No Government: Enforcing Property Rights in Common Law Africa*. Oxford: Oxford University Press.

Justino, Patricia. (2009) "Poverty and Violent Conflict: A Micro-Level Perspective on the Causes and Duration of Warfare." *Journal of Peace Research* 46(3): 315–333.

Kahl, Colin. (1998). "Population Growth, Environmental Degradation, and State-Sponsored Violence: The Case of Kenya, 1991–93." *International Security* 23(2): 80–119.

Kalyvas, Stathis. (2003). The Ontology of Political Violence. *Perspectives on Politics* 1(3): 475–494.

Kalyvas, Stathis. (2006). *The Logic of Violence in Civil War*. Cambridge: Cambridge University Press.

Kalyvas, Stathis. (2008.) "Ethnic Defection in Civil War." *Comparative Political Studies* 41(8): 1043–1068.

Kalyvas, Stathis, & Adam Kocher. (2007). "How 'Free' Is Free Riding in Civil Wars? Violence, Insurgency and the Collective Action Problem." *World Politics* 59(2): 177–217.

Kanyinga, Karuti. (1998). "Politics and Struggles for Access to Land: 'Grants from above' and 'Squatters' in Coastal Kenya." *The European Journal of Development Research* 10(28): 50–69.

Kanyinga, Karuti. (2000). *Re-Distribution from above: The Politics of Land Rights and Squatting in Coastal Kenya*. Research Report No.115. Uppsala: The Nordic Africa Institute.

Kanyinga, Karuti. (2009). "The Legacy of the White Highlands: Land Rights, Ethnicity and the Post-2007 Election Violence in Kenya." *Journal of Contemporary African Studies* 27(3): 325–344.

Kanyinga, Karuti, Peter Gibbon, Andrew SZ Kiondo, & Per Tidemand. (1994). *The New Local Level Politics in East Africa: Studies on Uganda, Tanzania and Kenya*. Uppsala: Nordiska Afrikainstitutet.

Kapstein, Ethan B. (2017). *Seeds of Stability: Land Reform and US Foreign Policy*. New York: Cambridge University Press.

Kasara, Kimuli. (2013). "Separate and Suspicious: Local Social and Political Context and Ethnic Tolerance in Kenya." *The Journal of Politics* 75(4): 921–936.

Kasara, Kimuli. (2016). "Electoral Geography and Conflict: Examining the Redistricting Through Violence in Kenya." Working paper. New York: Columbia University.

Kaufmann, Chaim. (1998). "When All Else Fails: Ethnic Population Transfers and Partitions in the Twentieth Century." *International Security* 23(2): 120–156.

Keenan, Jillian. (2015). "The Blood Cries Out." *Foreign Policy*, March 27. https://foreignpolicy.com/2015/03/27/the-blood-cries-out-burundi-land-conflict/

Kemei, Kipchumba. (2016). "Obituary: Life and Times of William ole Ntimama." September 2. *Business Today Kenya*.

Kenya National Bureau of Statistics. (2010). *The 2009 Kenya Population and Housing Census*. Nairobi: Kenya National Bureau of Statistics.

KHRC (Kenya Human Rights Commission). (2008). "Violating the Vote: A Report on the 2007 General Elections." Final Report. www.khrc.or.ke /publications/37-violating-the-vote/file.html

Kitschelt, Herbert, & Steven Wilkinson. (2007). *Patrons, Clients, and Policies: Patterns of Democratic Accountability and Political Competition*. Cambridge: Cambridge University Press.

Klaus, Kathleen & Mitchell, Matthew. (2015). "Land Grievances and the Mobilization of Electoral Violence: Evidence from Côte d'Ivoire and Kenya." *Journal of Peace Research* 52(5): 622–635.

Klaus, Kathleen, & Jeffery Paller. (2017). "Defending the City, Defending Votes: Campaign Strategies in Urban Ghana." *The Journal of Modern African Studies* 55(4): 681–708.

Klopp, Jacqueline. (2000). "Pilfering the Public: The Problem of Land Grabbing in Contemporary Kenya." *Africa Today* 47(1): 7–26.

Klopp, Jacqueline. (2001a). "'Ethnic Clashes' and Winning Elections: The Case of Kenya's Electoral Despotism." *Canadian Journal of African Studies* 35(3): 473–518

Klopp, Jacqueline. (2001b). "Electoral Despotism in Kenya: Land, Patronage and Resistance in the Multi-Party Context." PhD thesis. Montreal: McGill University.

Klopp, Jacqueline M. (2002). "Can Moral Ethnicity Trump Political Tribalism? The Struggle for Land and Nation in Kenya." *African Studies* 61(2): 270–294.

Klopp, Jacqueline M., & Elke Zuern. 2007. "The Politics of Violence in Democratization: Lessons from Kenya and South Africa." *Comparative Politics* 127–146.

KNCHR (Kenya National Commission on Human Rights). (2008). "On the Brink of the Precipice: A Human Rights Account of Kenya's Post-2007 Election Violence." www.knchr.org/Portals/0/Reports/KNCHR_REPOR T_ON_THE_BRINK_OF_THE_PRECIPE.pdf

Koter, Dominika. (2013)."King Makers: Local Leaders and Ethnic Politics in Africa." *World Politics* 65(2): 187–232.

Krause, Jana. (2016). "Non-Violence and Civilian Agency in Communal War: Evidence from Jos, Nigeria." *African Affairs* 116 (463): 261–283.

Kuo, Lily. "A Kenyan Crisis Tracking Team Has Deployed to Monitor US Election Violence and Voter Suppression" Quartz Africa, November 2. https://qz.com/africa/825442/kenyas-crisis-mapping-startup-ushahidi-will-monitor-the-us-presidential-election/

Laitin, David D. (1986). *Hegemony and Culture: Politics and Change Among the Yoruba.* Chicago: University of Chicago Press.

Laitin, David. (2007). *Nations, States, and Violence.* Oxford: Oxford University Press.

Lemarchand, René. (1972). "Political Clientelism and Ethnicity in Tropical Africa: Competing Solidarities in Nation-Building." *American Political Science Review* 66(1): 68–90.

Lemarchand, René. (2008). "The Burundi Killings." Online Encyclopedia of Mass Violence/ Sciences Po, June 2008.

Lentz, Carola. (2013). *Land, Mobility, and Belonging in West Africa.* Bloomington: Indiana University Press.

Leo, Christopher. (1981). "Who Benefited from the Million-Acre Scheme? Toward a Class Analysis of Kenya's Transition to Independence." *Canadian Journal of African Studies* 15(2): 201–222.

Leys, Colin. (1975). Underdevelopment in Kenya: The Political Economy of Neo-Colonialism. Berkeley: University of California Press.

Lieberman, Evan, & Prerna Singh. (2012). "The Institutional Origins of Ethnic Violence." *Comparative Politics* 45(1): 1–24.

Lindberg, Staffan I., & Minion KC Morrison. (2008). "Are African Voters Really Ethnic or Clientelistic? Survey Evidence from Ghana." *Political Science Quarterly* 123(1): 95–122.

Linke, Andrew. (2013). "The Aftermath of an Election Crisis: Kenyan Attitudes and the Influence of Individual-Level and Locality Violence." *Political Geography* 37: 5–17.

Linkow, Benjamin. (2016). "Causes and Consequences of Perceived Land Tenure Insecurity: Survey Evidence from Burkina Faso." *Land Economics* 92(2): 308–327.

Lonsdale, John. (1992). "The Moral Economy of Mau Mau: Wealth, Poverty and Civic Virtue in Kikuyu Political Thought." In Bruce Berman (ed.)

Unhappy Valley: Conflict in Kenya and Africa Book 2. Athens, OH: Ohio University Press, 315–504.

Lonsdale, John. (2008). "Soil, Work, Civilization, and Citizenship in Kenya." *Journal of Eastern African Studies* 2(2): 305–314.

Lukalo, Fibian, & Samuel Odari (2016) "Exploring the Status of Settlement Schemes in Kenya." Working Papers Series. Nairobi: National Land Commission.

Lund, Christian. (2003). "'Bawku is Still Volatile': Ethno-political Conflict and State Recognition in Northern Ghana." *Journal of Modern African Studies* 41(4): 587–610.

Lund, Christian. (2008). *Local Politics and the Dynamics of Property in Africa.* Cambridge: Cambridge University Press.

Lund, Christian, & Catherine Boone. (2013). "Introduction: Land Politics in Africa–Constituting Authority over Territory, Property and Persons." *Africa* 83(1): 1–13.

Lupu, Noam, & Leonid Peisakhin. (2017). "The Legacy of Political Violence Across Generations." *American Journal of Political Science* 61(4): 836–851.

Lynch, Gabrielle. (2008). "Courting the Kalenjin: The Failure of Dynastisicm and the Strength of the ODM Wave in Kenya's Rift Valley Province." *African Affairs* 107: 541–568.

Lynch, Gabrielle. (2011). *I Say to You: Ethnic Politics and the Kalenjin in Kenya.* Chicago: University of Chicago Press.

Lynch, Gabrielle. (2018). *Performances of Injustice: The Politics of Truth, Justice and Reconciliation in Kenya.* Cambridge: Cambridge University Press.

Mahoney, James, & Gary Goertz. (2004). "The Possibility Principle: Choosing Negative Cases in Comparative Research." *American Political Science Review* 98(4): 653–669.

Malik, Aditi. (2018). "Constitutional Reform and New Patterns of Electoral Violence: Evidence from Kenya's 2013 Elections." *Commonwealth & Comparative Politics* 56(3): 340–359.

Manji, Ambreena. (2015). "Whose Land Is It Anyway? the Failure of Land Law Reform in Kenya." August 1. *Africa Research Institute Counterpoint.* www.africaresearchinstitute.org/newsite/publications/whose-land-is-it -anyway/

Mansfield, Edward, & Jack Snyder. (1995). "Democratization and the Danger of War." *International Security* 20(1): 5–38.

Mansfield, Edward, & Jack Snyder. (2002). "Democratic Transitions, Institutional Strength, and War." *International Organization* 56(2): 297–337.

Mares, Isabela, & Lauren Young. (2016). "Buying, Expropriating, and Stealing Votes." *Annual Review of Political Science* 19: 267–288.

Marshall-Fratani, Ruth. (2006). "The War of 'Who Is Who': Autochthony, Nationalism, and Citizenship in the Ivoirian Crisis." *African Studies Review* 49(2): 9–43.

Mason, David. (1998). "'Take Two Acres and Call Me in the Morning': Is Land Reform a Prescription for Peasant Unrest?" *The Journal of Politics* 60: 199–230.

Matter, Scott. (2010). "Clashing Claims: Neopatrimonial Governance, Land Tenure Transformation, and Violence at Enoosupukia, Kenya." *PoLAR: Political and Legal Anthropology Review* 33(1): 67–88.

Midlarsky, Manus (1988). "Rulers and the Ruled: Patterned Inequality and the Onset of Mass Political Violence." *The American Political Science Review* 82: 491–509

Miguel, Edward. (2004). "Tribe or Nation? Nation Building and Public Goods in Kenya Versus Tanzania." *World Politics* 56(3): 327–362.

Minorities at Risk Project. (2009) "Minorities at Risk Dataset." College Park, MD: Center for International Development and Conflict Management. www.mar.umd.edu/

Mironova, Vera, & Sam Whitt. (2018). "Social Norms after Conflict Exposure and Victimization by Violence: Experimental Evidence from Kosovo." *British Journal of Political Science* 48(3): 749–765.

Mitchell, Matthew. (2018). "Migration, Sons of the Soil Conflict, and International Relations." *International Area Studies Review* 21(1): 51–67.

MOE(Misión de Observación Electoral). (2011) "Violencia Politica." https://moe.org.co/wp-content/uploads/2017/07/Informe_MOE_violencia_pol%C3%ADtica_2011.pdf

Mueller, Susanne. (1984). "Government and Opposition in Kenya, 1966–9." *The Journal of Modern African Studies* 22(3): 399–427.

Mueller, Susanne. (2008). "The Political Economy of Kenya's Crisis." *Journal of Eastern African Studies* 2(2): 185–210.

Muller, Edward, Mitchell A. Seligson, Hung-der Fu, & Manus I. Midlarsky. (1989). "Land Inequality and Political Violence." *American Political Science Review* 83(2): 577–596.

Muller, Edward, & Mitchell Seligson. (1987). "Inequality and Insurgency." *The American Political Science Review* 81(2): 425–451.

Mwakale, Steve. (2015). "Squatters on Agricultural Development Corporation's Mau Land Warned." *Standard Media*, 11 November. www.standardmedia.co.ke/article/2000182268/squatters-on-agricultural-development-corporation-s-mau-land-warned/?pageNo=2

Mwiandi, Sheila. (2008). "Moving Beyond Relief: The Challenges of Settling Kenya's Internally Displaced." United States Institute of Peace. www.usip.org/publications/2008/08/moving-beyond-relief-challenges-settling-kenyas-internally-displaced

Nathan, Noah. (2019). *Electoral Politics and Africa's Urban Transition: Class and Ethnicity in Ghana*. Cambridge: Cambridge University Press.

Ndegwa, Stephen N. (1997). "Citizenship and Ethnicity: An Examination of Two Transition Moments in Kenyan Politics." *American Political Science Review* 91(3): 599–616.

Newbury, David. (1997). "Irredentist Rwanda: Ethnic and Territorial Frontiers in Central Africa." *Africa Today* 44(2): 211–221.

Nieto-Matiz, Camilo. (2019). "Democracy in the Countryside: The Rural Sources of Violence Against Voters in Colombia." *Journal of Peace Research* 56(2): 264–278.

Njenga, Stanley. (2013). "Nyakinyua Warned Against Fraud." June 17. *The Star*. https://allafrica.com/stories/201306180097.html

Njogu, Kimani. (2009). *Healing the Wound. Personal Narratives about the 2007 Post-Election Violence in Kenya*. Oxford: African Books Collective.

Njonjo, Apollo. (1977). "The Africanisation of the 'White Highlands': A Study in Agrarian Class Struggles in Kenya." Unpublished PhD thesis. Princeton, NJ: Princeton University.

Nkurunziza, Janvier D. (2018). "The Origin and Persistence of State Fragility in Burundi." LSE-Oxford Commission on State Fragility, Growth and Development. www.theigc.org/wp-content/uploads/2018/04/Burundi-report-v2.pdf

Norris, Pippa. (2015). *Why Elections Fail*. Cambridge: Cambridge University Press.

Norris, Pippa, Frank, Richard, & Ferran Martínez Coma. (eds.). (2015). *Contentious Elections: From Ballots to Barricades*. New York: Routledge.

Okoth-Ogendo, H. W. O. (1991). Tenants of the Crown: Evolution of Agrarian Law and Institutions in Kenya. Nairobi: ACTS Press.

Olson, Mancur (1965). *The Theory of Collective Action: Public Goods and the Theory of Groups*. Cambridge, MA: Harvard University Press.

Onoma, Ato Kwamena. (2009). *The Politics of Property Rights Institutions in Africa*. Cambridge: Cambridge University Press.

Østby, Gudrun. (2008). "Polarization, Horizontal Inequalities and Violent Civil Conflict." *Journal of Peace Research* 45(2): 143–62.

Østby, Gudrun, Henrik Urdal, Mohammad Zulfan Tadjoeddin, S. Mansoob Murshed, & Håvard Strand. (2011). "Population Pressure, Horizontal Inequality and Political Violence: A Disaggregated Study of Indonesian Provinces, 1990–2003." The Journal of Development Studies 47(3): 377–398.

Oucho, John. (2002). *Undercurrents of Ethnic Conflicts in Kenya*. Vol. 3. Leiden: Brill.

Oyuke, John. (2012) "Coast Bets on Ramisi Sugar Comeback." January 19. *Standard Media*. www.standardmedia.co.ke/article/2000050299/coast-bets-on-ramisi-sugar-comeback

Paige, Jeffery. (1975). *Agrarian Revolution*. New York: The Free Press.

Paller, Jeffrey. (2019). *Democracy in Ghana: Everyday Politics in Urban Africa*. Cambridge: Cambridge University Press.

Patterson, Molly, & Kristen Monroe. (1998). "Narrative in Political Science." *Annual Review of Political Science* (1): 315–31.

Petersen, Roger D. (2002). *Understanding Ethnic Violence: Fear, Hatred, and Resentment in Twentieth-Century Eastern Europe*. Cambridge: Cambridge University Press.

Polletta, Francesca. (2006). *It Was Like a Fever: Storytelling in Protest and Politics*. Chicago: University of Chicago Press.

Posner, Daniel. (2004). The Political Salience of Cultural Difference: Why Chewas and Tumbukas Are Allies in Zambia and Adversaries in Malawi. *American Political Science Review* 98(4): 529–545.

Posner, Daniel. (2005). *Institutions and Ethnic Politics in Africa*. Cambridge: Cambridge University Press.

Prestholdt, Jeremy. (2014). "Politics of the Soil: Separatism, Autochthony, and Decolonization at the Kenyan Coast." *Journal of African History* 55 (2): 249–270.

Przeworski, Adam. (1991). *Democracy and the Market: Political and Economic Reforms in Eastern Europe and Latin America*. Cambridge: Cambridge University Press.

Raleigh, Clionadh. (2010). "Political Marginalization, Climate Change, and Conflict in African Sahel States." *International Studies Review* 12(1): 69–86.

Raleigh, Clionadh, & Henrik Urdal. (2007). Climate Change, Environmental Degradation and Armed Conflict. *Political Geography*, 26(6): 674–694.

Raleigh, Clionadh, Andrew Linke, Håvard Hegre, & Joackim Karlsen. (2010). Introducing ACLED: An Armed Conflict Location and Event Dataset. *Journal of Peace Research* 47(5): 1–10.

Ramsey, Geoffrey. (2011). "Ahead of Colombia's Elections, Violence Stalks Candidates." 31 October. *Christian Science Monitor*. https://reliefweb.int/report/colombia/ahead-colombias-elections-violence-stalks-candidates

Rasmussen, Jacob. (2010). "Outwitting the Professor of Politics? Mungiki Narratives of Political Deception and Their Role in Kenyan Politics." *Journal of Eastern African Studies* 4(3): 435–449.

Reno, William. (2011). *Warfare in Independent Africa*. Cambridge: Cambridge University Press

Reno, William. (2007). "Patronage Politics and the Behavior of Armed Groups." *Civil Wars* 9(4): 324–342.

Republic of Kenya. (1999). "Report of the Judicial Commission Appointed to Inquire into Tribal Clashes in Kenya." http://kenyalaw.org/kl/filead min/CommissionReports/ReportoftheJudicialCommissionAppointedtoIn quireintoTribalClashesinKenya.pdf

Republic of Kenya. (2004). "Report of the Commission of Inquiry into Illegal/Irregular Allocation of Land." (Ndung'u Report) Nairobi: Government Printers.

Republic of Kenya. (2008). "Report of the Commission of Inquiry into Post Election Violence (CIPEV). Nairobi." (aka "Waki Report"). https://relief web.int/report/kenya/kenya-commission-inquiry-post-election-violence-cip ev-final-report

Republic of Kenya. (2013a). "Report of the Truth Justice and Reconciliation Commission." http://knchr.org/Portals/0/Reports/TJRC_Volume_4.pdf

Republic of Kenya (2013b). "Kilifi County: First Integrated Development Plan (2013–2017)." www.kilifi.go.ke/lib.php?com=6&res_id=62

Republic of Kenya. (2013c). "County of Kwale: First County Integrated Development Plan, 2013." http://www.kpda.or.ke/documents/CIDP/Kw ale.pdf

Republic of Kenya/World Bank. (2017). "Climate Risk Profile: Tana River County." Kenya County Climate Risk Profile Series. https://cgspace .cgiar.org/rest/bitstreams/119958/retrieve

Reyntjens, Filip. (2005). "Briefing: Burundi: A Peaceful Transition after a Decade of War?" *African Affairs* 105(418): 117–135.

Romero, Mauricio. (2000). "Changing Identities and Contested Settings: Regional Elites and the Paramilitaries in Colombia." *International Journal of Politics, Culture, and Society* 14(1): 151–69.

Rosenzweig, Steven. (2016). "Dangerous Disconnect: Voter Backlash, Elite Misperception, and the Costs of Violence as an Electoral Tactic." Working Paper. New Haven, CT: Yale University.

Russett, Bruce. (1964). "Inequality and Instability: The Relation of Land Tenure to Politics." *World Politics: A Quarterly Journal of International Relations* 16(3): 442–454.

Rutten, Marcel, Alamin M. Mazrui, & François Grignon (eds.) (2001). *Out for the Count: The 1997 General Elections and Prospects for Democracy in Kenya*. Kampala: Fountain.

Sacks, Audrey, & Marco Larizza. (2012). "Why Quality Matters: Rebuilding Trustworthy Local Government in Post-Conflict Sierra Leone." The World Bank Policy Research Working Papers WPS6021.

Salehyan, Idean, & Christopher Linebarger. (2015). "Elections and Social Conflict in Africa, 1990–2009." *Studies in Comparative International Development* 50(1): 23–49.

Sambanis, Nicholas. (2001). "Do Ethnic and Nonethnic Civil Wars Have the Same Causes? A Theoretical and Empirical Inquiry (Part 1)." *Journal of Conflict Resolution* 45(3): 259–282.

Sambanis, Nicholas. (2004). "Using Case Studies to Expand Economic Models of Civil War." *Perspectives on Politics* 2(2): 259–279.

Sanin, Francisco Gutierrez, & Elisabeth Wood. (2014). "Ideology in Civil War: Instrumental Adoption and Beyond." *Journal of Peace Research* 51 (2) 213–226.

Sansom, Robert L. (1970). *The Economics of Insurgency in the Mekong Delta of Vietnam.* Cambridge, MA: MIT Press.

Schatzberg, Michael (ed). (1987) *The Political Economy of Kenya.* Santa Barbara, CA: Praeger Publishers

Schatzberg, Michael. (2001). *Political Legitimacy in Middle Africa: Father, Family, Food.* Bloomington: Indiana University Press.

Schwartz, Stephanie. (2019). "Home, Again: Refugee Return and Post-Conflict Violence in Burundi." *International Security* 44(2): 110–145.

Shimoli, Eric. (2007). "Violence Erupts After Kibaki Sworn In." December 31. *Daily Nation.* www.nation.co.ke/news/1056-224116-lu3osez/index.html

Scott, James C. (1976). *The Moral Economy of the Peasant: Rebellion and Subsistence in Southeast Asia.* New Haven, CT: Yale University Press.

Seawright, Jason, & John Gerring. (2008). "Case Selection Techniques in Case Study Research: A Menu of Qualitative and Quantitative Options." *Political Research Quarterly* 61(2): 294–308.

Sen, Amartya. (1992). *Inequality Reexamined.* Cambridge, MA: Harvard University Press.

Simmons, Erica. (2014). "Grievances Do Matter in Mobilization." *Theory and Society* 43(5): 513–536.

Simmons, Erica. (2016). *Meaningful Resistance: Market Reforms and the Roots of Social Protest in Latin America.* Cambridge: Cambridge University Press.

Skocpol, Theda. (1979). *States and Social Revolutions: A Comparative Analysis of France, Russia, and China.* Cambridge: Cambridge University Press.

Smith, Lahra. (2009). "Explaining Violence after Recent Elections in Ethiopia and Kenya." *Democratization* 16(5): 867–897.

Snow, David, & Robert Benford. (1992). "Master Frames and Cycles of Protest." In Aldon Morris & Carol Mueller (eds.) *Frontiers in Social Movement Theory.* New Haven, CT: Yale University Press, 133–155.

Snyder, David, & Charles Tilly. (1972). "Hardship and Collective Violence in France, 1830 to 1960." *American Sociological Review* 37(5): 520–532.

Snyder, Jack. (2000). *From Voting to Violence: Democratization and Nationalist Conflict*. New York: Norton.

Söderberg Kovacs, Mimmi, & Jesper Bjarnesen (eds.) (2018). *Violence in African Elections: Between Democracy and Big Man Politics*. London: Zed Books.

Staniland, Paul. (2014). "Violence and Democracy." *Comparative Politics* 47(1): 99–118.

Stearns, Jason. (2012). *North Kivu: The Background to Conflict in North Kivu Province of Eastern Congo*. London: Rift Valley Institute.

Steele, Abbey. (2011). "Electing Displacement: Political Cleansing in Apartado,' Colombia." *Journal of Conflict Resolution* 55(3): 423–445.

Steele, Abbey. (2018). "IDP Resettlement and Collective Targeting During Civil War: Evidence from Colombia." *Journal of Peace Research* 55(6): 810–824.

Stewart, Frances. (ed.) (2008). *Horizontal Inequalities and Conflict: Understanding Group Violence in Multiethnic Societies*. New York: Springer.

Stokes, Susan, and Thad Dunning. (2013). *Brokers, Voters, and Clientelism: The Puzzle of Distributive Politics*. Cambridge: Cambridge University Press.

Straus, Scott. (2006). *The Order of Genocide: Race, Power and War in Rwanda*. Ithaca, NY: Cornell University Press.

Straus, Scott. (2011). "'It's Sheer Horror Here': Patterns of Violence During the First Four Months of Côte d'Ivoire's Post-Electoral Crisis." *African Affairs* 110(440): 481–489.

Straus, Scott. (2012). "Retreating from the Brink: Theorizing Mass Violence and the Dynamics of Restraint." *Perspectives on Politics* 10(2): 343–362.

Straus, Scott. (2015). *Making and Unmaking Nations: War, Leadership, and Genocide in Modern Africa*. Ithaca, NY: Cornell University Press.

Straus, Scott, & Charlie Taylor. (2012). "Democratization and Electoral Violence in Sub-Saharan Africa, 1990–2008." In Dorina A. Bekoe (ed.) *Voting in Fear: Electoral Violence in Sub-Saharan Africa*. Washington, DC: United States Institute of Peace, 15–38.

Tajfel, Henri (ed.). (1982). *Social Identity and Intergroup Relations*. Cambridge: Cambridge University Press.

Tajfel, Henri, & John C. Turner. (1979). "An Integrative Theory of Intergroup Conflict." In William Austin & Stephen Worchel (eds.) *The Social Psychology of Intergroup Relations*. Monterey, CA: Brooks/Cole, 33–47.

Tarrow, Sidney. (2011). *Power in Movement: Social Movements and Contentious Politics*. Cambridge: Cambridge University Press.

Taylor, Charles, Jon Pevehouse, & Scott Straus. (2017). "Perils of Pluralism: Electoral Violence and Incumbency in Sub-Saharan Africa." *Journal of Peace Research* 54(3): 397–411.

Tellez, Juan Fernando. (2019). "Worlds Apart: Conflict Exposure and Preferences for Peace." *Journal of Conflict Resolution* 63(4): 1053–1076.

Thachil, Tariq. (2014). "Elite Parties and Poor Voters: Theory and Evidence from India." *American Political Science Review* 108(2): 454–477.

Themnér, Lotta, & Peter Wallensteen. (2014). "Armed Conflict, 1946–2013." *Journal of Peace Research* 51(4): 541–554.

Thomson, Henry. (2016). "Rural Grievances, Landholding Inequality, and Civil Conflict." *International Studies Quarterly* 60(3): 511–519.

Throup, David. (2003). "The Kenya General Election: December 27, 2002–January 2003." January 6. *CSIS: Africa Notes*. www.csis.org/analysis/afr ica-notes-kenya-general-election-december-27-2002-january-2003

Throup, David, & Charles Hornsby. (1998). *Multi-Party Politics in Kenya*. Oxford: James Currey.

Tilly. Charles. (1978). *From Mobilization to Revolution*. Boston, MA: Addison-Wesley.

Tilly, Charles. (1998). *Durable Inequality*. Berkeley: University of California Press.

Tilly, Charles. (2003). *The Politics of Collective Violence*. Cambridge: Cambridge University Press.

TJRC (Truth, Justice and Reconciliation Commission of Kenya). (2013). Final Report, vol. 1. Chicago: University of Chicago Press.

Toft, Monica D. (2003). *The Geography of Ethnic Violence: Identity, Interests, and the Indivisibility of Territory*. Princeton, NJ: Princeton University.

UNHCR-WFP (United Nations High Commissioner for Refugees / World Food Programme. (2007). "Joint Assessment Mission of Burundian Returnees. Burundi." http://documents.wfp.org/stellent/groups/public/do cuments/ena/wfp145774.pdf

Van de Walle, Nicolas. (2007). "Meet the New Boss, Same As the Old Boss? the Evolution of Political Clientelism in Africa." In Herbert Kitschelt & Steven Wilkinson (eds.) *Patrons, Clients, and Policies: Patterns of Democratic Accountability and Political Competition*. Cambridge: Cambridge University Press.

Van Ham, Carolien, & Staffan I. Lindberg. (2015). "From Sticks to Carrots: Electoral Manipulation in Africa, 1986–2012." *Government and Opposition* 50(3): 521–548.

Varshney, Ashutosh. (2002). *Ethnic Conflict and Civic Life: Hindus and Muslims in India*. New Haven, CT: Yale University Press.

Von Uexkull, Nina, Mihai Croicu, Hanne Fjelde, & Halvard Buhaug. (2016). "Civil Conflict Sensitivity to Growing-Season Drought." *Proceedings of the National Academy of Sciences* 113(44): 12391–12396.

Voors, J. Maarten, Eleonora E. M. Nillesen, Philip Verwimp, Erwin H. Bulte, Robert Lensink, & Daan P. Soest. (2012). "Violent Conflict and Behavior: A Field Experiment in Burundi." *American Economic Review* 102(2): 941–964.

Wanyande, Peter. (2001). "Management Politics in Kenya's Sugar Industry: Towards an Effective Framework." *African Journal of Political Science* 6 (1): 123–140.

Wasserman, Gary. (1973). "Continuity and Counter-Insurgency: The Role of Land Reform in Decolonizing Kenya, 1962–70." *Canadian Journal of African Studies* 7(1): 133–148.

Wedeen, Lisa. (2002). "Conceptualizing Culture: Possibilities for Political Science." *American Political Science Review* 96(4): 713–738.

Weidmann, Nils B., & Christoph Zürcher. (2013). "How Wartime Violence Affects Social Cohesion: The Spatial–Temporal Gravity Model." *Civil Wars* 15(1): 1–18.

Weidmann, Nils B., Jan Ketil Rød, & Lars-Erik Cederman. (2010). "Representing Ethnic Groups in Space: A New Dataset." *Journal of Peace Research* 47(4): 491–499.

Weiner, Myron. (1978). *Sons of the Soil: Migration and Ethnic Conflict in India*. Princeton, NJ: Princeton University.

Weinstein, Jeremy. (2006). *Inside Rebellion: The Politics of Insurgent Violence*. Cambridge: Cambridge University Press.

Weru, Job. (2016). "Meet Mau Mau Fighters Who Have Never Tasted Fruits of Independence." Standard [Nairobi], December 16. www.standardmedia.co.ke/article/2000226534/meet-mau-mau-fighters-who-have-never-tasted-fruits-of-independence

Wickham-Crowley, Timothy. (1992). *Guerrillas and Revolution in Latin America: A Comparative Study of Insurgents and Regimes since 1956*. Princeton, NJ: Princeton University.

Wig, Tore, & Daniela Kromrey. (2018). "Which Groups Fight? Customary Institutions and Communal Conflicts in Africa." *Journal of Peace Research* 55(4): 415–429.

Wilkinson, Steven. (2004). *Votes and Violence: Electoral Competition and Ethnic Riots in India*. Cambridge: Cambridge University Press

Willis, Justin, & Ngala Chome. (2014). "Marginalization and Political Participation on the Kenya Coast: The 2013 Elections." *Journal of Eastern African Studies* 8(1): 115–134.

Willis, Justin, & George Gona. (2013). "Pwani C Kenya? Memory, Document and Secessionist Politics in Coastal Kenya." *African Affairs* 112 (446): 48–71.

Wood, Elisabeth. (2003). *Insurgent Collective Action and Civil War in El Salvador*. New York: Cambridge University Press.

Wood, Reed, M., Jacob D. Kathman, & Stephen E. Gent. (2012). "Armed Intervention and Civilian Victimization in Intrastate Conflicts." *Journal of Peace Research* 49(5): 647–660.

Wucherpfennig, Julian, Hunziker, Philipp, & Cederman, Lars-Erik. (2016). "Who Inherits the State? Colonial Rule and Postcolonial Conflict." *American Journal of Political Science* 60(4): 882–898.

Wucherpfennig, Julian, Nils W. Metternich, Lars-Erik Cederman, & Kristian Skrede Gleditsch (2012) "Ethnicity, the State, and the Duration of Civil War." *World Politics* 64(1): 79–115.

Young, Crawford. (1979). *The Politics of Cultural Pluralism*. Madison: University of Wisconsin Press.

Index

methodology (cont.)
  paired case comparisons, list of,
    116–117
  research design and case selection,
    64–69
  socio-economic and demographic
    variables, 253–254
  summary of, 8–9
Mijikenda
  Arab-Swahili slave trade, 73
  fear of ethnic others, 273
  group size in logic of violence,
    232–233
  groups within, 71
  history of land patronage, 73
  insider-outsider narrative, 215
  in Kijipwa Settlement Scheme, 133
  land inequality, 215
  land reform, 79–80
  Land Title Ordinance of 1908,
    75–76
  majimboism, 80–81
  outsider land narratives, 233–237
  population percentage, 65, 99, 224
  in Ramisi Settlement Scheme, 136
Million-Acre-Scheme (MAS), 85–86
moderate land inequality, 6, 43–46
  contentious land narratives and,
    47–48, 283
  patronage politics and, 283–284
  qualitative measurement, 116
Moi, Daniel arap, 81
  land acquisition in Ogilgei, 154
  land politics under, 93–97, 145
  Mauche land rights, 142, 163, 164,
    182–183
  Oljorai and Nyakinyua paired case
    comparison, 125–126
  settlement schemes, 86, 88, 90,
    101–102
motivation. *See* logic of violence
Mpeketoni, 237–238
Mungiki, 206–208
Mwambao (Ten Mile Strip), 73–74
Mwisho wa Lami, 121–125

Naivasha flower farms paired case
  comparison, 129–132, 205–206
Nakuru County. *See also* Mauche
  description of, 140

electoral constituencies, 142
title deeds held, 114–115
Nakuru County, paired case
  comparisons
  Likia and Mauche, 121, 141–144,
    160–168, 179
  Naivasha flower farms, 129–132
  Ogilgei and Kerma, 117, 141–142,
    149–160
  Oljorai and Nyakinyua, 125–129
  Tipis and Mwisho wa Lami, 121–125
  Umoja and Belbar, 117–120
narratives. *See also* land narratives
  defined, 36
  grievances versus, 38–39
  injustice narratives, 39
  insecurity narratives, 40
National Alliance Rainbow Coalition
  (NARC), 15, 127
national citizenship, ethnic citizenship
  versus, 110
National Land Commission (CNTB),
  287
national-level electoral violence,
  317–319
national-level inequality, 112–113
Ndadye, Melchior, 286
Ndorobo. *See* Ogiek
neighboring, defined, 107
Ngala, Ronald, 81
Ngawataniro Land Buying Company,
  91
Nkurunziza, Pierre, 287
non-contentious land narratives, 39, 48
  criteria, 109
  defined, 141
  land equality and, 107
  in Ogilgei, 150–152
  "nothing is for free," 81–84
Ntimama, William Ole, 107, 190,
  222–223
Nyakinyua Co-operative Society (Ltd),
  125–129
Nyerere, Julius, 291

Odinga, Oginga, 82
Odinga, Raila, 1, 131, 192, 194, 223
Ogiek, 142, 164, 167
Ogilgei
  description of, 140, 142